Kingyo Used Books

4

Seimu Yoshizaki

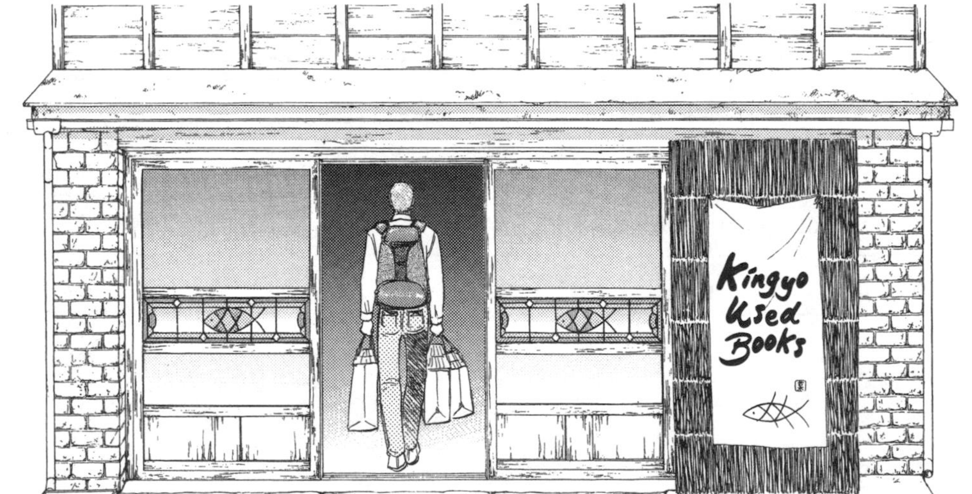
Kingyo
Used
Books

Kingyo Used Books 4

Contents

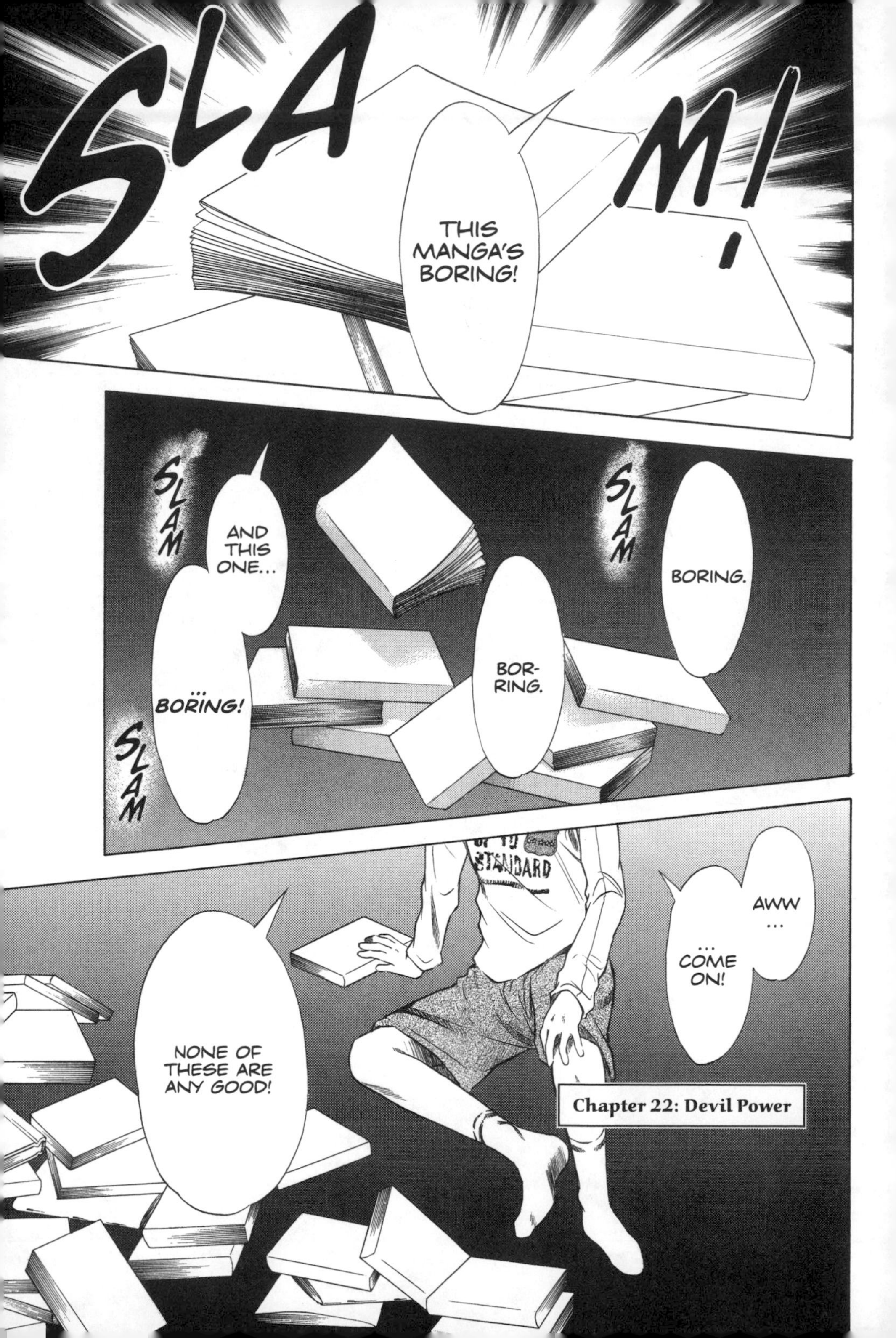
SLAM!
THIS MANGA'S BORING!
SLAM
BORING.
BOR-RING.
SLAM
AND THIS ONE...
...BORING!
SLAM
AWW...
...COME ON!
NONE OF THESE ARE ANY GOOD!
Chapter 22: Devil Power

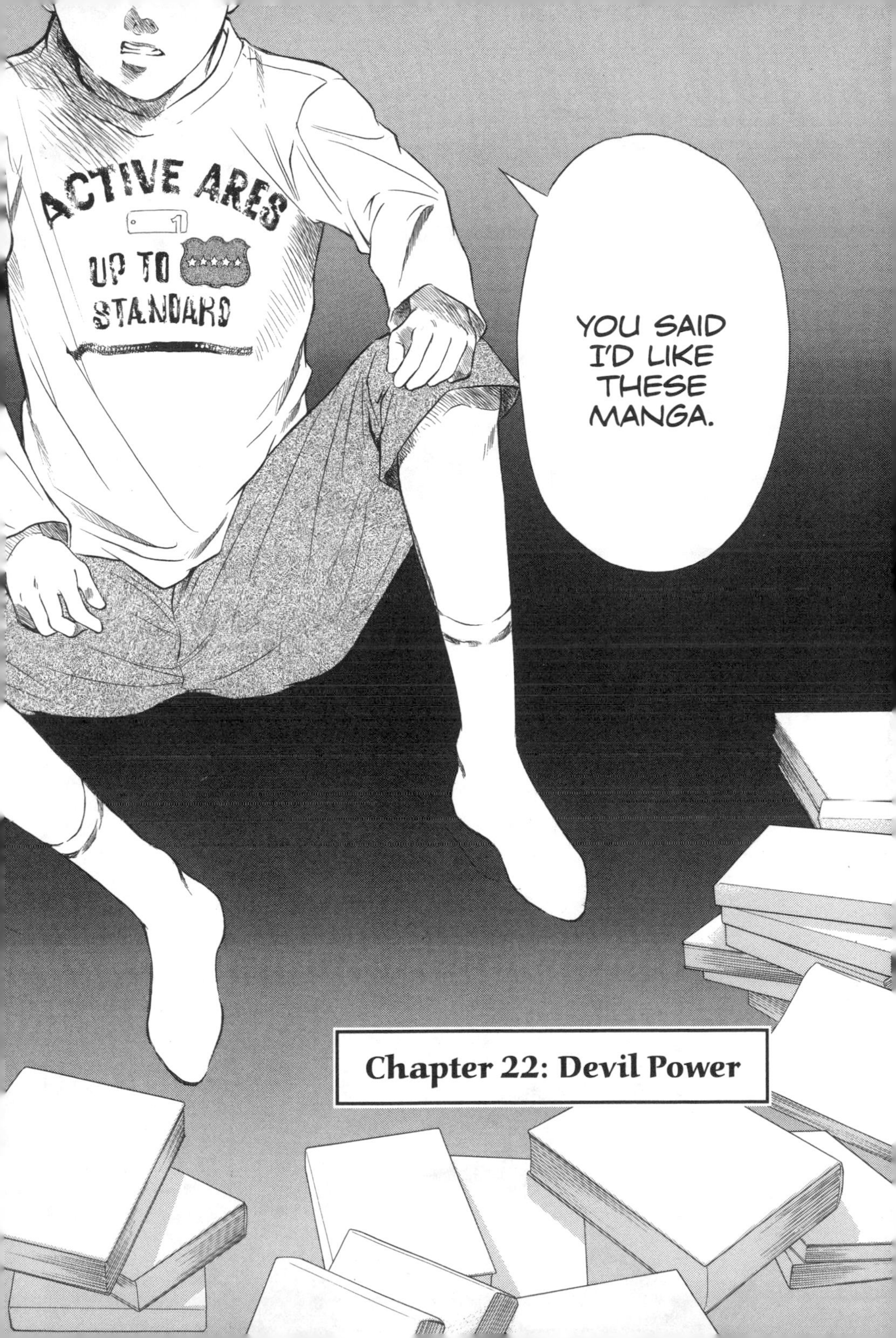
ACTIVE ARES
UP TO STANDARD
YOU SAID I'D LIKE THESE MANGA.
Chapter 22: Devil Power

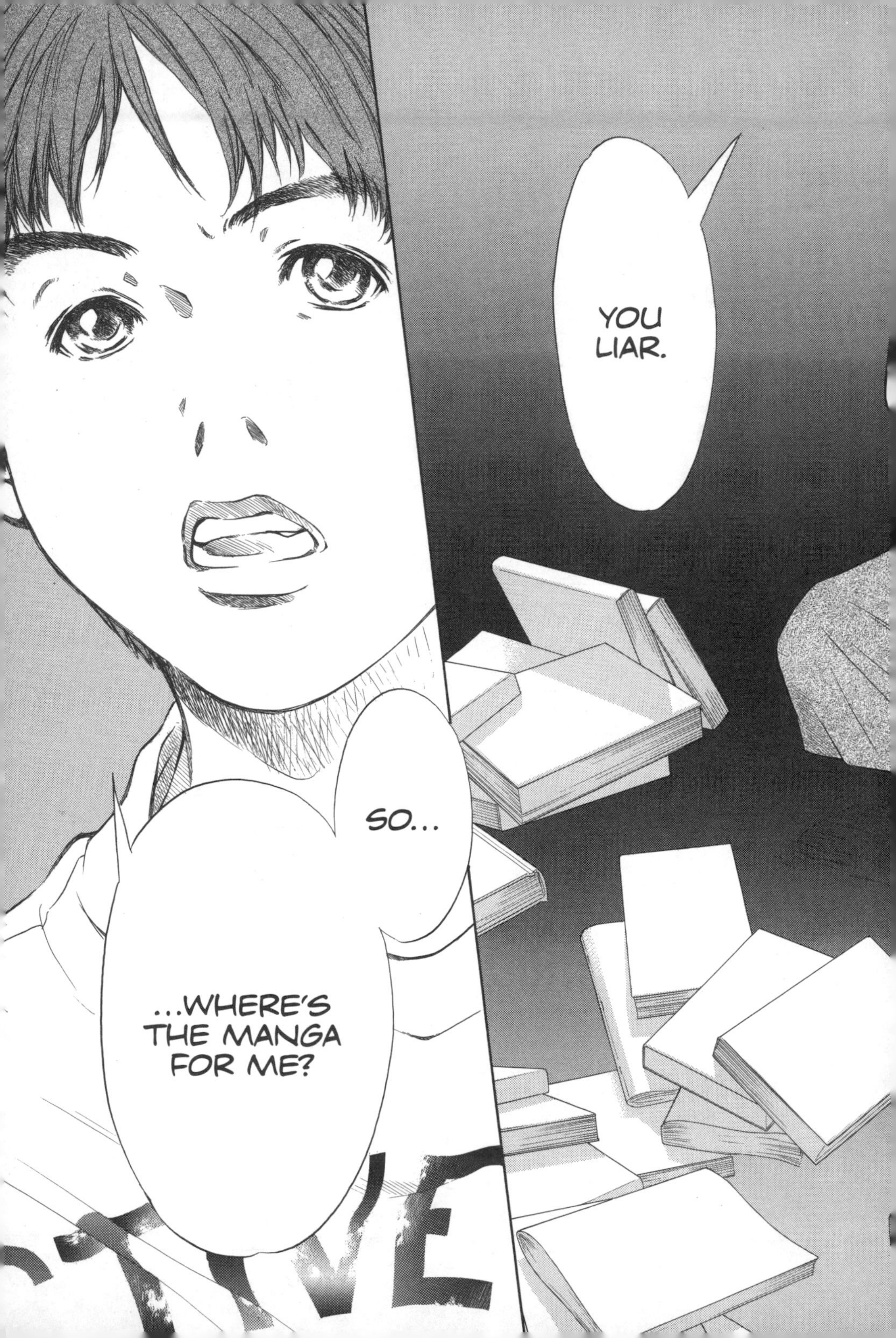
YOU LIAR.
SO...
...WHERE'S THE MANGA FOR ME?

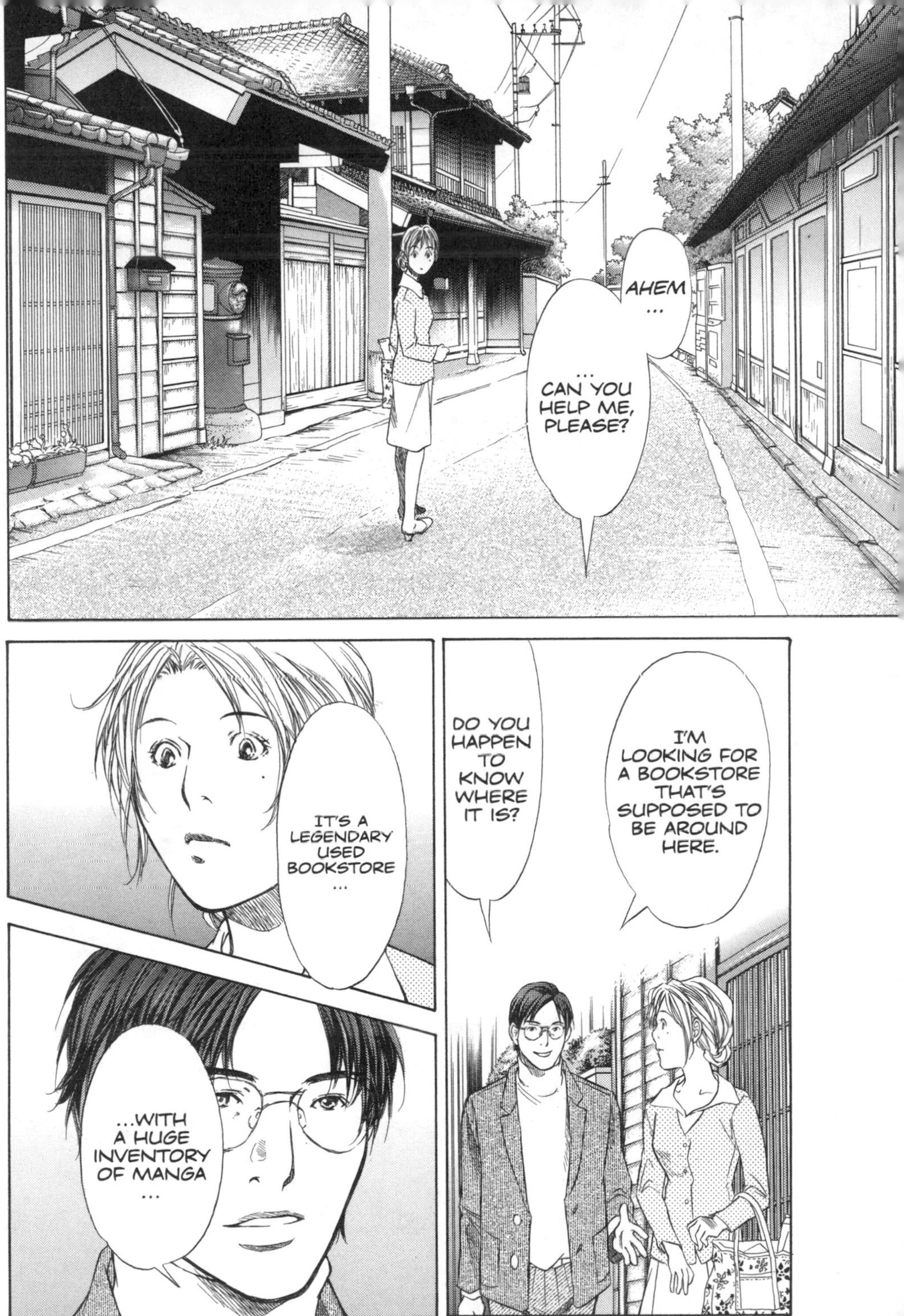
AHEM ...
... CAN YOU HELP ME, PLEASE?
I'M LOOKING FOR A BOOKSTORE THAT'S SUPPOSED TO BE AROUND HERE.
DO YOU HAPPEN TO KNOW WHERE IT IS?
IT'S A LEGENDARY USED BOOKSTORE ...
...WITH A HUGE INVENTORY OF MANGA ...

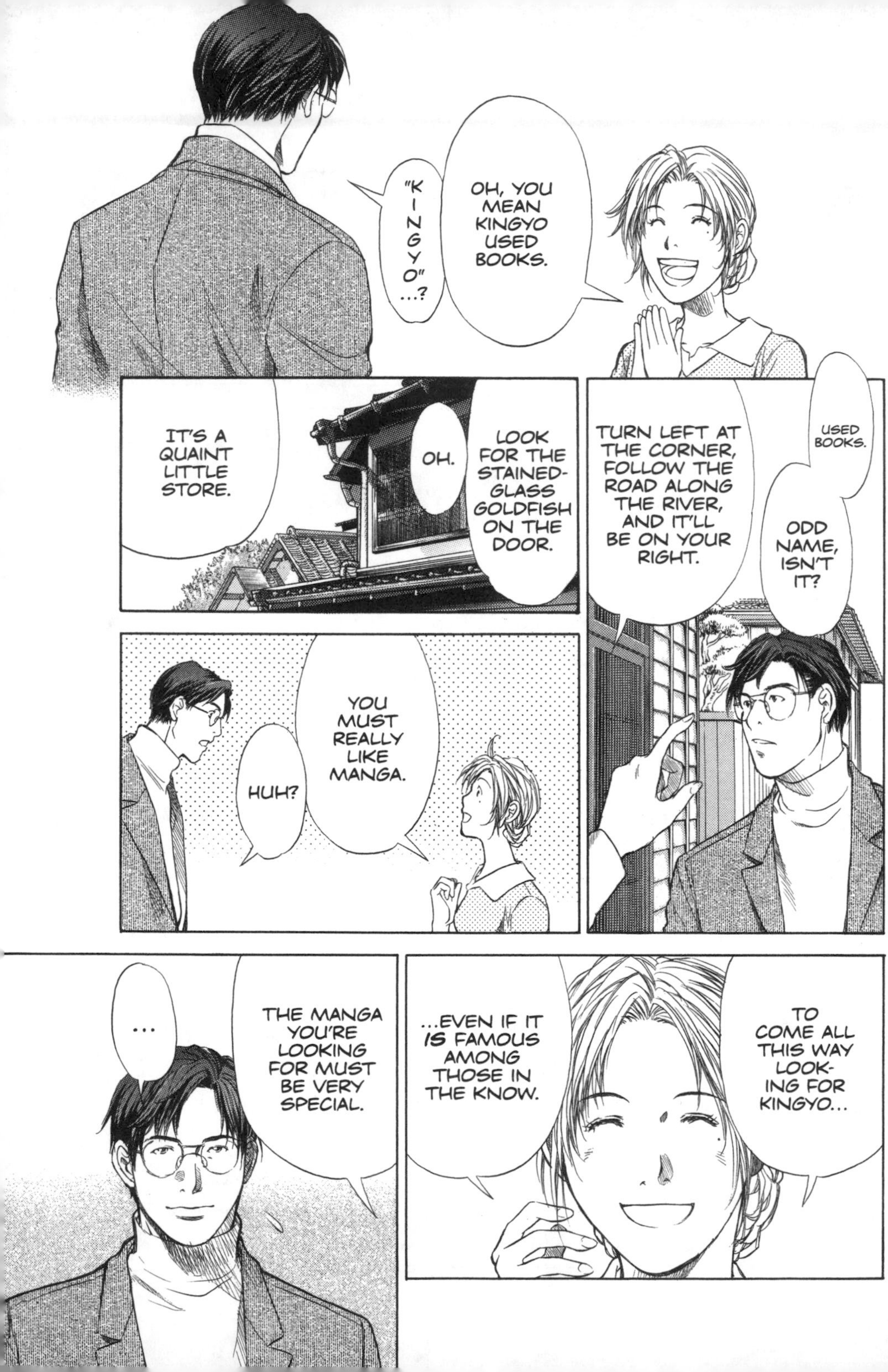

OH, YOU MEAN KINGYO USED BOOKS.
"KINGYO"...?
USED BOOKS.
ODD NAME, ISN'T IT?
TURN LEFT AT THE CORNER, FOLLOW THE ROAD ALONG THE RIVER, AND IT'LL BE ON YOUR RIGHT.
LOOK FOR THE STAINED-GLASS GOLDFISH ON THE DOOR.
OH.
IT'S A QUAINT LITTLE STORE.
YOU MUST REALLY LIKE MANGA.
HUH?
TO COME ALL THIS WAY LOOKING FOR KINGYO...
...EVEN IF IT *IS* FAMOUS AMONG THOSE IN THE KNOW.
THE MANGA YOU'RE LOOKING FOR MUST BE VERY SPECIAL.
...

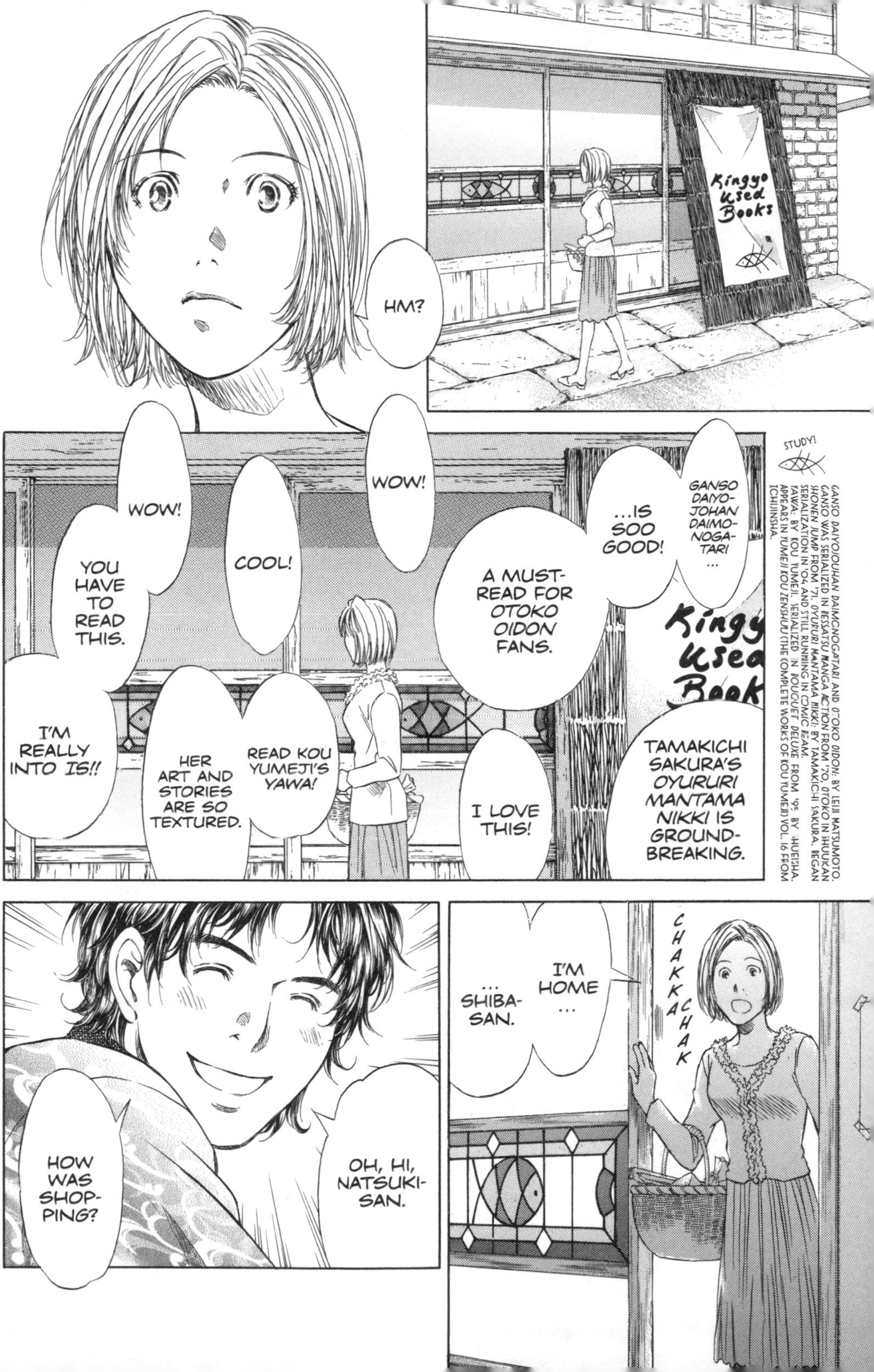
Kingyo Used Books
HM?
GANSO DAIYO-JOHAN DAIMO-NOGA-TARI...
...IS SOO GOOD!
A MUST-READ FOR OTOKO OIDON FANS.
WOW!
COOL!
WOW!
YOU HAVE TO READ THIS.
Kingyo Used Books
TAMAKICHI SAKURA'S OYURURI MANTAMA NIKKI IS GROUND-BREAKING.
I LOVE THIS!
READ KOU YUMEJI'S YAWA!
HER ART AND STORIES ARE SO TEXTURED.
I'M REALLY INTO IS!!
STUDY!
GANSO DAIYOJOUHAN DAIMONOGATARI AND OTOKO OIDON: BY LEIJI MATSUMOTO. GANSO WAS SERIALIZED IN BESSATSU MANGA ACTION FROM '70, OTOKO IN SHUUKAN SHONEN JUMP FROM '71. OYURURI MANTAMA NIKKI: BY TAMAKICHI SAKURA. BEGAN SERIALIZATION IN '04 AND STILL RUNNING IN COMIC BEAM. YAWA: BY KOU YUMEJI. SERIALIZED IN BOUQUET DELUXE FROM '95 BY SHUEISHA. APPEARS IN YUMEJI KOU ZENSHUU (THE COMPLETE WORKS OF KOU YUMEJI) VOL. 16 FROM ICHIJINSHA.
CHAKKA CHAK
I'M HOME...
...SHIBA-SAN.
OH, HI, NATSUKI-SAN.
HOW WAS SHOP-PING?

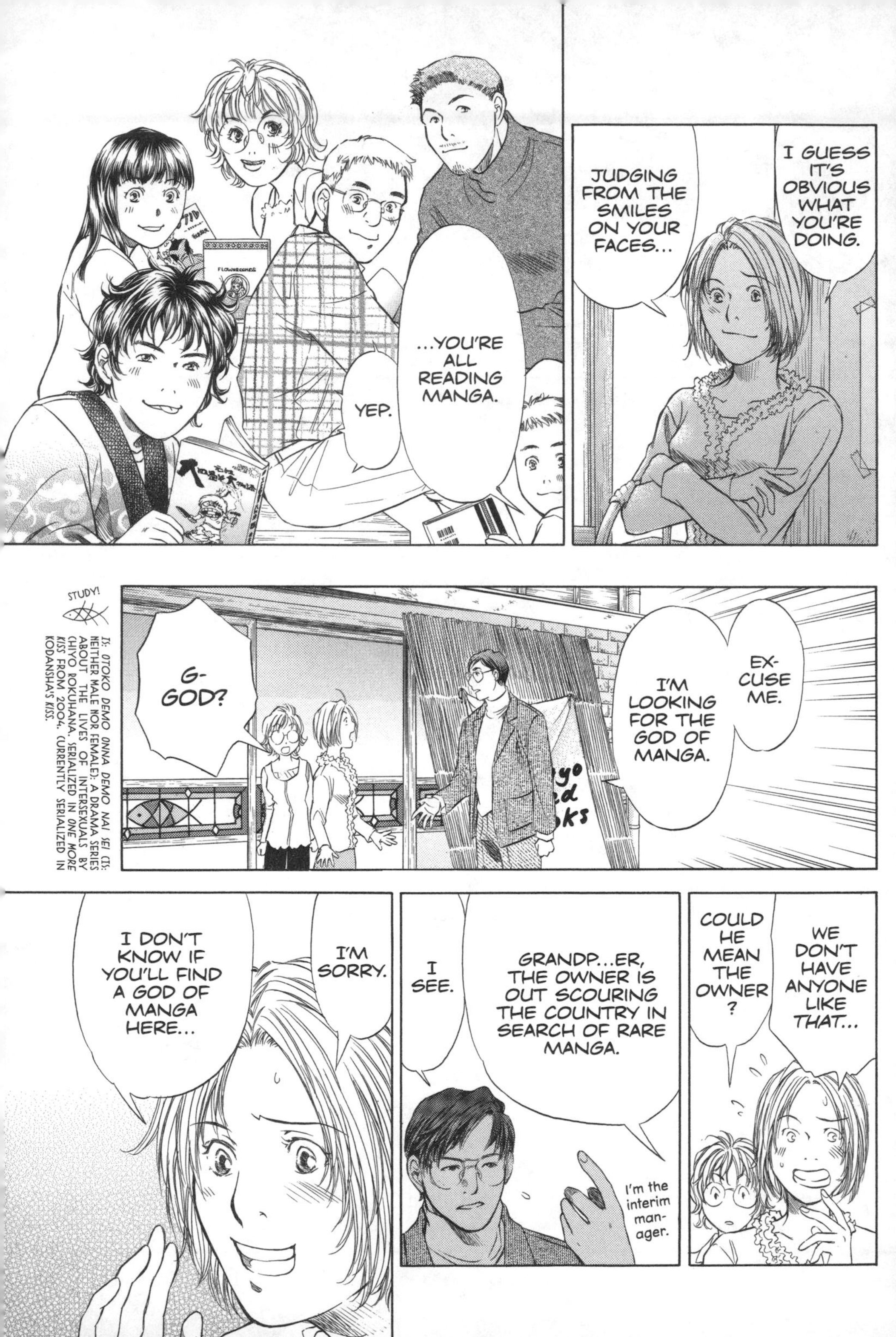
I GUESS IT'S OBVIOUS WHAT YOU'RE DOING.
JUDGING FROM THE SMILES ON YOUR FACES...
...YOU'RE ALL READING MANGA.
YEP.
EX-CUSE ME.
I'M LOOKING FOR THE GOD OF MANGA.
G-GOD?
WE DON'T HAVE ANYONE LIKE *THAT*...
COULD HE MEAN THE OWNER?
GRANDP...ER, THE OWNER IS OUT SCOURING THE COUNTRY IN SEARCH OF RARE MANGA.
I SEE.
I'm the interim man-ager.
I'M SORRY.
I DON'T KNOW IF YOU'LL FIND A GOD OF MANGA HERE...

STUDY!

IS: OTOKO DEMO ONNA DEMO NAI SEI (IS: NEITHER MALE NOR FEMALE): A DRAMA SERIES ABOUT THE LIVES OF INTERSEXUALS BY CHIYO ROKUHANA. SERIALIZED IN *ONE MORE KISS* FROM 2004. CURRENTLY SERIALIZED IN KODANSHA'S *KISS*.

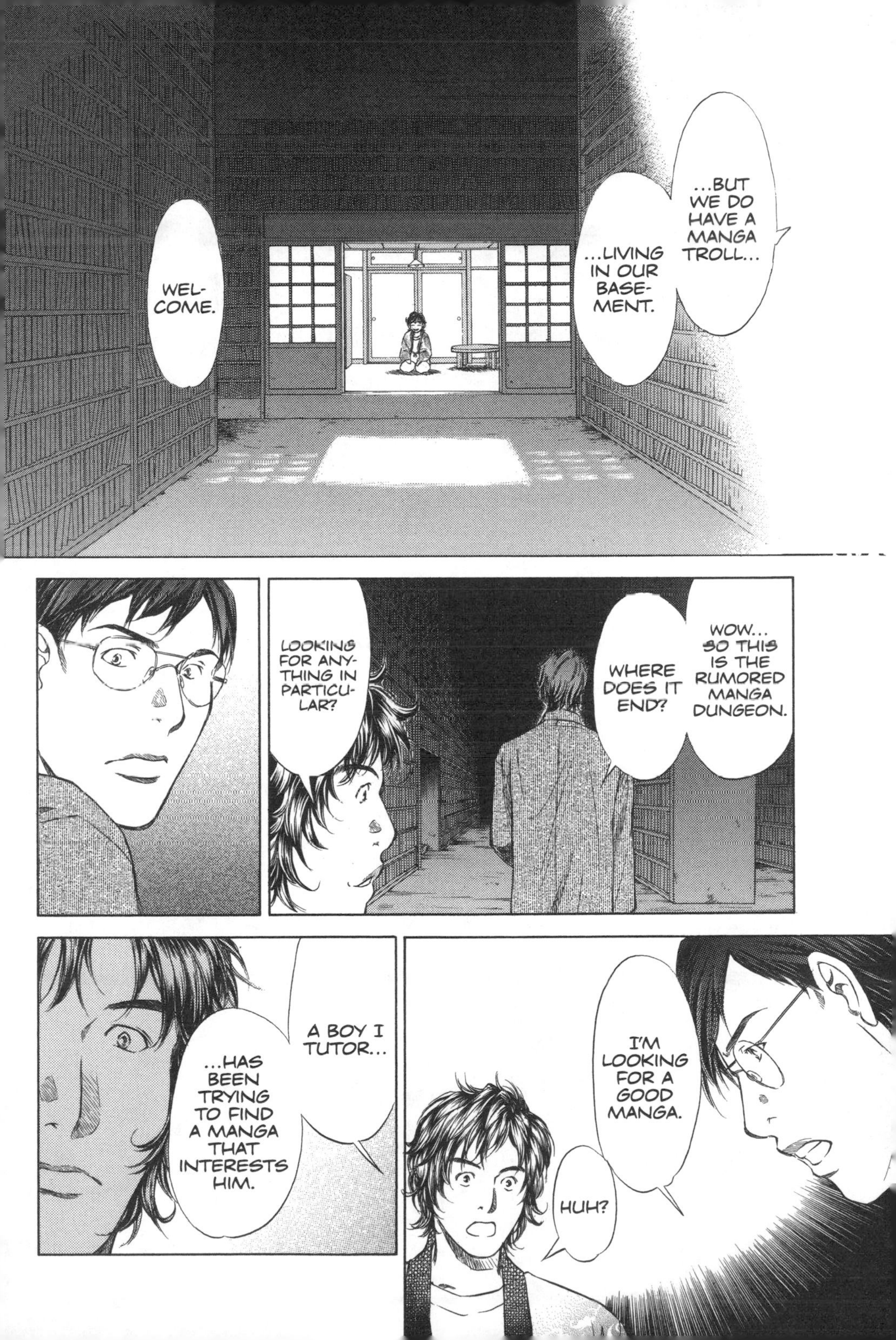
...BUT WE DO HAVE A MANGA TROLL...
...LIVING IN OUR BASE-MENT.
WEL-COME.
WOW... SO THIS IS THE RUMORED MANGA DUNGEON.
WHERE DOES IT END?
LOOKING FOR ANY-THING IN PARTICU-LAR?
I'M LOOKING FOR A GOOD MANGA.
HUH?
A BOY I TUTOR...
...HAS BEEN TRYING TO FIND A MANGA THAT INTERESTS HIM.

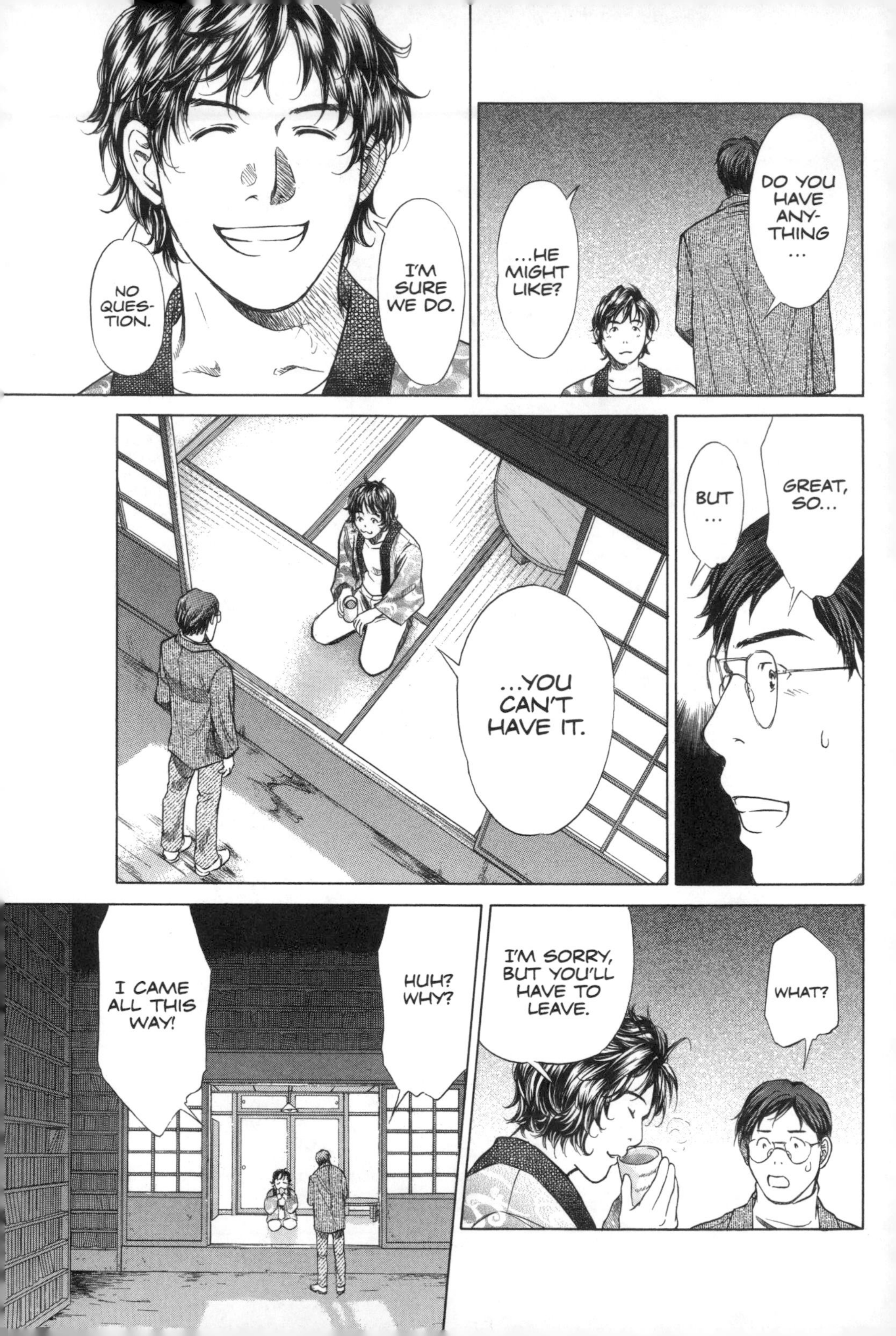
DO YOU HAVE ANY-THING...
...HE MIGHT LIKE?
I'M SURE WE DO.
NO QUES-TION.
GREAT, SO...
BUT...
...YOU CAN'T HAVE IT.
I'M SORRY, BUT YOU'LL HAVE TO LEAVE.
WHAT?
HUH? WHY?
I CAME ALL THIS WAY!

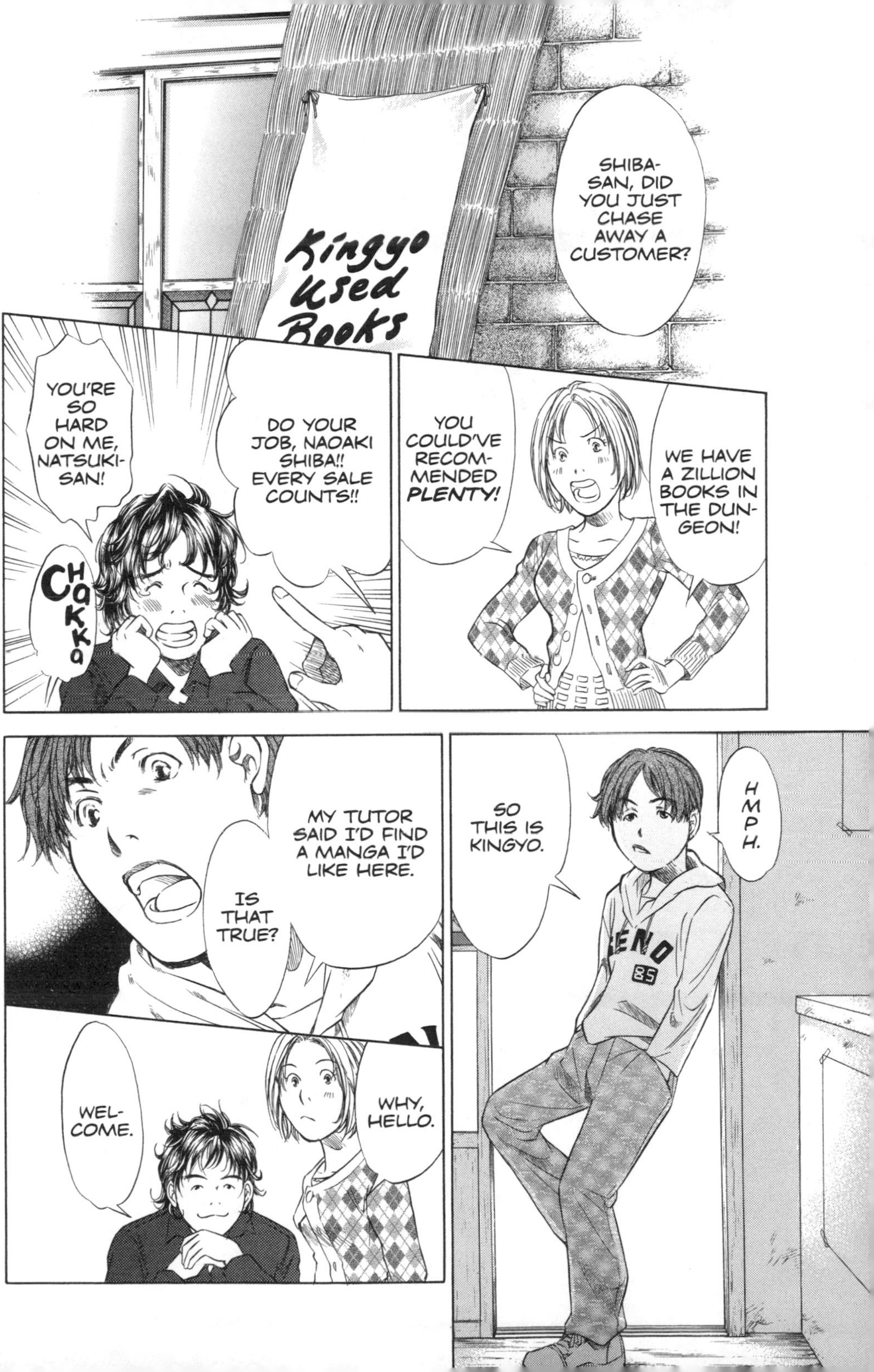
SHIBA-SAN, DID YOU JUST CHASE AWAY A CUSTOMER?
Kingyo Used Books
WE HAVE A ZILLION BOOKS IN THE DUNGEON!
YOU COULD'VE RECOMMENDED **PLENTY**!
DO YOUR JOB, NAOAKI SHIBA!! EVERY SALE COUNTS!!
YOU'RE SO HARD ON ME, NATSUKI-SAN!
Chakka
HMPH.
SO THIS IS KINGYO.
MY TUTOR SAID I'D FIND A MANGA I'D LIKE HERE.
IS THAT TRUE?
WHY, HELLO.
WELCOME.

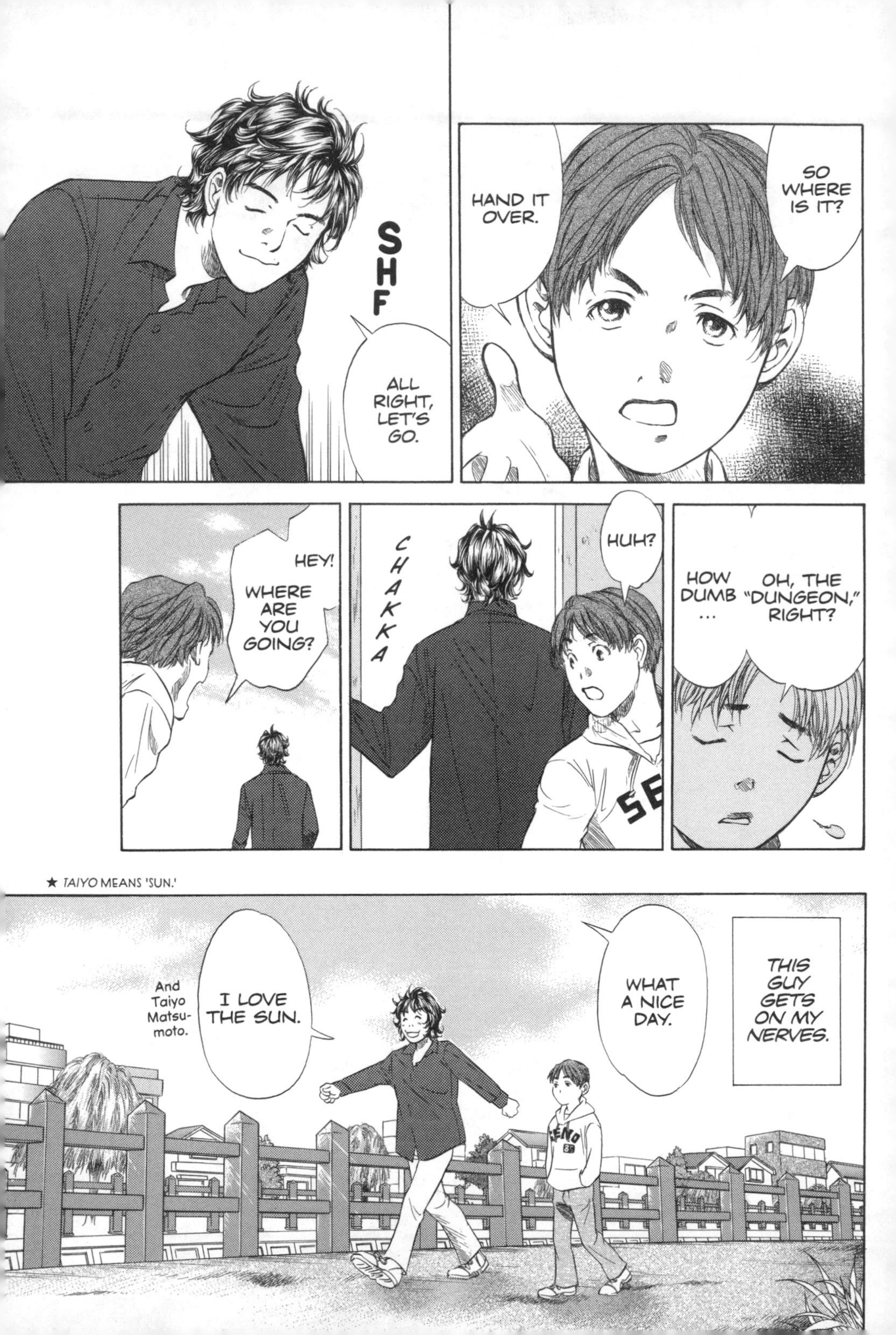
SO WHERE IS IT?
HAND IT OVER.
SHF
ALL RIGHT, LET'S GO.
OH, THE "DUNGEON," RIGHT?
HOW DUMB ...
HUH?
CHAKKA
HEY!
WHERE ARE YOU GOING?
THIS GUY GETS ON MY NERVES.
WHAT A NICE DAY.
I LOVE THE SUN.
And Taiyo Matsumoto.

★ *TAIYO* MEANS 'SUN.'

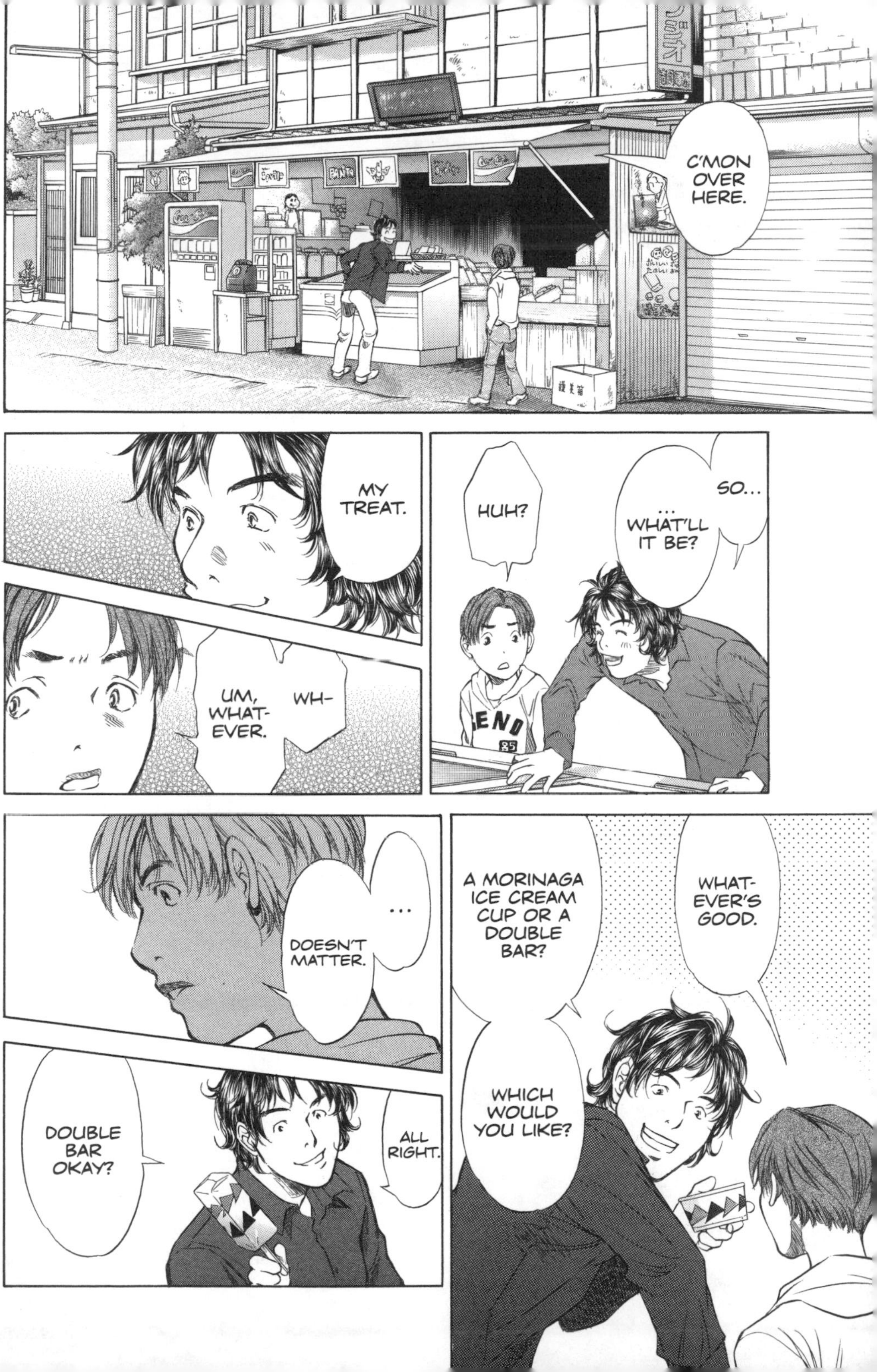
C'MON OVER HERE.
SO...
...WHAT'LL IT BE?
HUH?
MY TREAT.
WH-
UM, WHAT-EVER.
WHAT-EVER'S GOOD.
A MORINAGA ICE CREAM CUP OR A DOUBLE BAR?
WHICH WOULD YOU LIKE?
...
DOESN'T MATTER.
ALL RIGHT.
DOUBLE BAR OKAY?

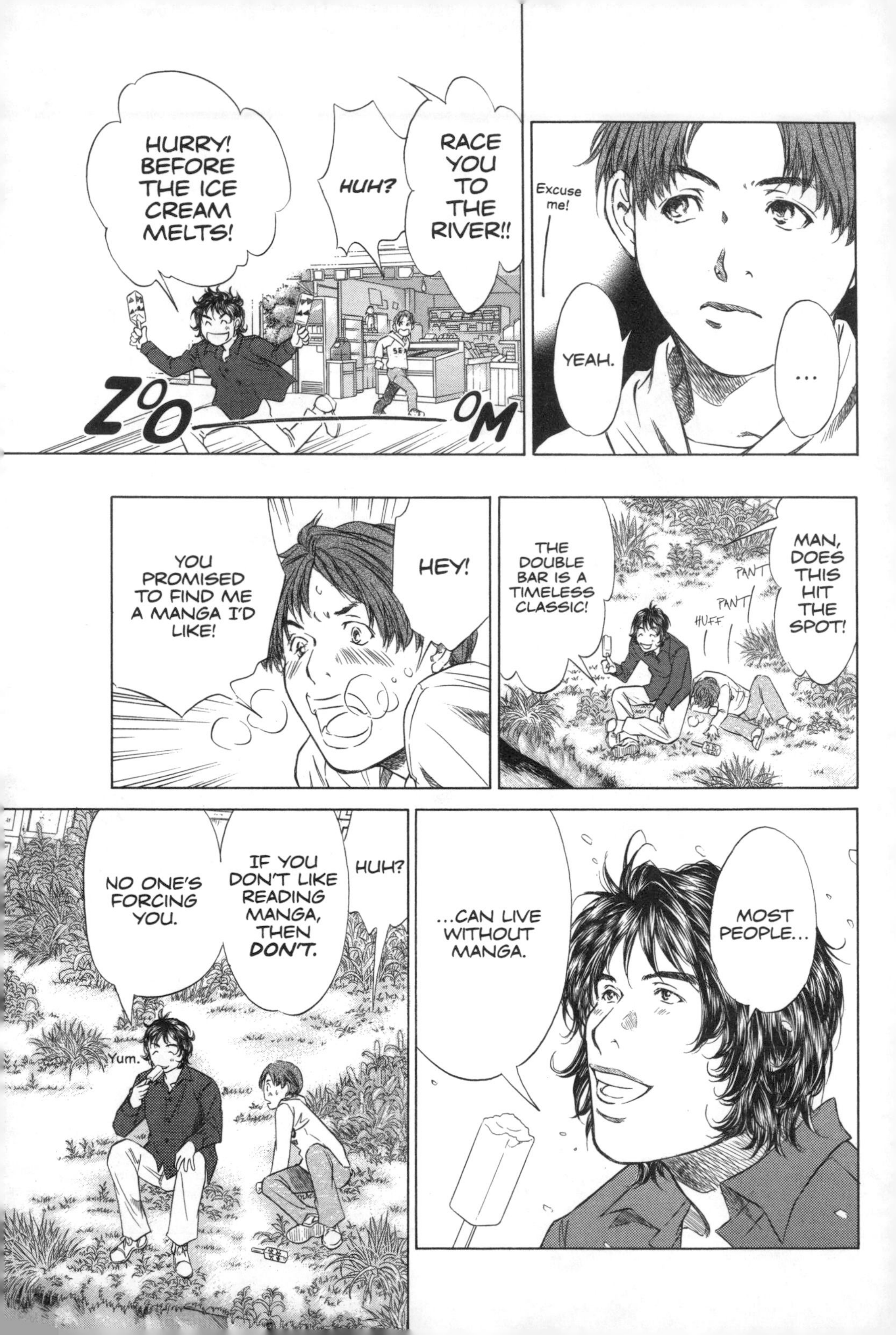
Excuse me!
...
YEAH.
RACE YOU TO THE RIVER!!
HUH?
HURRY! BEFORE THE ICE CREAM MELTS!
ZOOM
MAN, DOES THIS HIT THE SPOT!
PANT PANT
HUFF
THE DOUBLE BAR IS A TIMELESS CLASSIC!
HEY!
YOU PROMISED TO FIND ME A MANGA I'D LIKE!
MOST PEOPLE...
...CAN LIVE WITHOUT MANGA.
HUH?
IF YOU DON'T LIKE READING MANGA, THEN DON'T.
NO ONE'S FORCING YOU.
Yum.

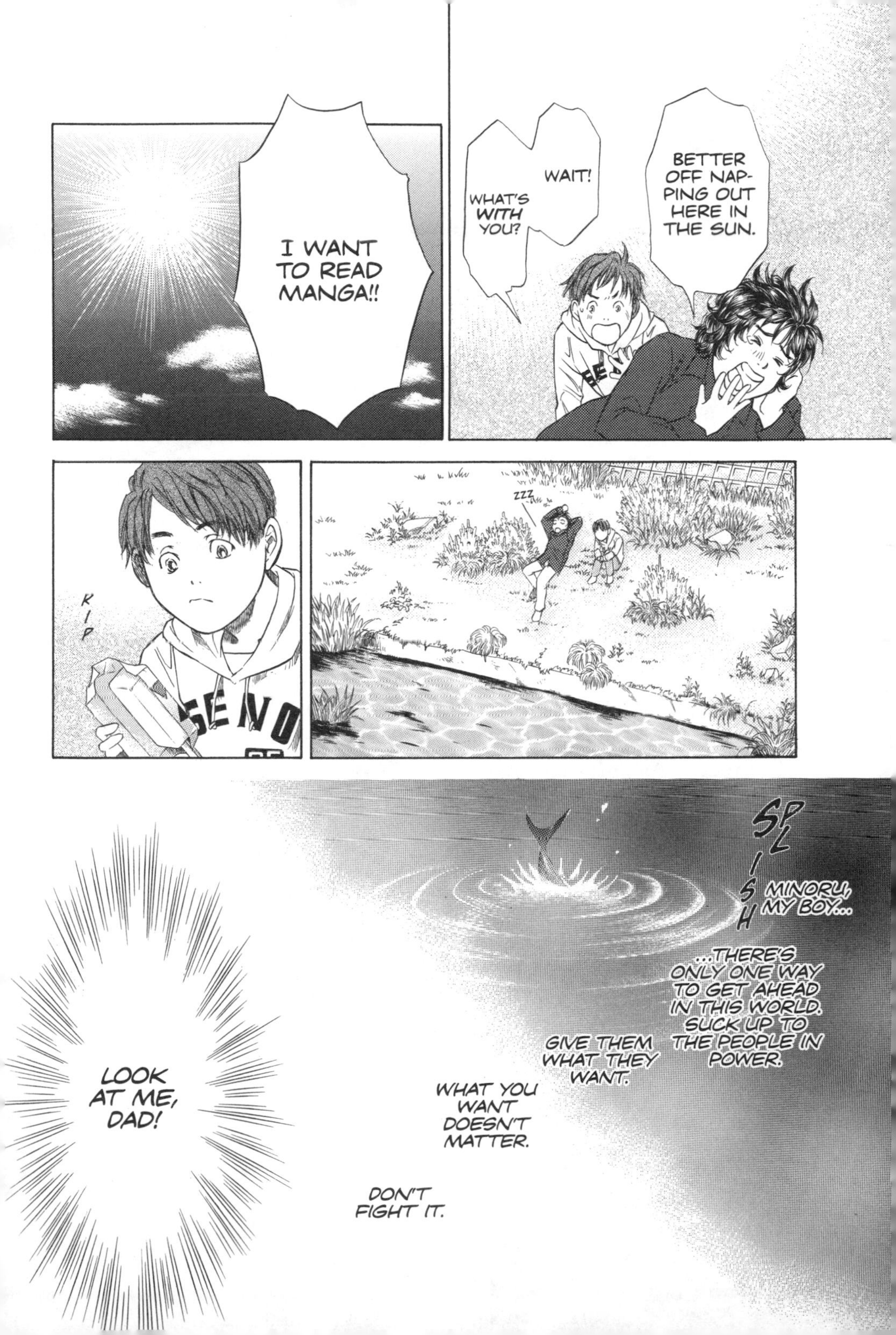
BETTER OFF NAP-PING OUT HERE IN THE SUN.
WAIT!
WHAT'S WITH YOU?
I WANT TO READ MANGA!!
ZZZ
RIP
SPLISH
MINORU, MY BOY...
...THERE'S ONLY ONE WAY TO GET AHEAD IN THIS WORLD. SUCK UP TO THE PEOPLE IN POWER.
GIVE THEM WHAT THEY WANT.
WHAT YOU WANT DOESN'T MATTER.
DON'T FIGHT IT.
LOOK AT ME, DAD!

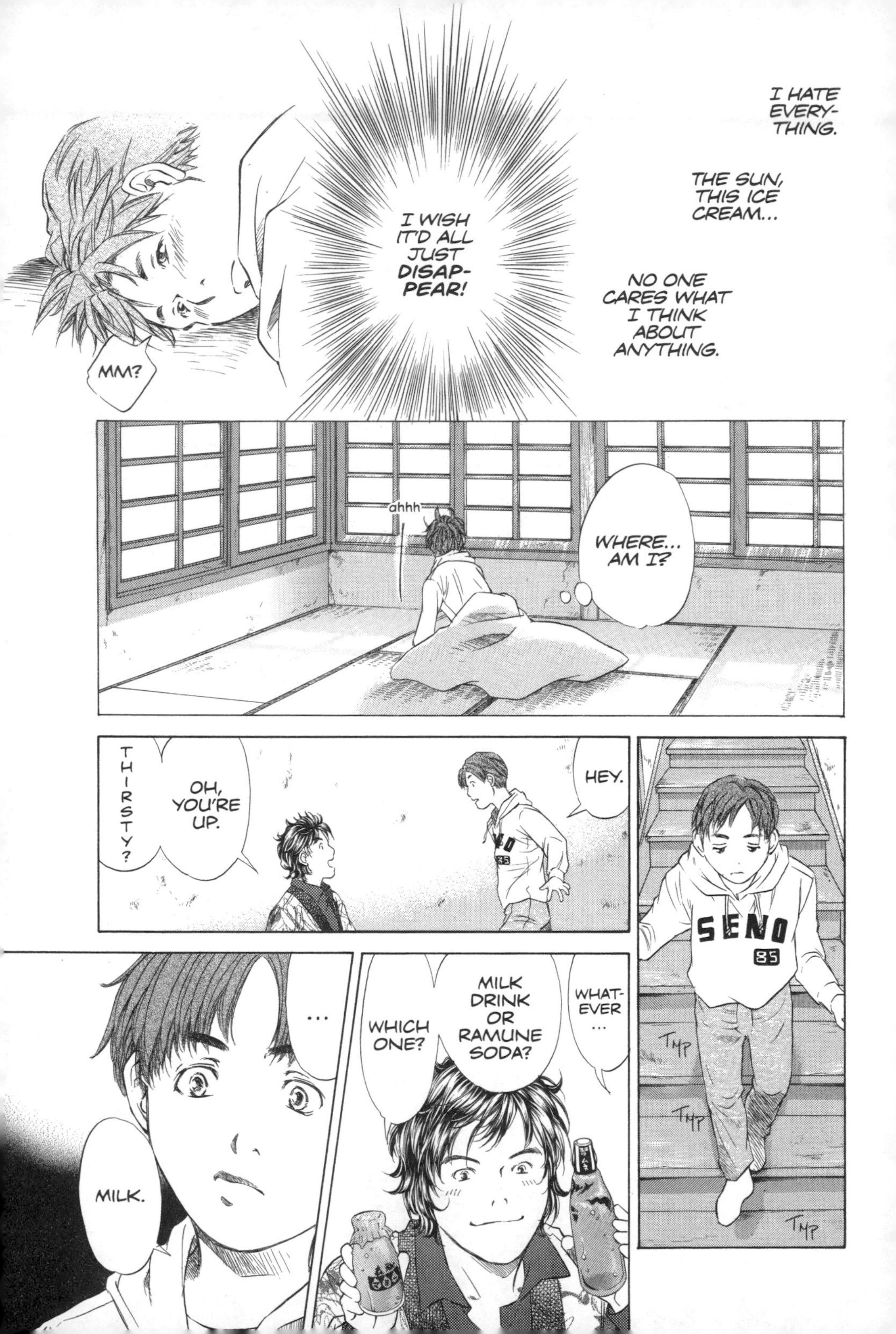
I HATE EVERYTHING.
THE SUN, THIS ICE CREAM...
NO ONE CARES WHAT I THINK ABOUT ANYTHING.
I WISH IT'D ALL JUST DISAPPEAR!
MM?
WHERE... AM I?
ahhh
SENO 85
TMP
TMP
TMP
HEY.
OH, YOU'RE UP.
THIRSTY?
WHAT-EVER...
MILK DRINK OR RAMUNE SODA?
WHICH ONE?
...
MILK.

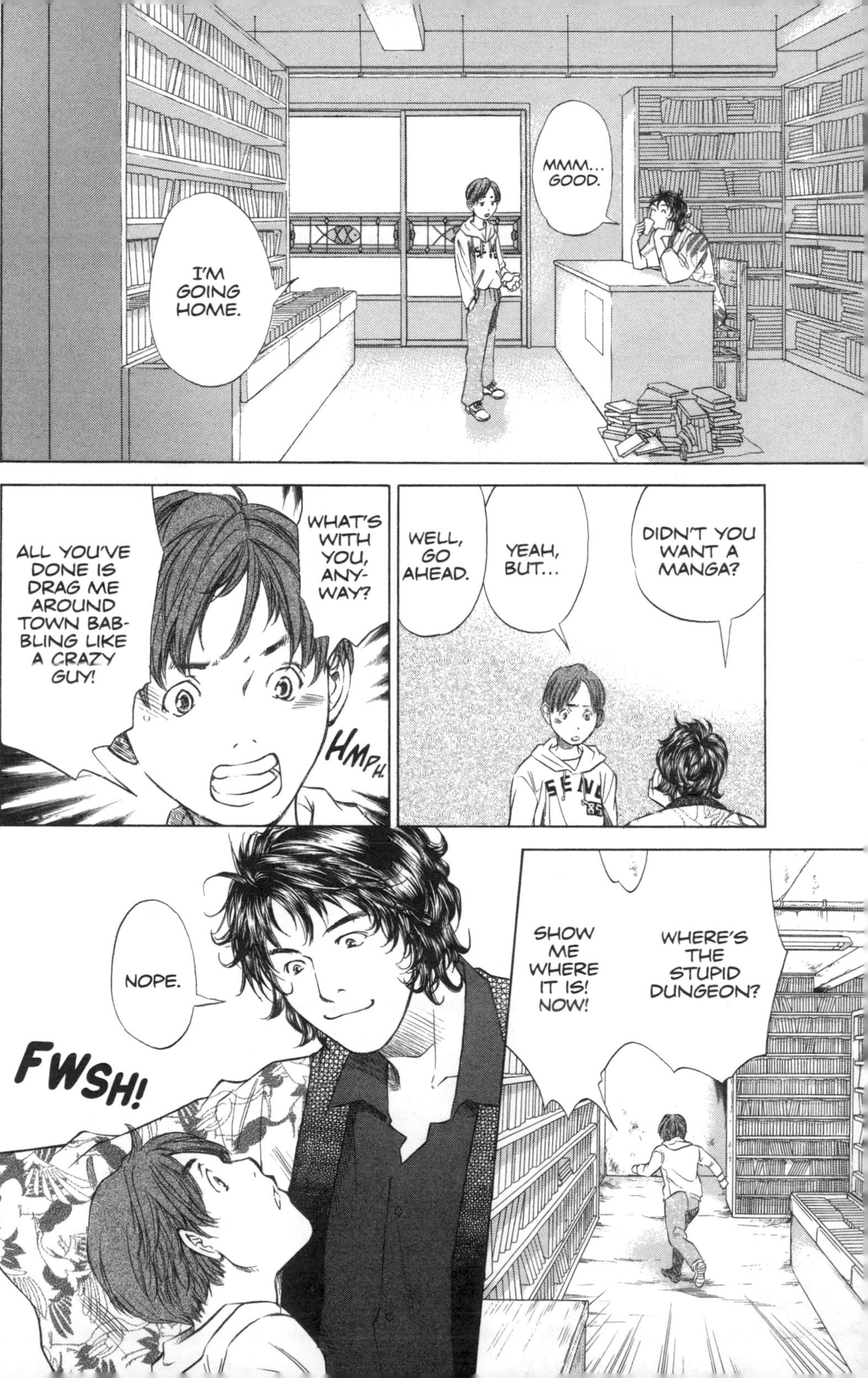
MMM... GOOD.
I'M GOING HOME.
DIDN'T YOU WANT A MANGA?
YEAH, BUT...
WELL, GO AHEAD.
WHAT'S WITH YOU, ANY-WAY?
ALL YOU'VE DONE IS DRAG ME AROUND TOWN BAB-BLING LIKE A CRAZY GUY!
HMPH.
WHERE'S THE STUPID DUNGEON?
SHOW ME WHERE IT IS! NOW!
NOPE.
FWSH!

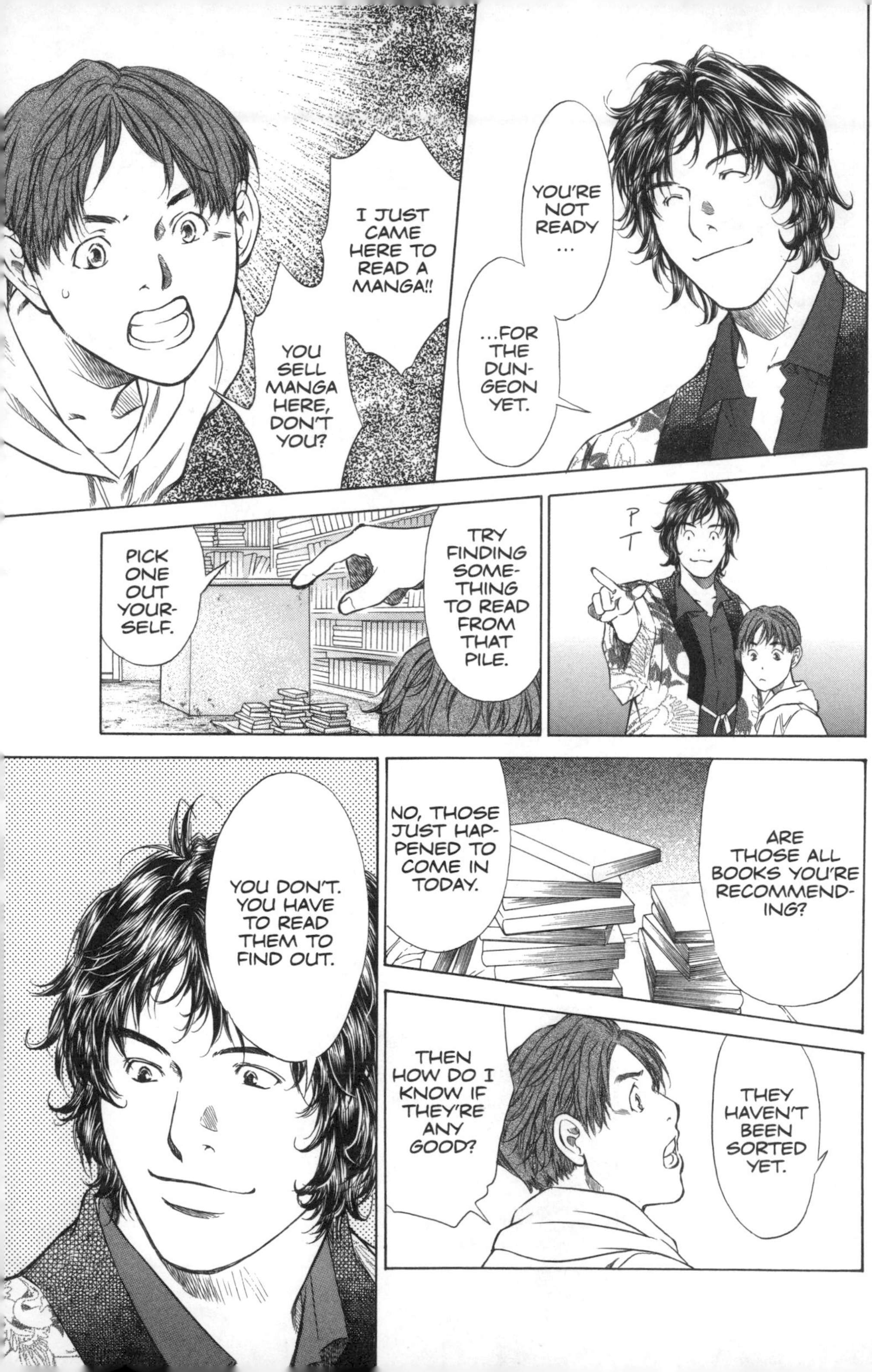
YOU'RE NOT READY ...
...FOR THE DUN-GEON YET.
I JUST CAME HERE TO READ A MANGA!!
YOU SELL MANGA HERE, DON'T YOU?
PT
TRY FINDING SOME-THING TO READ FROM THAT PILE.
PICK ONE OUT YOUR-SELF.
ARE THOSE ALL BOOKS YOU'RE RECOMMEND-ING?
NO, THOSE JUST HAP-PENED TO COME IN TODAY.
THEY HAVEN'T BEEN SORTED YET.
THEN HOW DO I KNOW IF THEY'RE ANY GOOD?
YOU DON'T. YOU HAVE TO READ THEM TO FIND OUT.

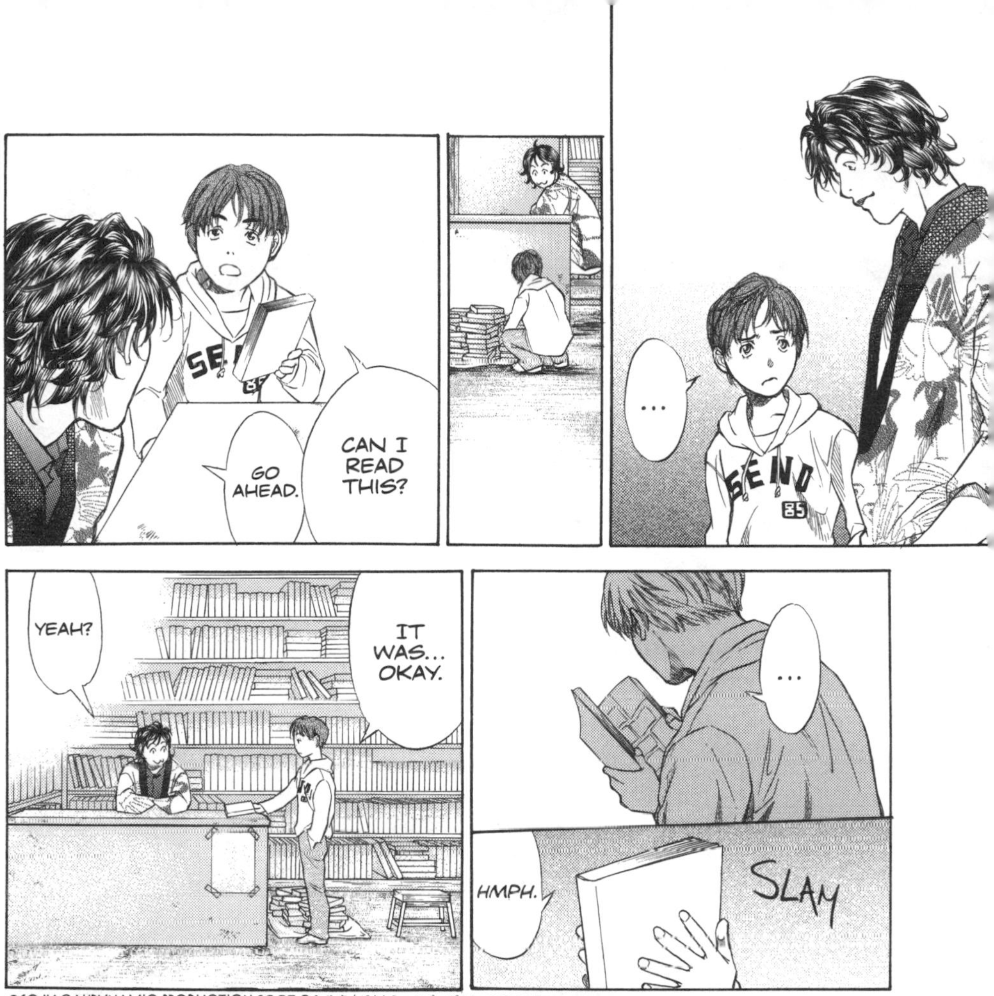
...
CAN I READ THIS?
GO AHEAD.
...
SLAM
HMPH.
IT WAS... OKAY.
YEAH?

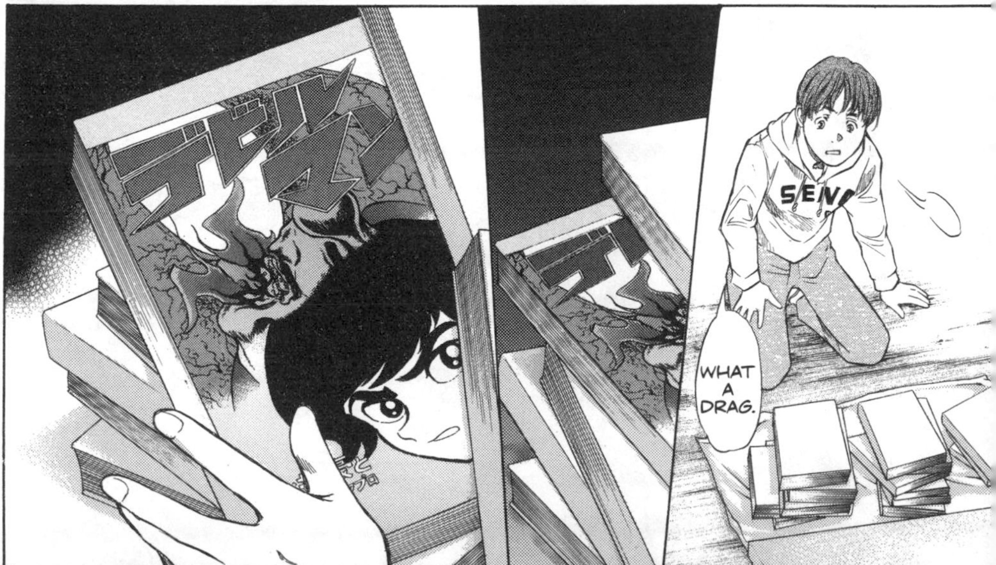
WHAT A DRAG.

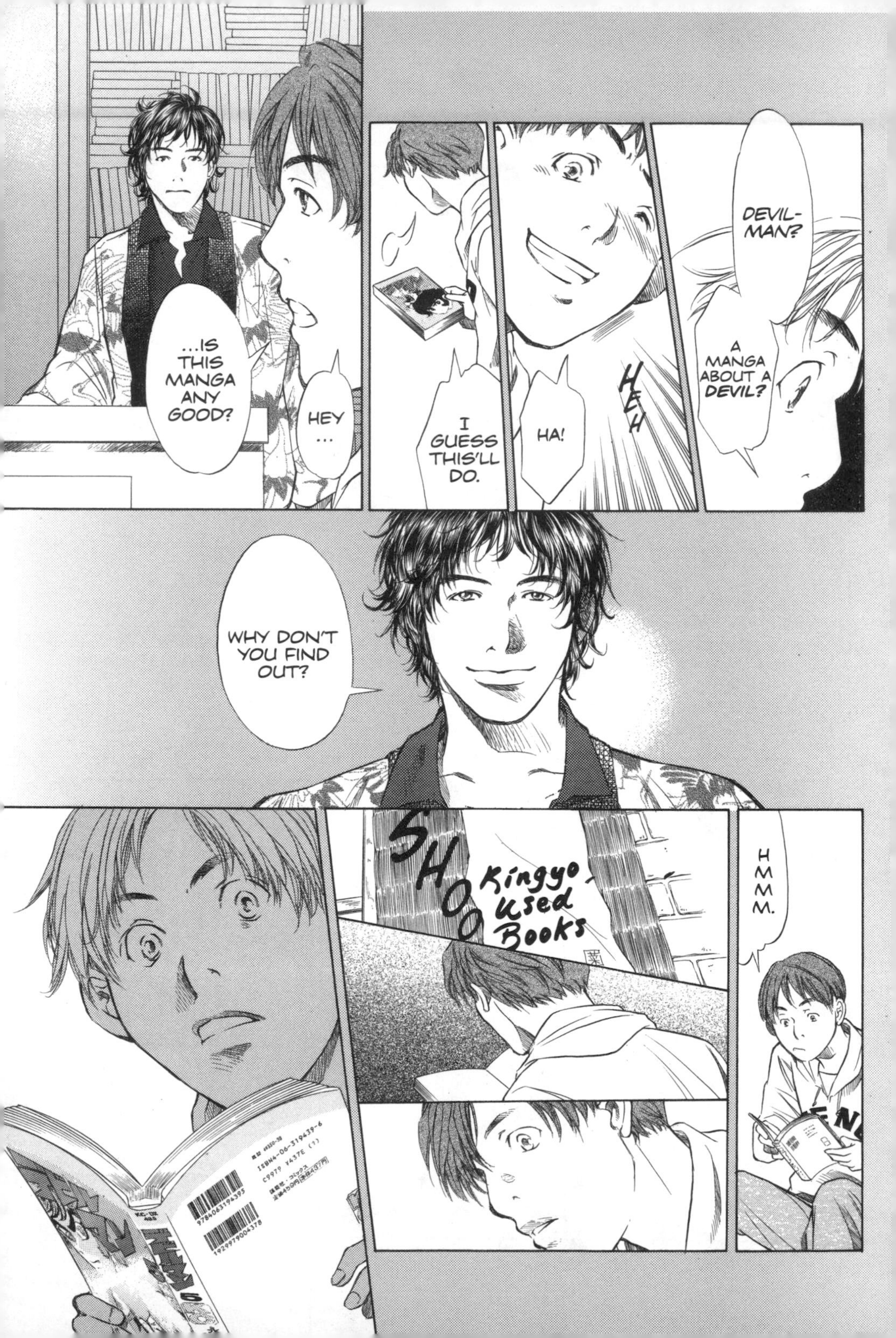
DEVIL-MAN?
A MANGA ABOUT A DEVIL?
HEH
HA!
I GUESS THIS'LL DO.
HEY ...
...IS THIS MANGA ANY GOOD?
WHY DON'T YOU FIND OUT?
HMMM.
SHOOO
Kingyo Used Books

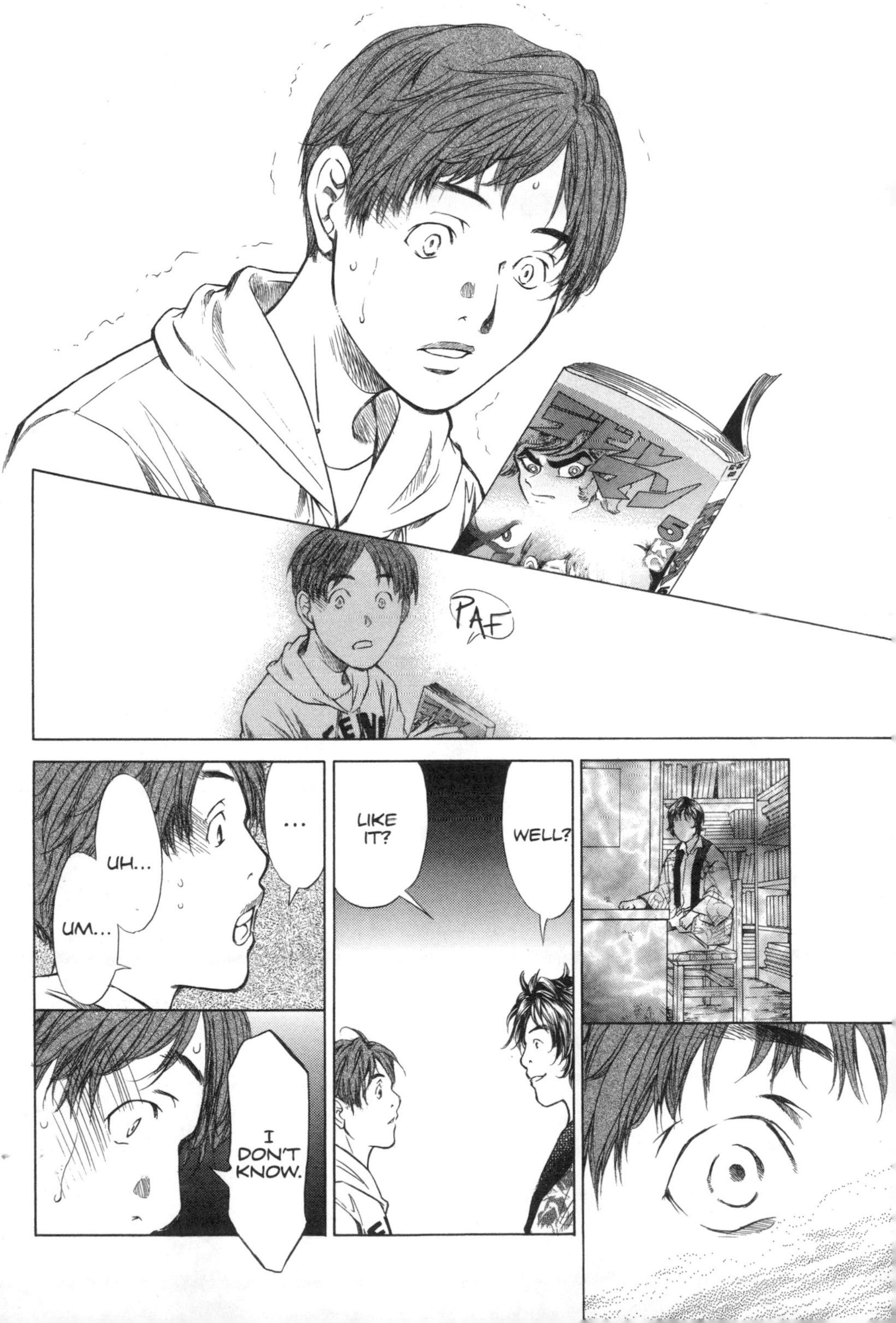
PAF
WELL?
LIKE IT?
...
UH...
UM...
I DON'T KNOW.

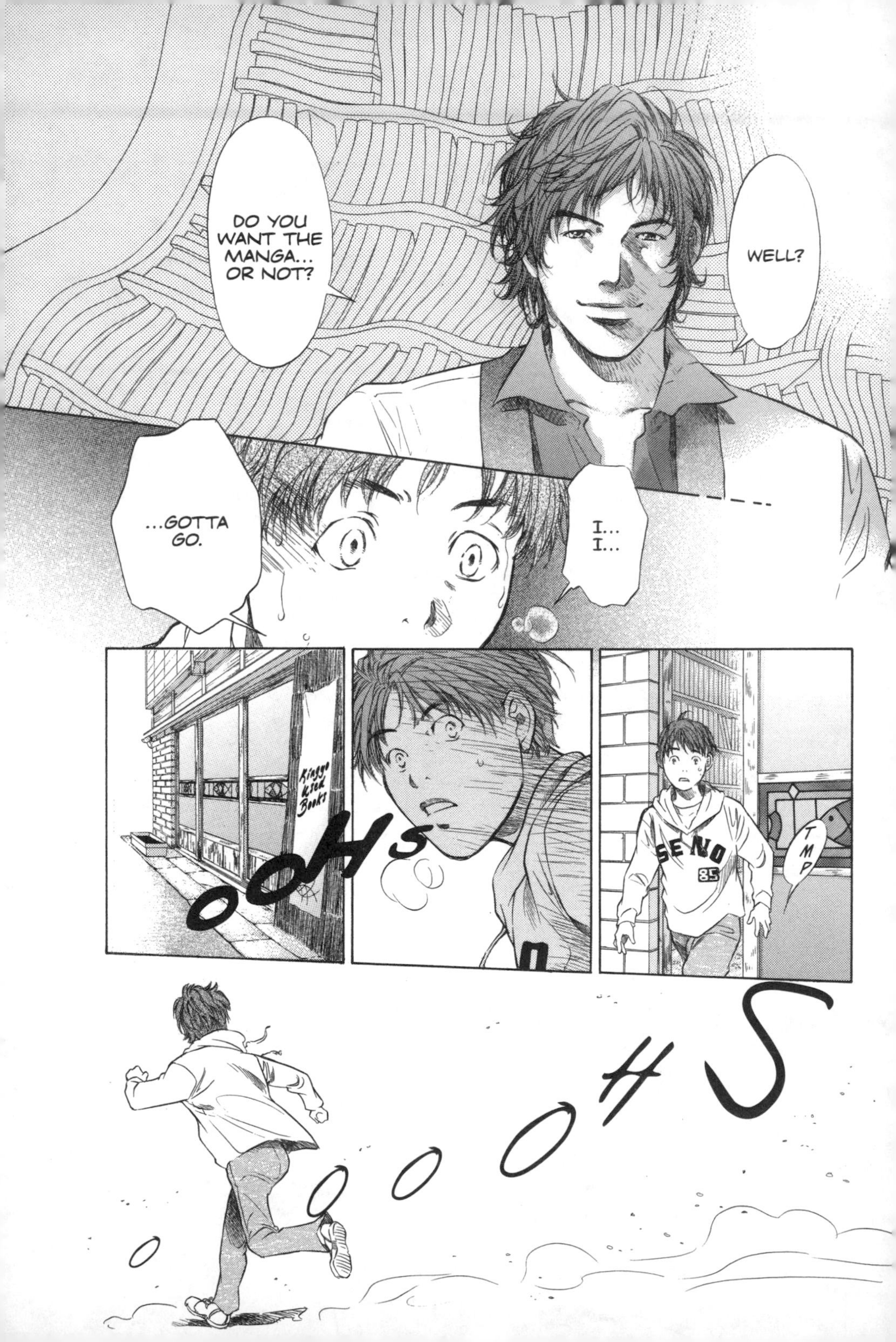
WELL?
DO YOU WANT THE MANGA... OR NOT?
I... I...
...GOTTA GO.
TMP
SHOO
Kingyo Used Books
SHOOOOO

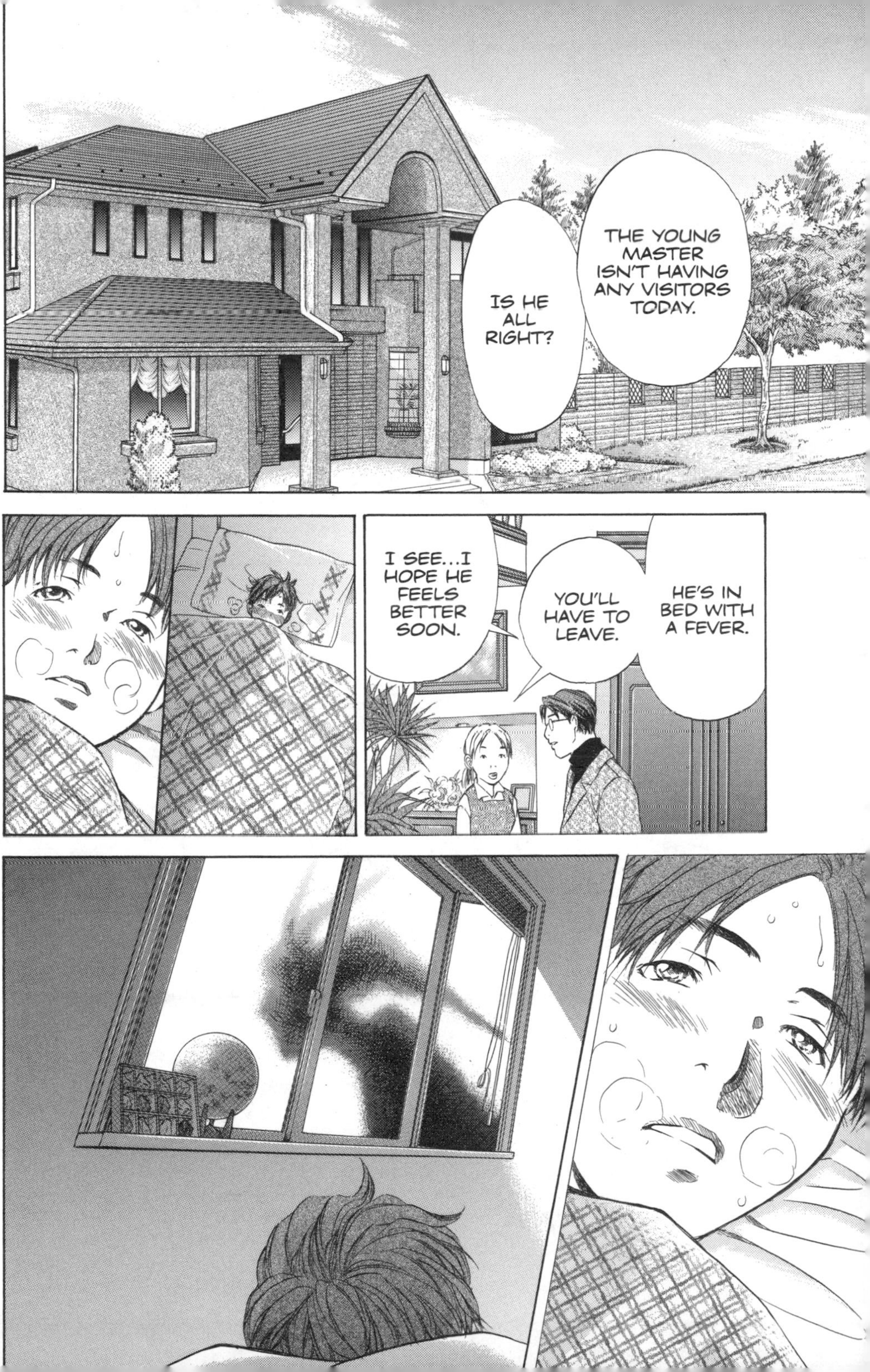
THE YOUNG MASTER ISN'T HAVING ANY VISITORS TODAY.
IS HE ALL RIGHT?
HE'S IN BED WITH A FEVER.
YOU'LL HAVE TO LEAVE.
I SEE...I HOPE HE FEELS BETTER SOON.

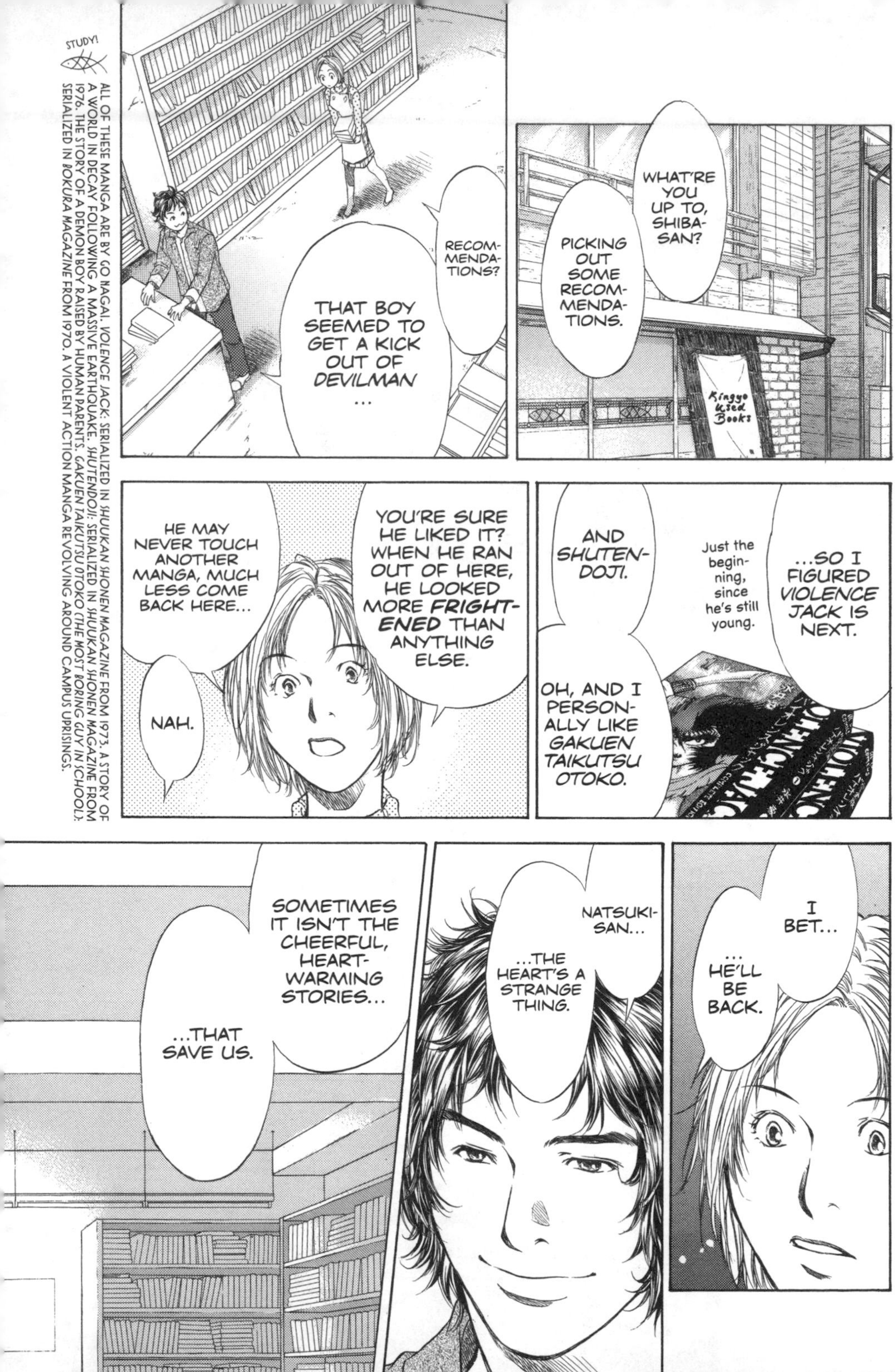
WHAT'RE YOU UP TO, SHIBA-SAN?
PICKING OUT SOME RECOMMENDATIONS.
Ringgo Used Books
RECOMMENDATIONS?
THAT BOY SEEMED TO GET A KICK OUT OF *DEVILMAN* ...
...SO I FIGURED *VIOLENCE JACK* IS NEXT.
Just the beginning, since he's still young.
AND *SHUTEN-DOJI*.
OH, AND I PERSONALLY LIKE *GAKUEN TAIKUTSU OTOKO*.
YOU'RE SURE HE LIKED IT? WHEN HE RAN OUT OF HERE, HE LOOKED MORE **FRIGHTENED** THAN ANYTHING ELSE.
HE MAY NEVER TOUCH ANOTHER MANGA, MUCH LESS COME BACK HERE...
NAH.
I BET...
...HE'LL BE BACK.
NATSUKI-SAN...
...THE HEART'S A STRANGE THING.
SOMETIMES IT ISN'T THE CHEERFUL, HEART-WARMING STORIES...
...THAT SAVE US.

STUDY!

ALL OF THESE MANGA ARE BY GO NAGAI. VOLENCE JACK: SERIALIZED IN SHUUKAN SHONEN MAGAZINE FROM 1973. A STORY OF A WORLD IN DECAY FOLLOWING A MASSIVE EARTHQUAKE. SHUTENDOJI: SERIALIZED IN SHUUKAN SHONEN MAGAZINE FROM 1976. THE STORY OF A DEMON BOY RAISED BY HUMAN PARENTS. GAKUEN TAIKUTSU OTOKO (THE MOST BORING GUY IN SCHOOL): SERIALIZED IN BOKURA MAGAZINE FROM 1970. A VIOLENT ACTION MANGA REVOLVING AROUND CAMPUS UPRISINGS.

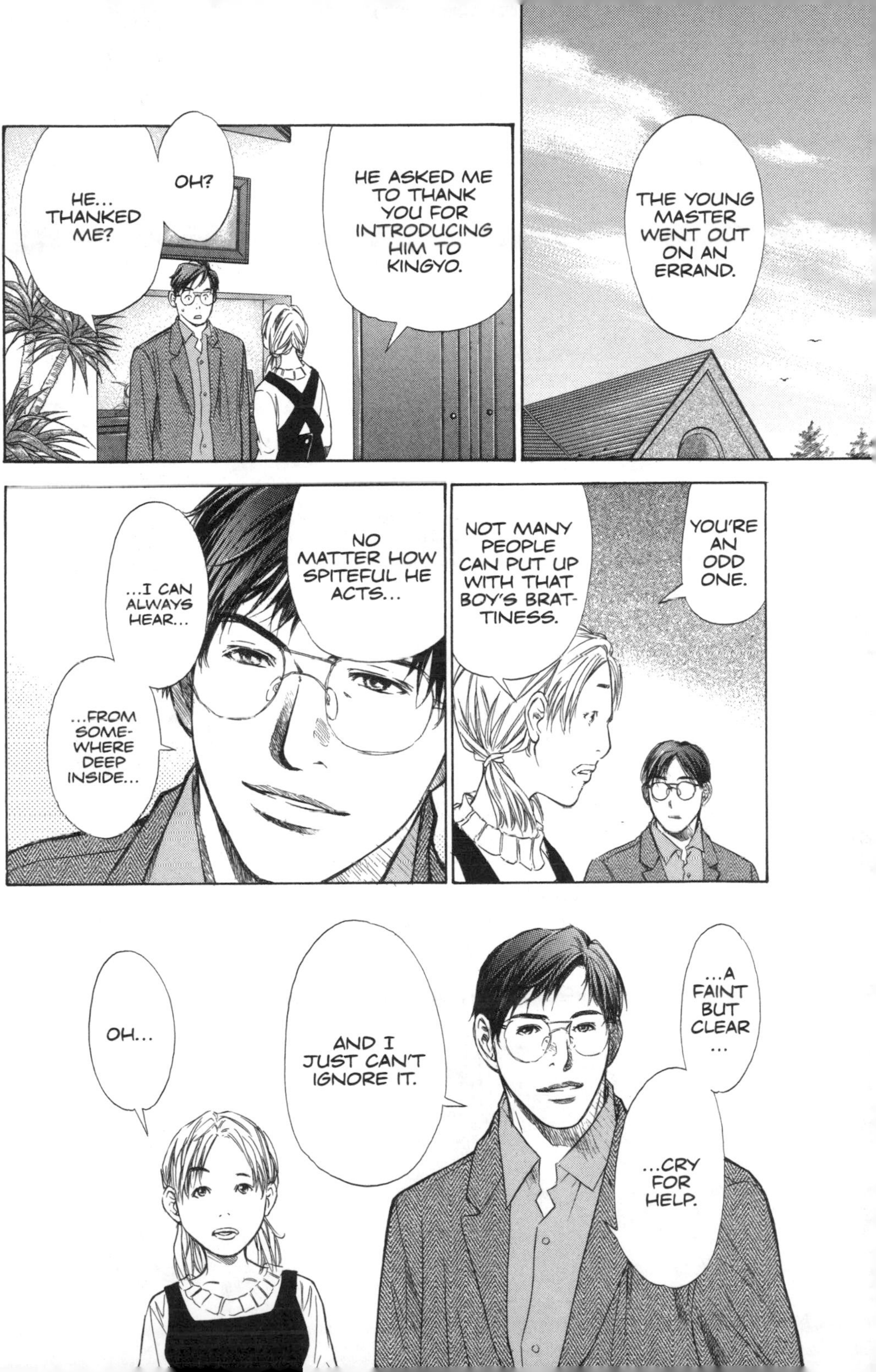
THE YOUNG MASTER WENT OUT ON AN ERRAND.
HE ASKED ME TO THANK YOU FOR INTRODUCING HIM TO KINGYO.
OH?
HE... THANKED ME?
YOU'RE AN ODD ONE.
NOT MANY PEOPLE CAN PUT UP WITH THAT BOY'S BRAT-TINESS.
NO MATTER HOW SPITEFUL HE ACTS...
...I CAN ALWAYS HEAR...
...FROM SOME-WHERE DEEP INSIDE...
...A FAINT BUT CLEAR...
...CRY FOR HELP.
AND I JUST CAN'T IGNORE IT.
OH...

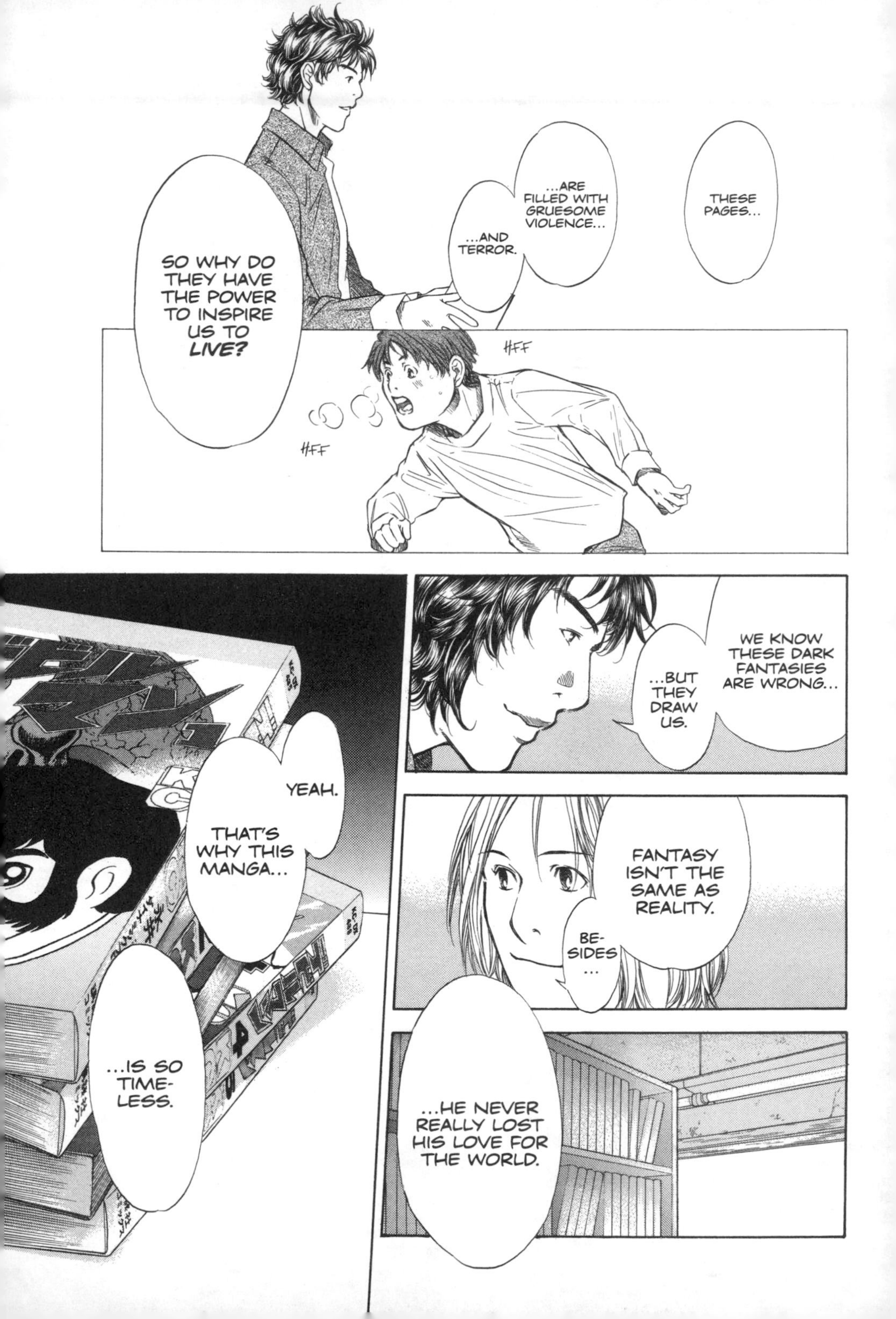
THESE PAGES...
...ARE FILLED WITH GRUESOME VIOLENCE...
...AND TERROR.
SO WHY DO THEY HAVE THE POWER TO INSPIRE US TO *LIVE?*
HFF
HFF
WE KNOW THESE DARK FANTASIES ARE WRONG...
...BUT THEY DRAW US.
FANTASY ISN'T THE SAME AS REALITY.
BE-SIDES...
...HE NEVER REALLY LOST HIS LOVE FOR THE WORLD.
YEAH.
THAT'S WHY THIS MANGA...
...IS SO TIME-LESS.

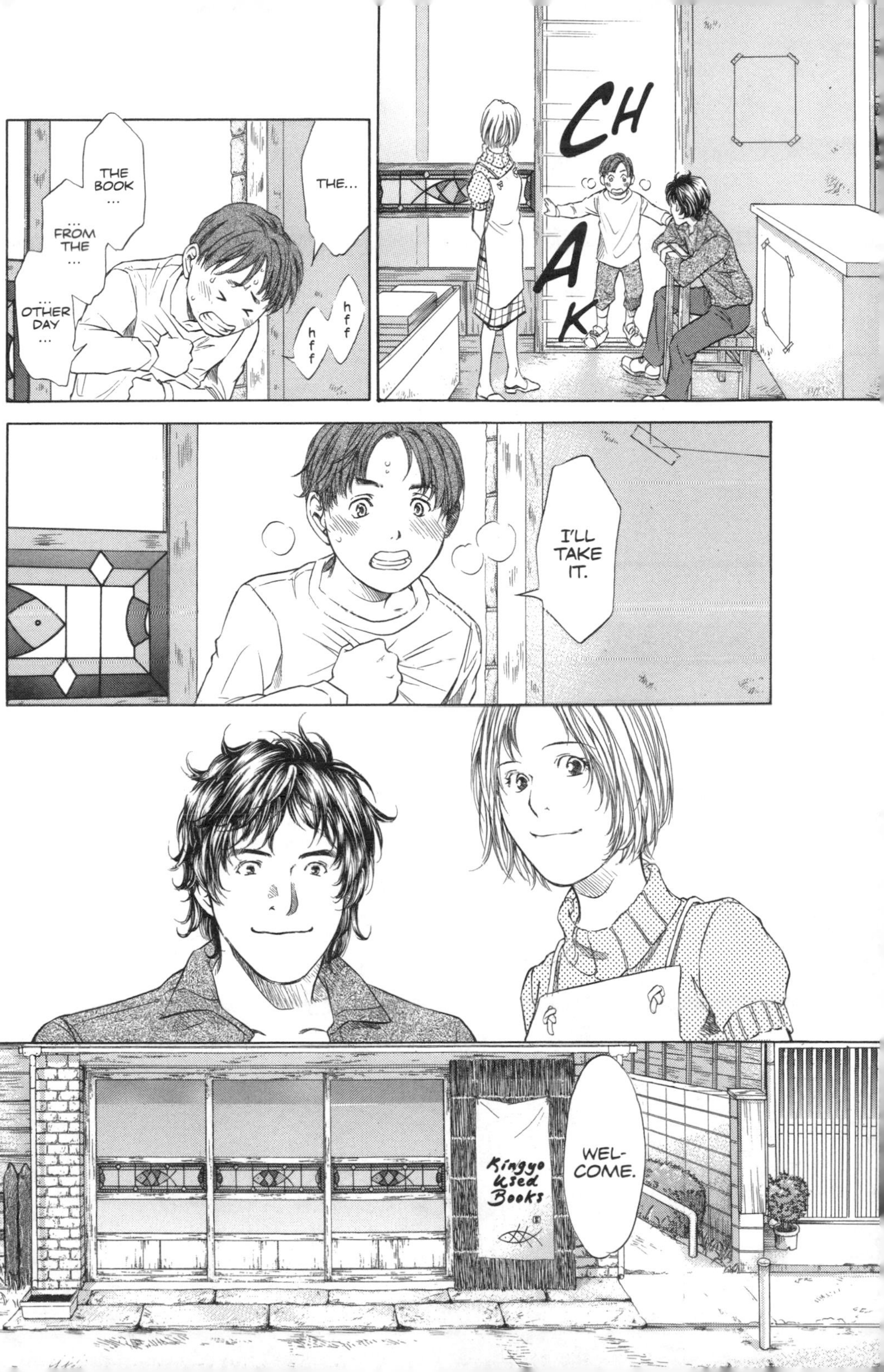
CHAK
THE...
hff hff
THE BOOK ...
... FROM THE ...
... OTHER DAY ...
I'LL TAKE IT.
Kingyo Used Books
WEL-COME.

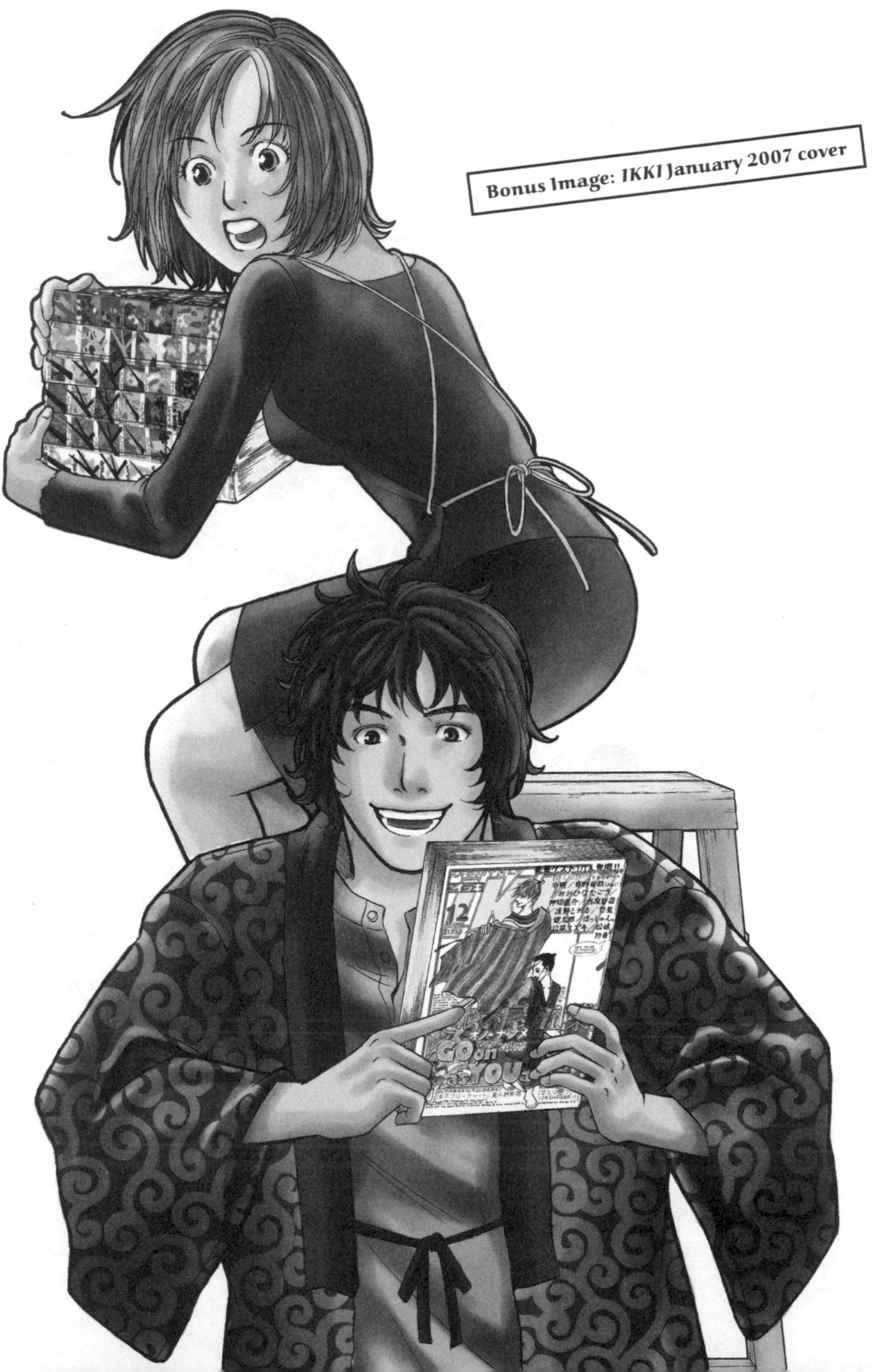

Bonus Image: *IKKI* January 2007 cover

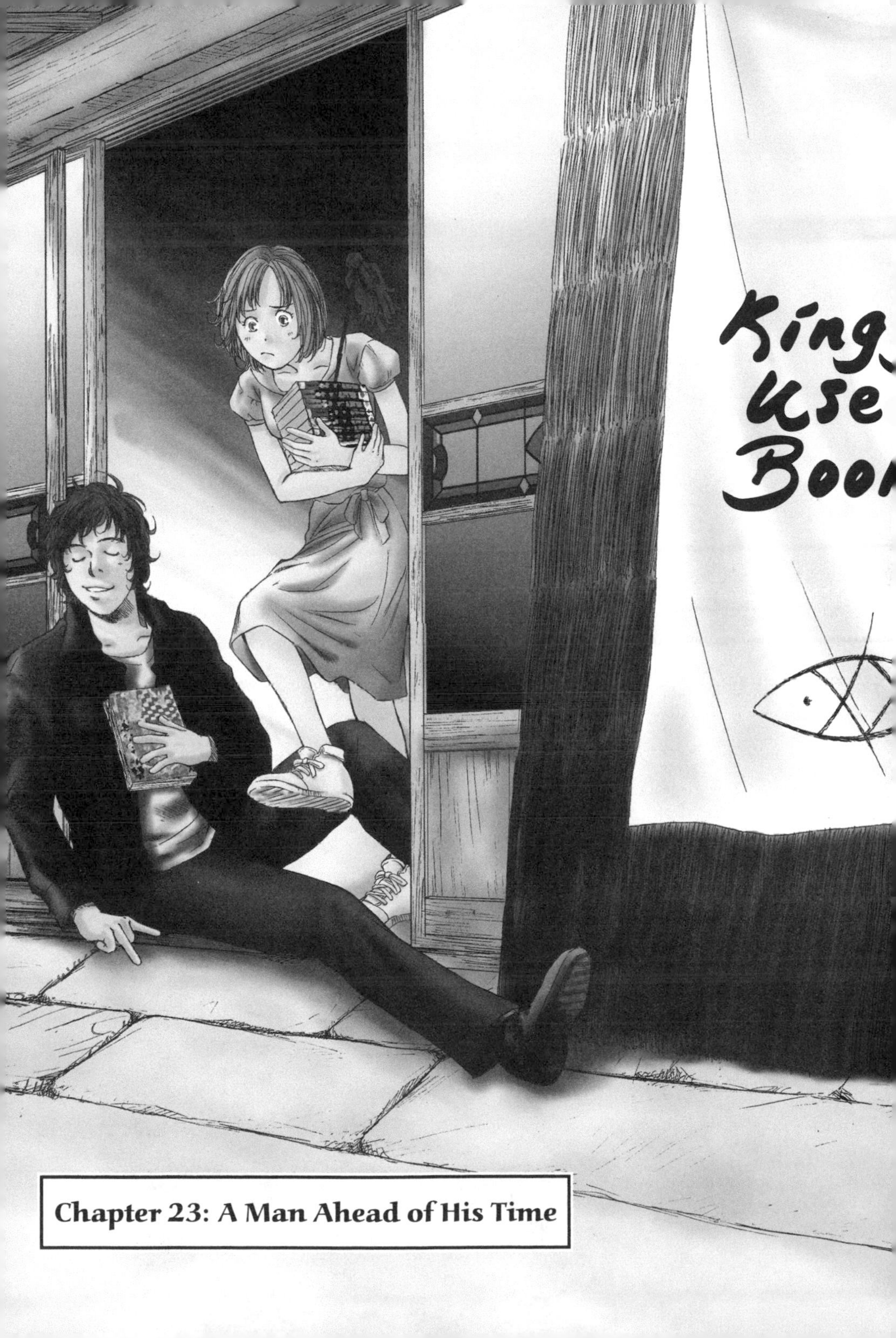

Chapter 23: A Man Ahead of His Time

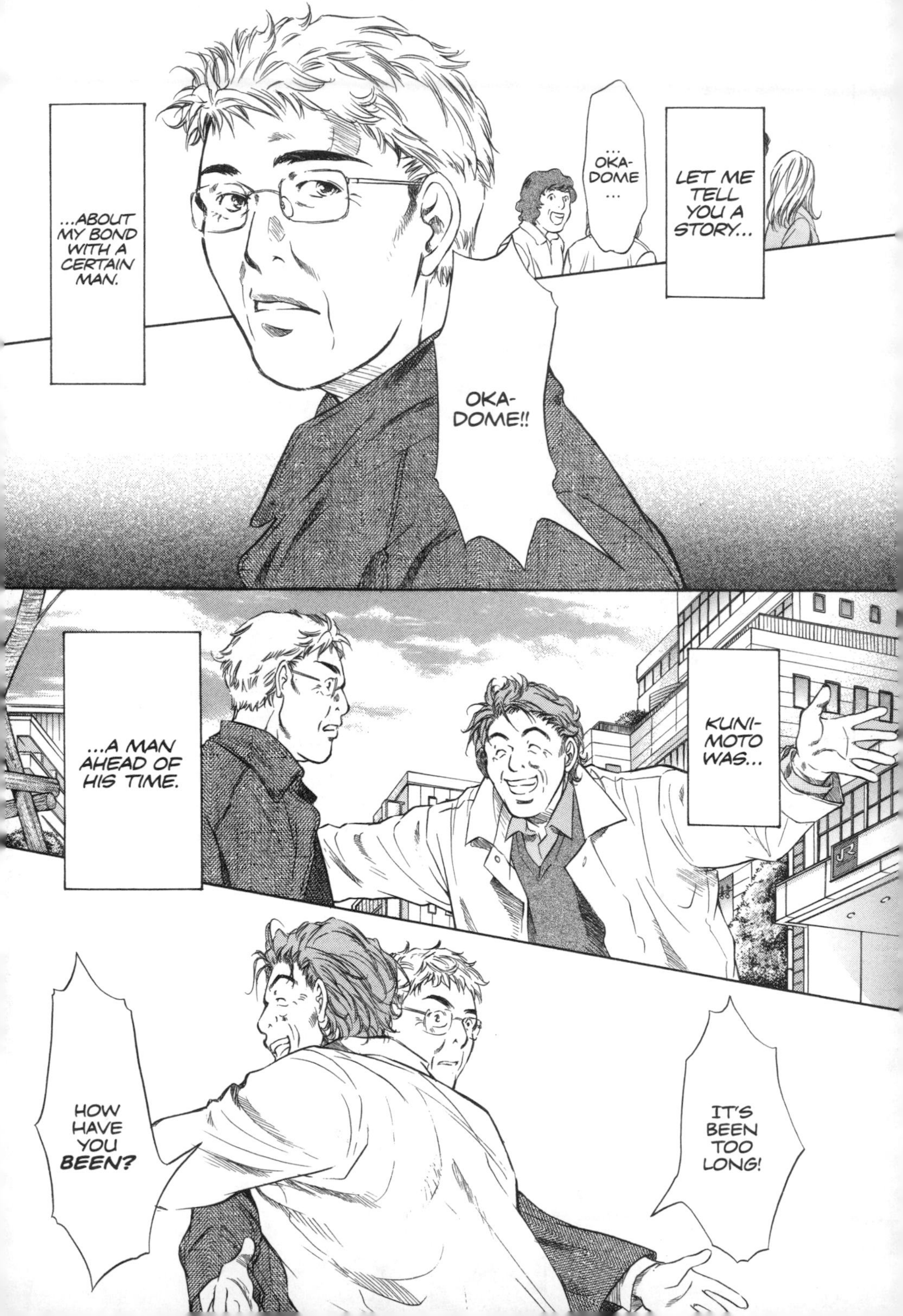
LET ME TELL YOU A STORY...
...OKA-DOME...
...ABOUT MY BOND WITH A CERTAIN MAN.
OKA-DOME!!
KUNI-MOTO WAS...
...A MAN AHEAD OF HIS TIME.
IT'S BEEN TOO LONG!
HOW HAVE YOU BEEN?

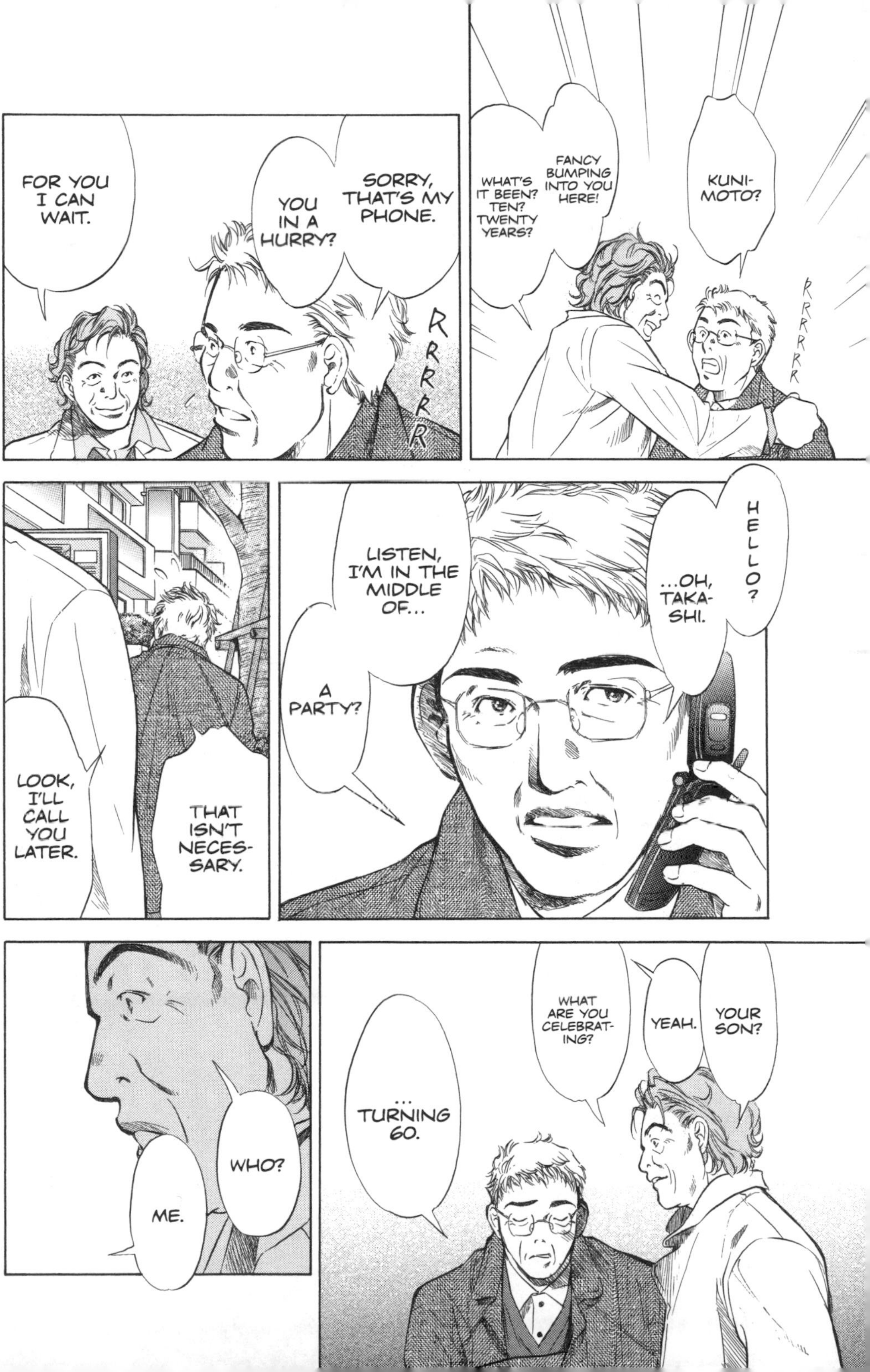
KUNI-MOTO?
FANCY BUMPING INTO YOU HERE!
WHAT'S IT BEEN? TEN? TWENTY YEARS?
RRRRRR
SORRY, THAT'S MY PHONE.
YOU IN A HURRY?
FOR YOU I CAN WAIT.
RRRRR
HELLO?
...OH, TAKA-SHI.
LISTEN, I'M IN THE MIDDLE OF...
A PARTY?
THAT ISN'T NECES-SARY.
LOOK, I'LL CALL YOU LATER.
YOUR SON?
YEAH.
WHAT ARE YOU CELEBRAT-ING?
... TURNING 60.
WHO?
ME.

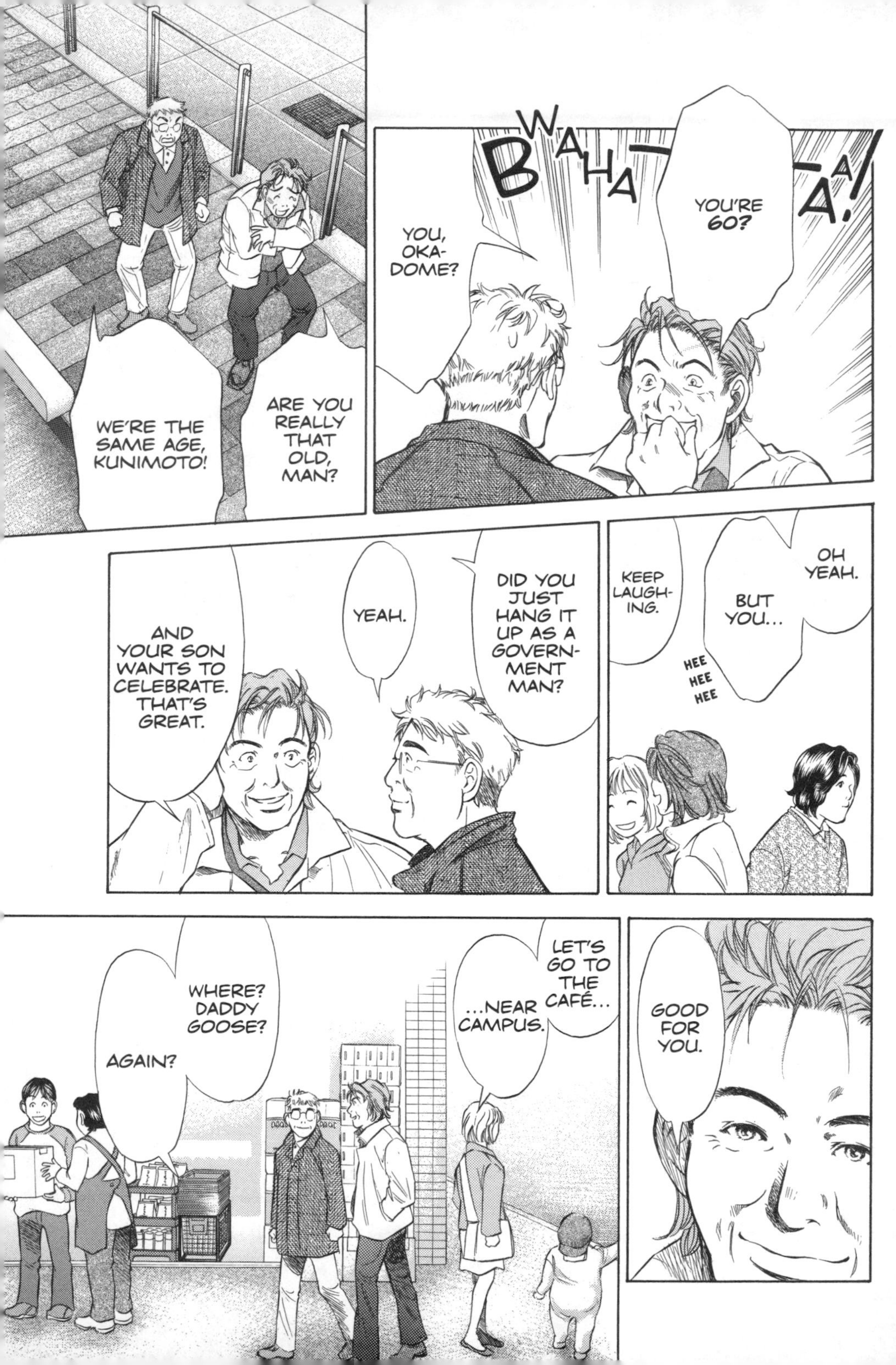
BWAHA——AA!
YOU'RE 60?
YOU, OKA-DOME?
ARE YOU REALLY THAT OLD, MAN?
WE'RE THE SAME AGE, KUNIMOTO!
OH YEAH.
BUT YOU...
KEEP LAUGH-ING.
HEE HEE HEE
DID YOU JUST HANG IT UP AS A GOVERN-MENT MAN?
YEAH.
AND YOUR SON WANTS TO CELEBRATE. THAT'S GREAT.
GOOD FOR YOU.
LET'S GO TO THE CAFÉ...
...NEAR CAMPUS.
WHERE? DADDY GOOSE?
AGAIN?

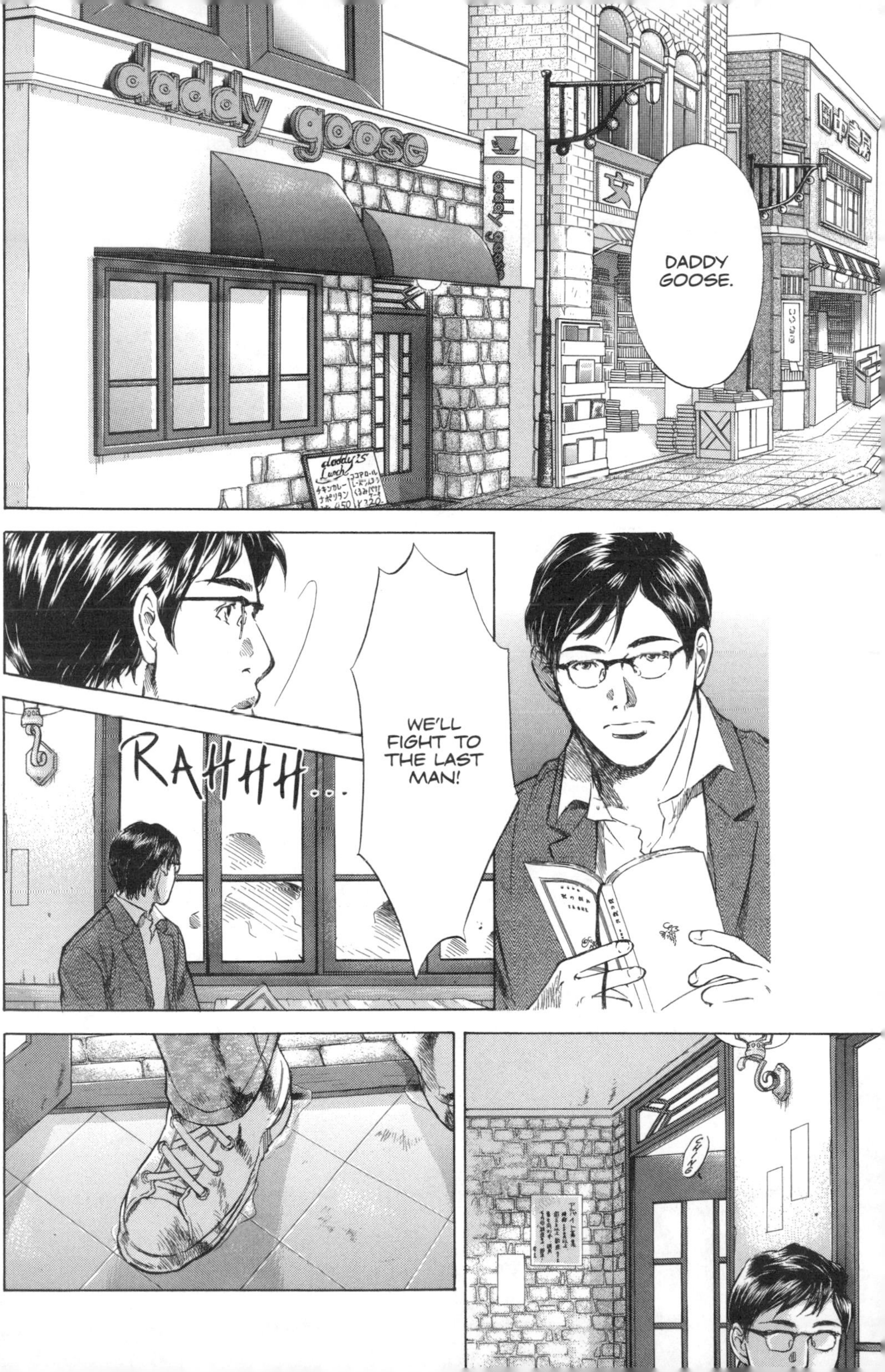
daddy goose
daddy goose
daddy's Lunch
チキンカレー
ナポリタン
ココアロール
くるみパン
DADDY GOOSE.
WE'LL FIGHT TO THE LAST MAN!
RAHHH...
CHING

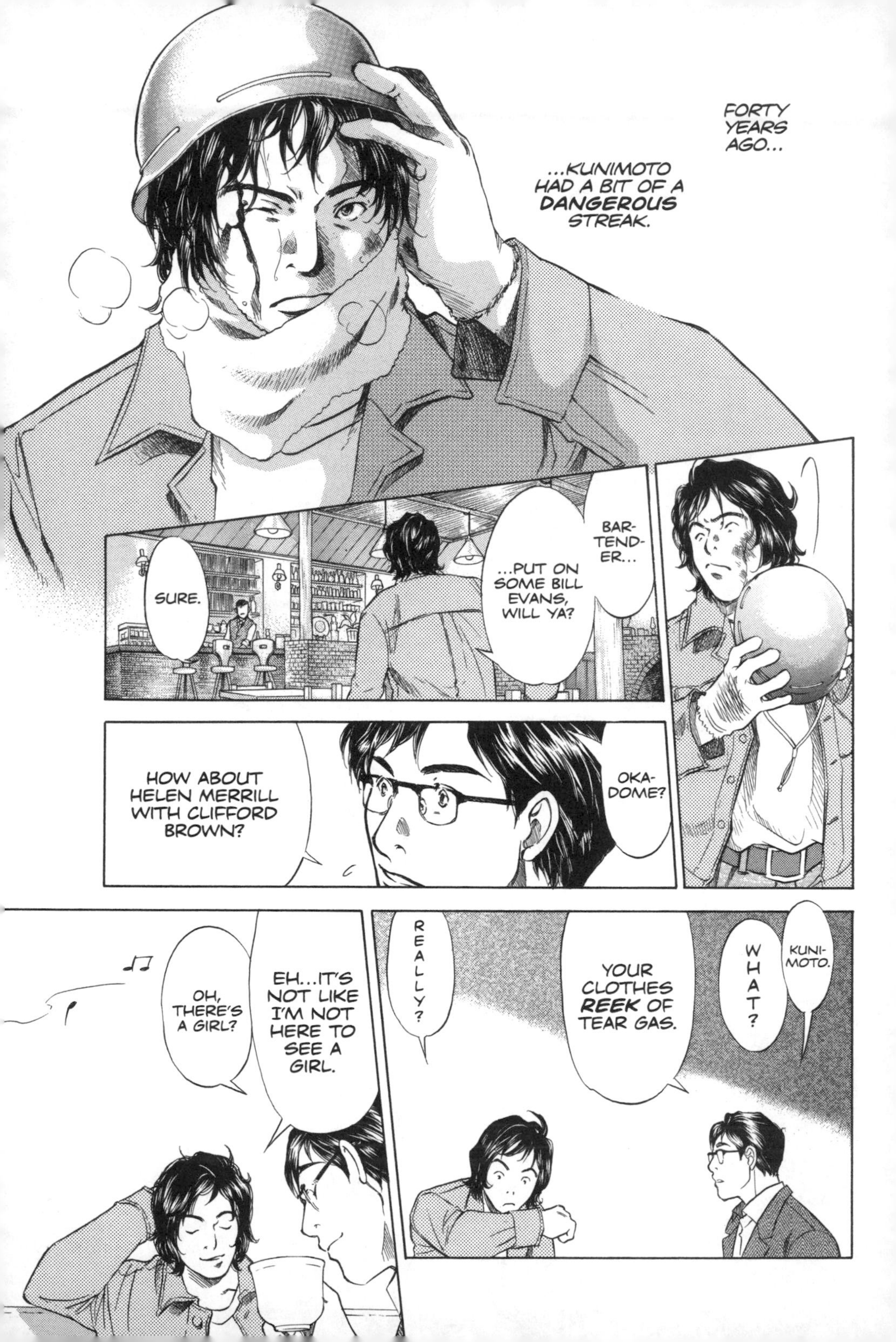
FORTY YEARS AGO...
...KUNIMOTO HAD A BIT OF A **DANGEROUS** STREAK.
BAR-TENDER...
...PUT ON SOME BILL EVANS, WILL YA?
SURE.
OKA-DOME?
HOW ABOUT HELEN MERRILL WITH CLIFFORD BROWN?
KUNI-MOTO.
WHAT?
YOUR CLOTHES ***REEK*** OF TEAR GAS.
REALLY?
EH...IT'S NOT LIKE I'M NOT HERE TO SEE A GIRL.
OH, THERE'S A GIRL?

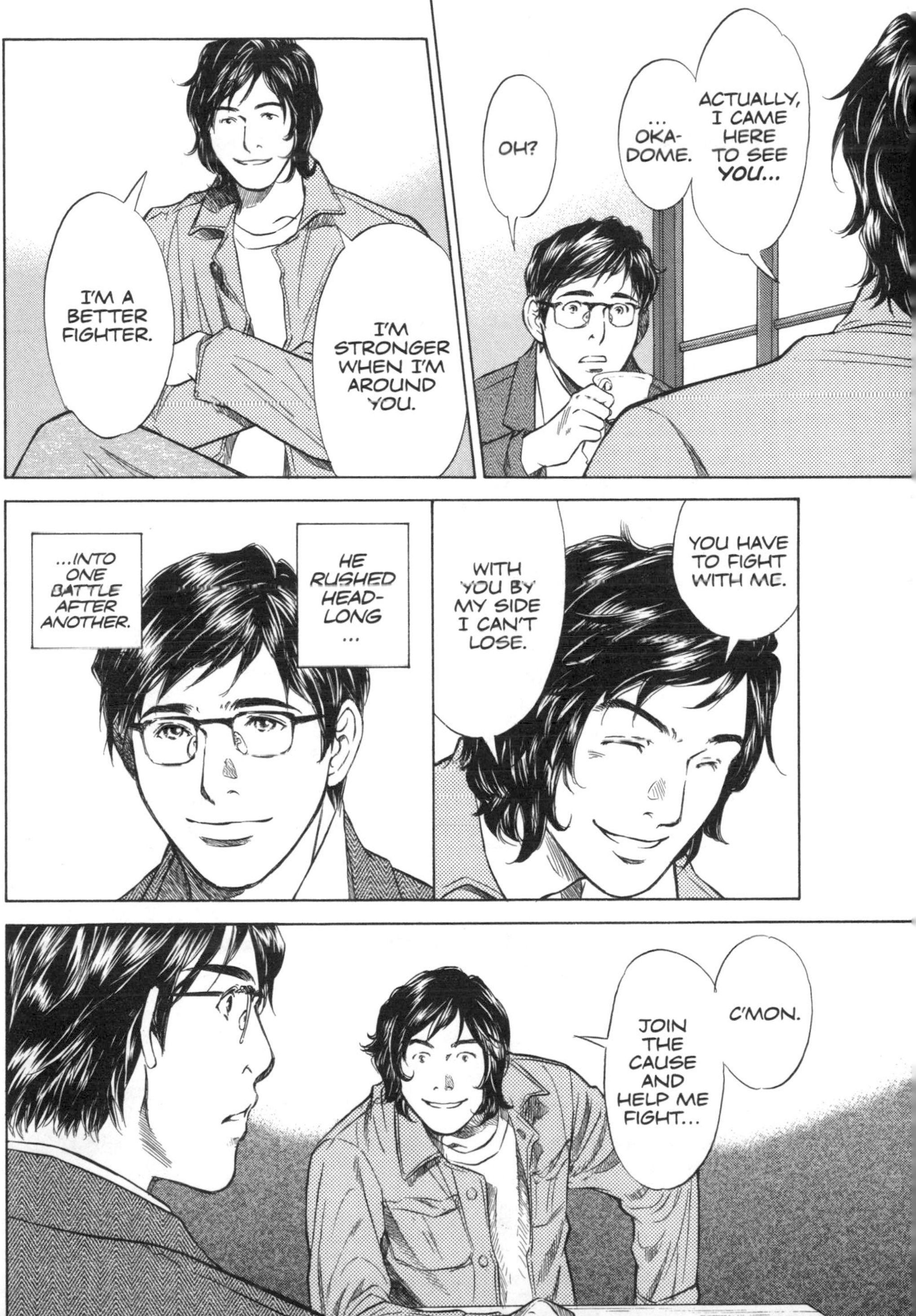
ACTUALLY, I CAME HERE TO SEE YOU...
... OKA-DOME.
OH?
I'M STRONGER WHEN I'M AROUND YOU.
I'M A BETTER FIGHTER.
YOU HAVE TO FIGHT WITH ME.
WITH YOU BY MY SIDE I CAN'T LOSE.
HE RUSHED HEAD-LONG ...
...INTO ONE BATTLE AFTER ANOTHER.
C'MON.
JOIN THE CAUSE AND HELP ME FIGHT...

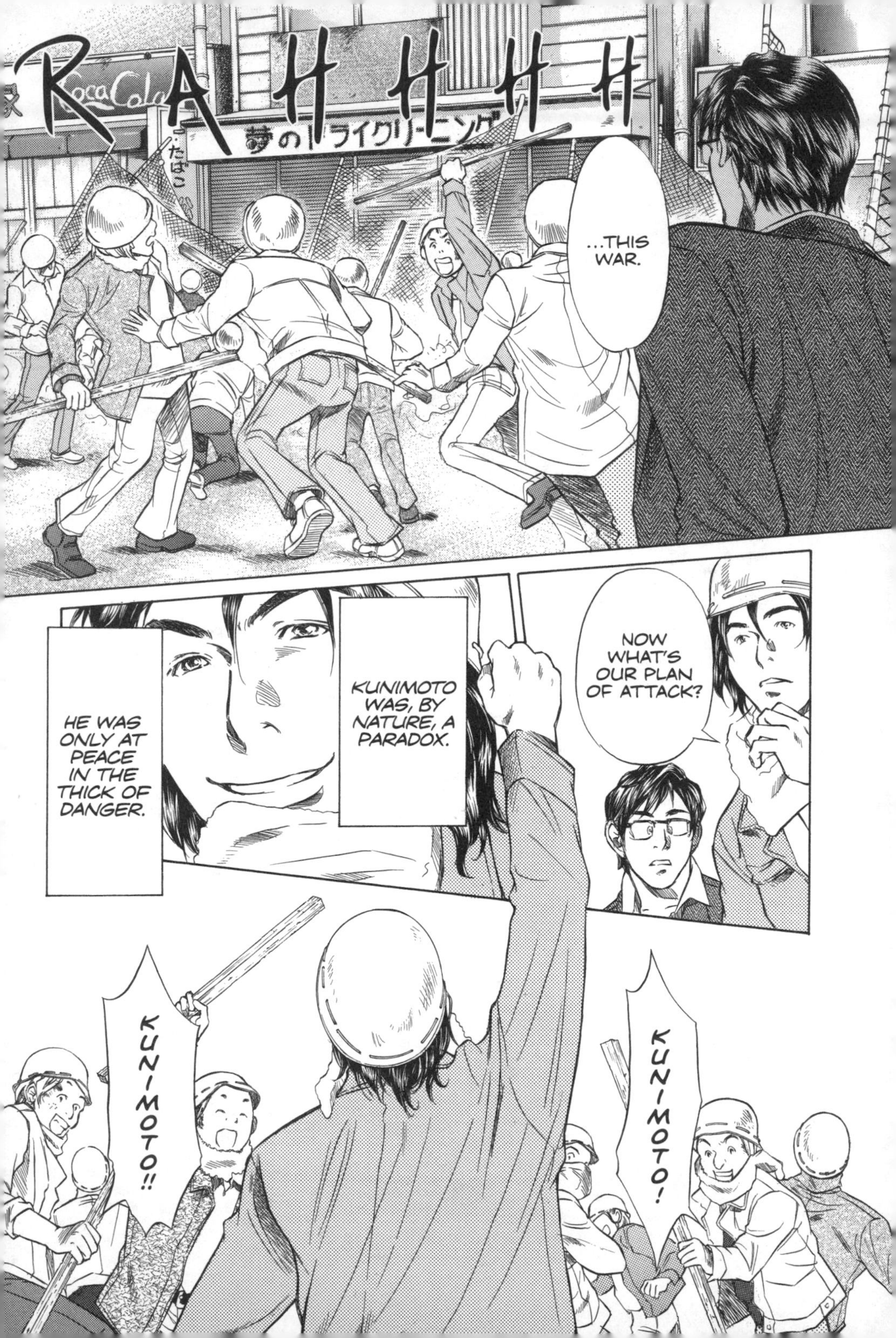
RAHHHHH
...THIS WAR.
NOW WHAT'S OUR PLAN OF ATTACK?
KUNIMOTO WAS, BY NATURE, A PARADOX.
HE WAS ONLY AT PEACE IN THE THICK OF DANGER.
KUNIMOTO!
KUNIMOTO!!

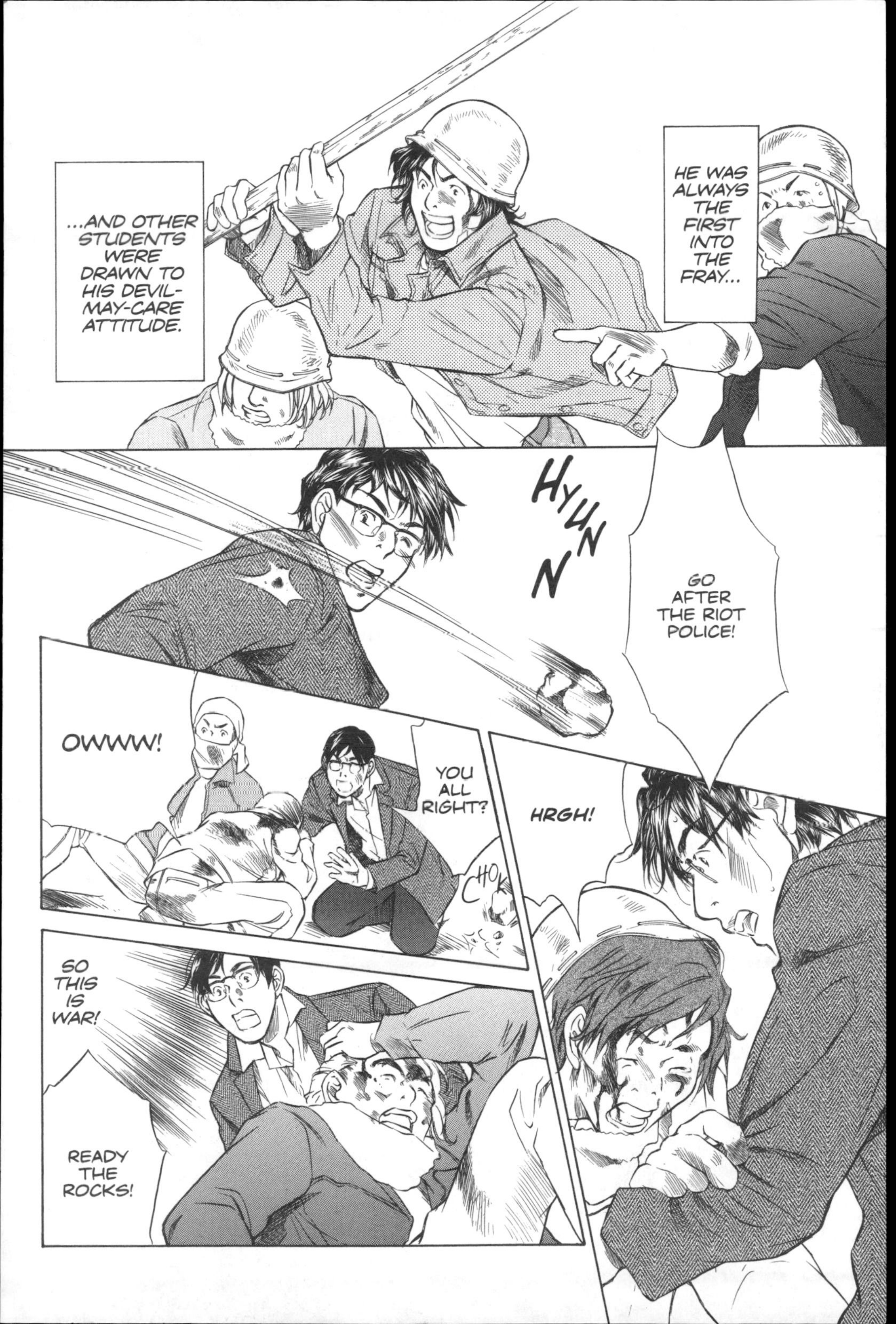
HE WAS ALWAYS THE FIRST INTO THE FRAY...
...AND OTHER STUDENTS WERE DRAWN TO HIS DEVIL-MAY-CARE ATTITUDE.
HYUNNN
GO AFTER THE RIOT POLICE!
HRGH!
YOU ALL RIGHT?
OWWW!
CHOK
SO THIS IS WAR!
READY THE ROCKS!

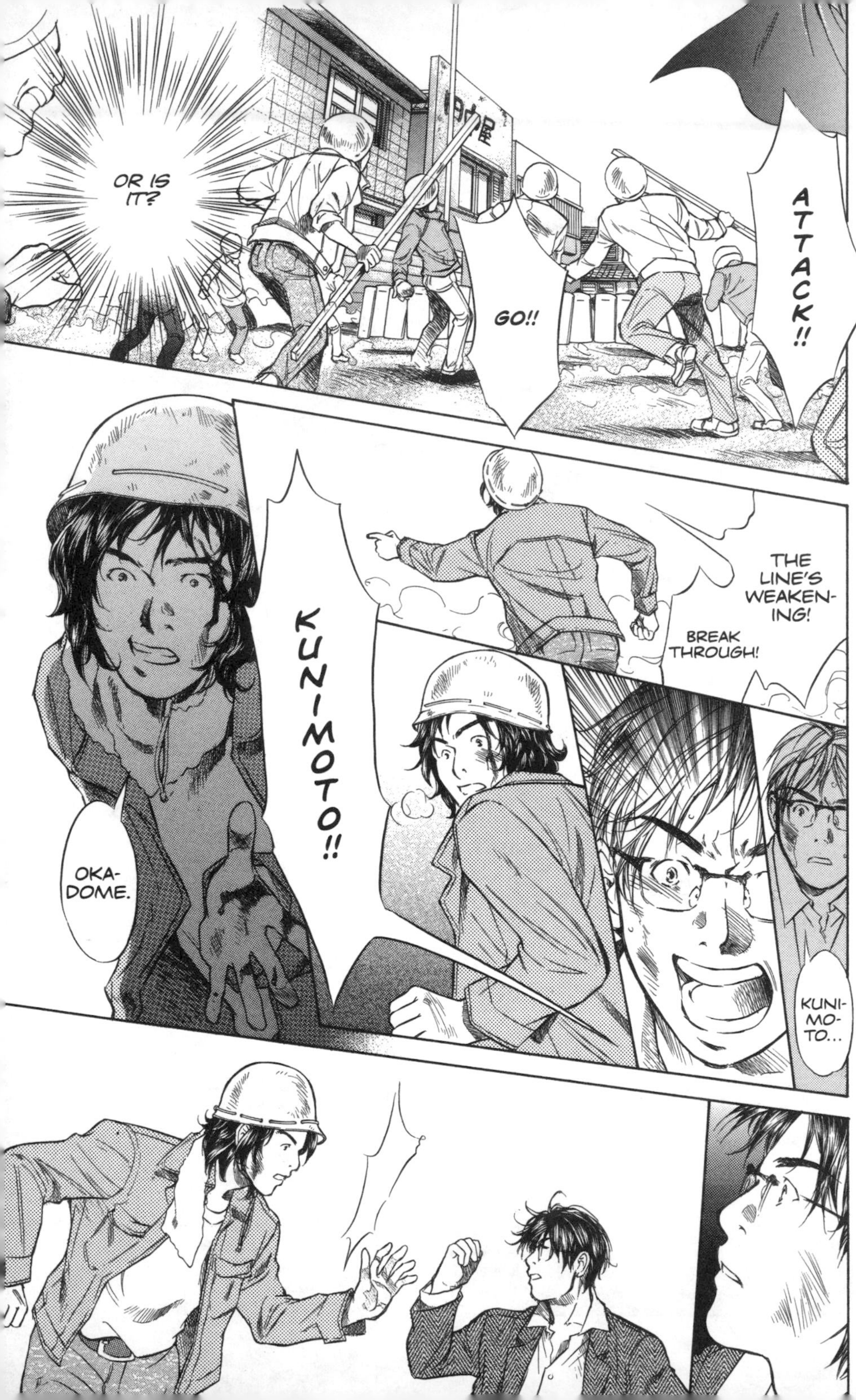
ATTACK!!
GO!!
OR IS IT?
THE LINE'S WEAKENING!
BREAK THROUGH!
KUNIMOTO!!
KUNI-MO-TO...
OKA-DOME.

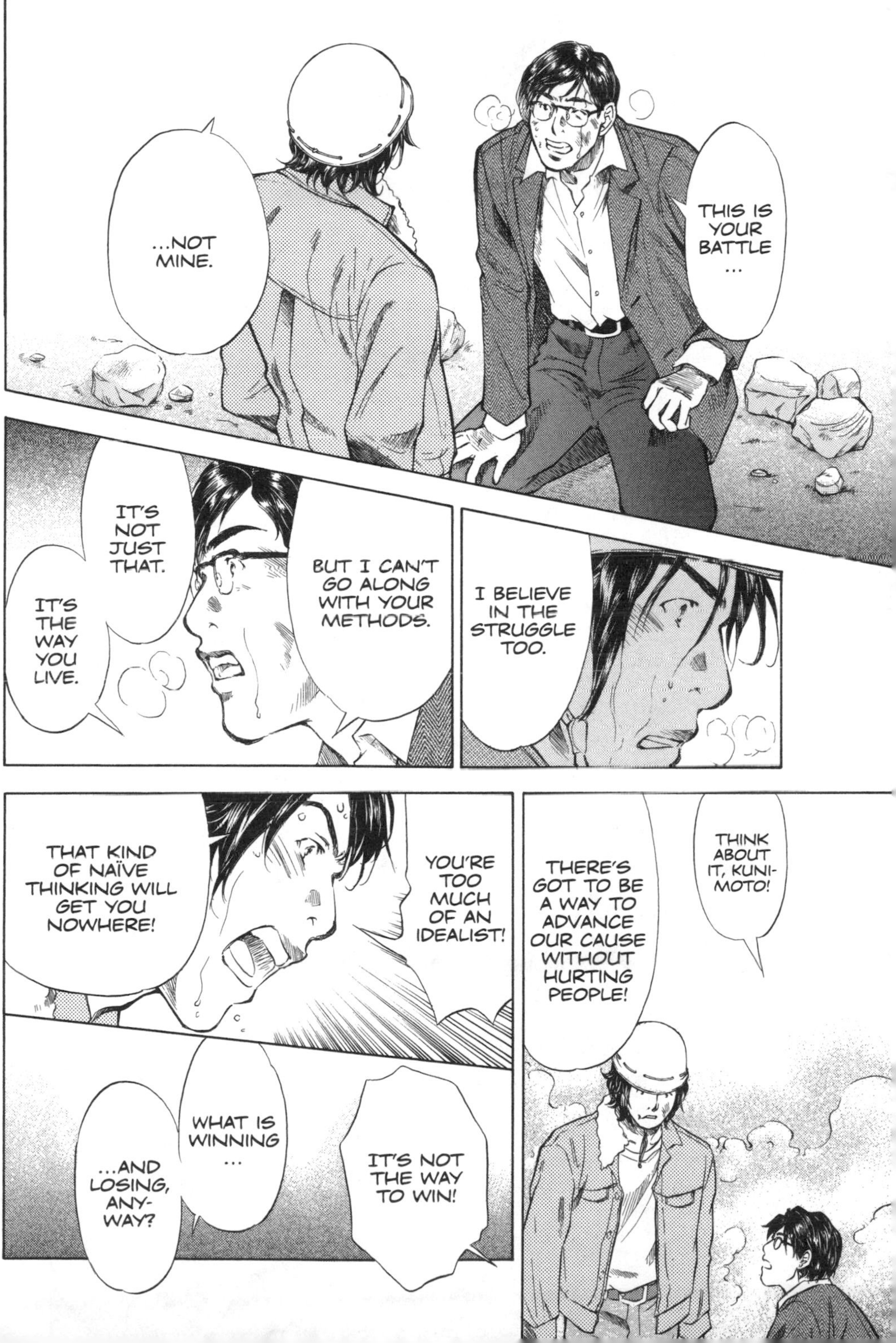
THIS IS YOUR BATTLE ...
...NOT MINE.
I BELIEVE IN THE STRUGGLE TOO.
BUT I CAN'T GO ALONG WITH YOUR METHODS.
IT'S NOT JUST THAT.
IT'S THE WAY YOU LIVE.
THINK ABOUT IT, KUNI-MOTO!
THERE'S GOT TO BE A WAY TO ADVANCE OUR CAUSE WITHOUT HURTING PEOPLE!
YOU'RE TOO MUCH OF AN IDEALIST!
THAT KIND OF NAÏVE THINKING WILL GET YOU NOWHERE!
IT'S NOT THE WAY TO WIN!
WHAT IS WINNING ...
...AND LOSING, ANY-WAY?

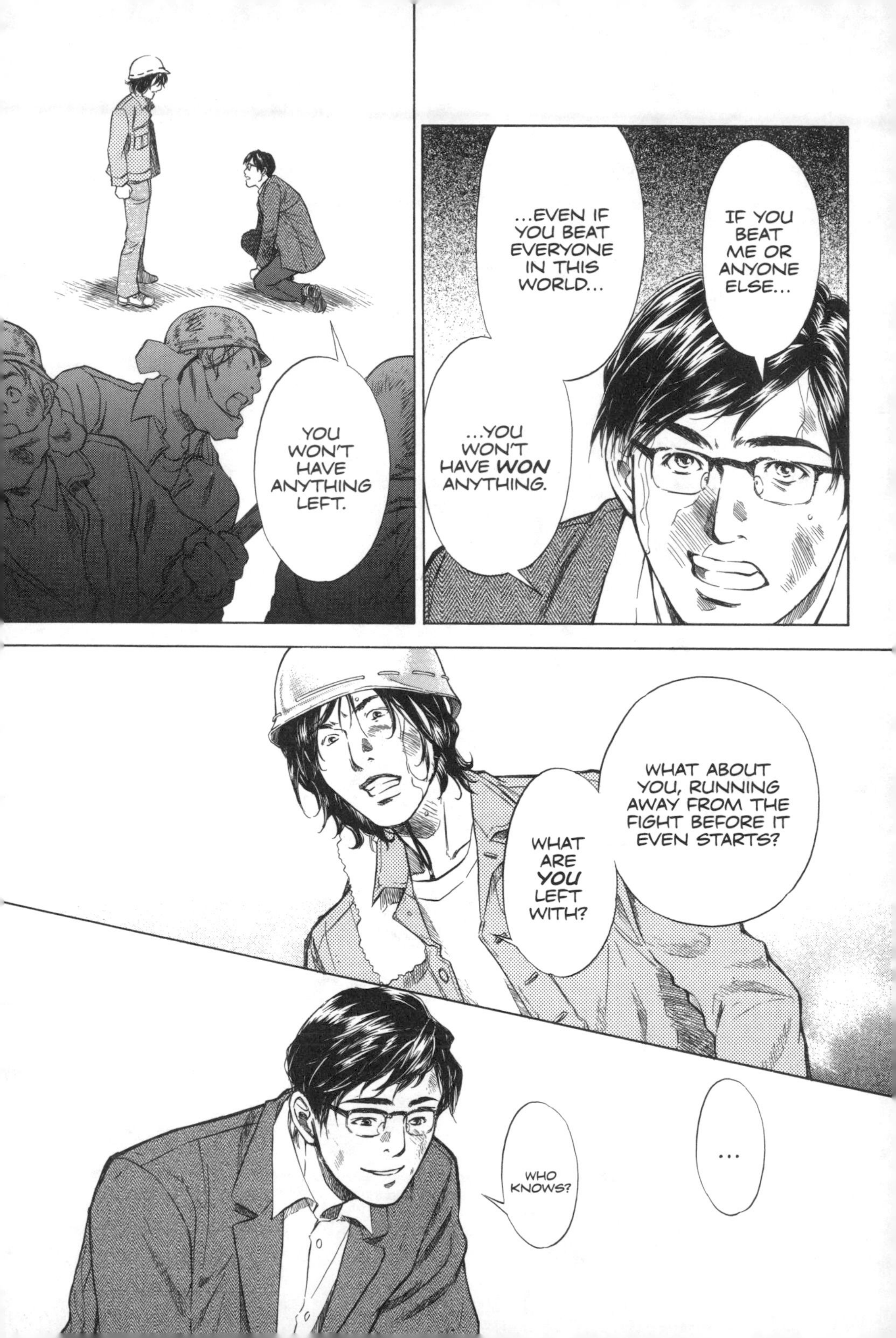
IF YOU BEAT ME OR ANYONE ELSE...
...EVEN IF YOU BEAT EVERYONE IN THIS WORLD...
...YOU WON'T HAVE **WON** ANYTHING.
YOU WON'T HAVE ANYTHING LEFT.
WHAT ABOUT YOU, RUNNING AWAY FROM THE FIGHT BEFORE IT EVEN STARTS?
WHAT ARE **YOU** LEFT WITH?
...
WHO KNOWS?

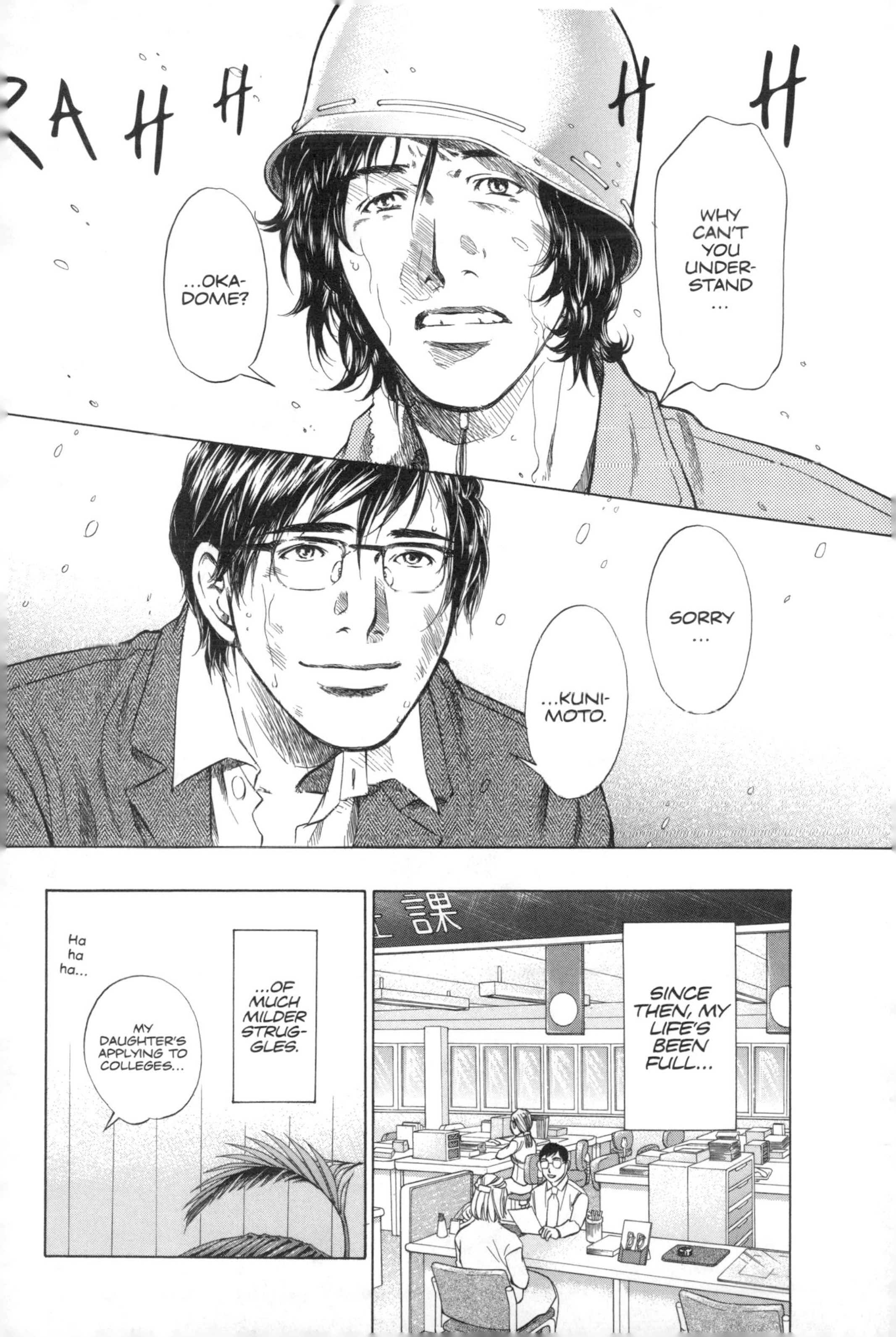
RAHH H H
WHY CAN'T YOU UNDER-STAND...
...OKA-DOME?
SORRY...
...KUNI-MOTO.
SINCE THEN, MY LIFE'S BEEN FULL...
...OF MUCH MILDER STRUG-GLES.
MY DAUGHTER'S APPLYING TO COLLEGES...
Ha ha ha...

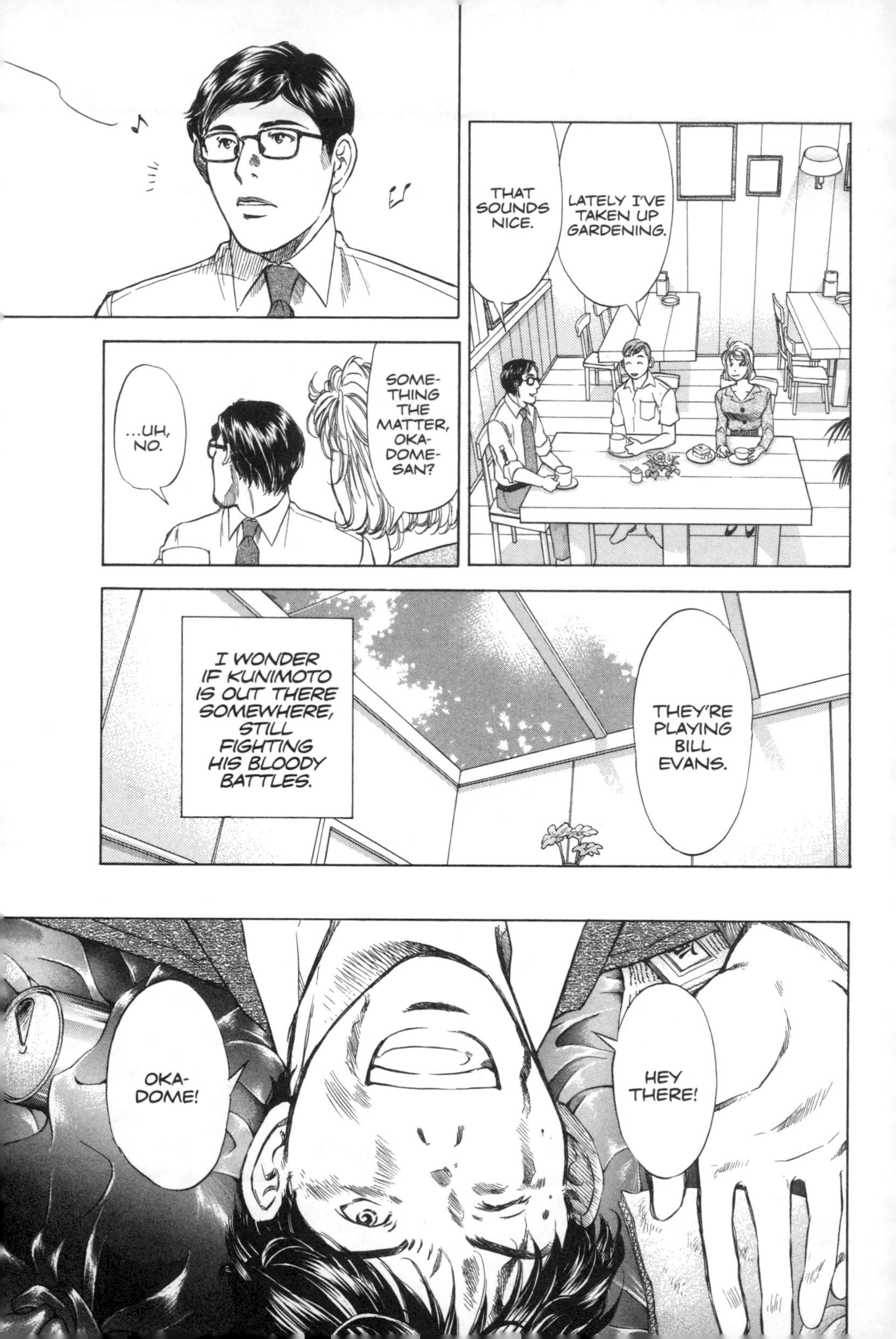
LATELY I'VE TAKEN UP GARDENING.
THAT SOUNDS NICE.
SOME-THING THE MATTER, OKA-DOME-SAN?
...UH, NO.
THEY'RE PLAYING BILL EVANS.
I WONDER IF KUNIMOTO IS OUT THERE SOMEWHERE, STILL FIGHTING HIS BLOODY BATTLES.
HEY THERE!
OKA-DOME!

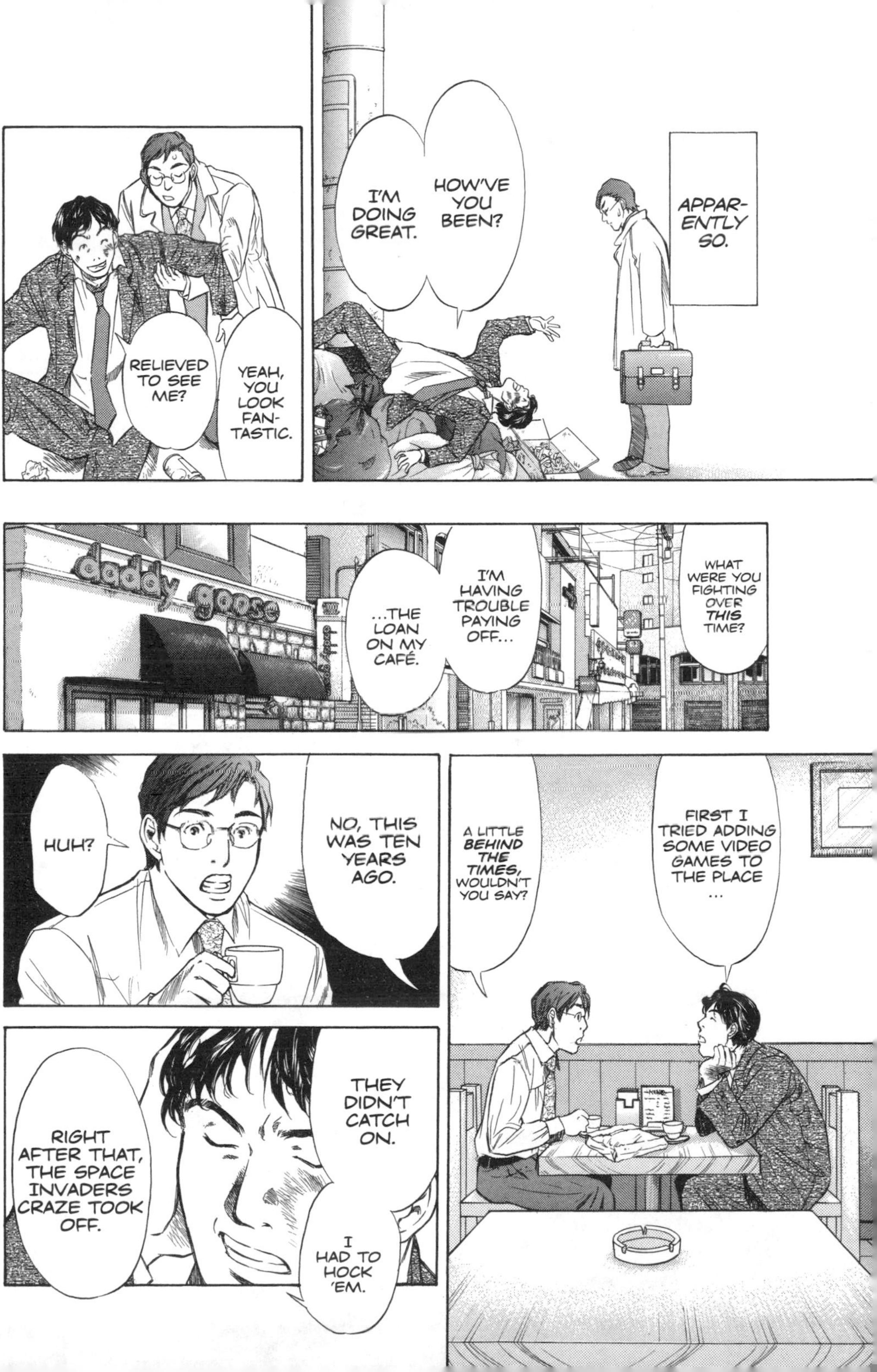
APPAR-ENTLY SO.
HOW'VE YOU BEEN?
I'M DOING GREAT.
YEAH, YOU LOOK FAN-TASTIC.
RELIEVED TO SEE ME?
WHAT WERE YOU FIGHTING OVER *THIS* TIME?
I'M HAVING TROUBLE PAYING OFF...
...THE LOAN ON MY CAFÉ.
daddy goose
FIRST I TRIED ADDING SOME VIDEO GAMES TO THE PLACE ...
A LITTLE *BEHIND THE TIMES*, WOULDN'T YOU SAY?
NO, THIS WAS TEN YEARS AGO.
HUH?
THEY DIDN'T CATCH ON.
RIGHT AFTER THAT, THE SPACE INVADERS CRAZE TOOK OFF.
I HAD TO HOCK 'EM.

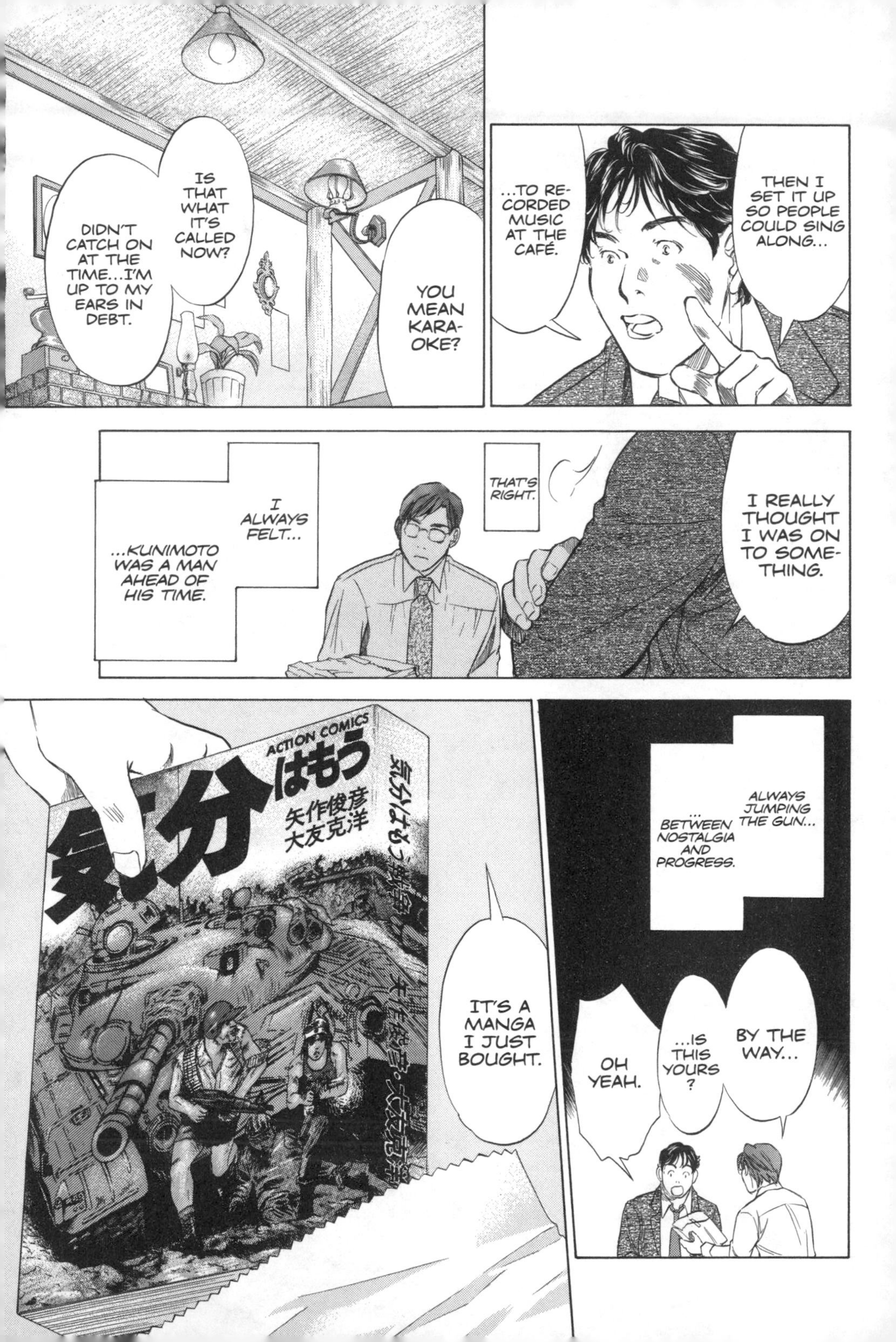
THEN I SET IT UP SO PEOPLE COULD SING ALONG...
...TO RE-CORDED MUSIC AT THE CAFÉ.
YOU MEAN KARA-OKE?
IS THAT WHAT IT'S CALLED NOW?
DIDN'T CATCH ON AT THE TIME...I'M UP TO MY EARS IN DEBT.
I REALLY THOUGHT I WAS ON TO SOME-THING.
THAT'S RIGHT.
I ALWAYS FELT...
...KUNIMOTO WAS A MAN AHEAD OF HIS TIME.
ALWAYS JUMPING THE GUN...
...BETWEEN NOSTALGIA AND PROGRESS.
BY THE WAY...
...IS THIS YOURS?
OH YEAH.
IT'S A MANGA I JUST BOUGHT.
ACTION COMICS
分はもう
矢作俊彦
大友克洋

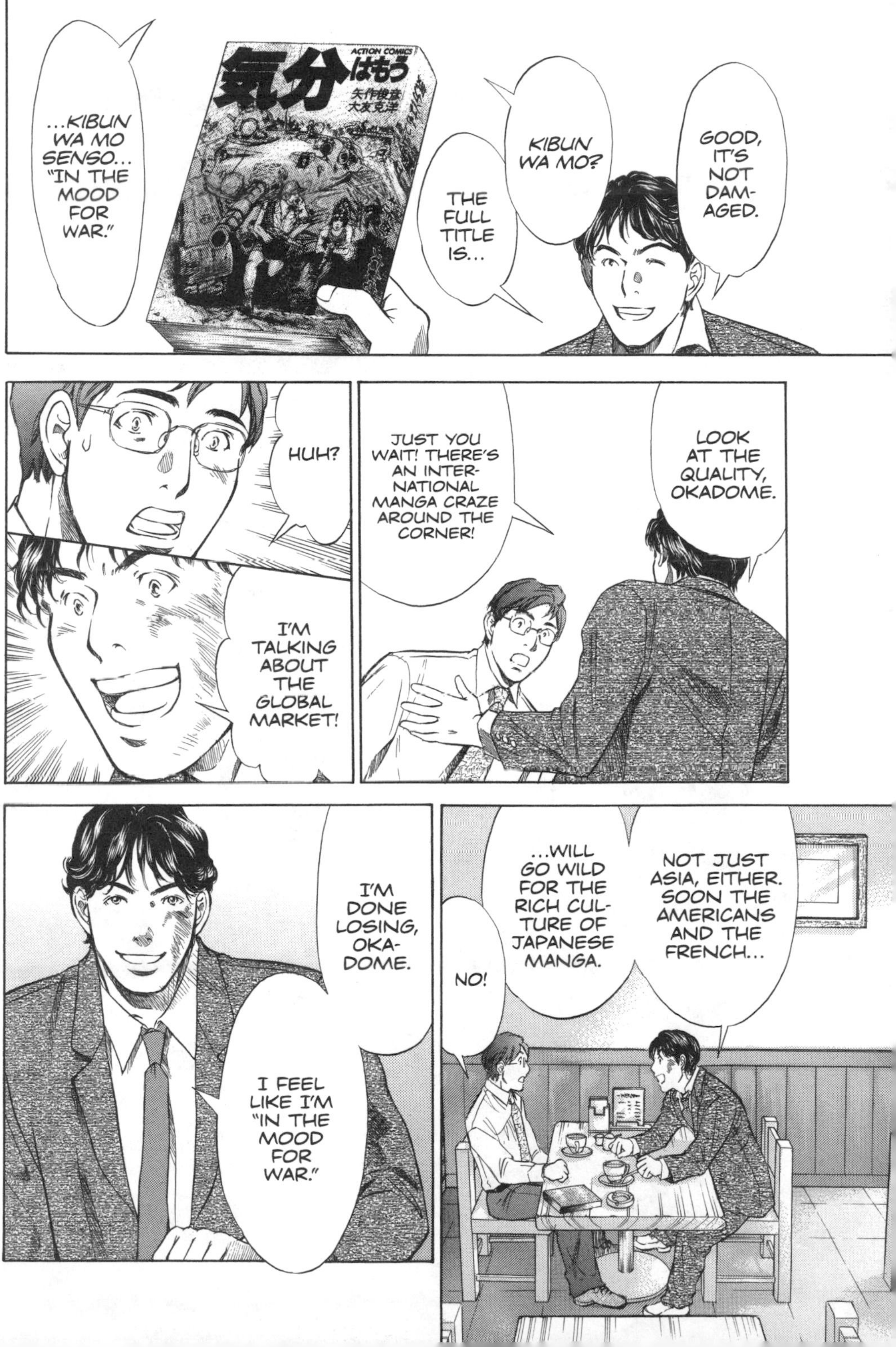
GOOD, IT'S NOT DAMAGED.
KIBUN WA MO?
ACTION COMICS
気分はもう
矢作俊彦
大友克洋
THE FULL TITLE IS...
...KIBUN WA MO SENSO... "IN THE MOOD FOR WAR."
LOOK AT THE QUALITY, OKADOME.
JUST YOU WAIT! THERE'S AN INTERNATIONAL MANGA CRAZE AROUND THE CORNER!
HUH?
I'M TALKING ABOUT THE GLOBAL MARKET!
NOT JUST ASIA, EITHER. SOON THE AMERICANS AND THE FRENCH...
...WILL GO WILD FOR THE RICH CULTURE OF JAPANESE MANGA.
NO!
I'M DONE LOSING, OKADOME.
I FEEL LIKE I'M "IN THE MOOD FOR WAR."

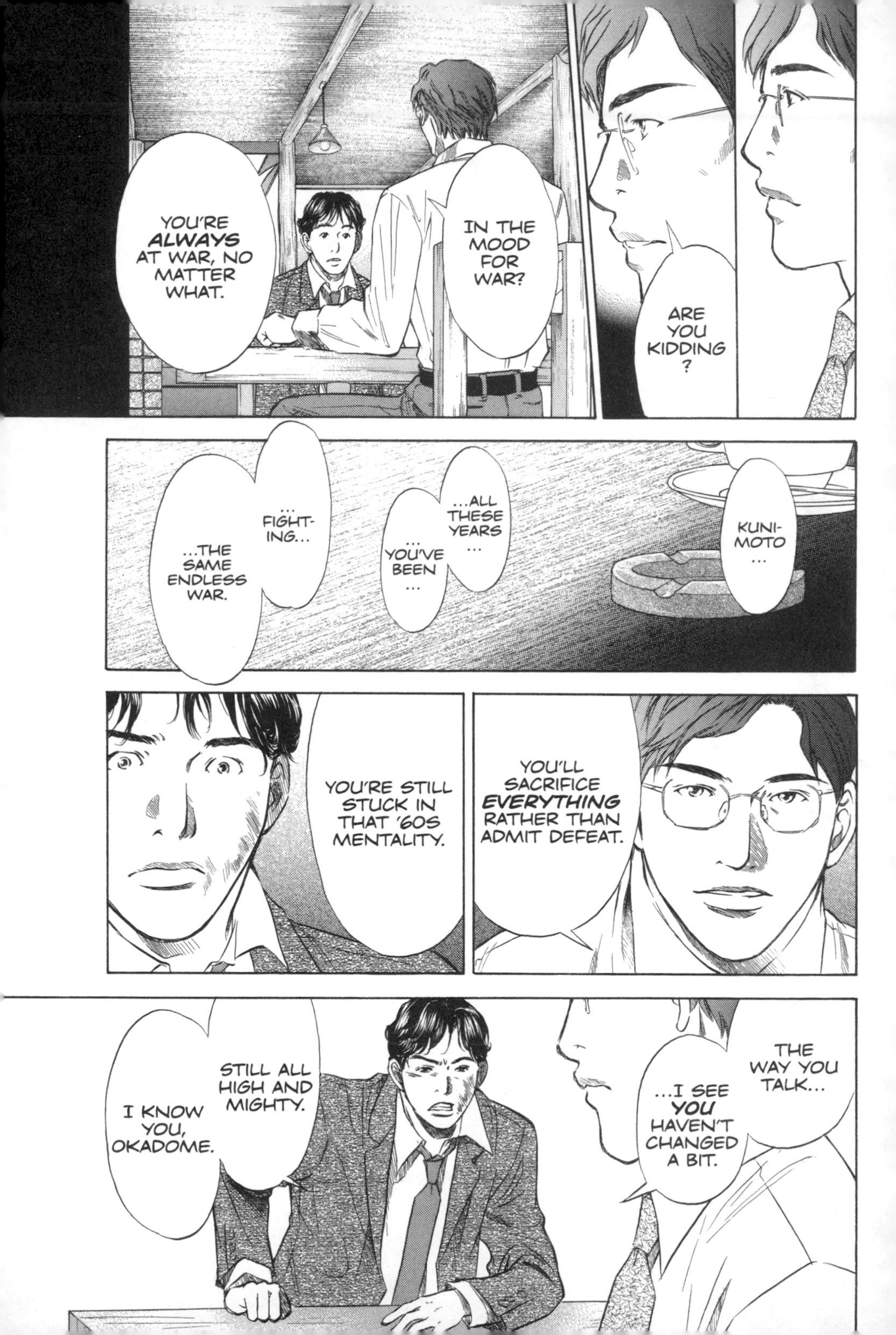
ARE YOU KIDDING?
IN THE MOOD FOR WAR?
YOU'RE **ALWAYS** AT WAR, NO MATTER WHAT.
KUNI-MOTO...
...ALL THESE YEARS...
...YOU'VE BEEN...
...FIGHT-ING...
...THE SAME ENDLESS WAR.
YOU'LL SACRIFICE **EVERYTHING** RATHER THAN ADMIT DEFEAT.
YOU'RE STILL STUCK IN THAT '60S MENTALITY.
THE WAY YOU TALK...
...I SEE **YOU** HAVEN'T CHANGED A BIT.
STILL ALL HIGH AND MIGHTY.
I KNOW YOU, OKADOME.

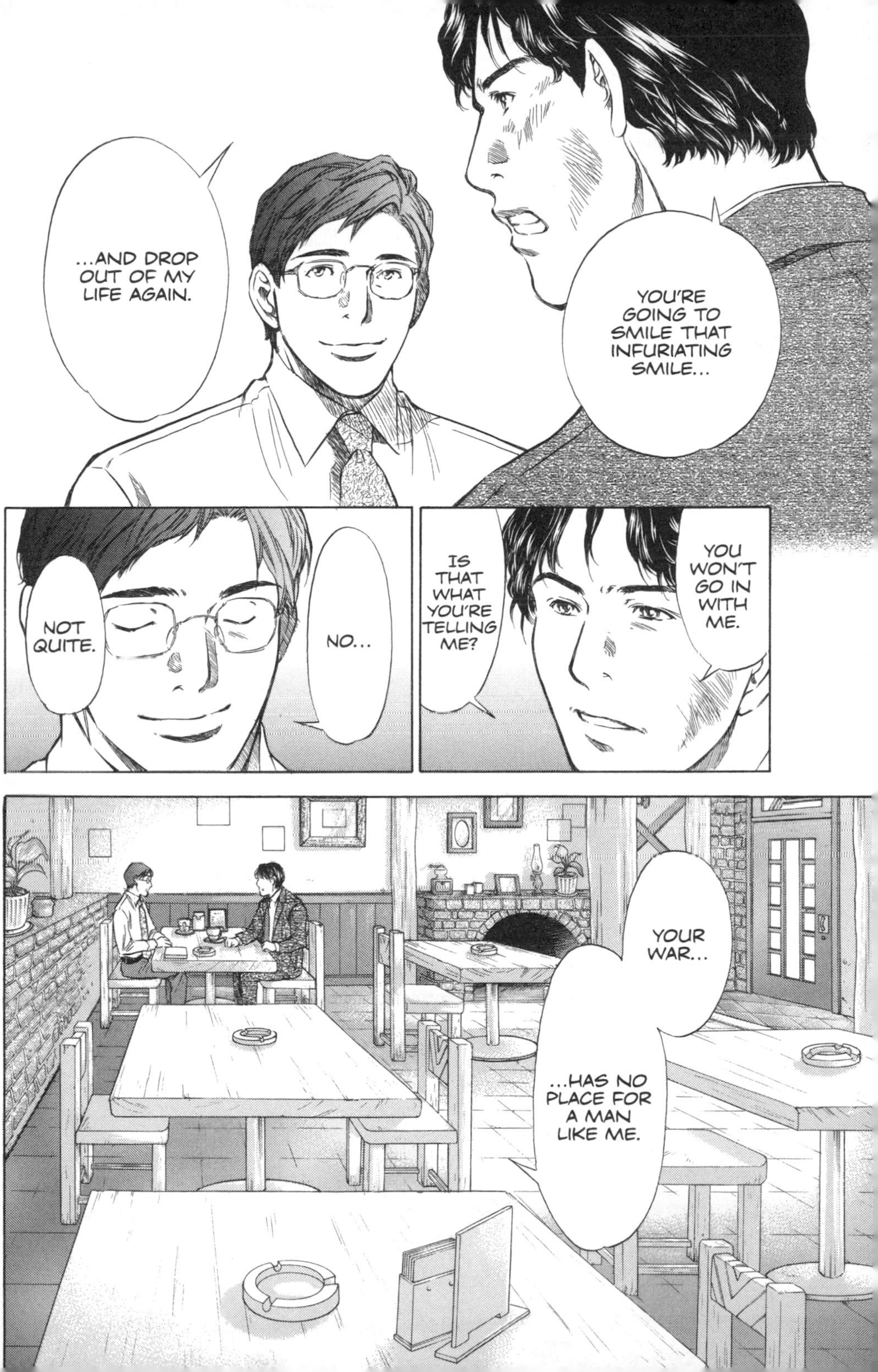
YOU'RE GOING TO SMILE THAT INFURIATING SMILE...
...AND DROP OUT OF MY LIFE AGAIN.
YOU WON'T GO IN WITH ME.
IS THAT WHAT YOU'RE TELLING ME?
NO...
NOT QUITE.
YOUR WAR...
...HAS NO PLACE FOR A MAN LIKE ME.

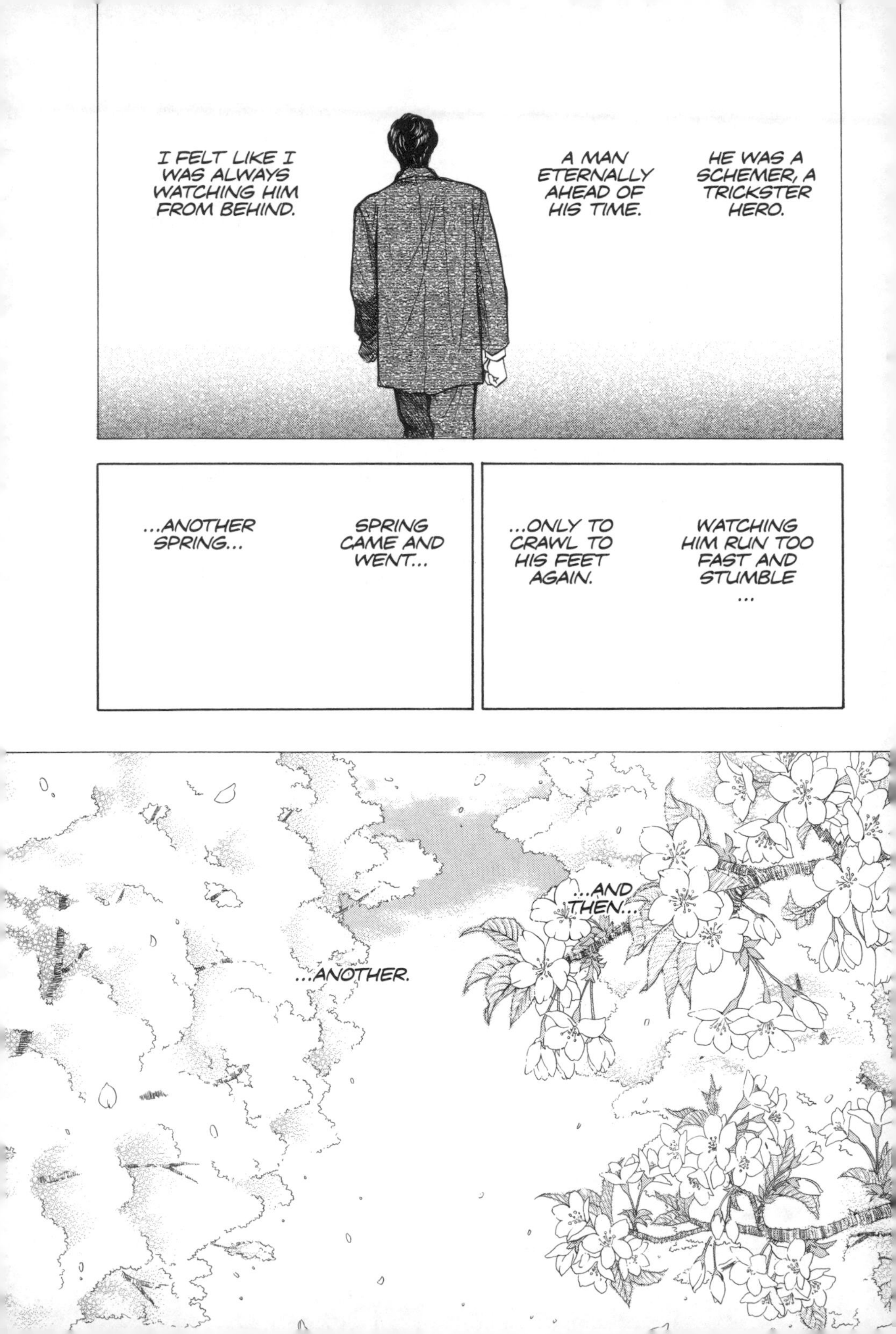
HE WAS A SCHEMER, A TRICKSTER HERO.
A MAN ETERNALLY AHEAD OF HIS TIME.
I FELT LIKE I WAS ALWAYS WATCHING HIM FROM BEHIND.
WATCHING HIM RUN TOO FAST AND STUMBLE ...
...ONLY TO CRAWL TO HIS FEET AGAIN.
SPRING CAME AND WENT...
...ANOTHER SPRING...
...AND THEN...
...ANOTHER.

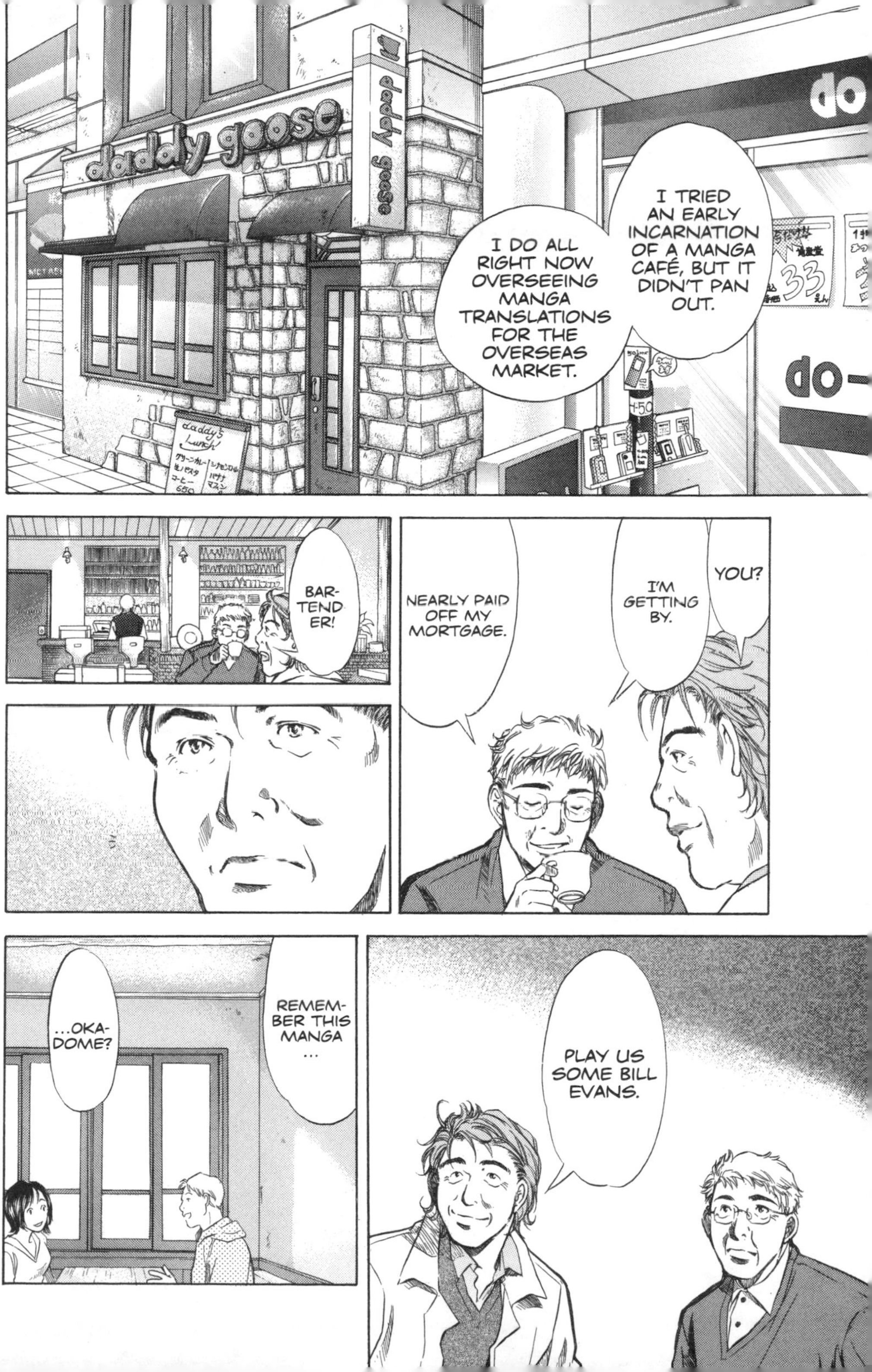
daddy goose
daddy goose
I TRIED AN EARLY INCARNATION OF A MANGA CAFÉ, BUT IT DIDN'T PAN OUT.
I DO ALL RIGHT NOW OVERSEEING MANGA TRANSLATIONS FOR THE OVERSEAS MARKET.
YOU?
I'M GETTING BY.
NEARLY PAID OFF MY MORTGAGE.
BAR-TENDER!
PLAY US SOME BILL EVANS.
REMEM-BER THIS MANGA ...
...OKA-DOME?

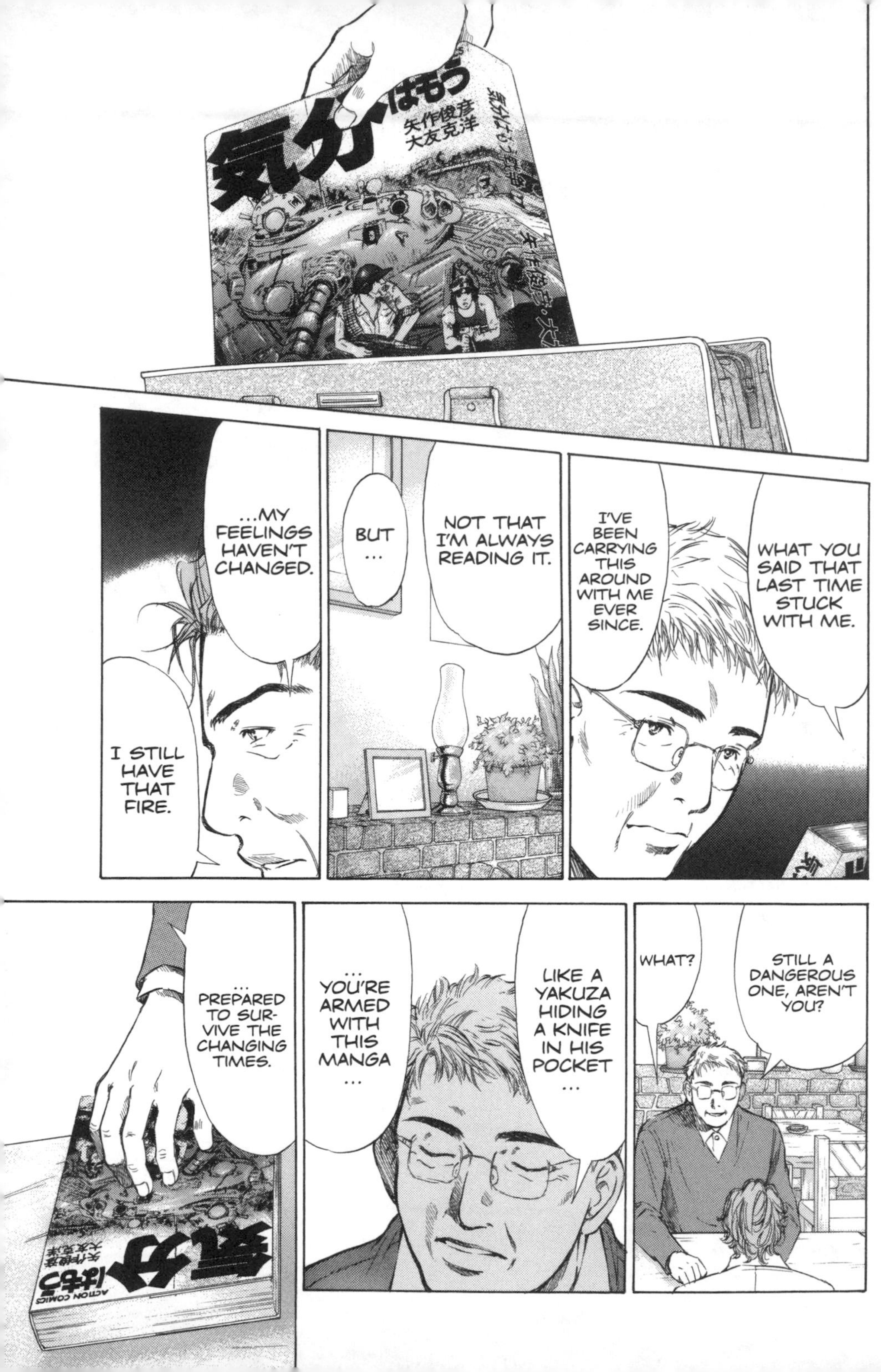
矢作俊彦
大友克洋
WHAT YOU SAID THAT LAST TIME STUCK WITH ME.
I'VE BEEN CARRYING THIS AROUND WITH ME EVER SINCE.
NOT THAT I'M ALWAYS READING IT.
BUT ...
...MY FEELINGS HAVEN'T CHANGED.
I STILL HAVE THAT FIRE.
STILL A DANGEROUS ONE, AREN'T YOU?
WHAT?
LIKE A YAKUZA HIDING A KNIFE IN HIS POCKET ...
... YOU'RE ARMED WITH THIS MANGA ...
... PREPARED TO SURVIVE THE CHANGING TIMES.
ACTION COMICS

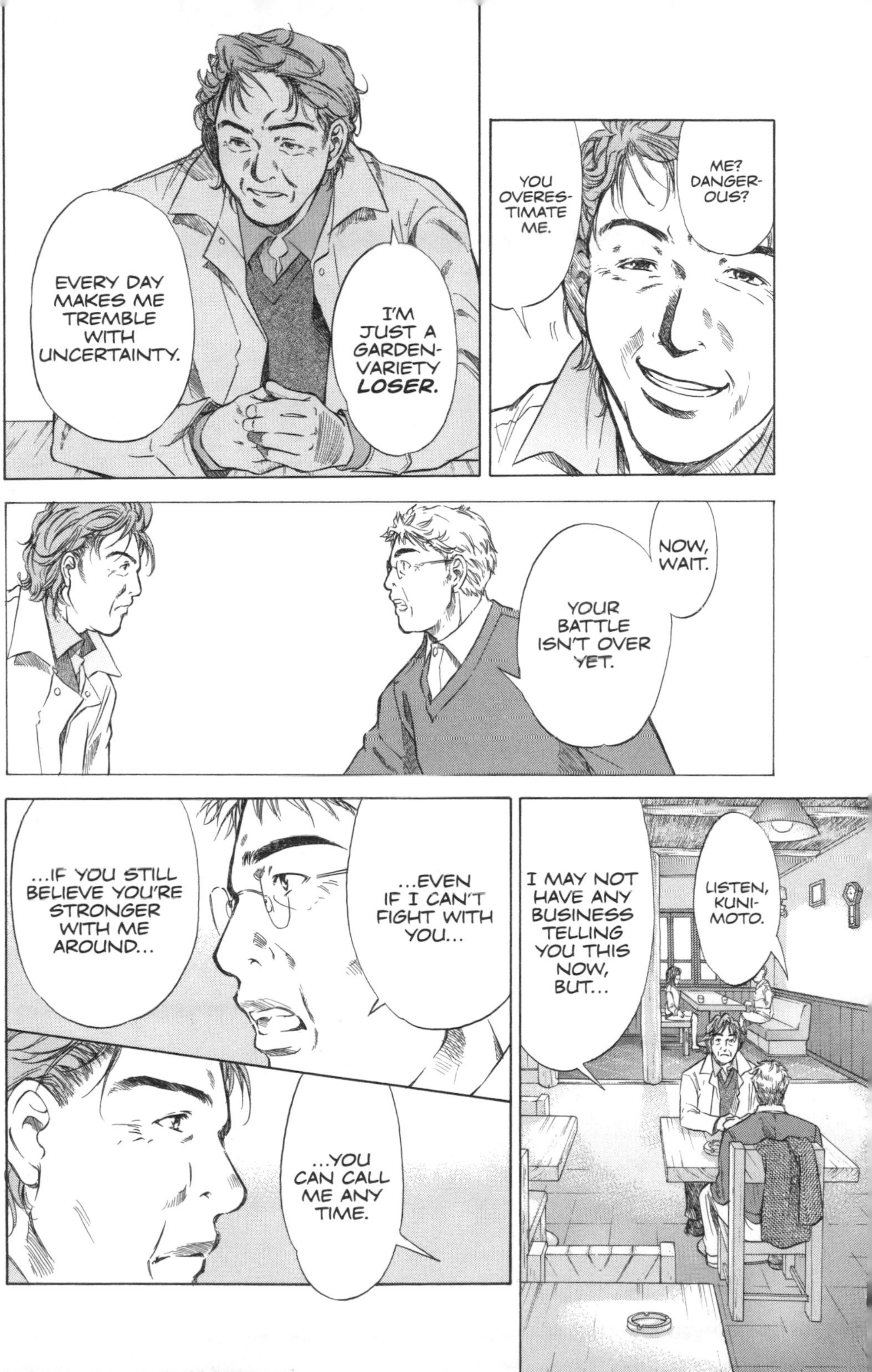
ME? DANGER-OUS?
YOU OVERES-TIMATE ME.
I'M JUST A GARDEN-VARIETY **LOSER.**
EVERY DAY MAKES ME TREMBLE WITH UNCERTAINTY.
NOW, WAIT.
YOUR BATTLE ISN'T OVER YET.
LISTEN, KUNI-MOTO.
I MAY NOT HAVE ANY BUSINESS TELLING YOU THIS NOW, BUT...
...EVEN IF I CAN'T FIGHT WITH YOU...
...IF YOU STILL BELIEVE YOU'RE STRONGER WITH ME AROUND...
...YOU CAN CALL ME ANY TIME.

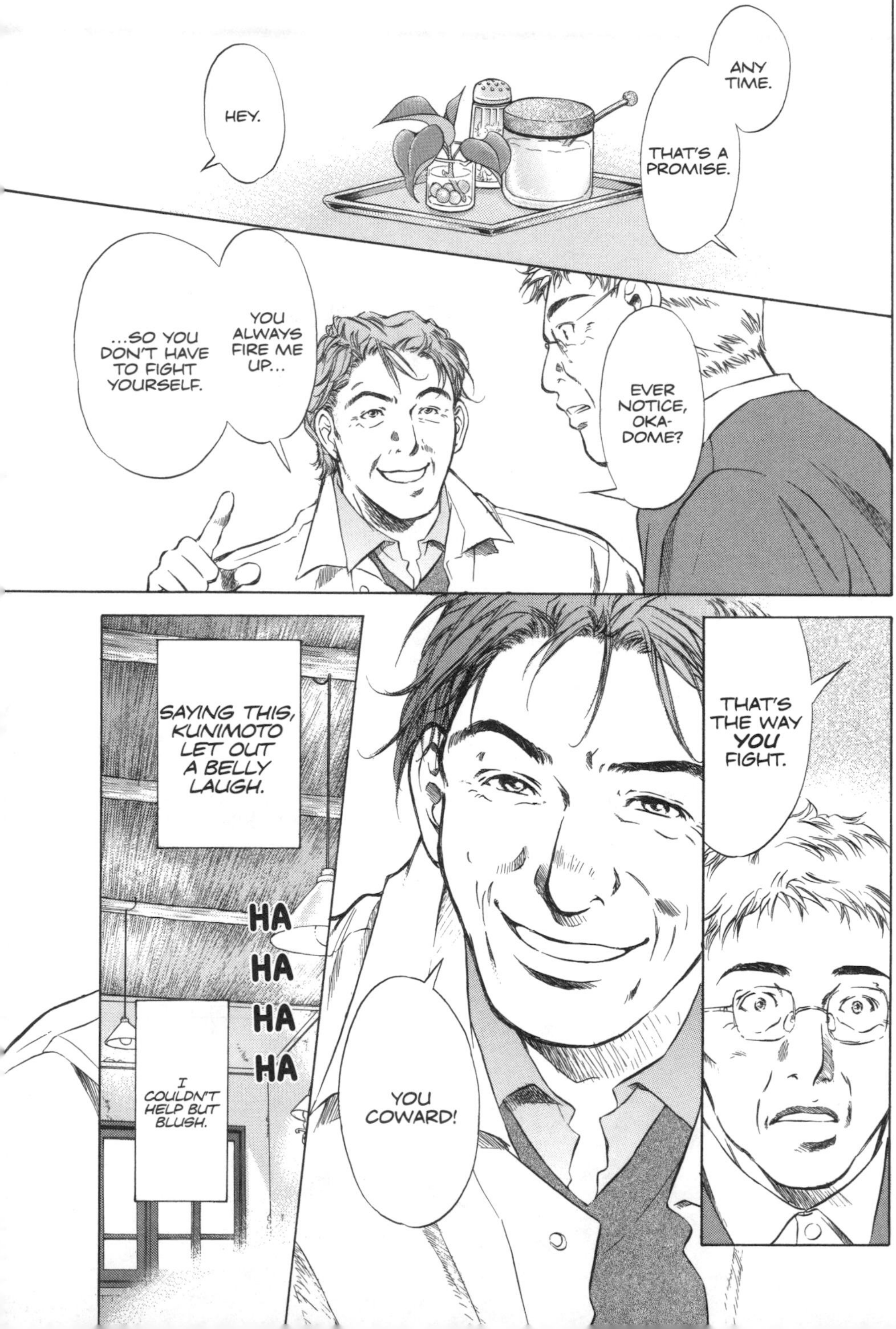
ANY TIME.
THAT'S A PROMISE.
HEY.
EVER NOTICE, OKA-DOME?
YOU ALWAYS FIRE ME UP...
...SO YOU DON'T HAVE TO FIGHT YOURSELF.
THAT'S THE WAY **YOU** FIGHT.
SAYING THIS, KUNIMOTO LET OUT A BELLY LAUGH.
YOU COWARD!
HA HA HA HA
I COULDN'T HELP BUT BLUSH.

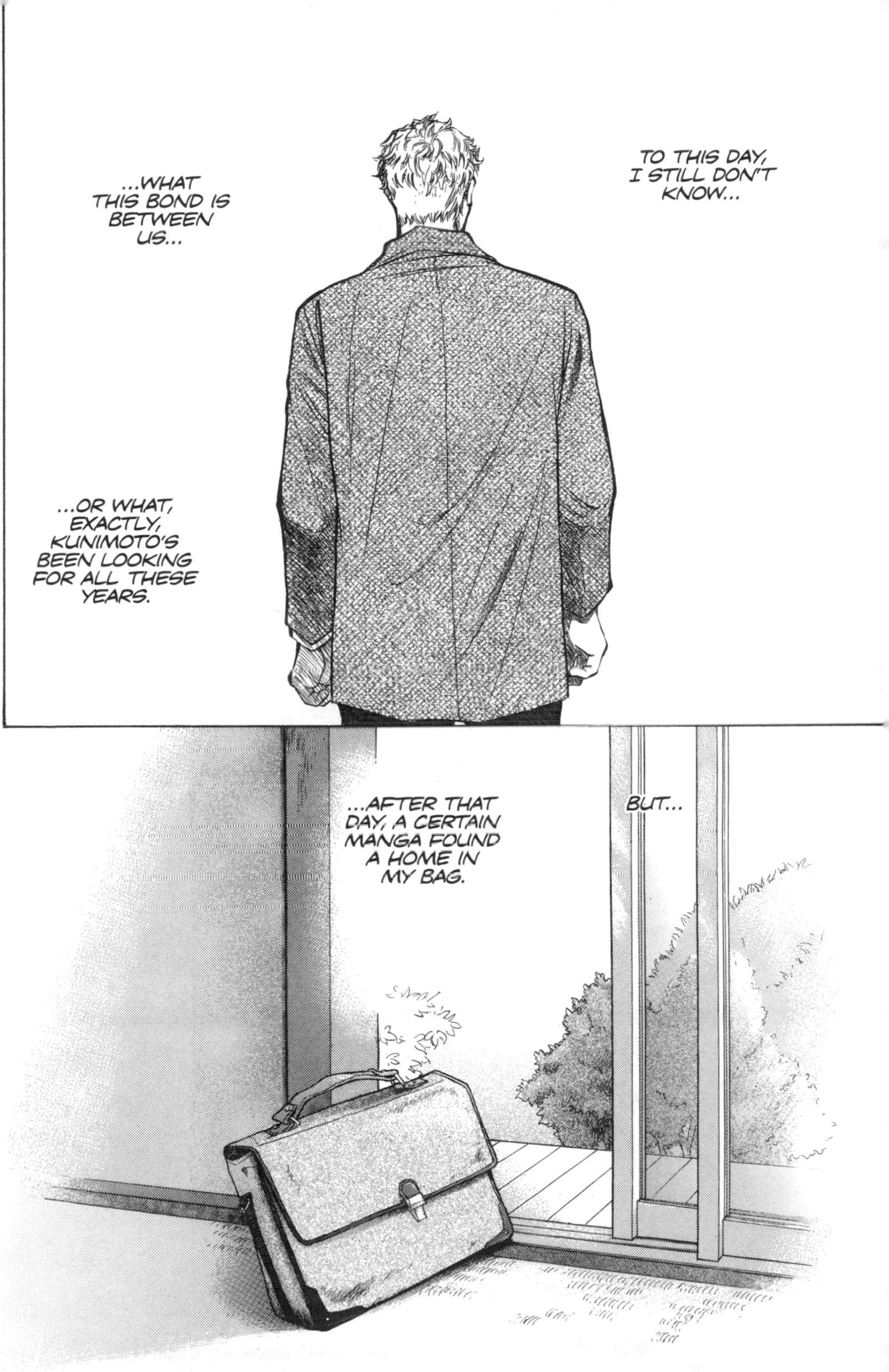
TO THIS DAY, I STILL DON'T KNOW...
...WHAT THIS BOND IS BETWEEN US...
...OR WHAT, EXACTLY, KUNIMOTO'S BEEN LOOKING FOR ALL THESE YEARS.
BUT...
...AFTER THAT DAY, A CERTAIN MANGA FOUND A HOME IN MY BAG.

Chapter 24: A Common Language

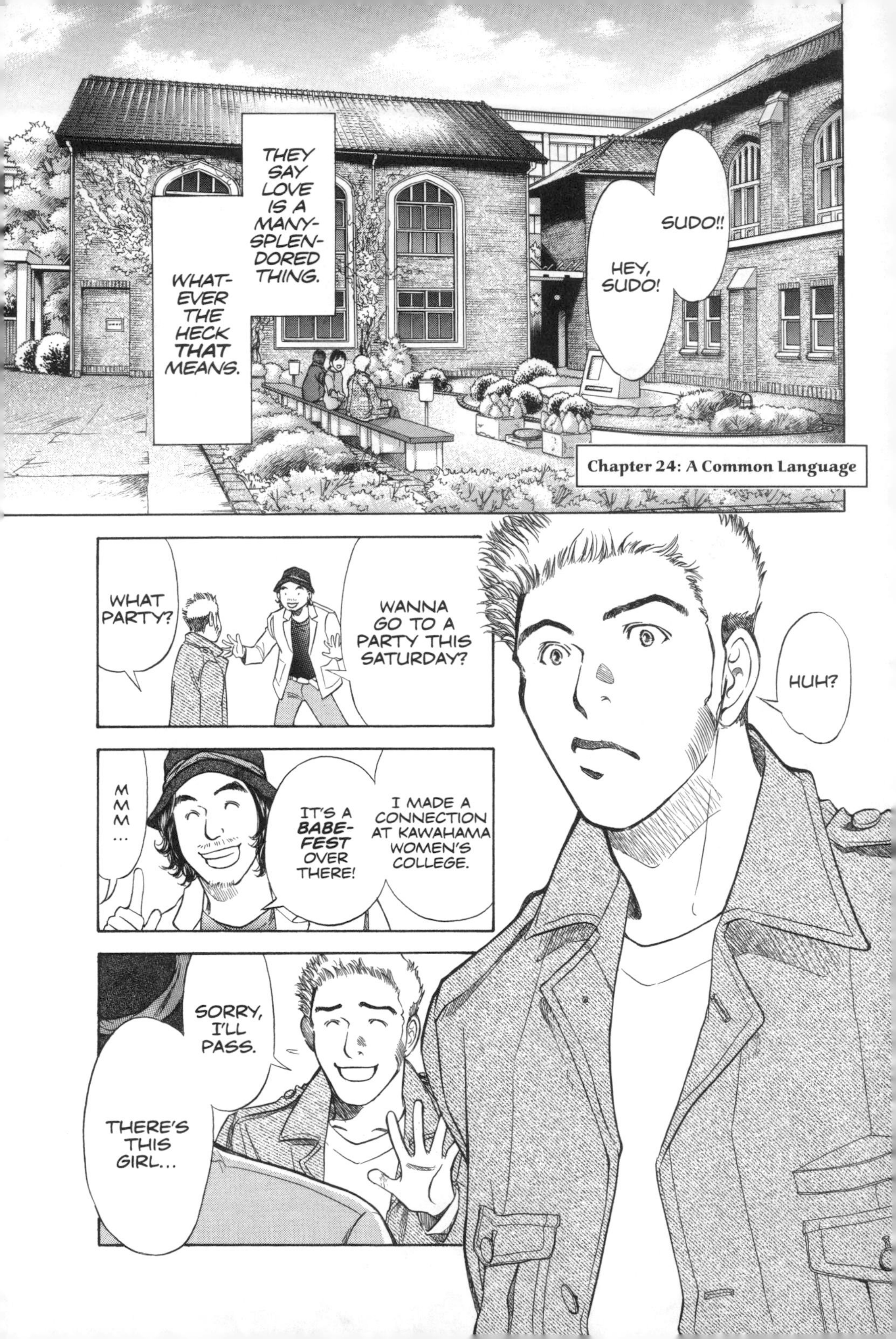
THEY SAY LOVE IS A MANY-SPLENDORED THING.
WHATEVER THE HECK THAT MEANS.
SUDO!!
HEY, SUDO!
HUH?
WANNA GO TO A PARTY THIS SATURDAY?
WHAT PARTY?
I MADE A CONNECTION AT KAWAHAMA WOMEN'S COLLEGE.
IT'S A BABE-FEST OVER THERE!
MMM...
SORRY, I'LL PASS.
THERE'S THIS GIRL...

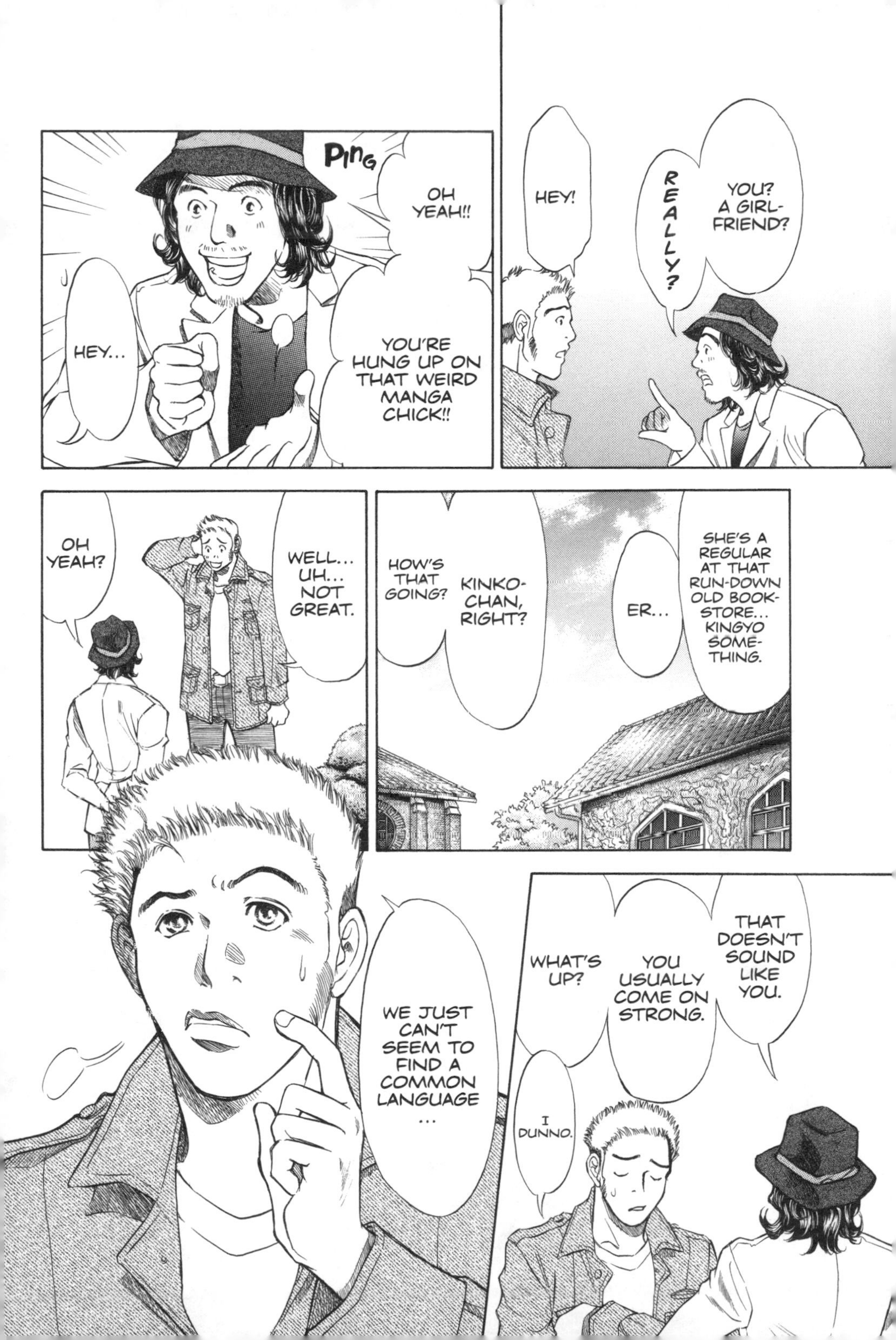
YOU? A GIRL-FRIEND?
REALLY?
HEY!
PING
OH YEAH!!
YOU'RE HUNG UP ON THAT WEIRD MANGA CHICK!!
HEY...
SHE'S A REGULAR AT THAT RUN-DOWN OLD BOOK-STORE... KINGYO SOMETHING.
ER...
KINKO-CHAN, RIGHT?
HOW'S THAT GOING?
WELL... UH... NOT GREAT.
OH YEAH?
THAT DOESN'T SOUND LIKE YOU.
YOU USUALLY COME ON STRONG.
WHAT'S UP?
I DUNNO.
WE JUST CAN'T SEEM TO FIND A COMMON LANGUAGE ...

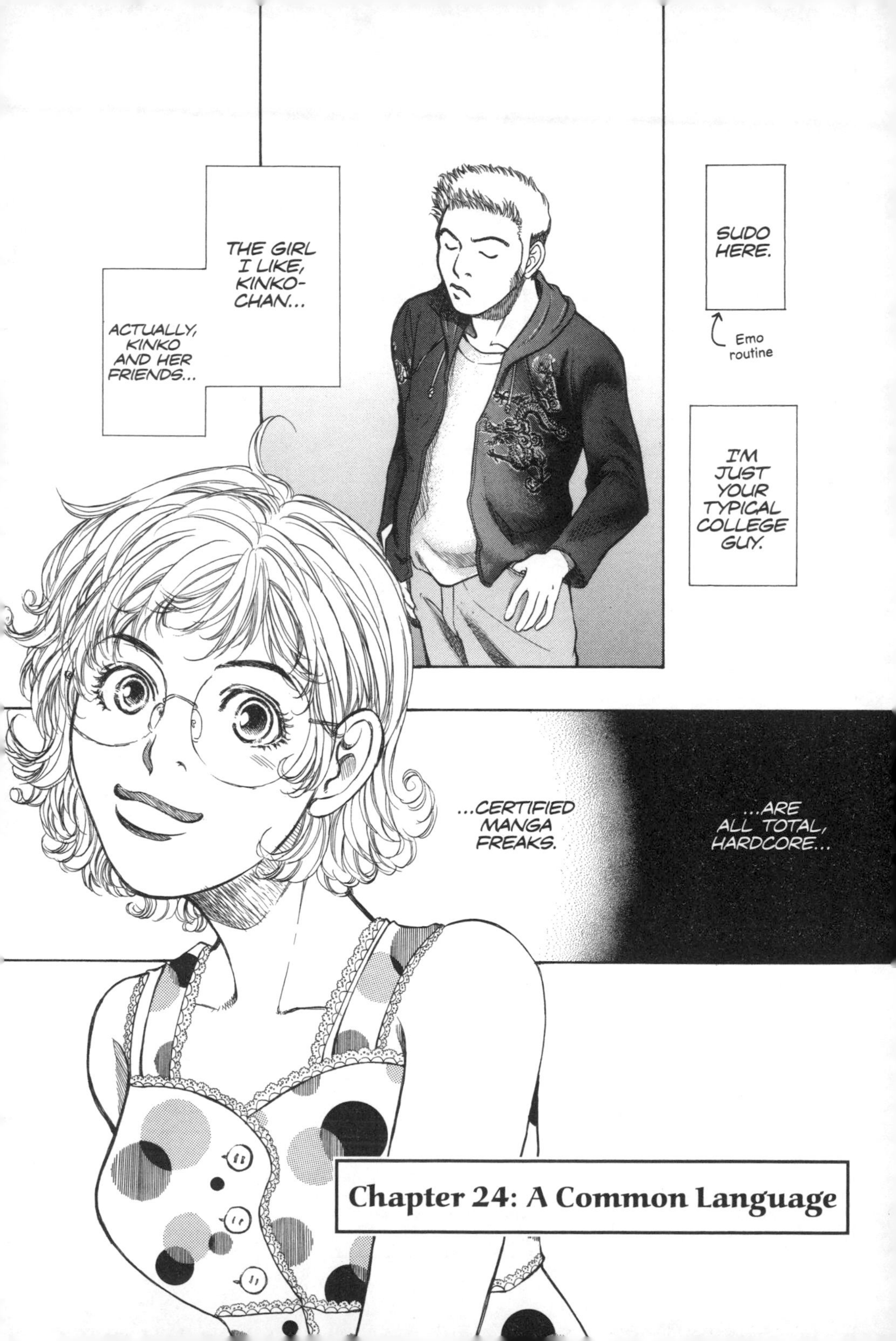
SUDO HERE.
Emo routine
I'M JUST YOUR TYPICAL COLLEGE GUY.
THE GIRL I LIKE, KINKO-CHAN...
ACTUALLY, KINKO AND HER FRIENDS...
...ARE ALL TOTAL, HARDCORE...
...CERTIFIED MANGA FREAKS.

Chapter 24: A Common Language

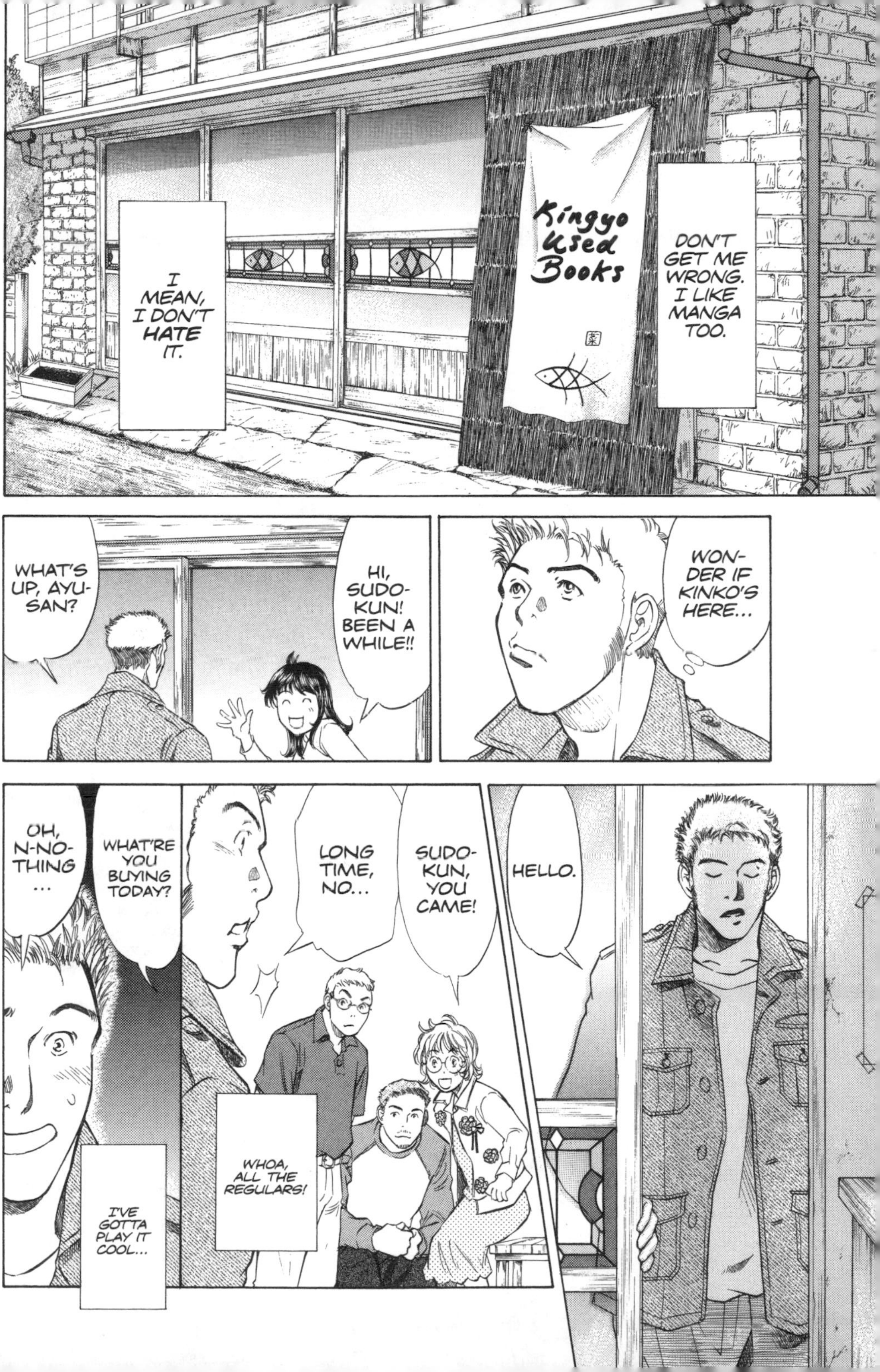
DON'T GET ME WRONG. I LIKE MANGA TOO.
Kingyo Used Books
I MEAN, I DON'T HATE IT.
WONDER IF KINKO'S HERE...
HI, SUDO-KUN! BEEN A WHILE!!
WHAT'S UP, AYU-SAN?
HELLO.
SUDO-KUN, YOU CAME!
LONG TIME, NO...
WHOA, ALL THE REGULARS!
WHAT'RE YOU BUYING TODAY?
OH, N-NOTHING...
I'VE GOTTA PLAY IT COOL...

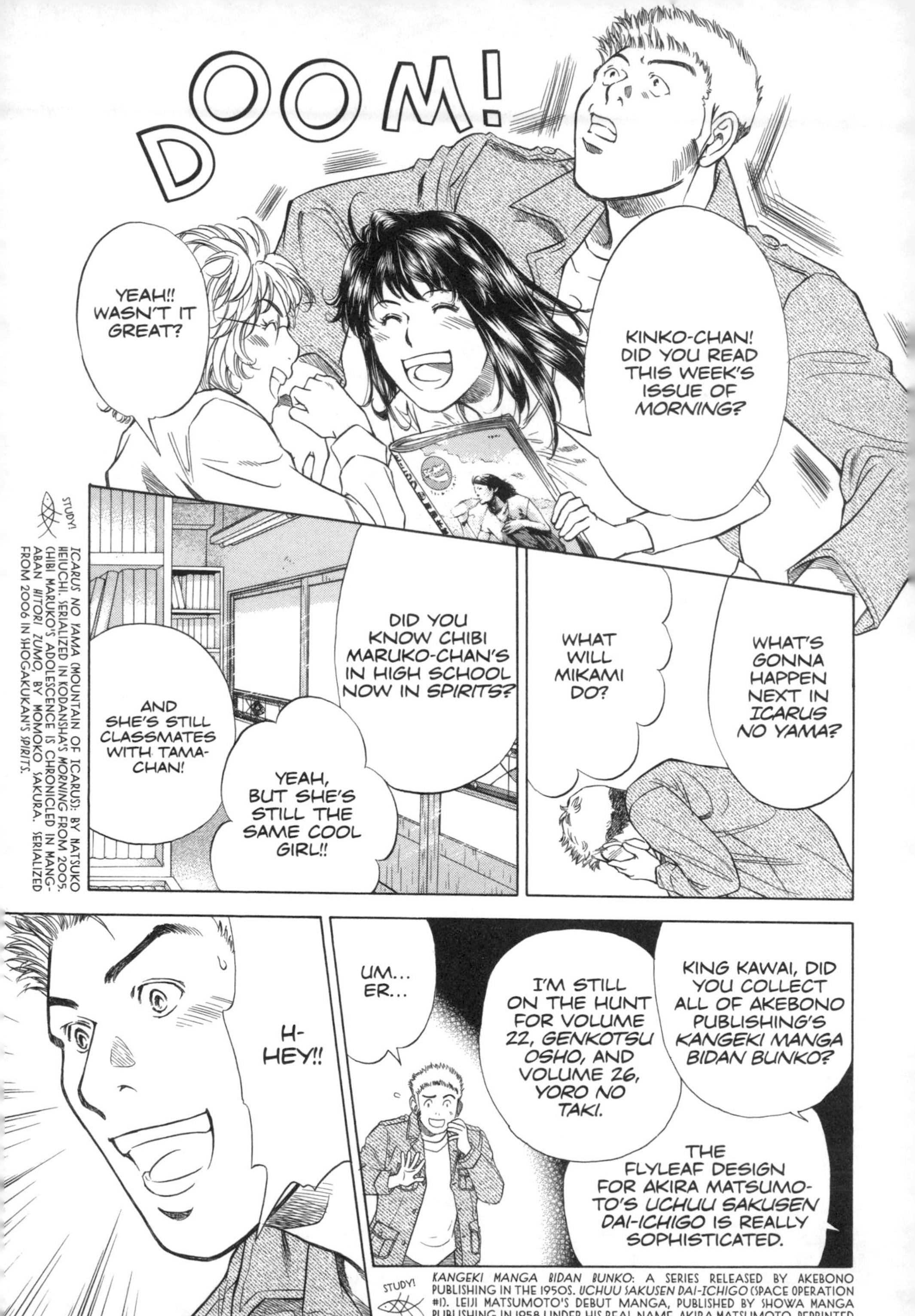
DOOM!
KINKO-CHAN! DID YOU READ THIS WEEK'S ISSUE OF *MORNING*?
YEAH!! WASN'T IT GREAT?
WHAT'S GONNA HAPPEN NEXT IN *ICARUS NO YAMA*?
WHAT WILL MIKAMI DO?
DID YOU KNOW CHIBI MARUKO-CHAN'S IN HIGH SCHOOL NOW IN *SPIRITS*?
AND SHE'S STILL CLASSMATES WITH TAMA-CHAN!
YEAH, BUT SHE'S STILL THE SAME COOL GIRL!!
KING KAWAI, DID YOU COLLECT ALL OF AKEBONO PUBLISHING'S *KANGEKI MANGA BIDAN BUNKO*?
I'M STILL ON THE HUNT FOR VOLUME 22, GENKOTSU OSHO, AND VOLUME 26, YORO NO TAKI.
UM... ER...
THE FLYLEAF DESIGN FOR AKIRA MATSUMOTO'S *UCHUU SAKUSEN DAI-ICHIGO* IS REALLY SOPHISTICATED.
H-HEY!!

STUDY!

ICARUS NO YAMA (MOUNTAIN OF ICARUS): BY MATSUKO HEIUCHI. SERIALIZED IN KODANSHA'S *MORNING* FROM 2005. CHIBI MARUKO'S ADOLESCENCE IS CHRONICLED IN *MANGABAN HITORI ZUMO*, BY MOMOKO SAKURA. SERIALIZED FROM 2006 IN SHOGAKUKAN'S *SPIRITS*.

STUDY!

KANGEKI MANGA BIDAN BUNKO: A SERIES RELEASED BY AKEBONO PUBLISHING IN THE 1950S. *UCHUU SAKUSEN DAI-ICHIGO* (SPACE OPERATION #1). LEIJI MATSUMOTO'S DEBUT MANGA, PUBLISHED BY SHOWA MANGA PUBLISHING IN 1958 UNDER HIS REAL NAME, AKIRA MATSUMOTO. REPRINTED IN 2006 BY SHOGAKUKAN.

★ *AINORI* (LOVE RIDE) IS A POPULAR REALITY TV SHOW.

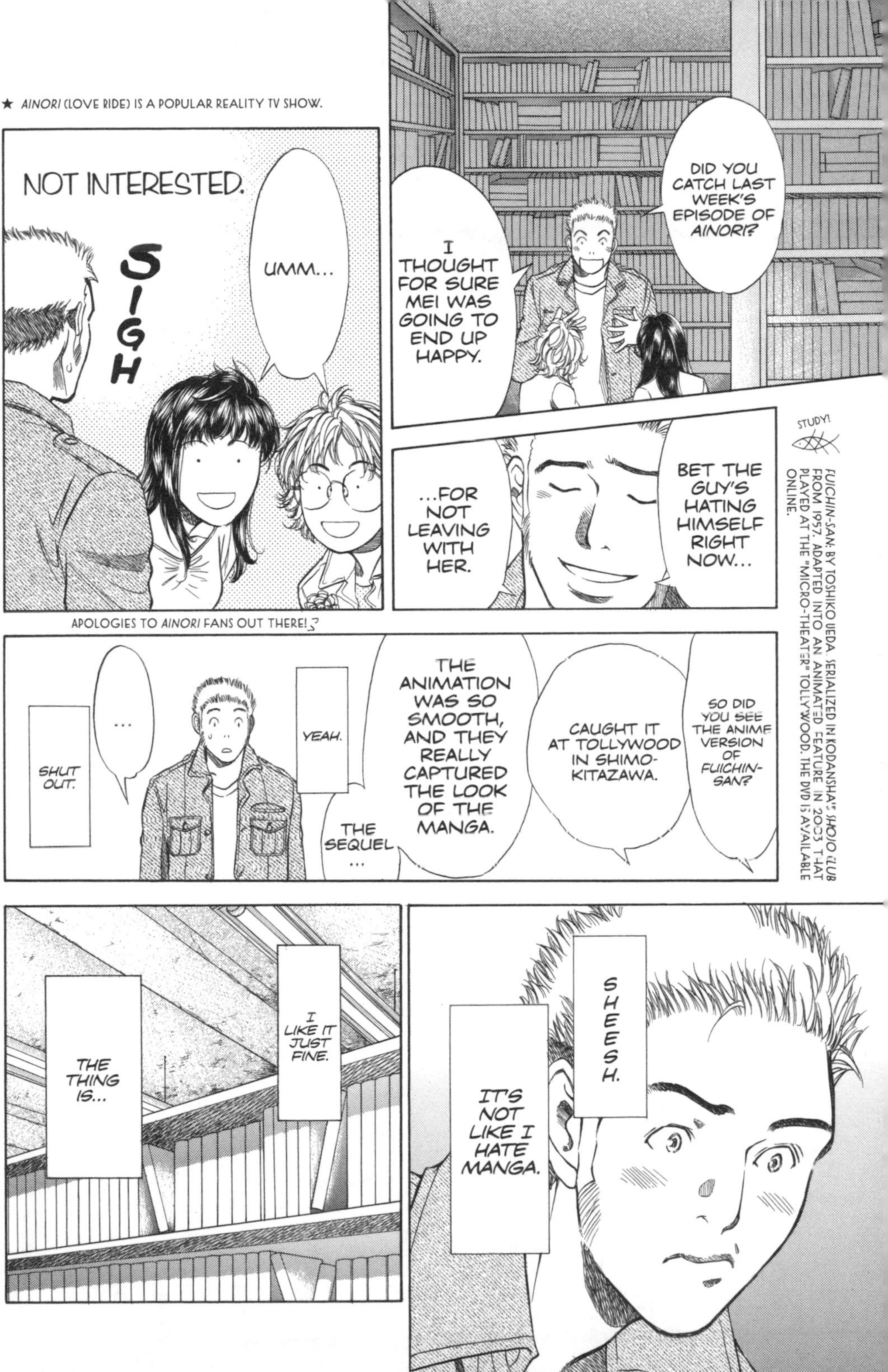
DID YOU CATCH LAST WEEK'S EPISODE OF AINORI?
I THOUGHT FOR SURE MEI WAS GOING TO END UP HAPPY.
BET THE GUY'S HATING HIMSELF RIGHT NOW...
...FOR NOT LEAVING WITH HER.
NOT INTERESTED.
SIGH
UMM...
SO DID YOU SEE THE ANIME VERSION OF FUICHIN-SAN?
CAUGHT IT AT TOLLYWOOD IN SHIMO-KITAZAWA.
THE ANIMATION WAS SO SMOOTH, AND THEY REALLY CAPTURED THE LOOK OF THE MANGA.
THE SEQUEL...
YEAH.
...
SHUT OUT.
SHEESH.
IT'S NOT LIKE I HATE MANGA.
I LIKE IT JUST FINE.
THE THING IS...

APOLOGIES TO *AINORI* FANS OUT THERE!

STUDY!

FUICHIN-SAN: BY TOSHIKO UEDA. SERIALIZED IN KODANSHA'S *SHOJO CLUB* FROM 1957. ADAPTED INTO AN ANIMATED FEATURE IN 2003 THAT PLAYED AT THE "MICRO-THEATER" TOLLYWOOD. THE DVD IS AVAILABLE ONLINE.

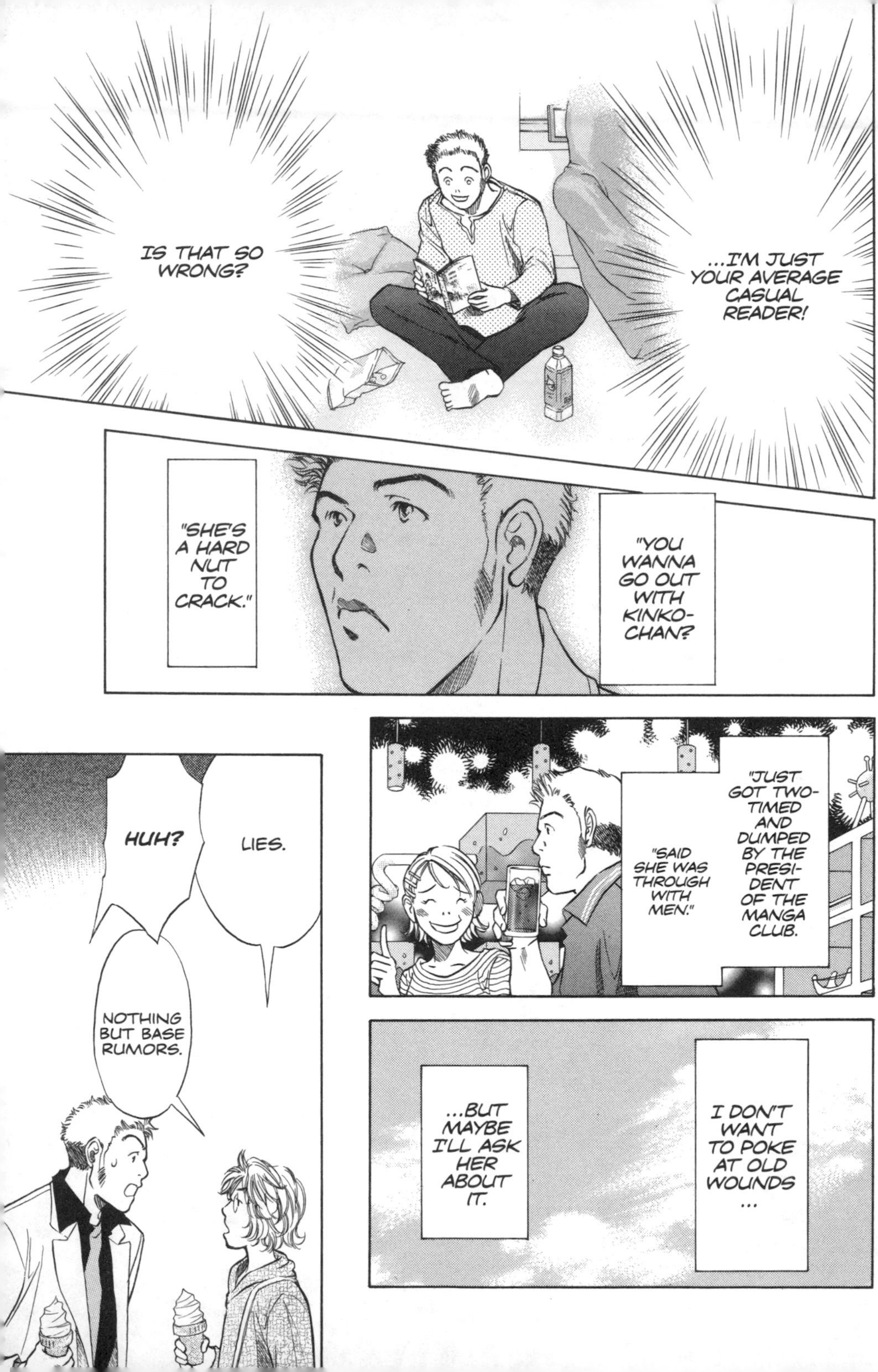
...I'M JUST YOUR AVERAGE CASUAL READER!
IS THAT SO WRONG?
"YOU WANNA GO OUT WITH KINKO-CHAN?
"SHE'S A HARD NUT TO CRACK."
"JUST GOT TWO-TIMED AND DUMPED BY THE PRESIDENT OF THE MANGA CLUB.
"SAID SHE WAS THROUGH WITH MEN."
I DON'T WANT TO POKE AT OLD WOUNDS ...
...BUT MAYBE I'LL ASK HER ABOUT IT.
LIES.
HUH?
NOTHING BUT BASE RUMORS.

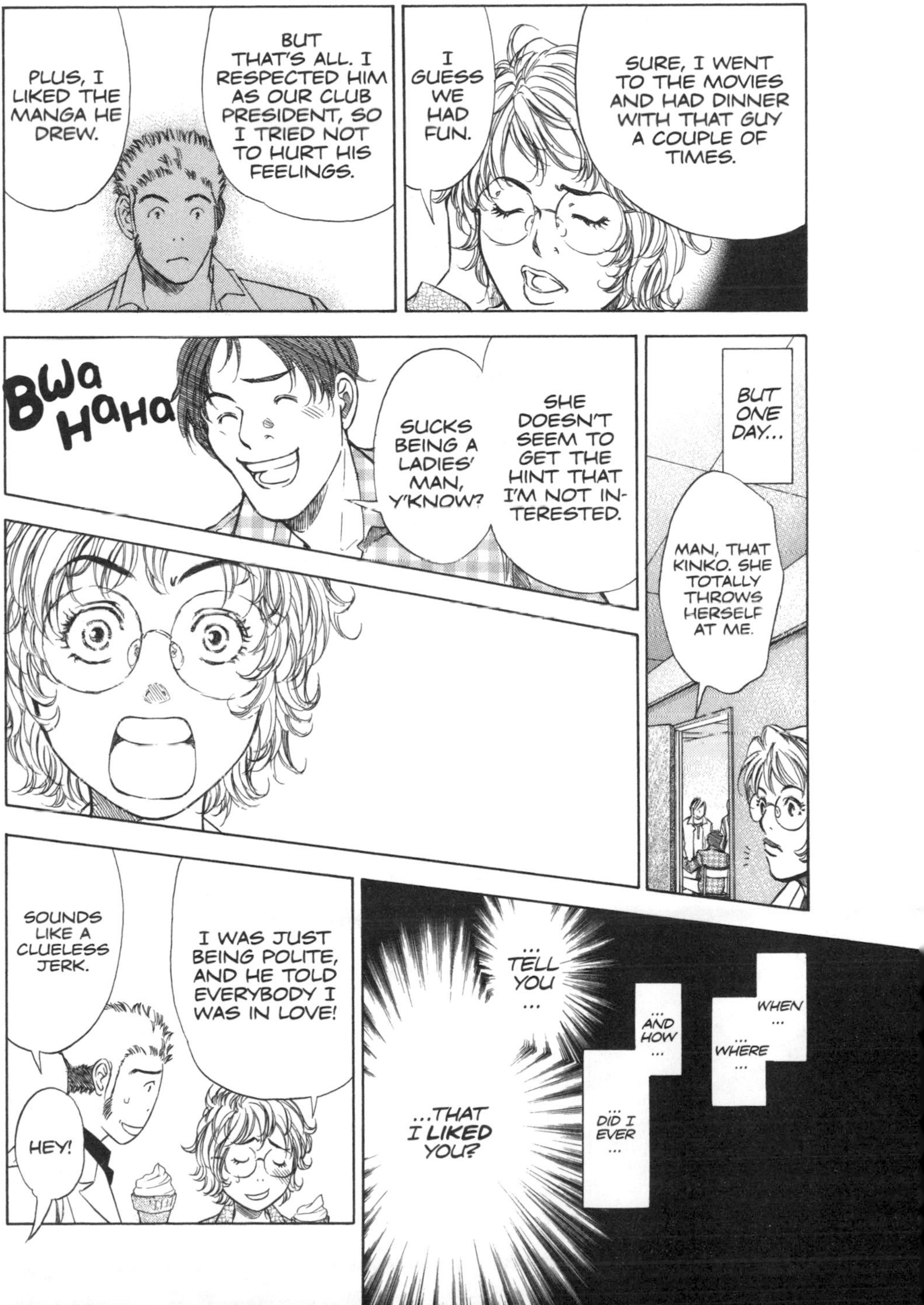
SURE, I WENT TO THE MOVIES AND HAD DINNER WITH THAT GUY A COUPLE OF TIMES.
I GUESS WE HAD FUN.
BUT THAT'S ALL. I RESPECTED HIM AS OUR CLUB PRESIDENT, SO I TRIED NOT TO HURT HIS FEELINGS.
PLUS, I LIKED THE MANGA HE DREW.
BUT ONE DAY...
MAN, THAT KINKO. SHE TOTALLY THROWS HERSELF AT ME.
SHE DOESN'T SEEM TO GET THE HINT THAT I'M NOT INTERESTED.
SUCKS BEING A LADIES' MAN, Y'KNOW?
BWA HAHA
WHEN...
...WHERE...
...AND HOW...
...DID I EVER...
...TELL YOU...
...THAT I **LIKED** YOU?
I WAS JUST BEING POLITE, AND HE TOLD EVERYBODY I WAS IN LOVE!
SOUNDS LIKE A CLUELESS JERK.
HEY!

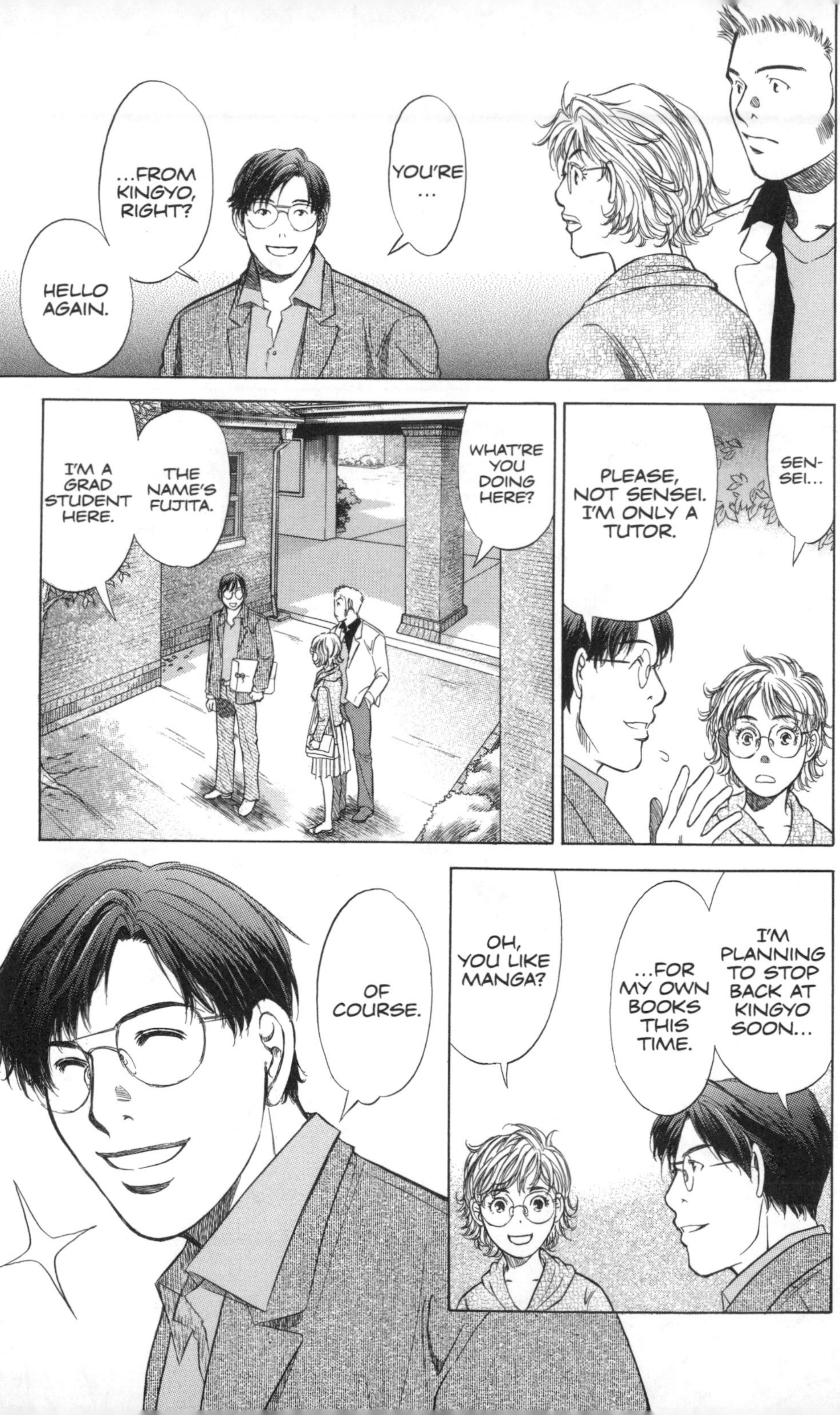
YOU'RE ...
...FROM KINGYO, RIGHT?
HELLO AGAIN.
SEN-SEI...
PLEASE, NOT SENSEI. I'M ONLY A TUTOR.
WHAT'RE YOU DOING HERE?
THE NAME'S FUJITA.
I'M A GRAD STUDENT HERE.
I'M PLANNING TO STOP BACK AT KINGYO SOON...
...FOR MY OWN BOOKS THIS TIME.
OH, YOU LIKE MANGA?
OF COURSE.

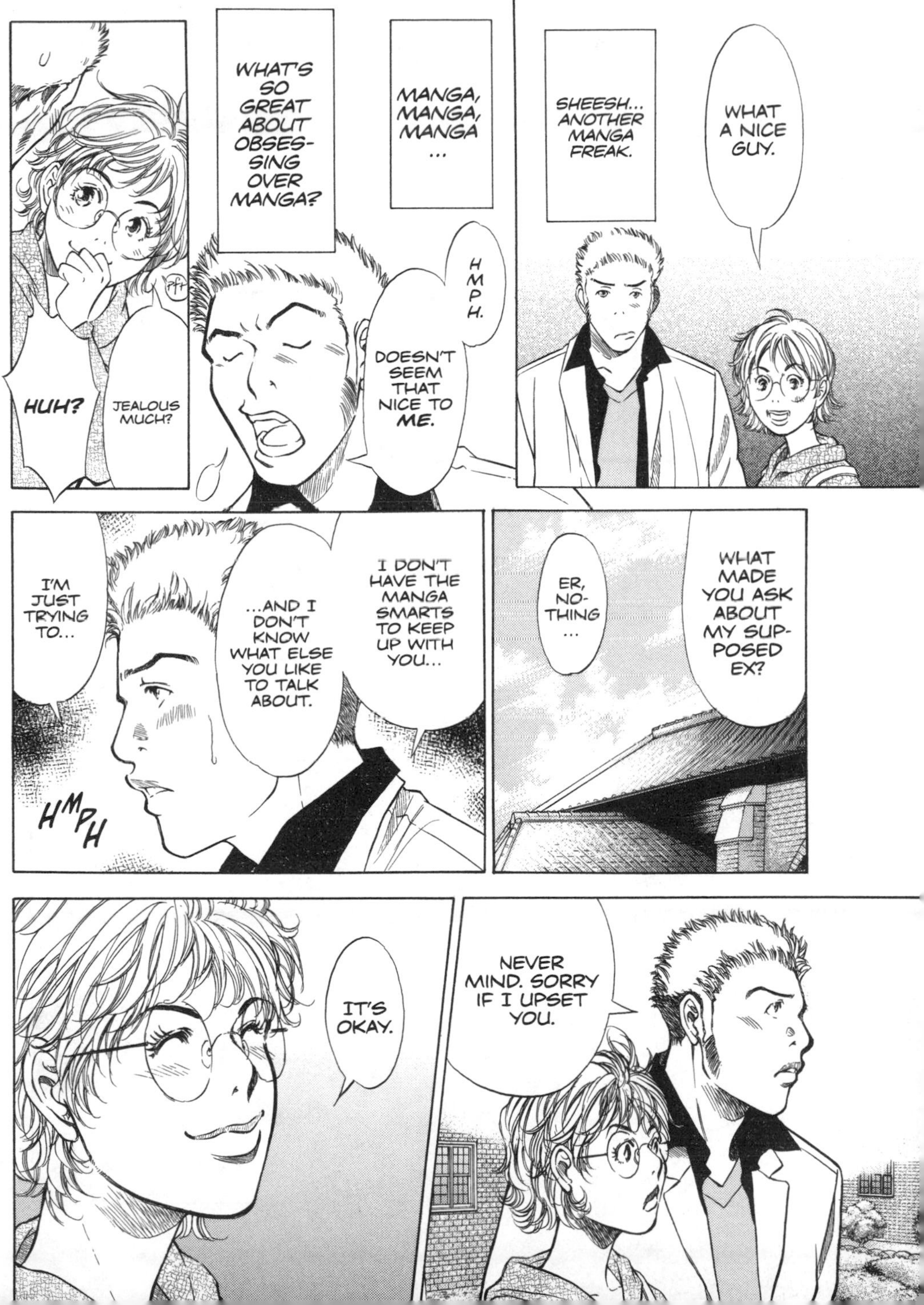
WHAT A NICE GUY.
SHEESH... ANOTHER MANGA FREAK.
MANGA, MANGA, MANGA...
HMPH.
DOESN'T SEEM THAT NICE TO **ME.**
WHAT'S SO GREAT ABOUT OBSES-SING OVER MANGA?
JEALOUS MUCH?
HUH?
WHAT MADE YOU ASK ABOUT MY SUP-POSED EX?
ER, NO-THING...
I DON'T HAVE THE MANGA SMARTS TO KEEP UP WITH YOU...
...AND I DON'T KNOW WHAT ELSE YOU LIKE TO TALK ABOUT.
I'M JUST TRYING TO...
HMPH
NEVER MIND. SORRY IF I UPSET YOU.
IT'S OKAY.

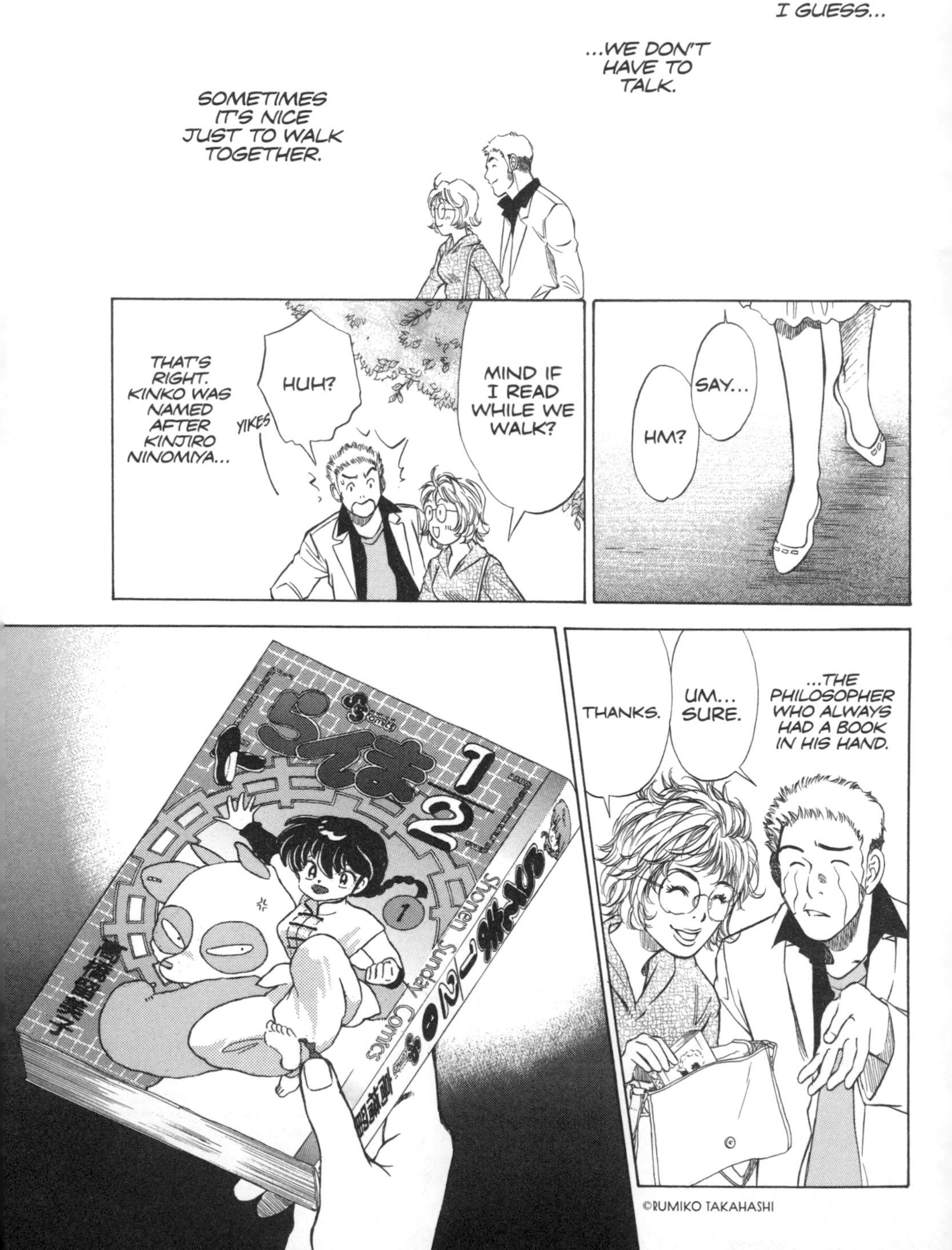

I GUESS...
...WE DON'T HAVE TO TALK.
SOMETIMES IT'S NICE JUST TO WALK TOGETHER.
SAY...
HM?
MIND IF I READ WHILE WE WALK?
HUH?
YIKES
THAT'S RIGHT. KINKO WAS NAMED AFTER KINJIRO NINOMIYA...
...THE PHILOSOPHER WHO ALWAYS HAD A BOOK IN HIS HAND.
UM... SURE.
THANKS.
Shonen Sunday Comics
©RUMIKO TAKAHASHI

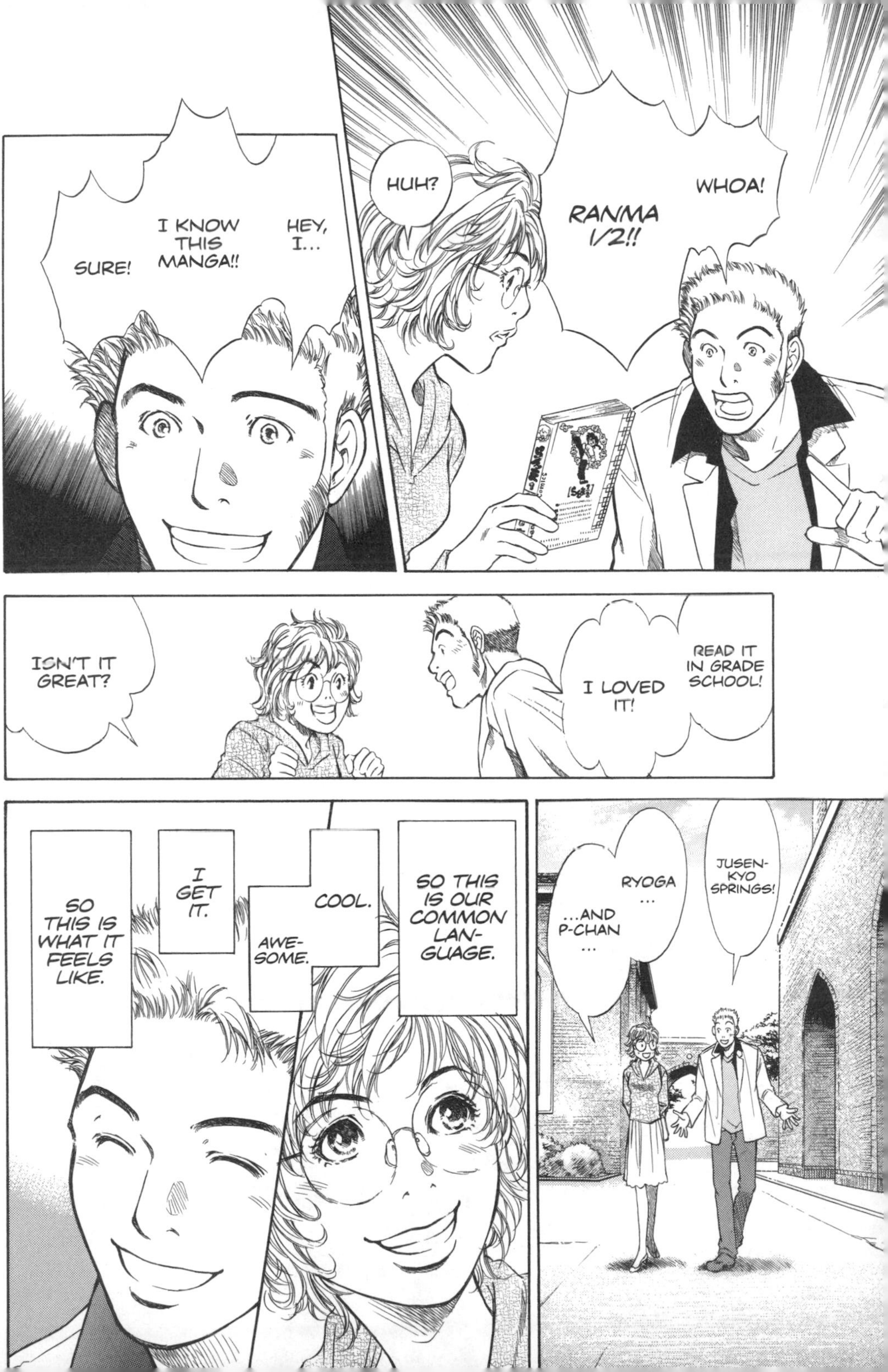
WHOA!
RANMA 1/2!!
HUH?
HEY, I... I KNOW THIS MANGA!! SURE!
READ IT IN GRADE SCHOOL! I LOVED IT!
ISN'T IT GREAT?
JUSEN-KYO SPRINGS!
RYOGA ... ...AND P-CHAN ...
SO THIS IS OUR COMMON LAN-GUAGE.
COOL.
AWE-SOME.
I GET IT.
SO THIS IS WHAT IT FEELS LIKE.

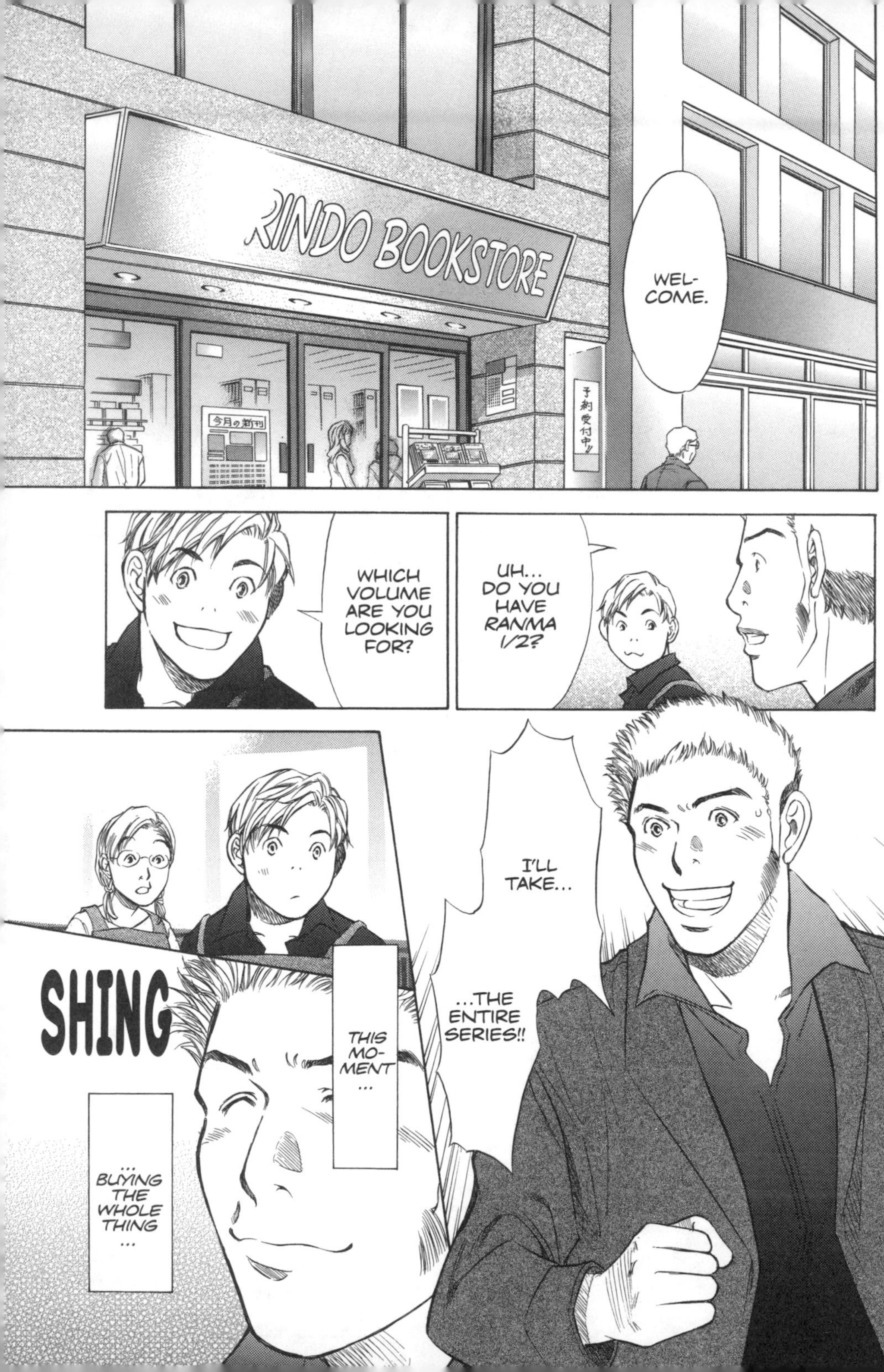
INDO BOOKSTORE
今月の新刊
予約受付中!!
WEL-COME.
UH... DO YOU HAVE RANMA 1/2?
WHICH VOLUME ARE YOU LOOKING FOR?
I'LL TAKE...
...THE ENTIRE SERIES!!
SHING
THIS MO-MENT...
...BUYING THE WHOLE THING...

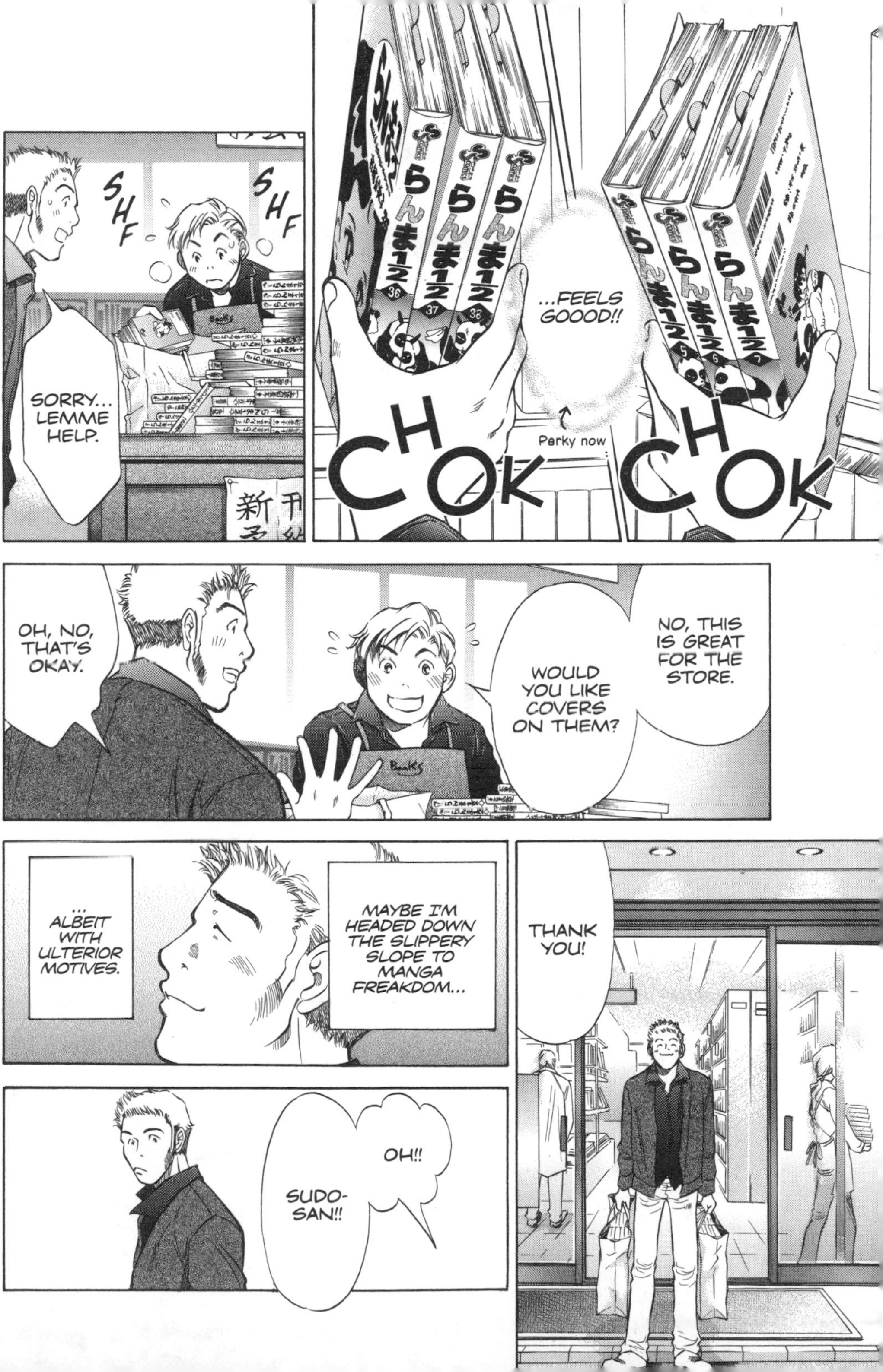
...FEELS GOOOD!!
Perky now
CHOK
CHOK
SHF
SHF
SORRY... LEMME HELP.
NO, THIS IS GREAT FOR THE STORE.
WOULD YOU LIKE COVERS ON THEM?
OH, NO, THAT'S OKAY.
THANK YOU!
MAYBE I'M HEADED DOWN THE SLIPPERY SLOPE TO MANGA FREAKDOM...
... ALBEIT WITH ULTERIOR MOTIVES.
OH!!
SUDO-SAN!!

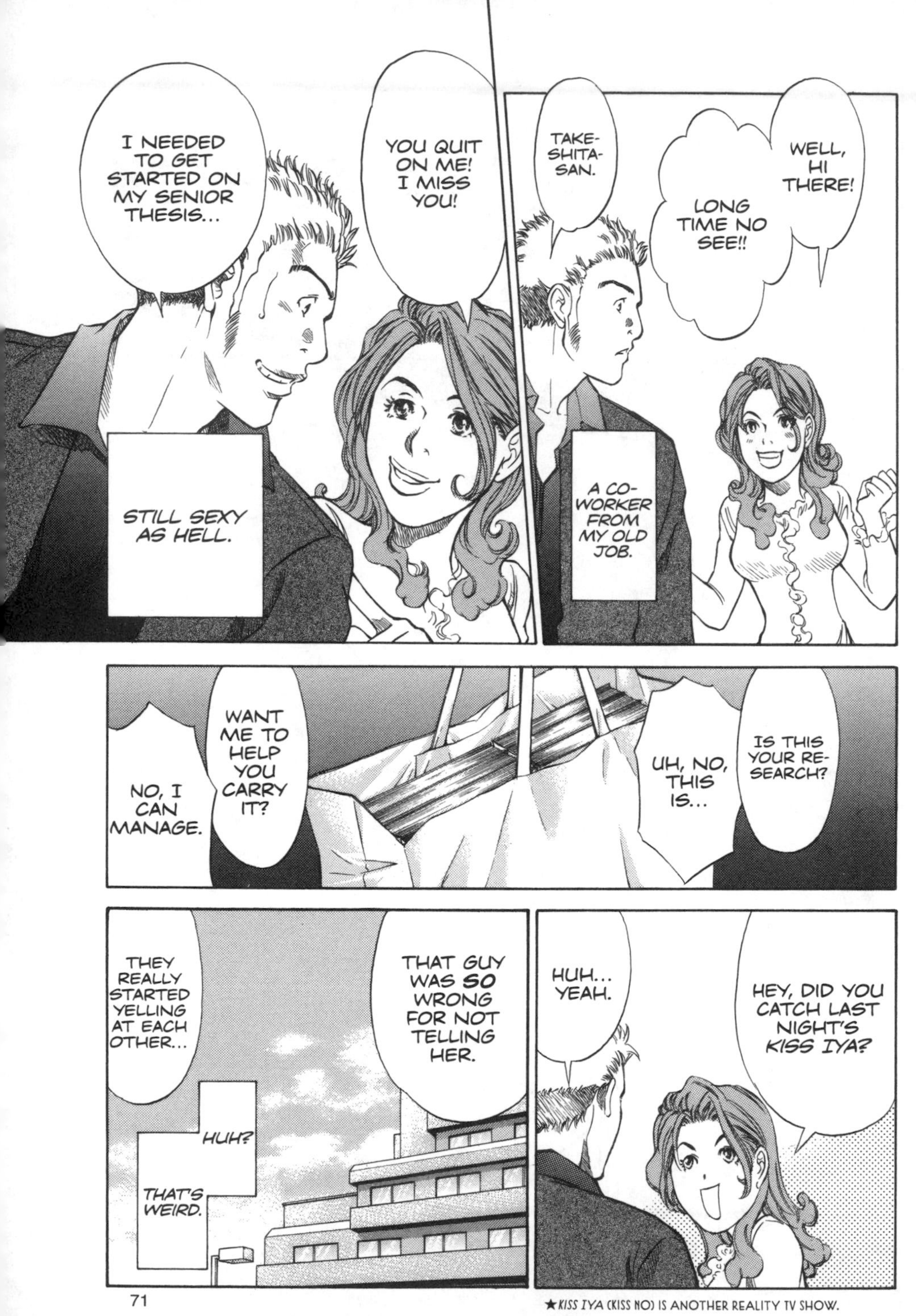
WELL, HI THERE!
LONG TIME NO SEE!!
TAKE-SHITA-SAN.
A CO-WORKER FROM MY OLD JOB.
YOU QUIT ON ME! I MISS YOU!
I NEEDED TO GET STARTED ON MY SENIOR THESIS...
STILL SEXY AS HELL.
IS THIS YOUR RE-SEARCH?
UH, NO, THIS IS...
WANT ME TO HELP YOU CARRY IT?
NO, I CAN MANAGE.
HEY, DID YOU CATCH LAST NIGHT'S *KISS IYA*?
HUH... YEAH.
THAT GUY WAS **SO** WRONG FOR NOT TELLING HER.
THEY REALLY STARTED YELLING AT EACH OTHER...
HUH?
THAT'S WEIRD.

★*KISS IYA* (KISS NO) IS ANOTHER REALITY TV SHOW.

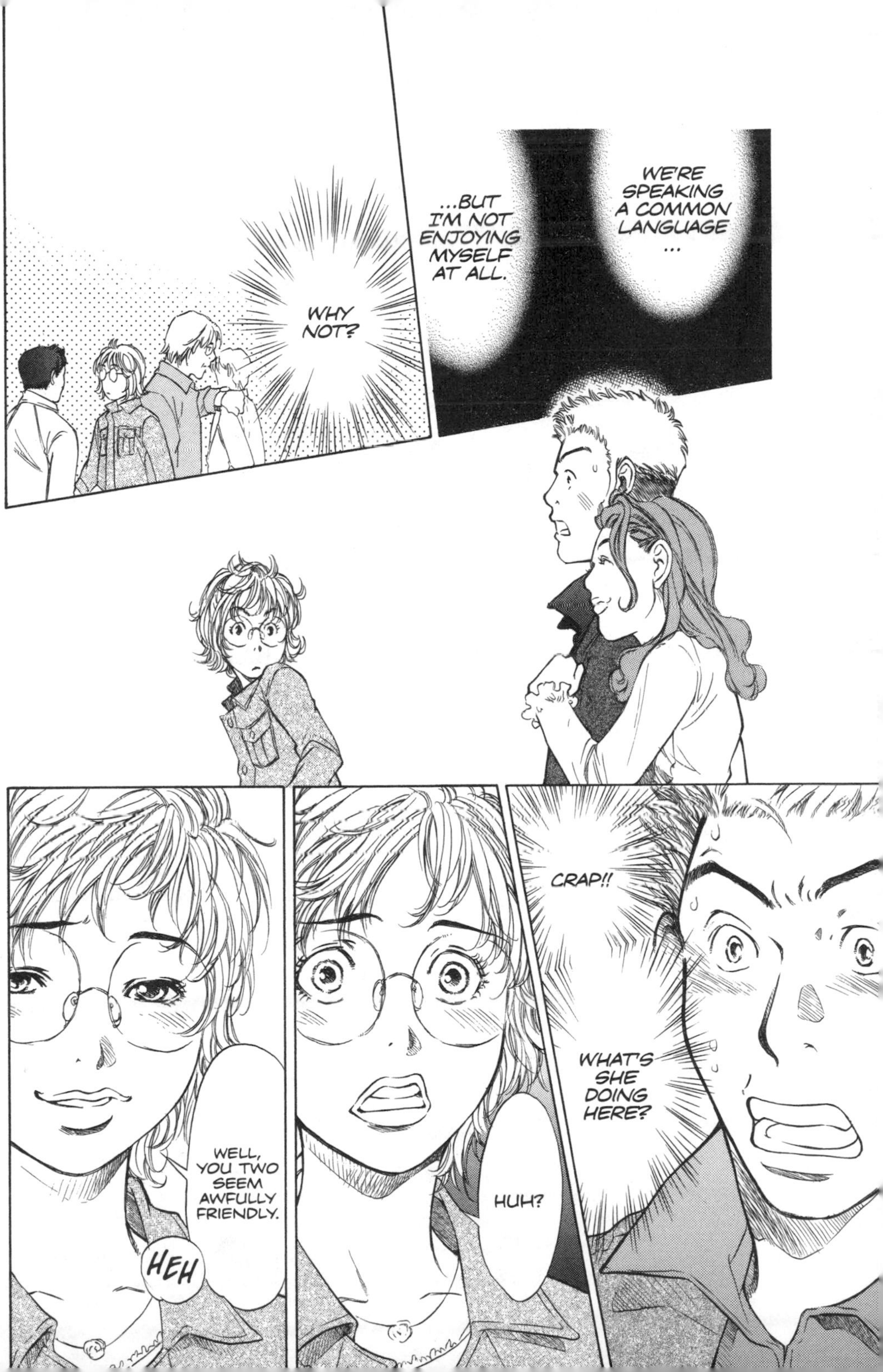
WE'RE SPEAKING A COMMON LANGUAGE ...
...BUT I'M NOT ENJOYING MYSELF AT ALL.
WHY NOT?
CRAP!!
WHAT'S SHE DOING HERE?
HUH?
WELL, YOU TWO SEEM AWFULLY FRIENDLY.
HEH

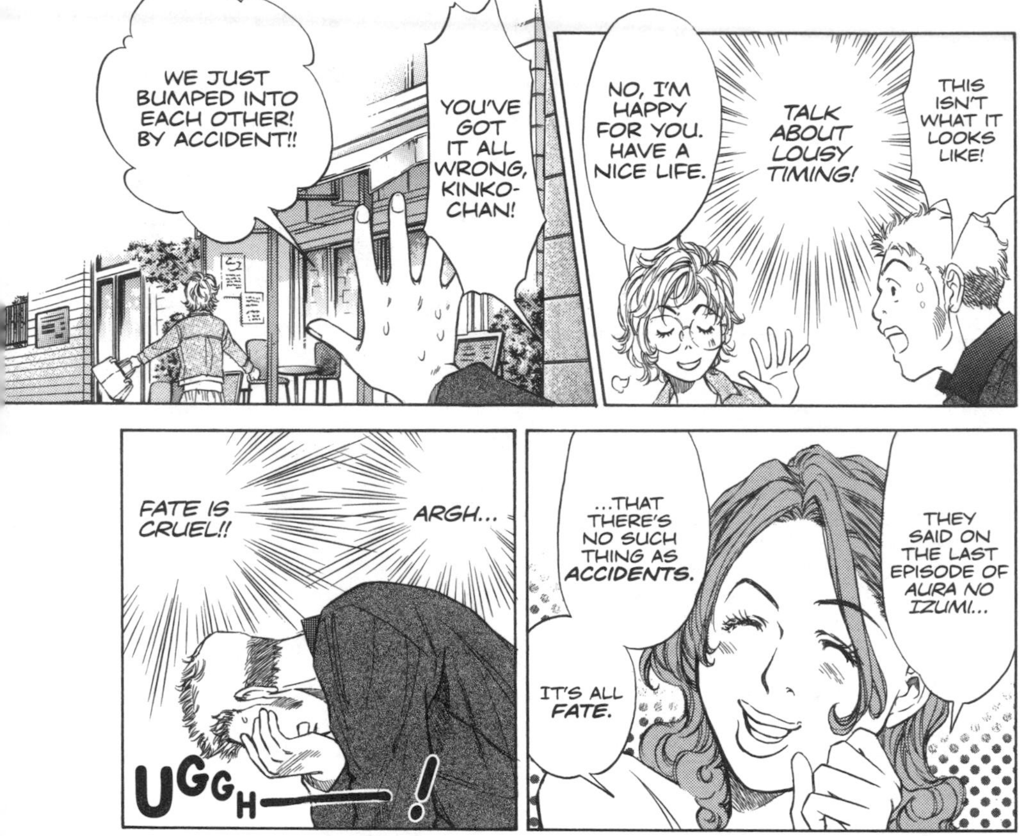
THIS ISN'T WHAT IT LOOKS LIKE!
TALK ABOUT LOUSY TIMING!
NO, I'M HAPPY FOR YOU. HAVE A NICE LIFE.
YOU'VE GOT IT ALL WRONG, KINKO-CHAN!
WE JUST BUMPED INTO EACH OTHER! BY ACCIDENT!!
THEY SAID ON THE LAST EPISODE OF AURA NO IZUMI...
...THAT THERE'S NO SUCH THING AS ACCIDENTS.
IT'S ALL FATE.
ARGH...
FATE IS CRUEL!!
UGGH—!

★*AURA NO IZUMI* (IZUMI'S AURA) IS A PSYCHIC "SPIRITUAL ADVICE" SHOW.

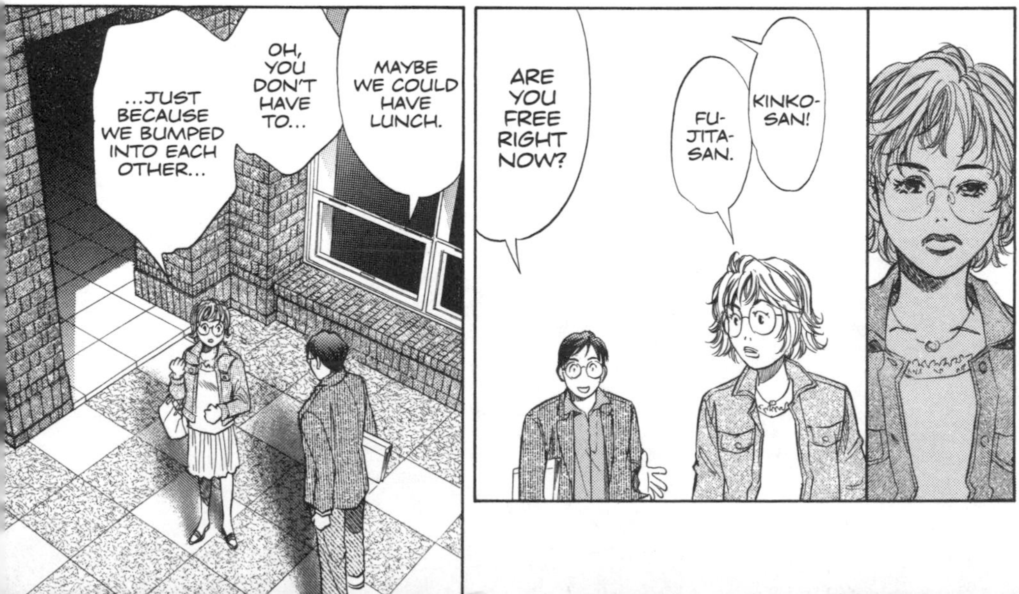
KINKO-SAN!
FU-JITA-SAN.
ARE YOU FREE RIGHT NOW?
MAYBE WE COULD HAVE LUNCH.
OH, YOU DON'T HAVE TO...
...JUST BECAUSE WE BUMPED INTO EACH OTHER...

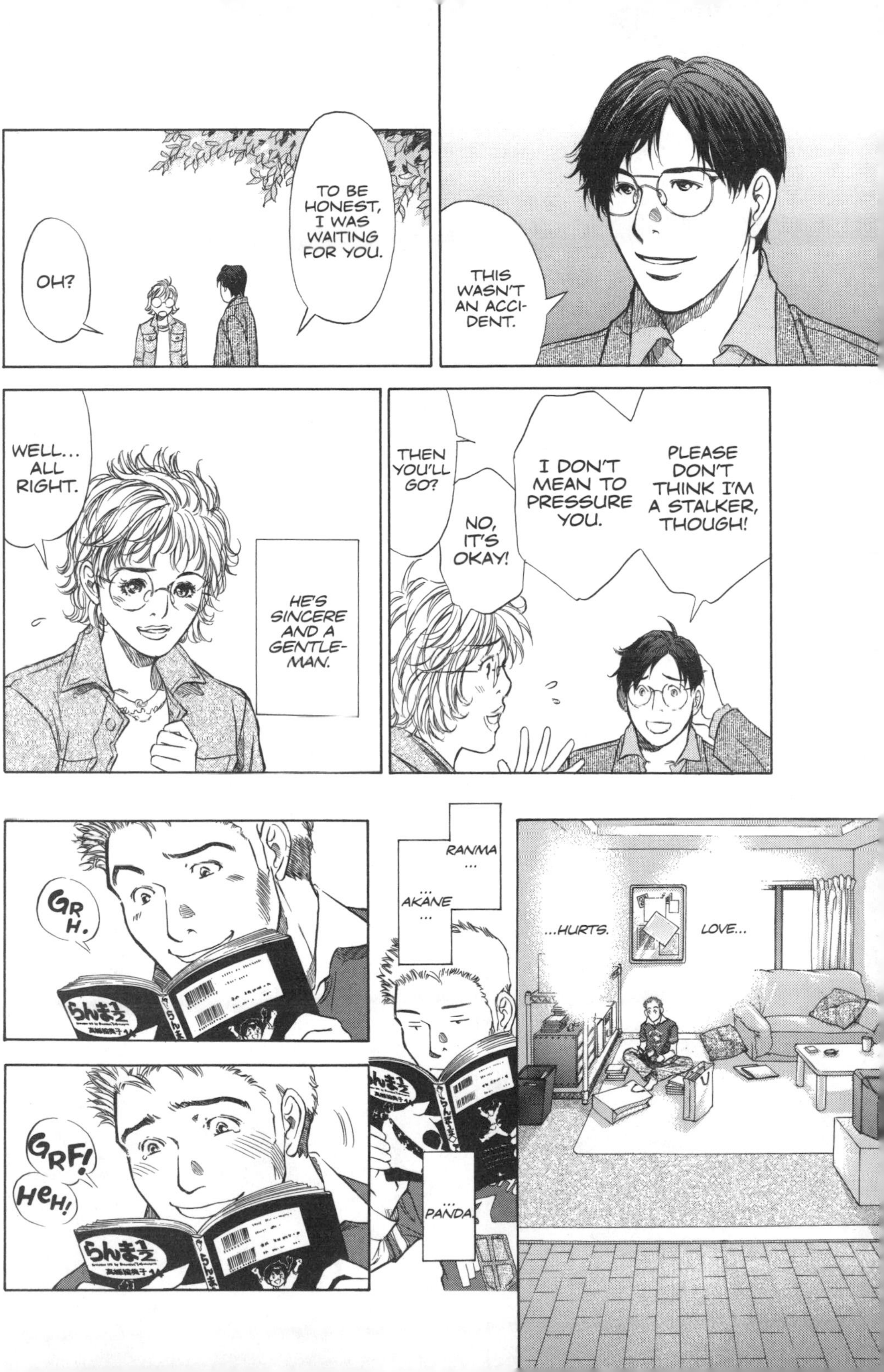
THIS WASN'T AN ACCI-DENT.
TO BE HONEST, I WAS WAITING FOR YOU.
OH?
PLEASE DON'T THINK I'M A STALKER, THOUGH!
I DON'T MEAN TO PRESSURE YOU.
THEN YOU'LL GO?
NO, IT'S OKAY!
WELL... ALL RIGHT.
HE'S SINCERE AND A GENTLE-MAN.
LOVE...
...HURTS.
RANMA ...
... AKANE ...
... PANDA.
GRH.
GRF!
HEH!

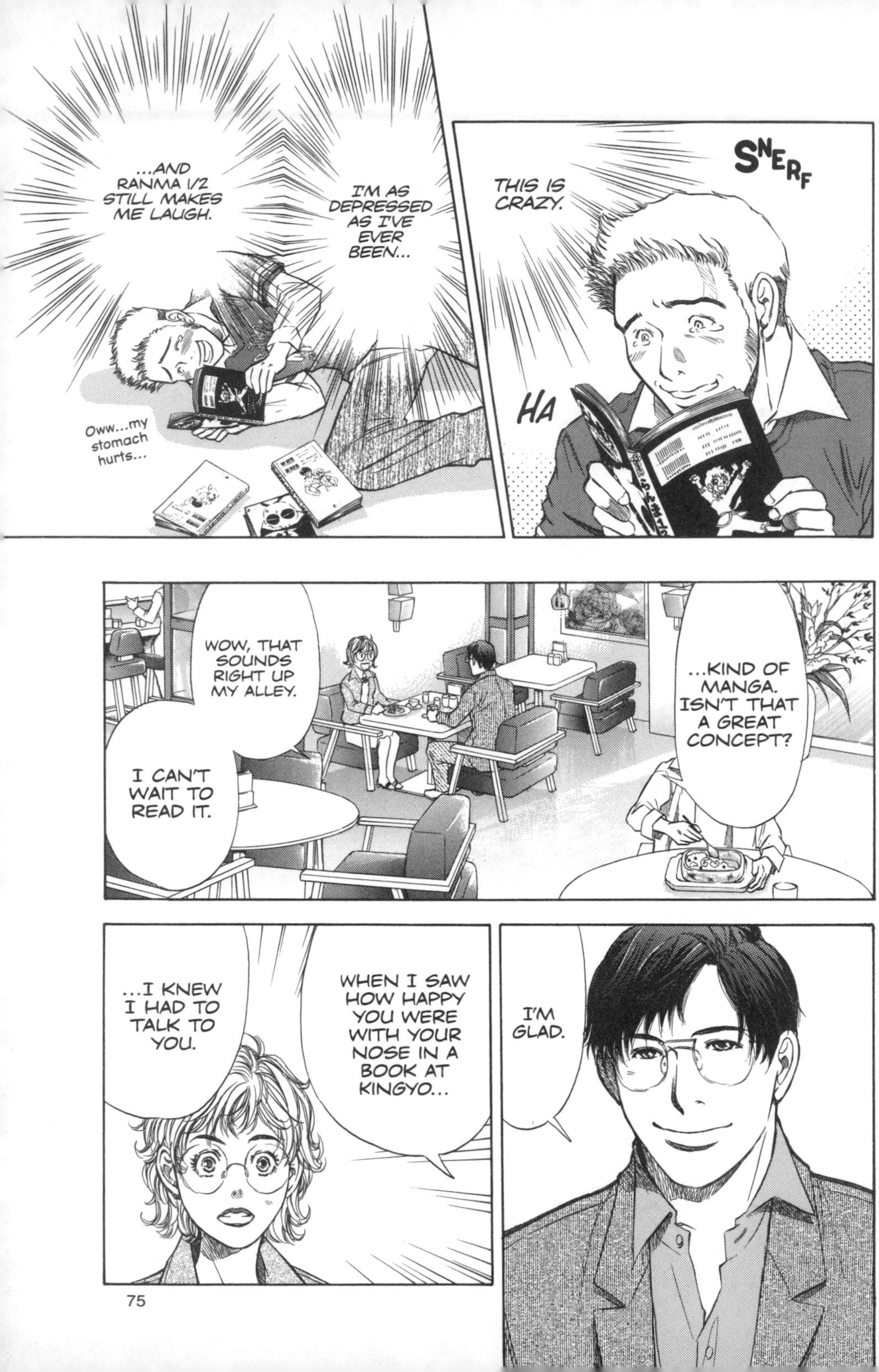
SNERF
THIS IS CRAZY.
HA
I'M AS DEPRESSED AS I'VE EVER BEEN...
...AND RANMA 1/2 STILL MAKES ME LAUGH.
Oww...my stomach hurts...
...KIND OF MANGA. ISN'T THAT A GREAT CONCEPT?
WOW, THAT SOUNDS RIGHT UP MY ALLEY.
I CAN'T WAIT TO READ IT.
I'M GLAD.
WHEN I SAW HOW HAPPY YOU WERE WITH YOUR NOSE IN A BOOK AT KINGYO...
...I KNEW I HAD TO TALK TO YOU.

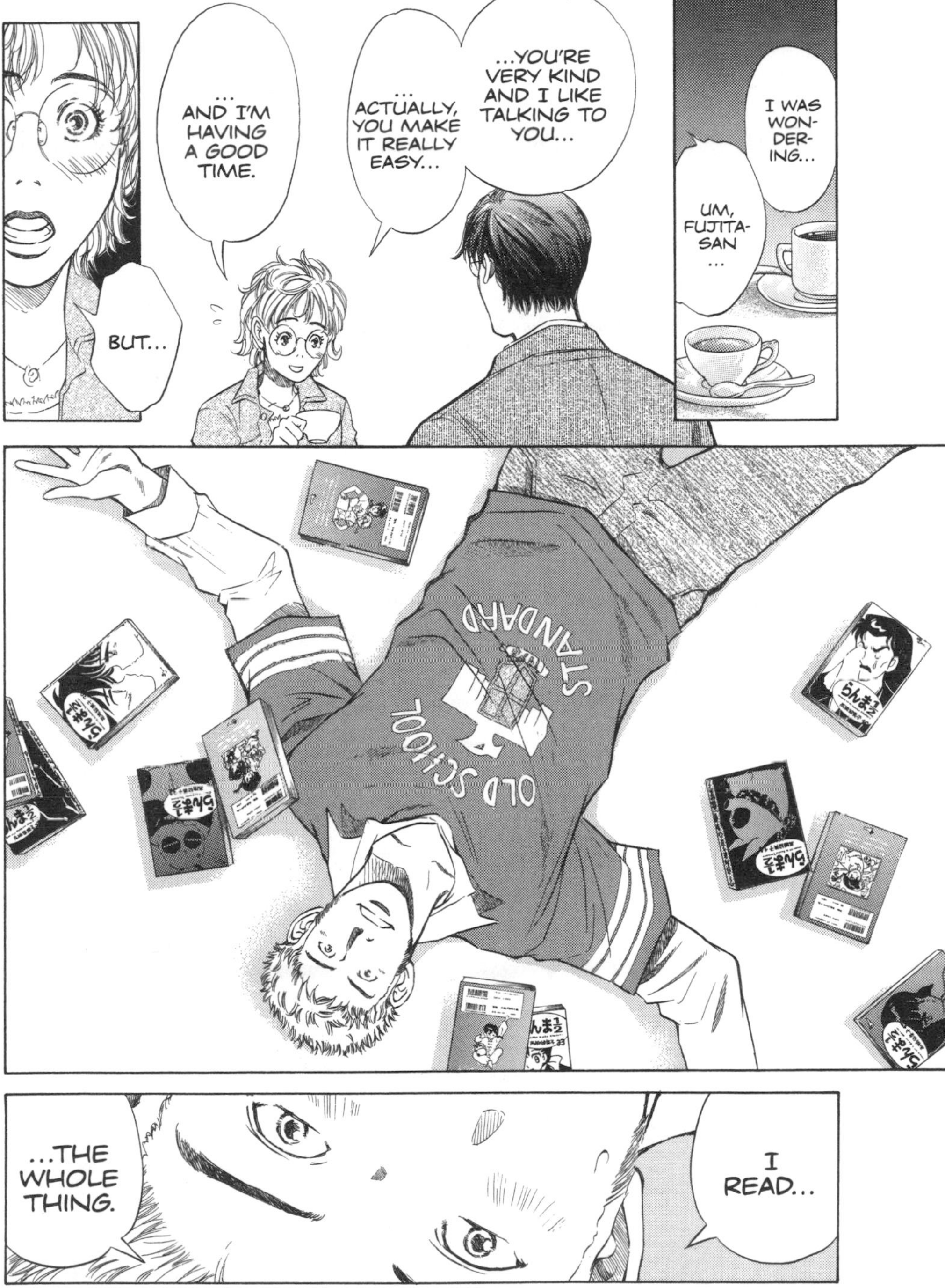
I WAS WON-DER-ING...
UM, FUJITA-SAN...
...YOU'RE VERY KIND AND I LIKE TALKING TO YOU...
...ACTUALLY, YOU MAKE IT REALLY EASY...
...AND I'M HAVING A GOOD TIME.
BUT...
I READ...
...THE WHOLE THING.

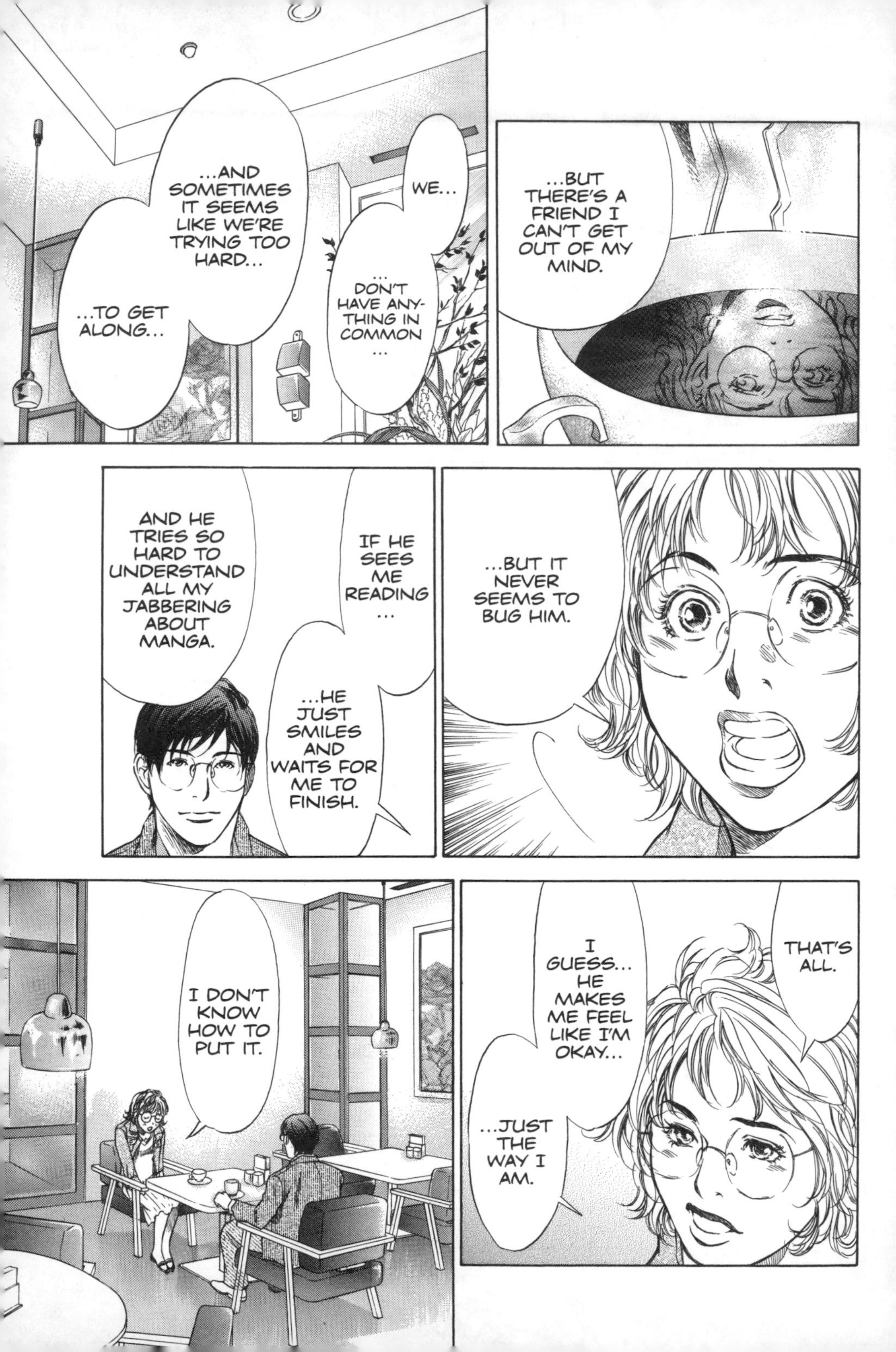
...BUT THERE'S A FRIEND I CAN'T GET OUT OF MY MIND.
WE...
...DON'T HAVE ANY-THING IN COMMON...
...AND SOMETIMES IT SEEMS LIKE WE'RE TRYING TOO HARD...
...TO GET ALONG...
...BUT IT NEVER SEEMS TO BUG HIM.
IF HE SEES ME READING...
...HE JUST SMILES AND WAITS FOR ME TO FINISH.
AND HE TRIES SO HARD TO UNDERSTAND ALL MY JABBERING ABOUT MANGA.
THAT'S ALL.
I GUESS... HE MAKES ME FEEL LIKE I'M OKAY...
...JUST THE WAY I AM.
I DON'T KNOW HOW TO PUT IT.

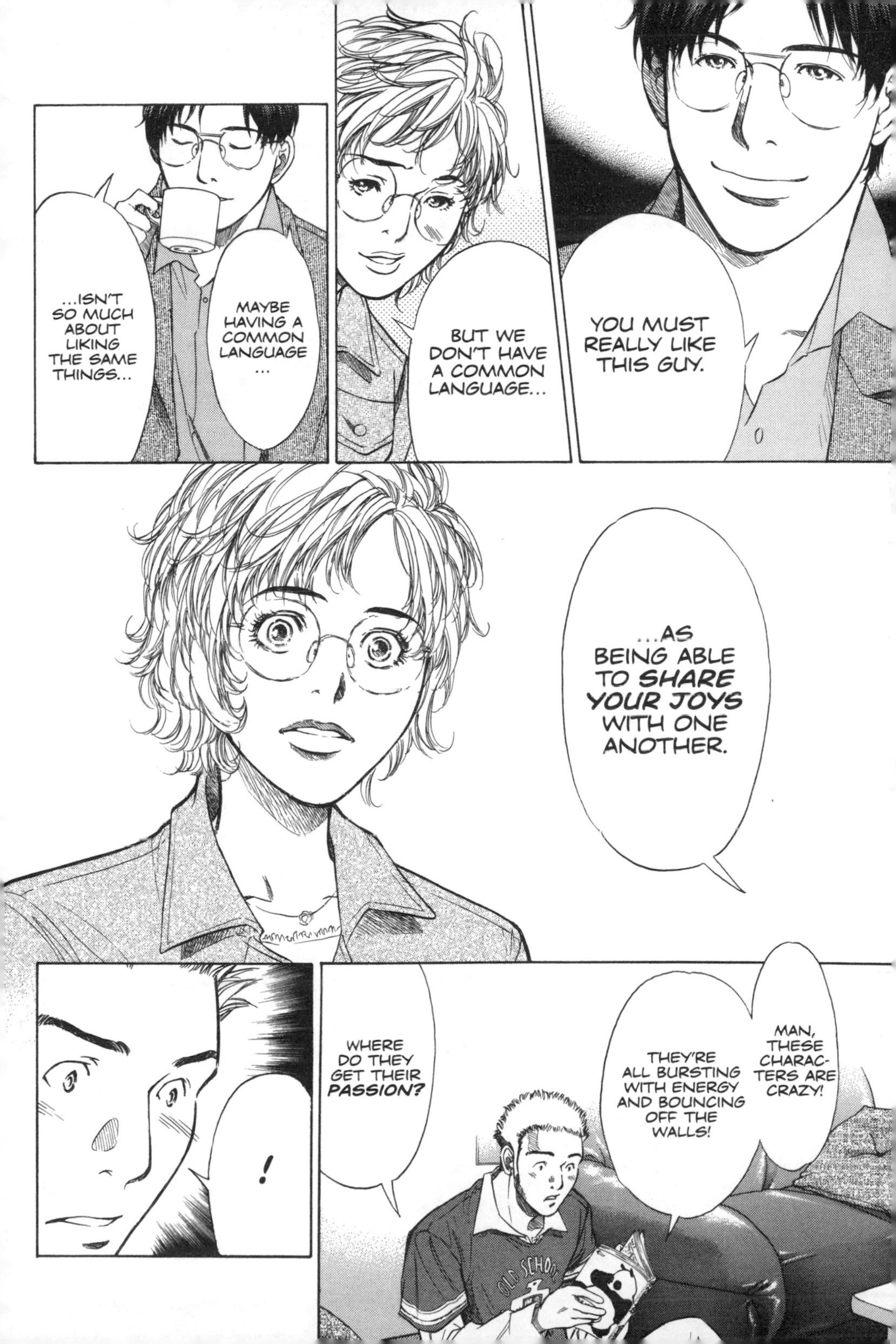
YOU MUST REALLY LIKE THIS GUY.
BUT WE DON'T HAVE A COMMON LANGUAGE...
MAYBE HAVING A COMMON LANGUAGE ...
...ISN'T SO MUCH ABOUT LIKING THE SAME THINGS...
...AS BEING ABLE TO SHARE YOUR JOYS WITH ONE ANOTHER.
MAN, THESE CHARAC-TERS ARE CRAZY!
THEY'RE ALL BURSTING WITH ENERGY AND BOUNCING OFF THE WALLS!
WHERE DO THEY GET THEIR PASSION?
!

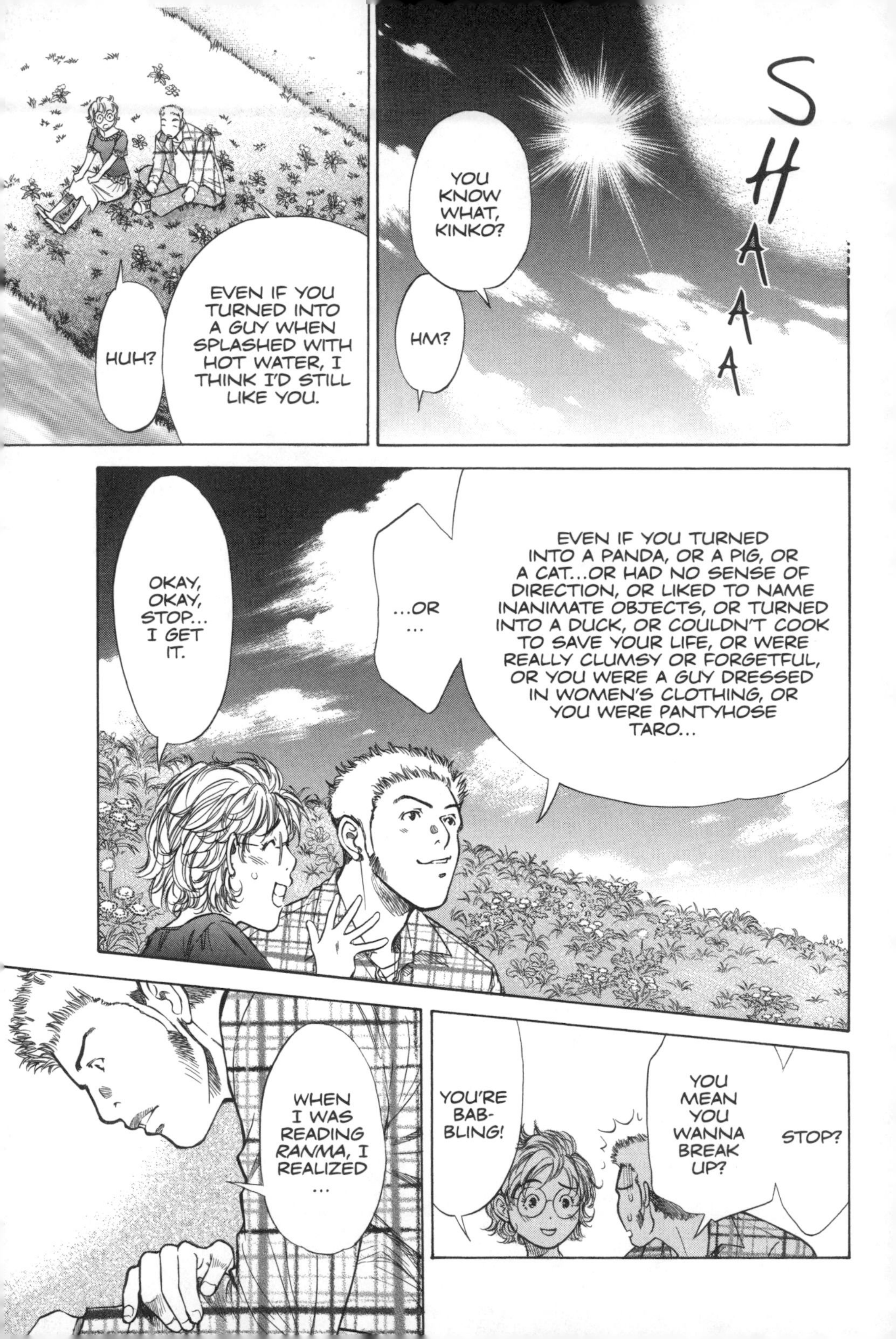
SHAAA
YOU KNOW WHAT, KINKO?
HM?
EVEN IF YOU TURNED INTO A GUY WHEN SPLASHED WITH HOT WATER, I THINK I'D STILL LIKE YOU.
HUH?
EVEN IF YOU TURNED INTO A PANDA, OR A PIG, OR A CAT…OR HAD NO SENSE OF DIRECTION, OR LIKED TO NAME INANIMATE OBJECTS, OR TURNED INTO A DUCK, OR COULDN'T COOK TO SAVE YOUR LIFE, OR WERE REALLY CLUMSY OR FORGETFUL, OR YOU WERE A GUY DRESSED IN WOMEN'S CLOTHING, OR YOU WERE PANTYHOSE TARO…
…OR …
OKAY, OKAY, STOP… I GET IT.
STOP?
YOU MEAN YOU WANNA BREAK UP?
YOU'RE BAB-BLING!
WHEN I WAS READING *RANMA*, I REALIZED …

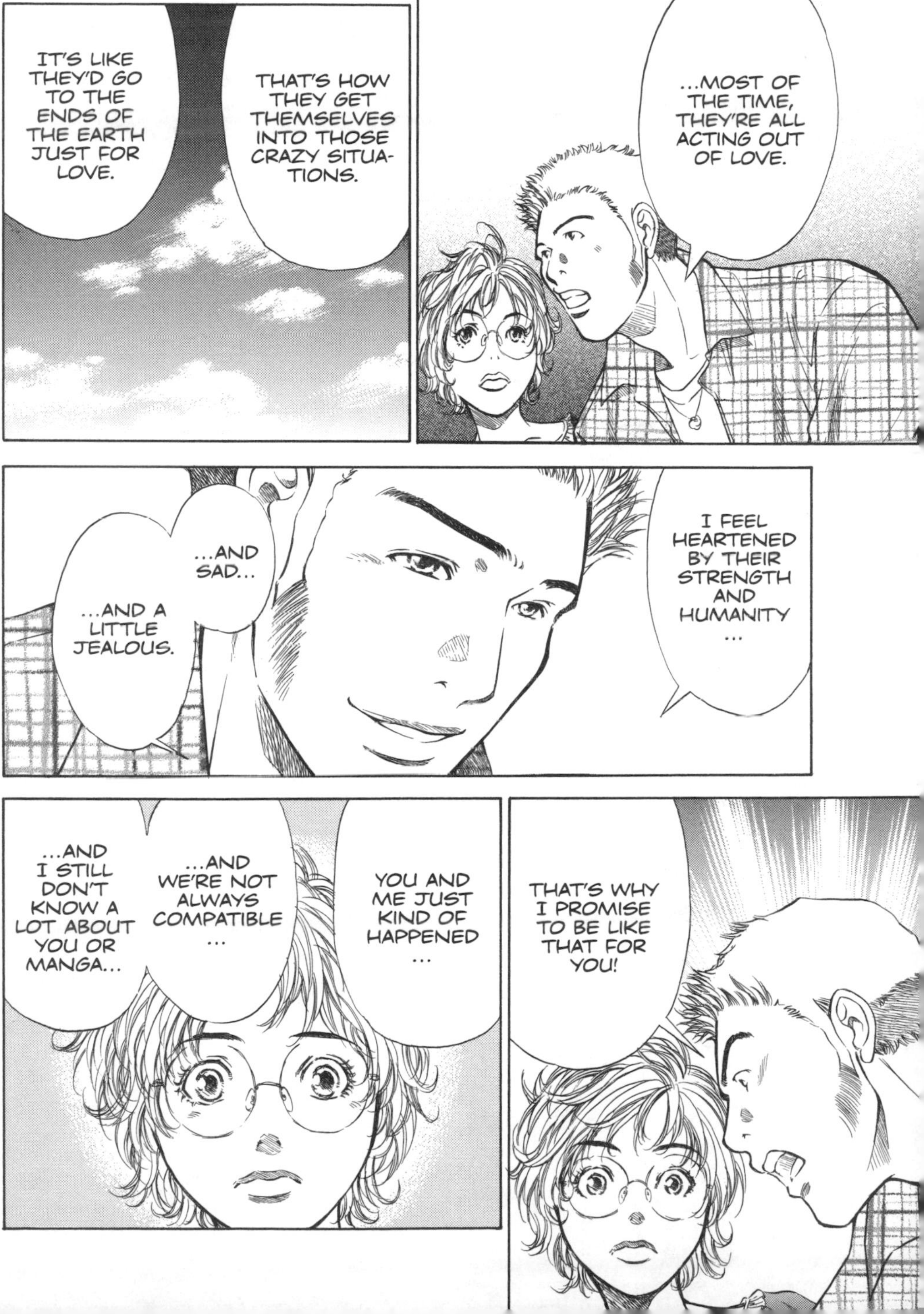
...MOST OF THE TIME, THEY'RE ALL ACTING OUT OF LOVE.
THAT'S HOW THEY GET THEMSELVES INTO THOSE CRAZY SITUATIONS.
IT'S LIKE THEY'D GO TO THE ENDS OF THE EARTH JUST FOR LOVE.
I FEEL HEARTENED BY THEIR STRENGTH AND HUMANITY...
...AND SAD...
...AND A LITTLE JEALOUS.
THAT'S WHY I PROMISE TO BE LIKE THAT FOR YOU!
YOU AND ME JUST KIND OF HAPPENED...
...AND WE'RE NOT ALWAYS COMPATIBLE...
...AND I STILL DON'T KNOW A LOT ABOUT YOU OR MANGA...

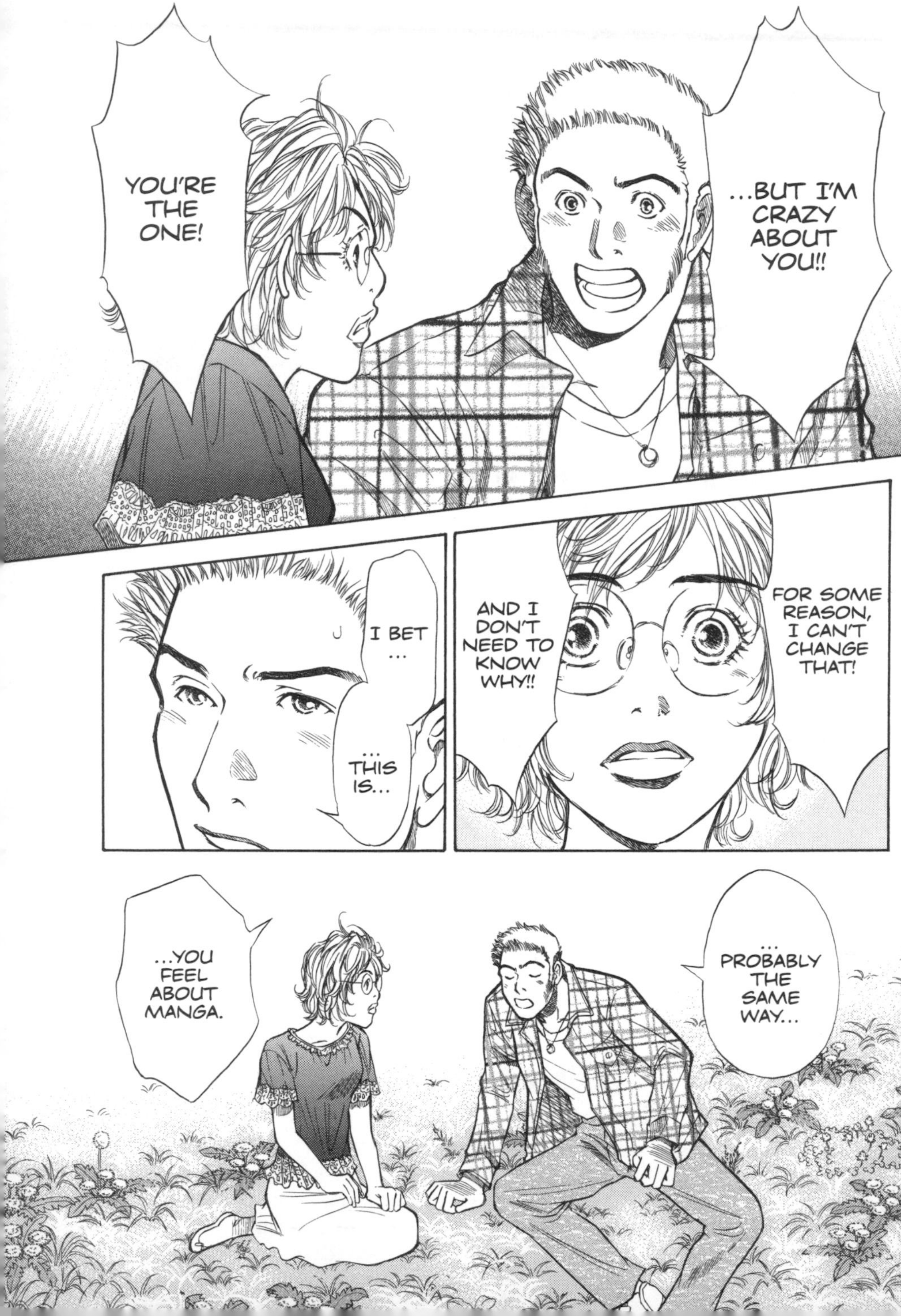
...BUT I'M CRAZY ABOUT YOU!!
YOU'RE THE ONE!
FOR SOME REASON, I CAN'T CHANGE THAT!
AND I DON'T NEED TO KNOW WHY!!
I BET ...
... THIS IS...
... PROBABLY THE SAME WAY...
...YOU FEEL ABOUT MANGA.

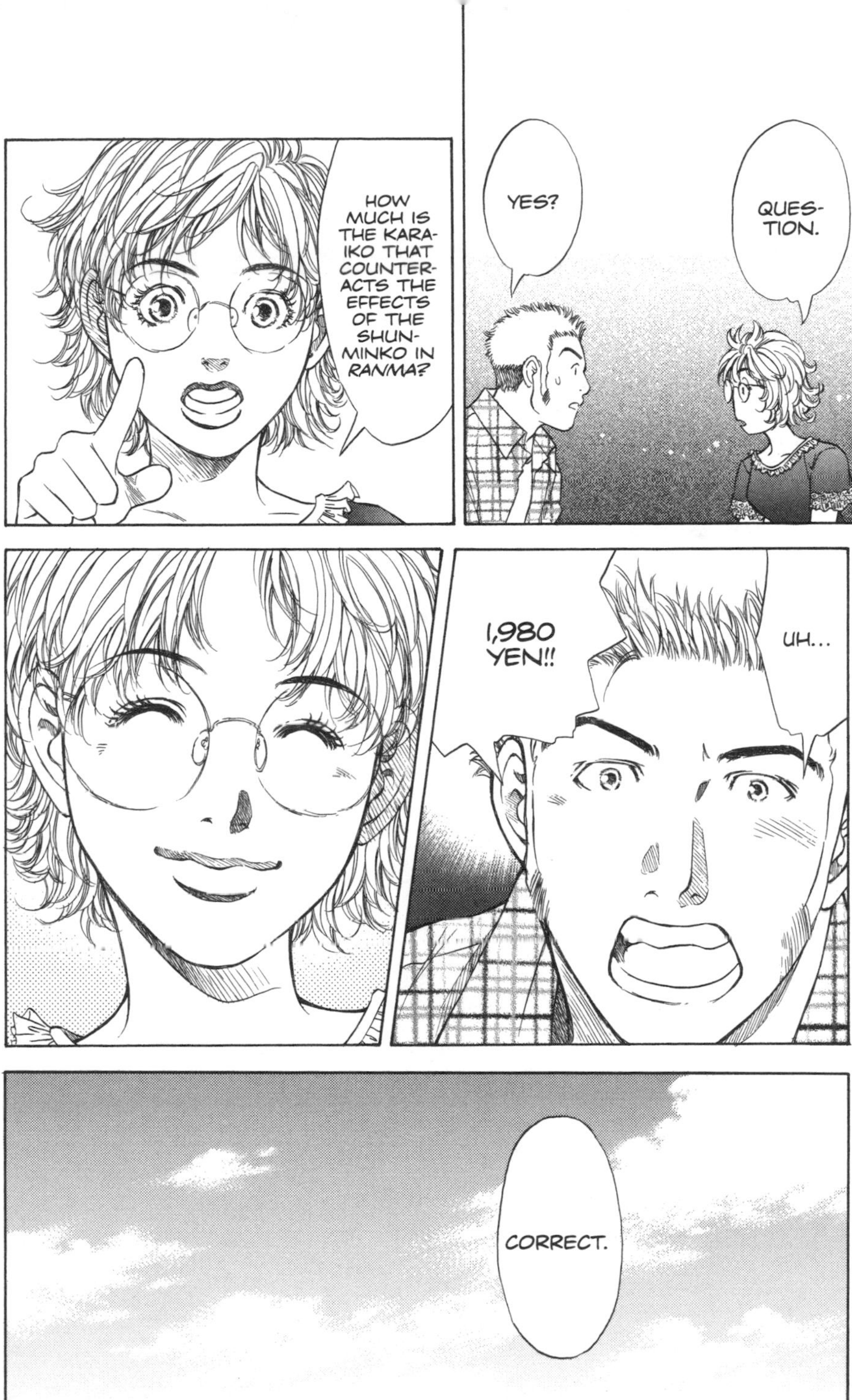
QUES-
TION.
YES?
HOW MUCH IS THE KARA-IKO THAT COUNTER-ACTS THE EFFECTS OF THE SHUN-MINKO IN *RANMA*?
UH...
1,980 YEN!!
CORRECT.

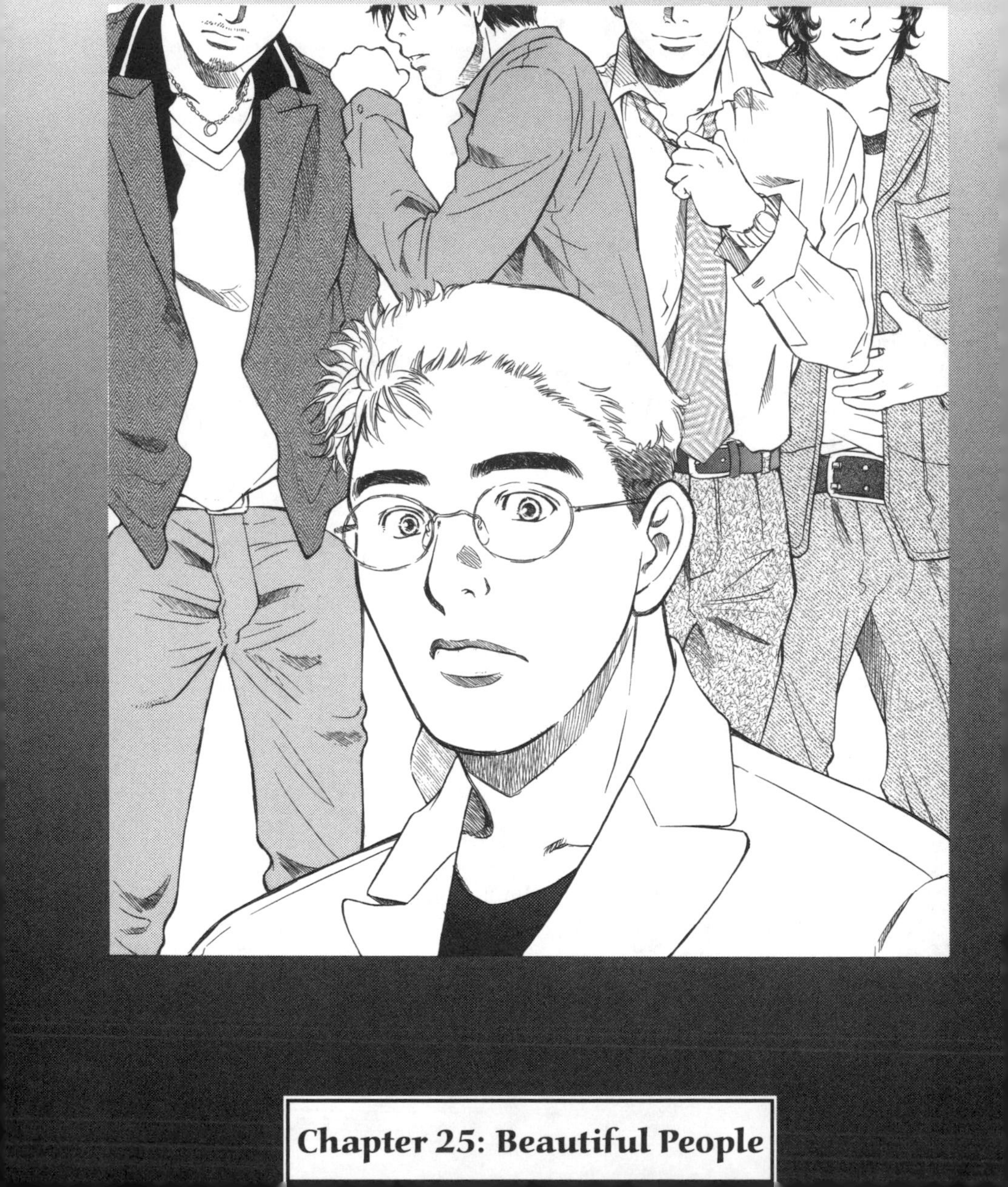

Chapter 25: Beautiful People

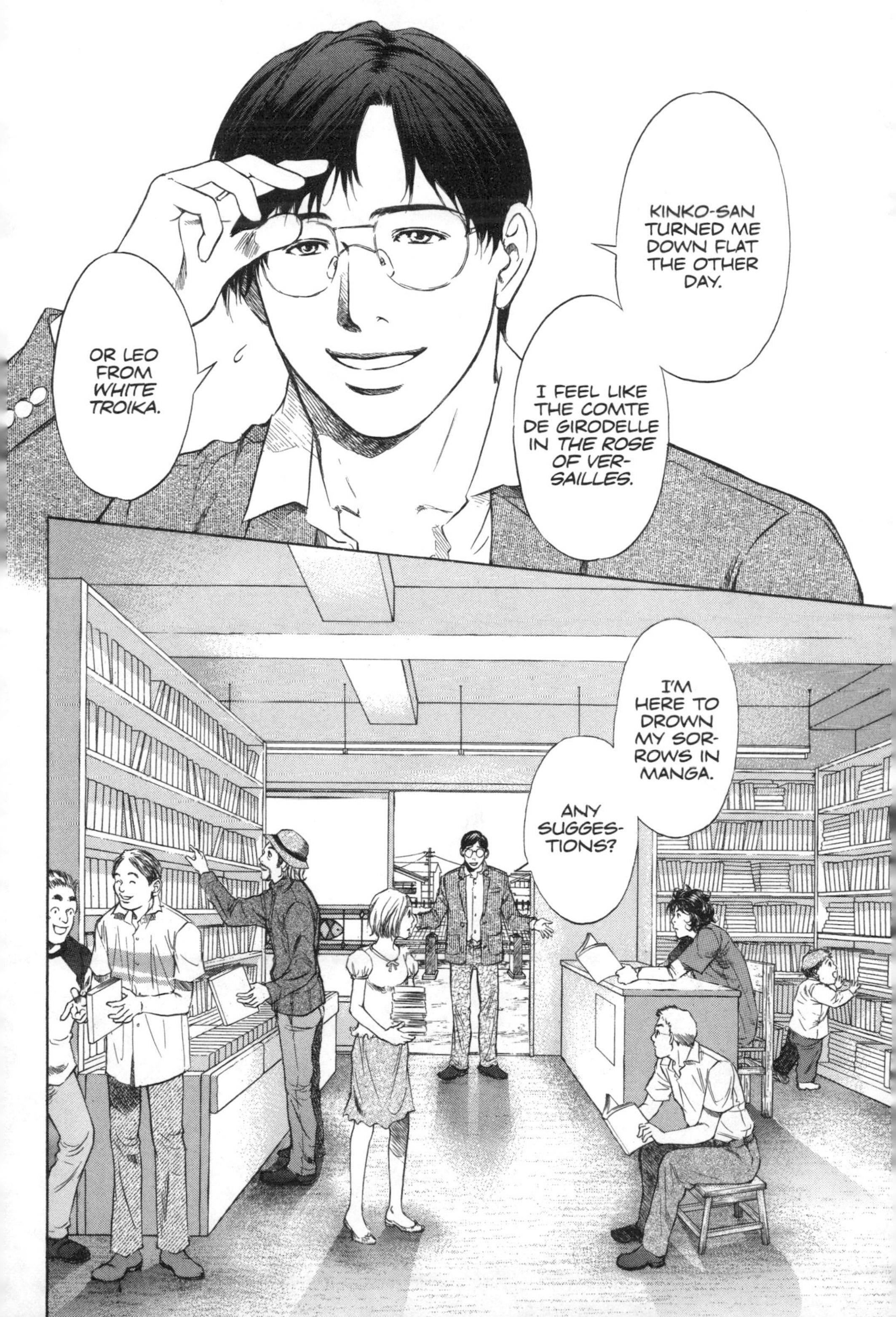
KINKO-SAN TURNED ME DOWN FLAT THE OTHER DAY.
I FEEL LIKE THE COMTE DE GIRODELLE IN *THE ROSE OF VERSAILLES.*
OR LEO FROM *WHITE TROIKA.*
I'M HERE TO DROWN MY SORROWS IN MANGA.
ANY SUGGESTIONS?

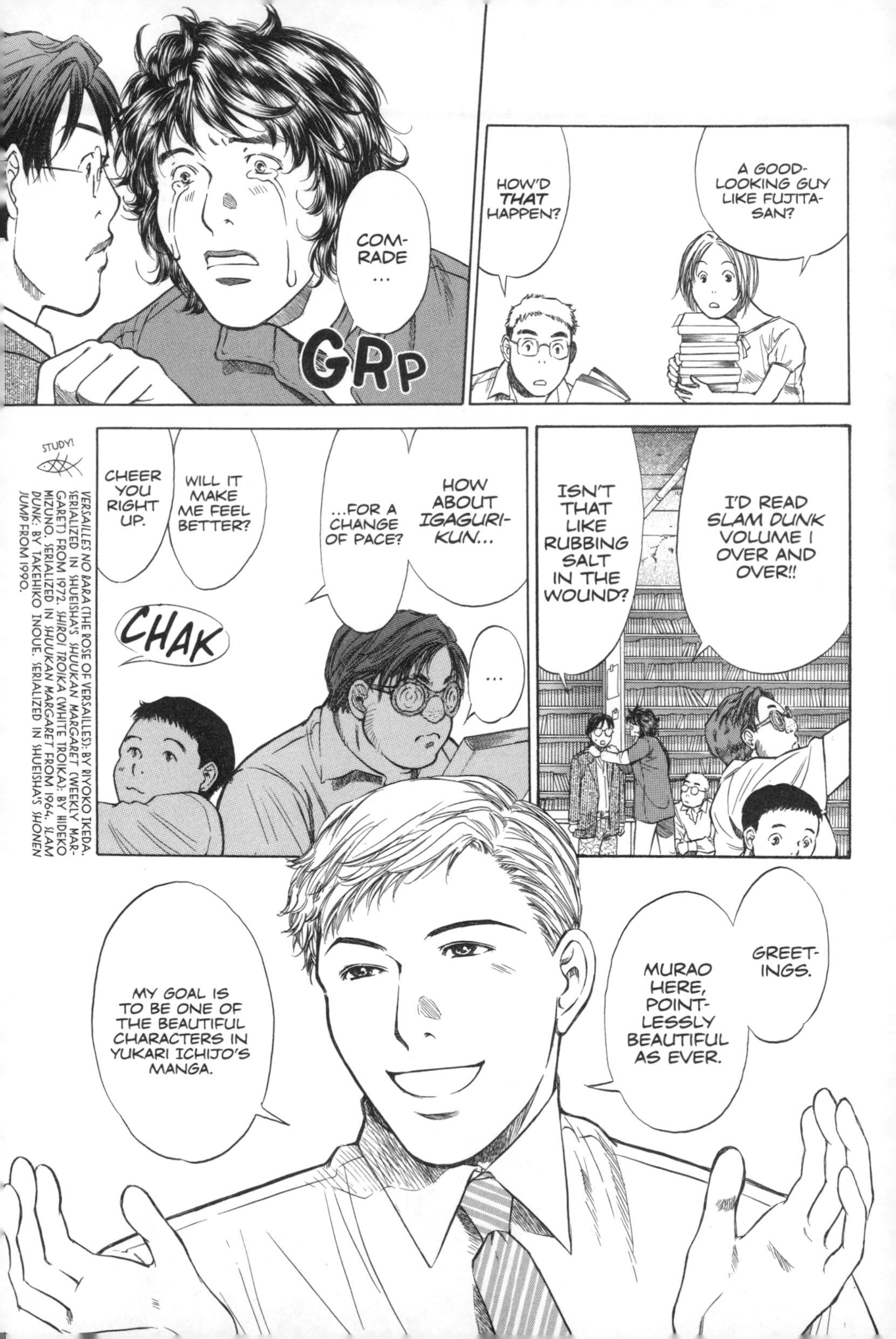
A GOOD-LOOKING GUY LIKE FUJITA-SAN?
HOW'D THAT HAPPEN?
COM-RADE ...
GRP
I'D READ SLAM DUNK VOLUME 1 OVER AND OVER!!
ISN'T THAT LIKE RUBBING SALT IN THE WOUND?
HOW ABOUT IGAGURI-KUN...
...FOR A CHANGE OF PACE?
...
WILL IT MAKE ME FEEL BETTER?
CHEER YOU RIGHT UP.
CHAK
GREET-INGS.
MURAO HERE, POINT-LESSLY BEAUTIFUL AS EVER.
MY GOAL IS TO BE ONE OF THE BEAUTIFUL CHARACTERS IN YUKARI ICHIJO'S MANGA.

STUDY!

VERSAILLES NO BARA (THE ROSE OF VERSAILLES): BY RIYOKO IKEDA. SERIALIZED IN SHUEISHA'S SHUUKAN MARGARET (WEEKLY MARGARET) FROM 1972. SHIROI TROIKA (WHITE TROIKA): BY HIDEKO MIZUNO. SERIALIZED IN SHUUKAN MARGARET FROM 1964. SLAM DUNK: BY TAKEHIKO INOUE. SERIALIZED IN SHUEISHA'S SHONEN JUMP FROM 1990.

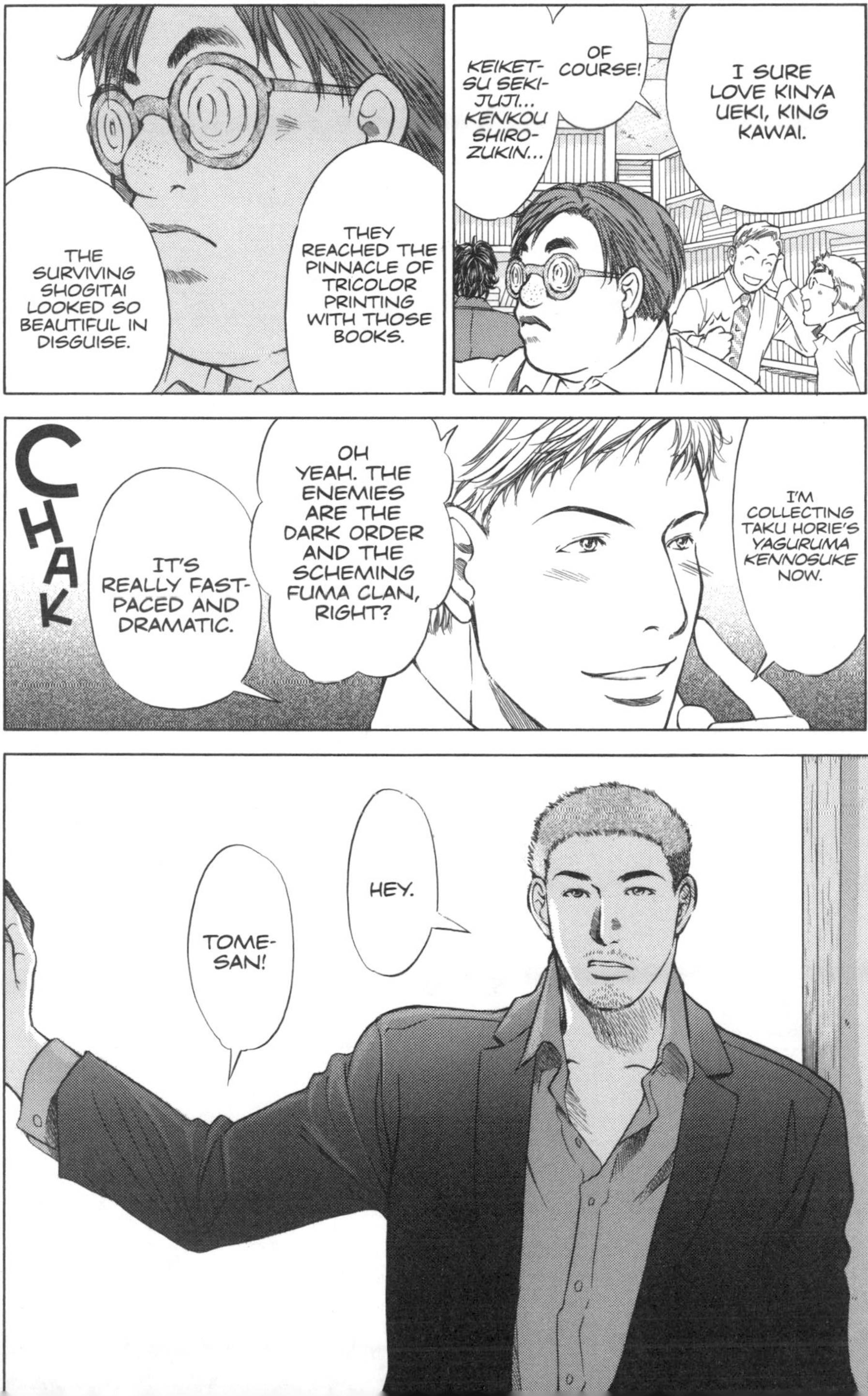
I SURE LOVE KINYA UEKI, KING KAWAI.
OF COURSE!
KEIKET-SU SEKI-JUJI... KENKOU SHIRO-ZUKIN...
THEY REACHED THE PINNACLE OF TRICOLOR PRINTING WITH THOSE BOOKS.
THE SURVIVING SHOGITAI LOOKED SO BEAUTIFUL IN DISGUISE.
I'M COLLECTING TAKU HORIE'S YAGURUMA KENNOSUKE NOW.
OH YEAH. THE ENEMIES ARE THE DARK ORDER AND THE SCHEMING FUMA CLAN, RIGHT?
IT'S REALLY FAST-PACED AND DRAMATIC.
CHAK
HEY.
TOME-SAN!

STUDY!

IGAGURI-KUN: BY EIICHI FUKUI. A MANGA ABOUT JUDO SERIALIZED IN AKITA SHOTEN'S BOUKEN-OH. THE CREATOR DIED LEAVING THE SERIES UNFINISHED. KEIKETSU SEKIJUJI AND KENKOU SHIROZUKIN: BY KINYA UEKI, AN ARTIST WHO SPECIALIZED IN SAMURAI MANGA. KENKOU WAS SERIALIZED IN SHONEN GAHOU FROM 1956. YAGURUMA KENNOSUKE: BY TAKU HORIE. SERIALIZED IN KOUBUNSHA'S SHONEN. KENNOSUKE FIGHTS EVIL WEARING A BLACK MASK.

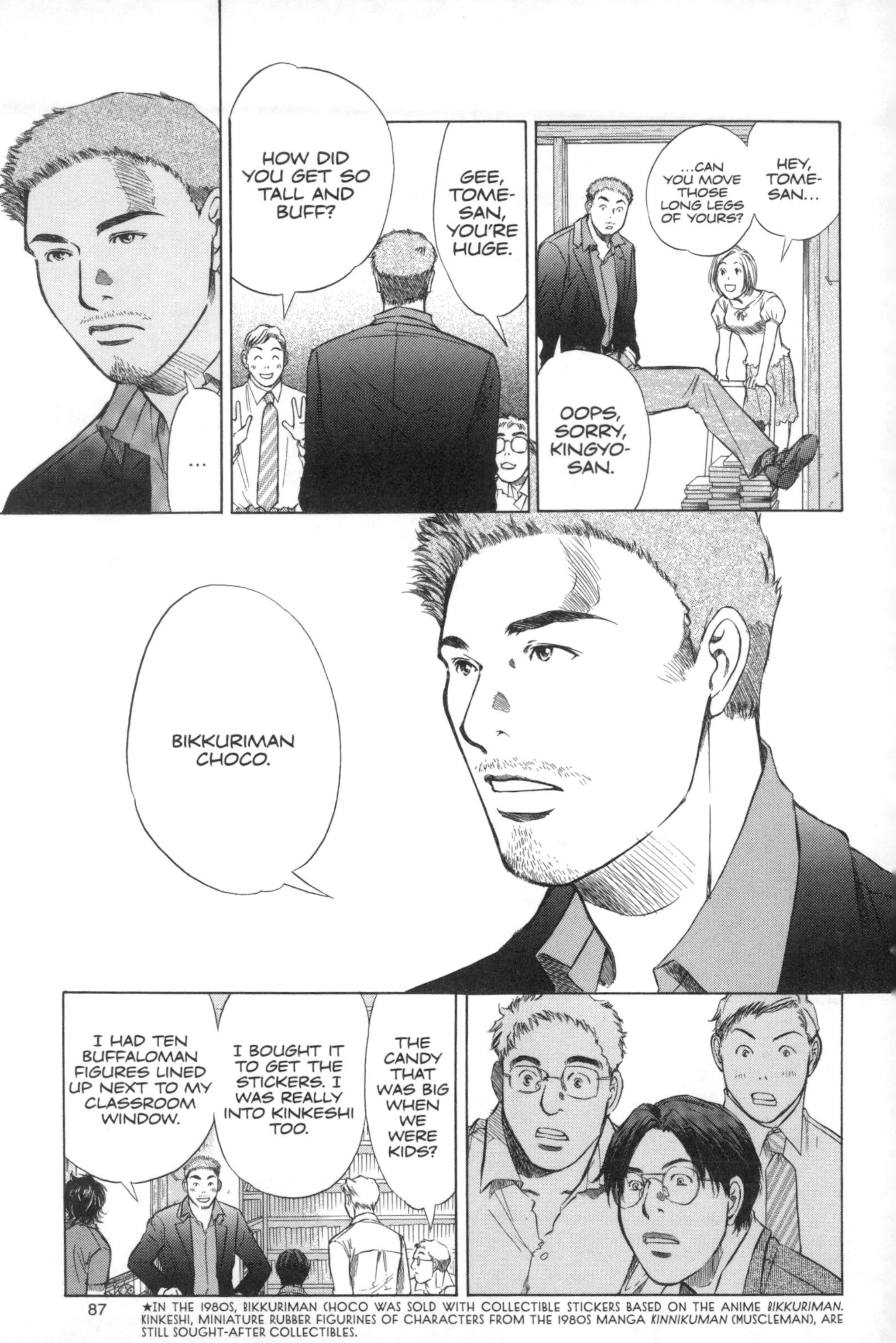
HEY, TOME-SAN...
...CAN YOU MOVE THOSE LONG LEGS OF YOURS?
OOPS, SORRY, KINGYO-SAN.
GEE, TOME-SAN, YOU'RE HUGE.
HOW DID YOU GET SO TALL AND BUFF?
...
BIKKURIMAN CHOCO.
THE CANDY THAT WAS BIG WHEN WE WERE KIDS?
I BOUGHT IT TO GET THE STICKERS. I WAS REALLY INTO KINKESHI TOO.
I HAD TEN BUFFALOMAN FIGURES LINED UP NEXT TO MY CLASSROOM WINDOW.

★IN THE 1980S, BIKKURIMAN CHOCO WAS SOLD WITH COLLECTIBLE STICKERS BASED ON THE ANIME *BIKKURIMAN*. KINKESHI, MINIATURE RUBBER FIGURINES OF CHARACTERS FROM THE 1980S MANGA *KINNIKUMAN* (MUSCLEMAN), ARE STILL SOUGHT-AFTER COLLECTIBLES.

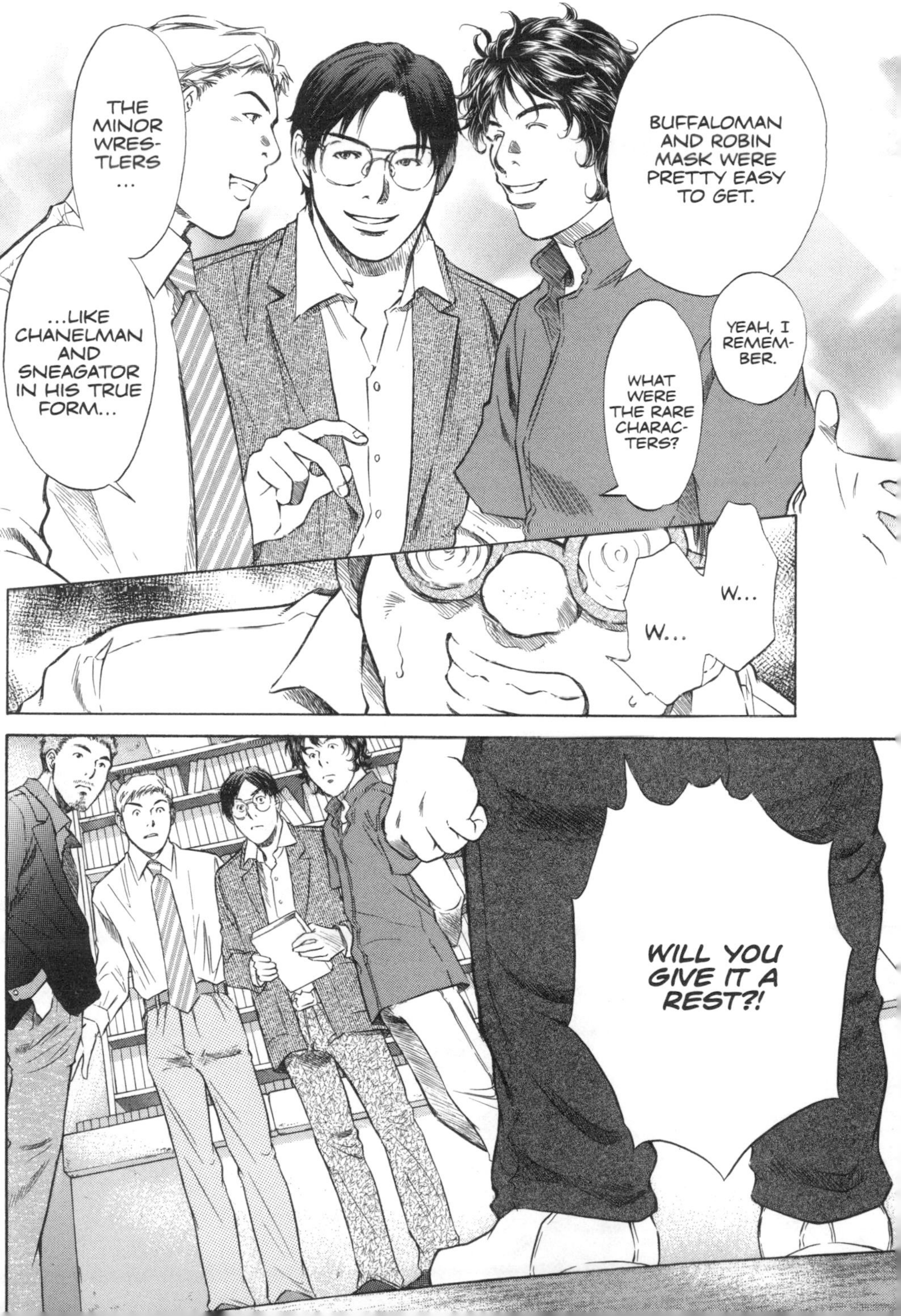
BUFFALOMAN AND ROBIN MASK WERE PRETTY EASY TO GET.
YEAH, I REMEMBER.
WHAT WERE THE RARE CHARACTERS?
THE MINOR WRESTLERS...
...LIKE CHANELMAN AND SNEAGATOR IN HIS TRUE FORM...
W...
W...
WILL YOU GIVE IT A REST?!

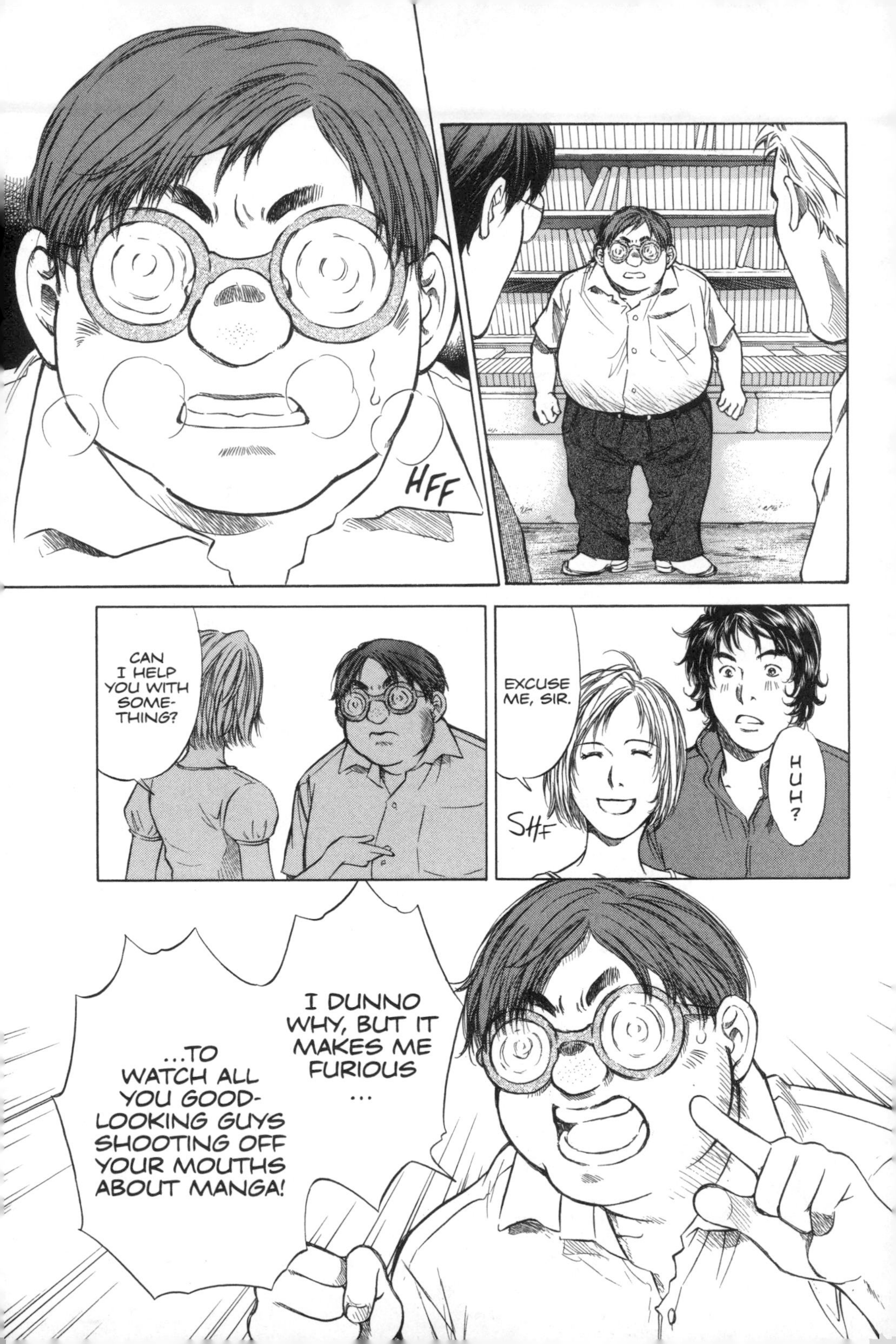
HFF
EXCUSE ME, SIR.
HUH?
SHF
CAN I HELP YOU WITH SOMETHING?
I DUNNO WHY, BUT IT MAKES ME FURIOUS...
...TO WATCH ALL YOU GOOD-LOOKING GUYS SHOOTING OFF YOUR MOUTHS ABOUT MANGA!

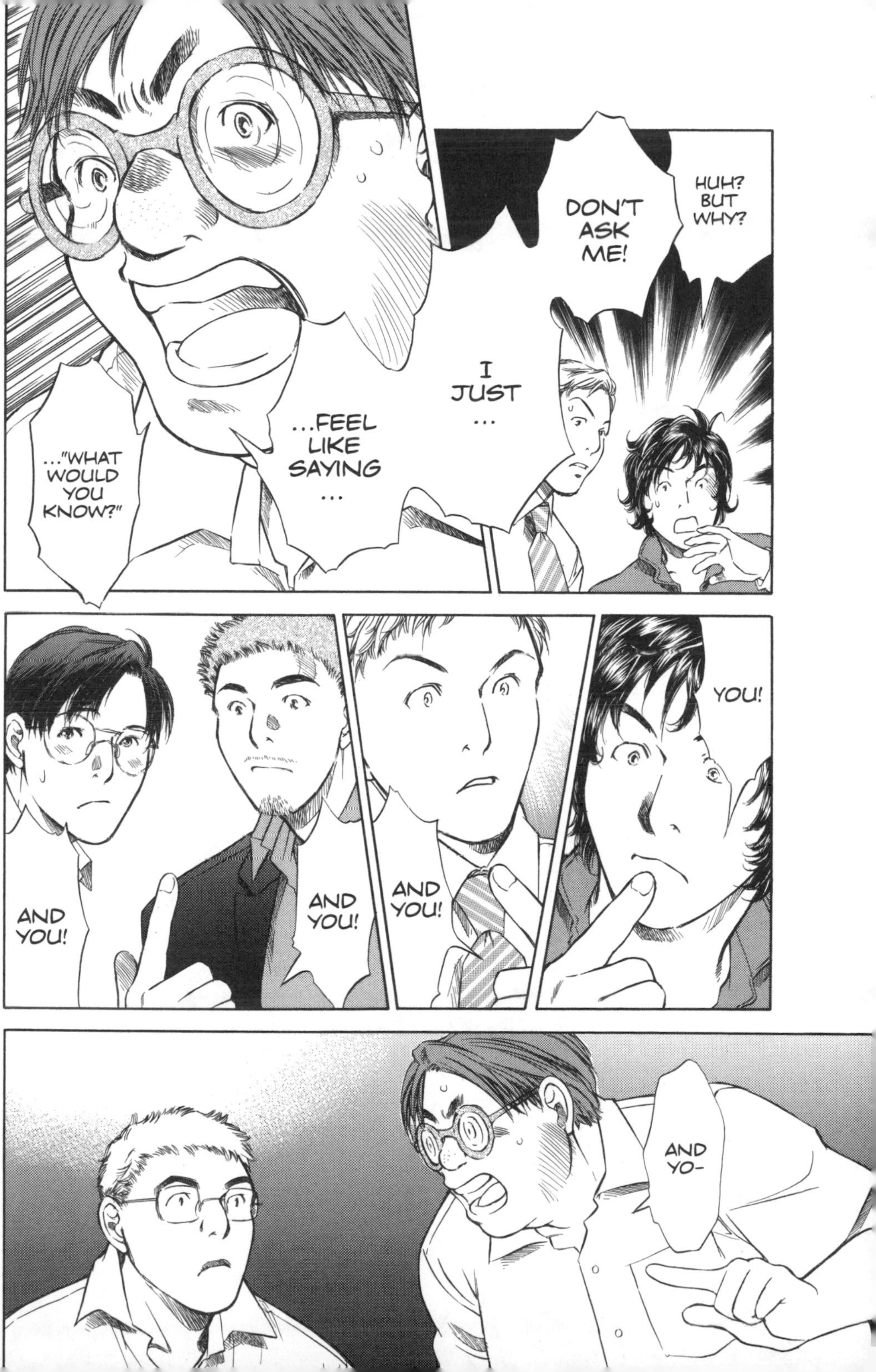
HUH? BUT WHY?
DON'T ASK ME!
I JUST ...
...FEEL LIKE SAYING ...
..."WHAT WOULD YOU KNOW?"
YOU!
AND YOU!
AND YOU!
AND YOU!
AND YO-

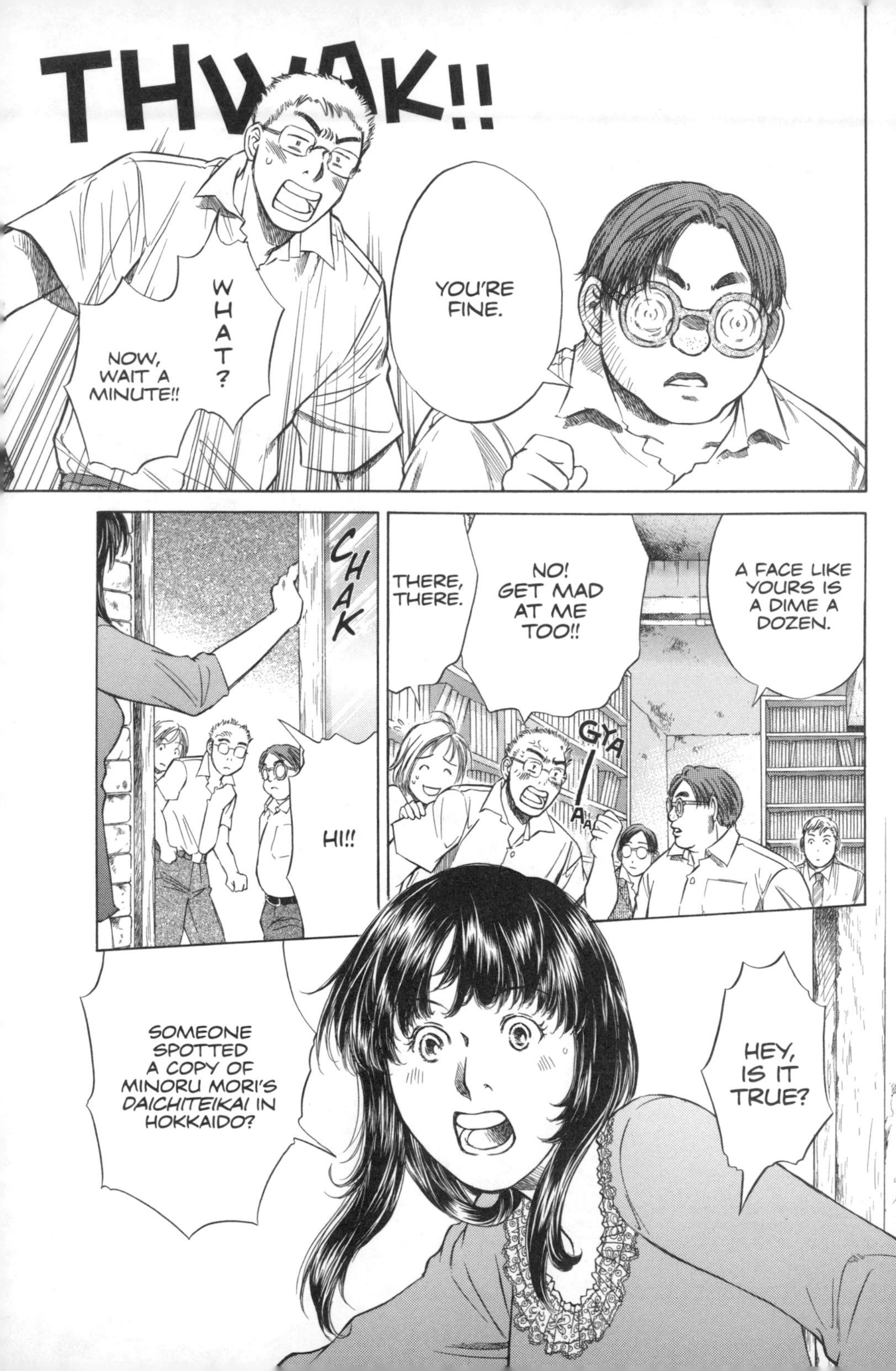
THWAK!!
YOU'RE FINE.
WHAT?
NOW, WAIT A MINUTE!!
A FACE LIKE YOURS IS A DIME A DOZEN.
NO! GET MAD AT ME TOO!!
GYA-AA
THERE, THERE.
CHAK
HI!!
HEY, IS IT TRUE?
SOMEONE SPOTTED A COPY OF MINORU MORI'S *DAICHITEIKAI* IN HOKKAIDO?

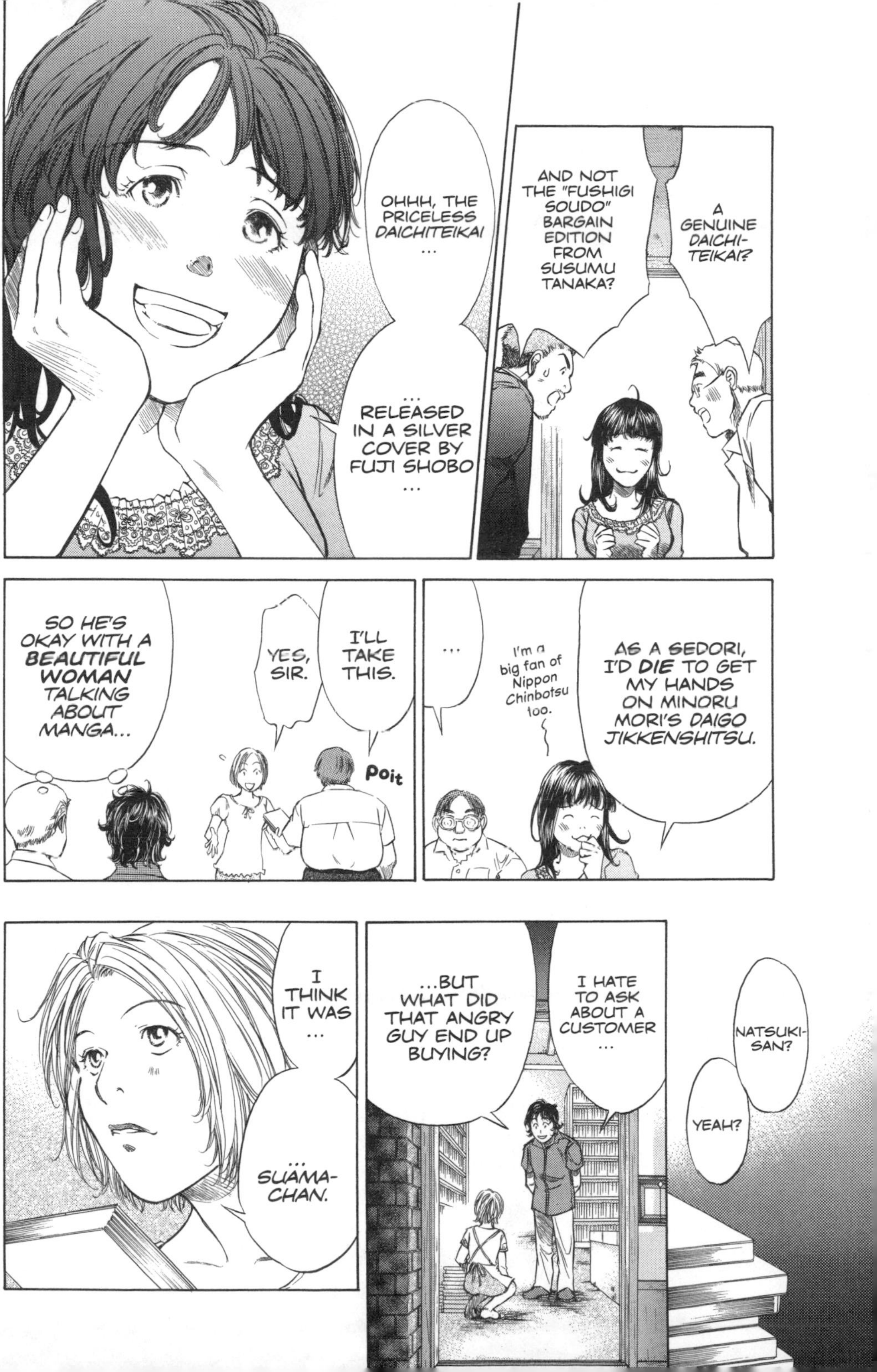
A GENUINE DAICHI-TEIKAI?
AND NOT THE "FUSHIGI SOUDO" BARGAIN EDITION FROM SUSUMU TANAKA?
OHHH, THE PRICELESS DAICHITEIKAI ...
... RELEASED IN A SILVER COVER BY FUJI SHOBO ...
AS A SEDORI, I'D **DIE** TO GET MY HANDS ON MINORU MORI'S DAIGO JIKKENSHITSU.
I'm a big fan of Nippon Chinbotsu too.
...
I'LL TAKE THIS.
YES, SIR.
Poit
SO HE'S OKAY WITH A **BEAUTIFUL WOMAN** TALKING ABOUT MANGA...
NATSUKI-SAN?
YEAH?
I HATE TO ASK ABOUT A CUSTOMER ...
...BUT WHAT DID THAT ANGRY GUY END UP BUYING?
I THINK IT WAS ...
... SUÄMA-CHAN.

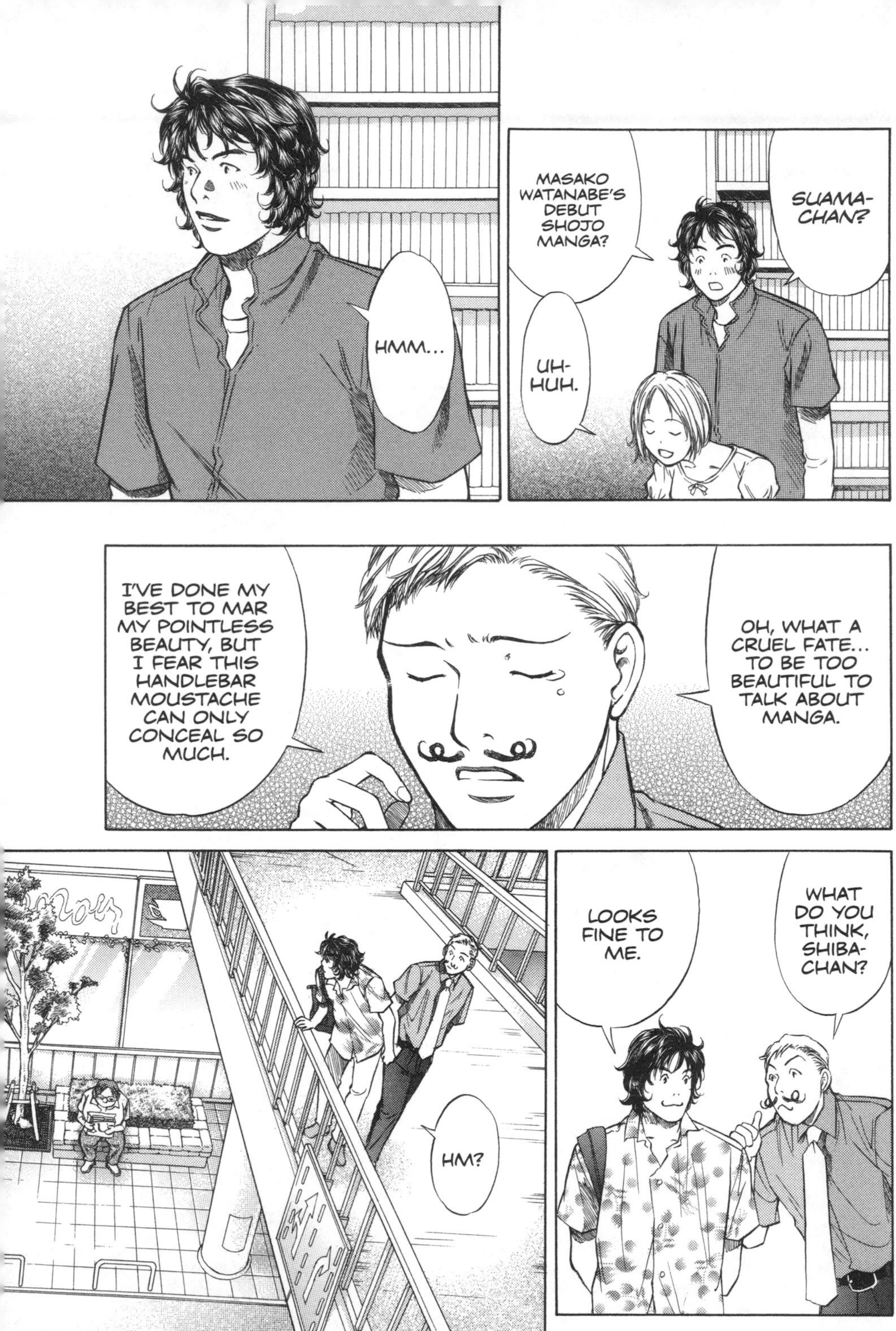
SUAMA-CHAN?
MASAKO WATANABE'S DEBUT SHOJO MANGA?
UH-HUH.
HMM...
OH, WHAT A CRUEL FATE... TO BE TOO BEAUTIFUL TO TALK ABOUT MANGA.
I'VE DONE MY BEST TO MAR MY POINTLESS BEAUTY, BUT I FEAR THIS HANDLEBAR MOUSTACHE CAN ONLY CONCEAL SO MUCH.
WHAT DO YOU THINK, SHIBA-CHAN?
LOOKS FINE TO ME.
HM?

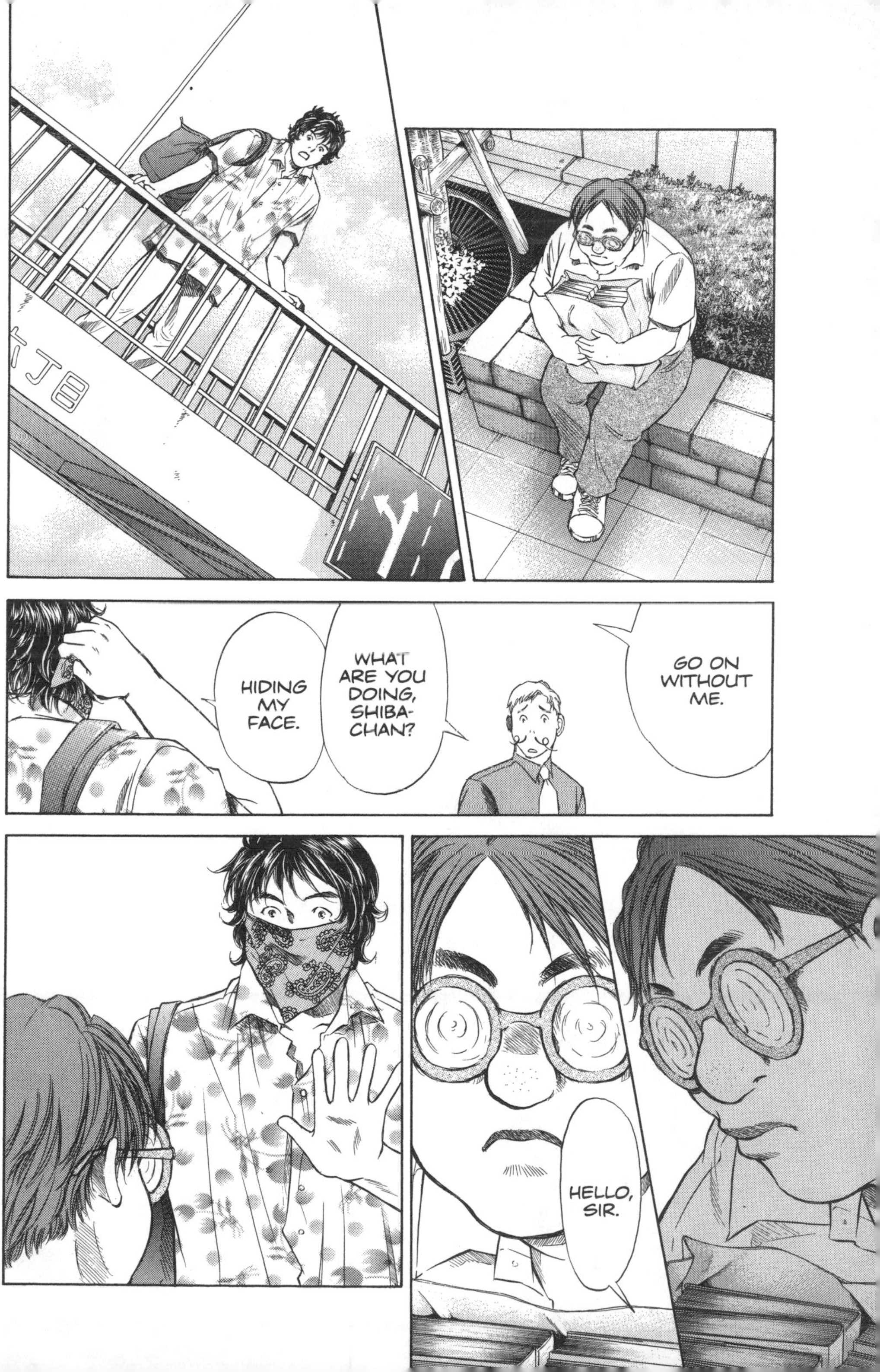
GO ON WITHOUT ME.
WHAT ARE YOU DOING, SHIBA-CHAN?
HIDING MY FACE.
HELLO, SIR.

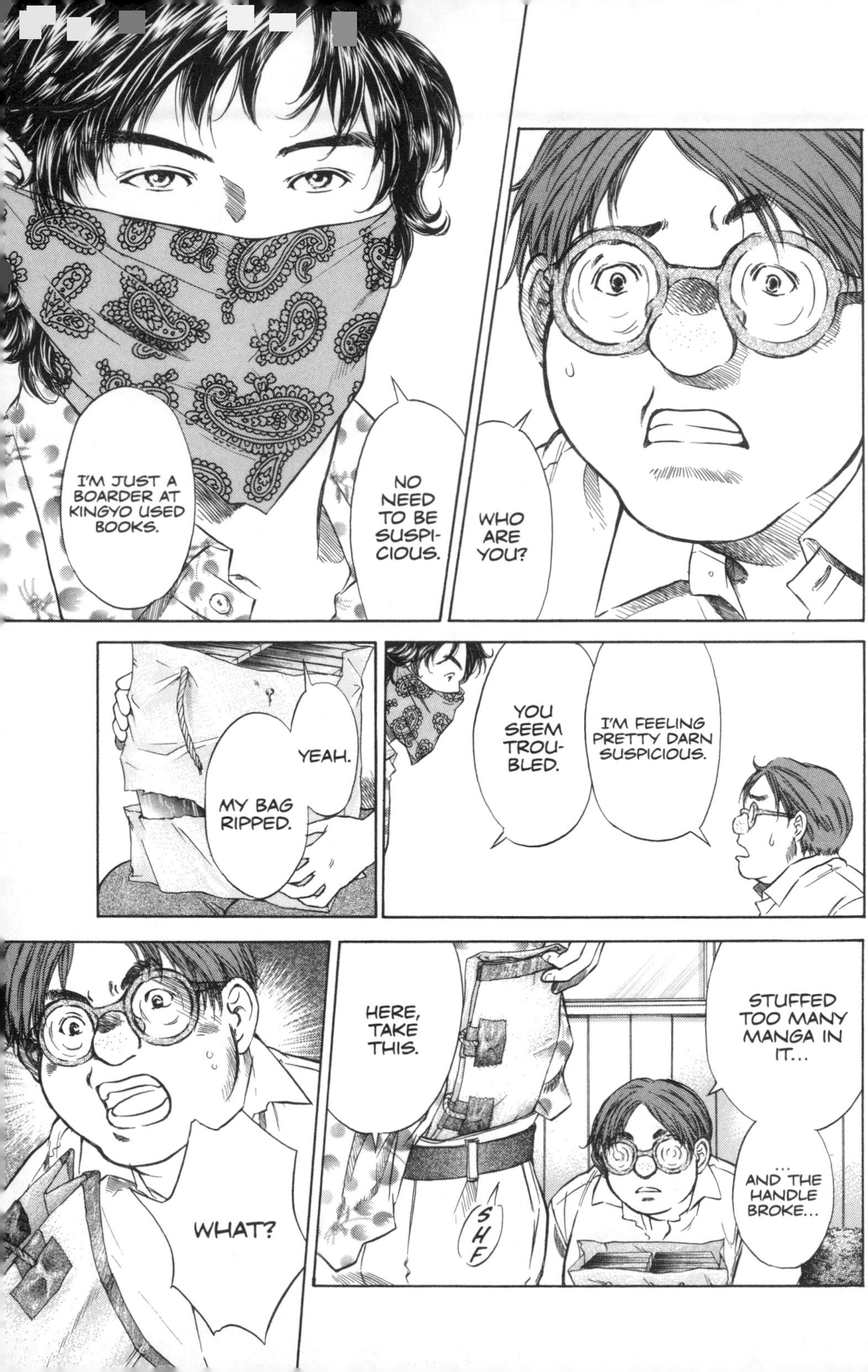
WHO ARE YOU?
NO NEED TO BE SUSPICIOUS.
I'M JUST A BOARDER AT KINGYO USED BOOKS.
I'M FEELING PRETTY DARN SUSPICIOUS.
YOU SEEM TROUBLED.
YEAH.
MY BAG RIPPED.
STUFFED TOO MANY MANGA IN IT...
...AND THE HANDLE BROKE...
HERE, TAKE THIS.
SHF
WHAT?

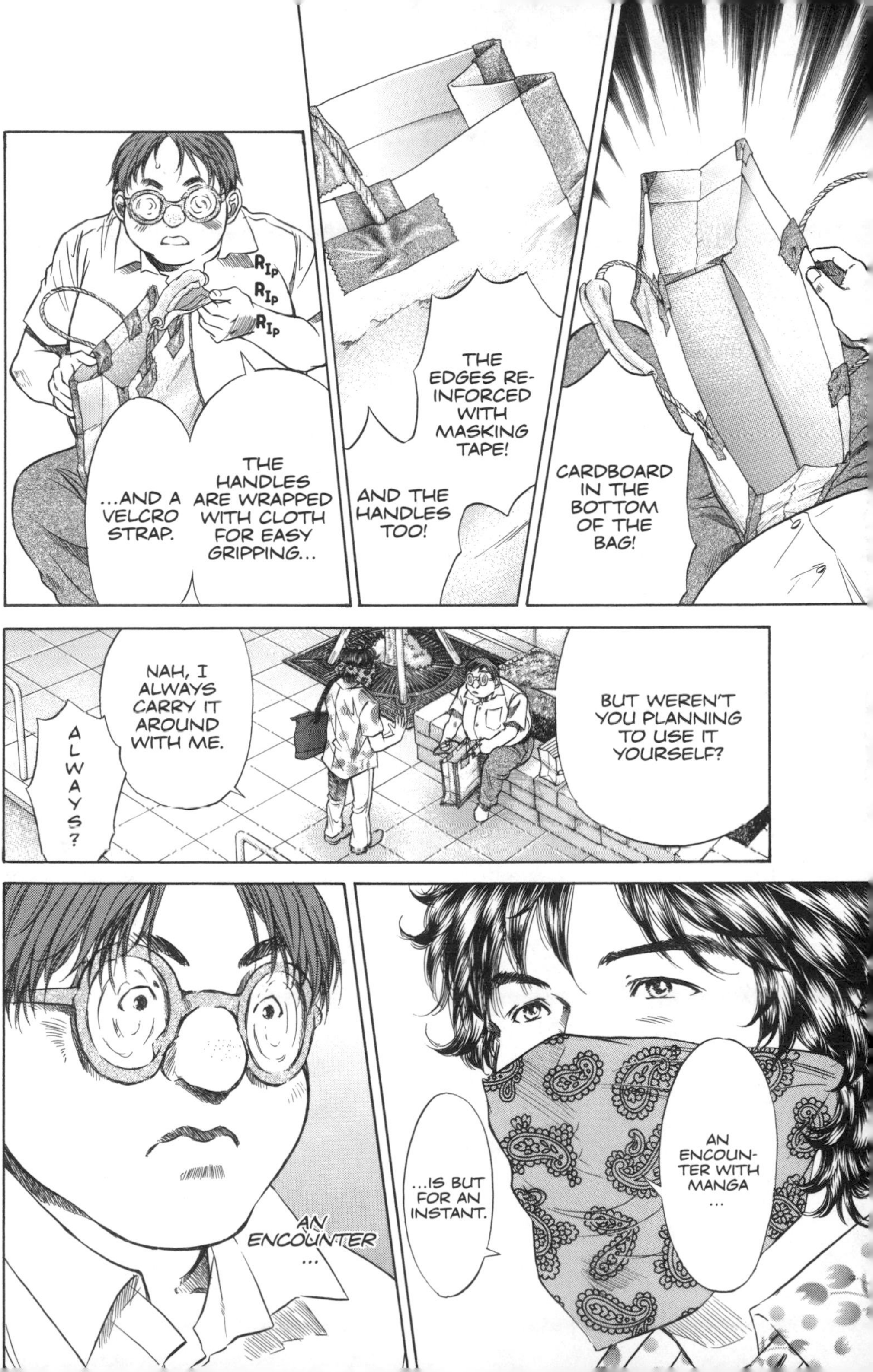
CARDBOARD IN THE BOTTOM OF THE BAG!
THE EDGES RE-INFORCED WITH MASKING TAPE!
AND THE HANDLES TOO!
RIp RIp RIp
THE HANDLES ARE WRAPPED WITH CLOTH FOR EASY GRIPPING...
...AND A VELCRO STRAP.
BUT WEREN'T YOU PLANNING TO USE IT YOURSELF?
NAH, I ALWAYS CARRY IT AROUND WITH ME.
ALWAYS?
AN ENCOUNTER WITH MANGA ...
...IS BUT FOR AN INSTANT.
AN ENCOUNTER ...

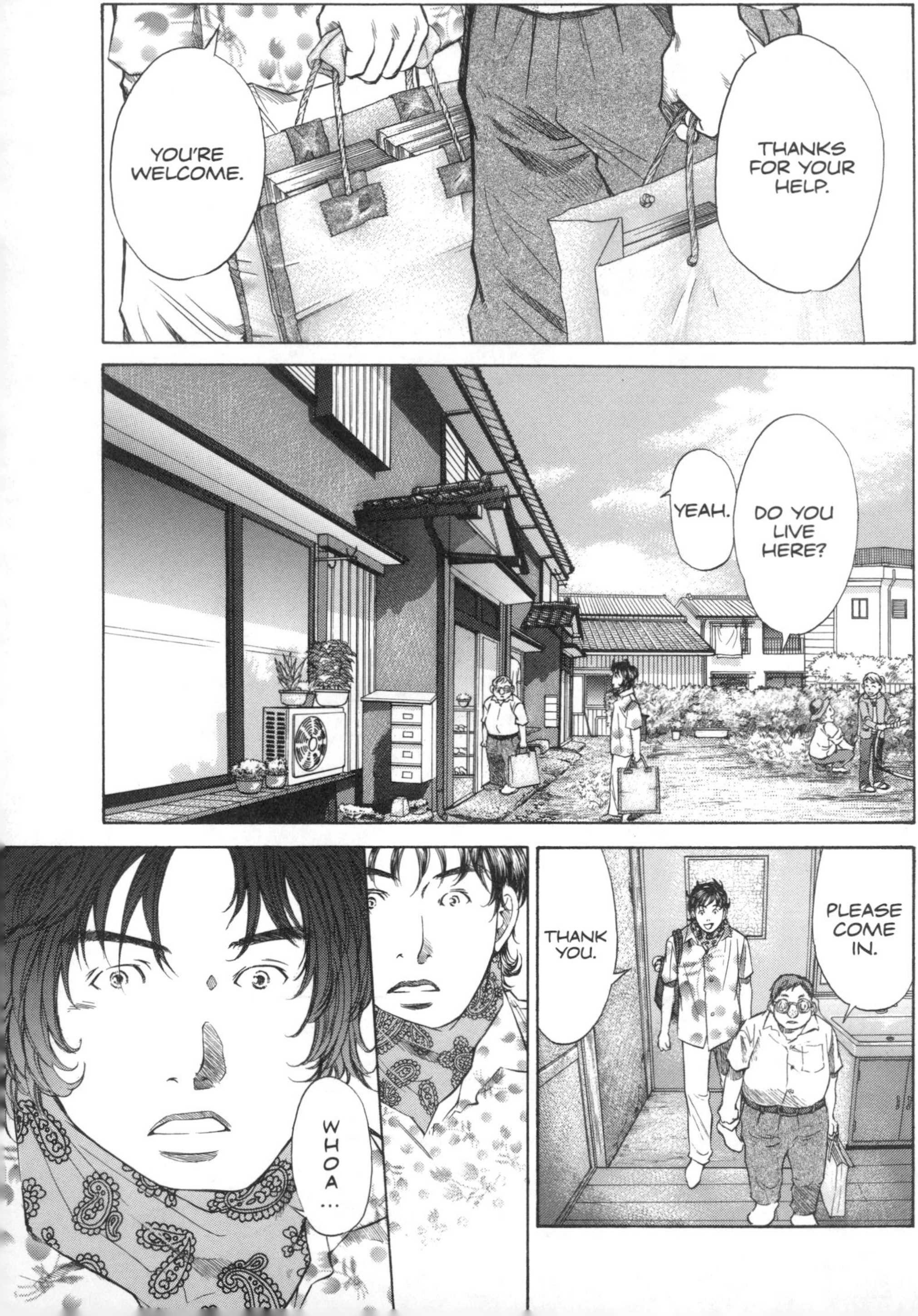
THANKS FOR YOUR HELP.
YOU'RE WELCOME.
DO YOU LIVE HERE?
YEAH.
PLEASE COME IN.
THANK YOU.
WHOA...

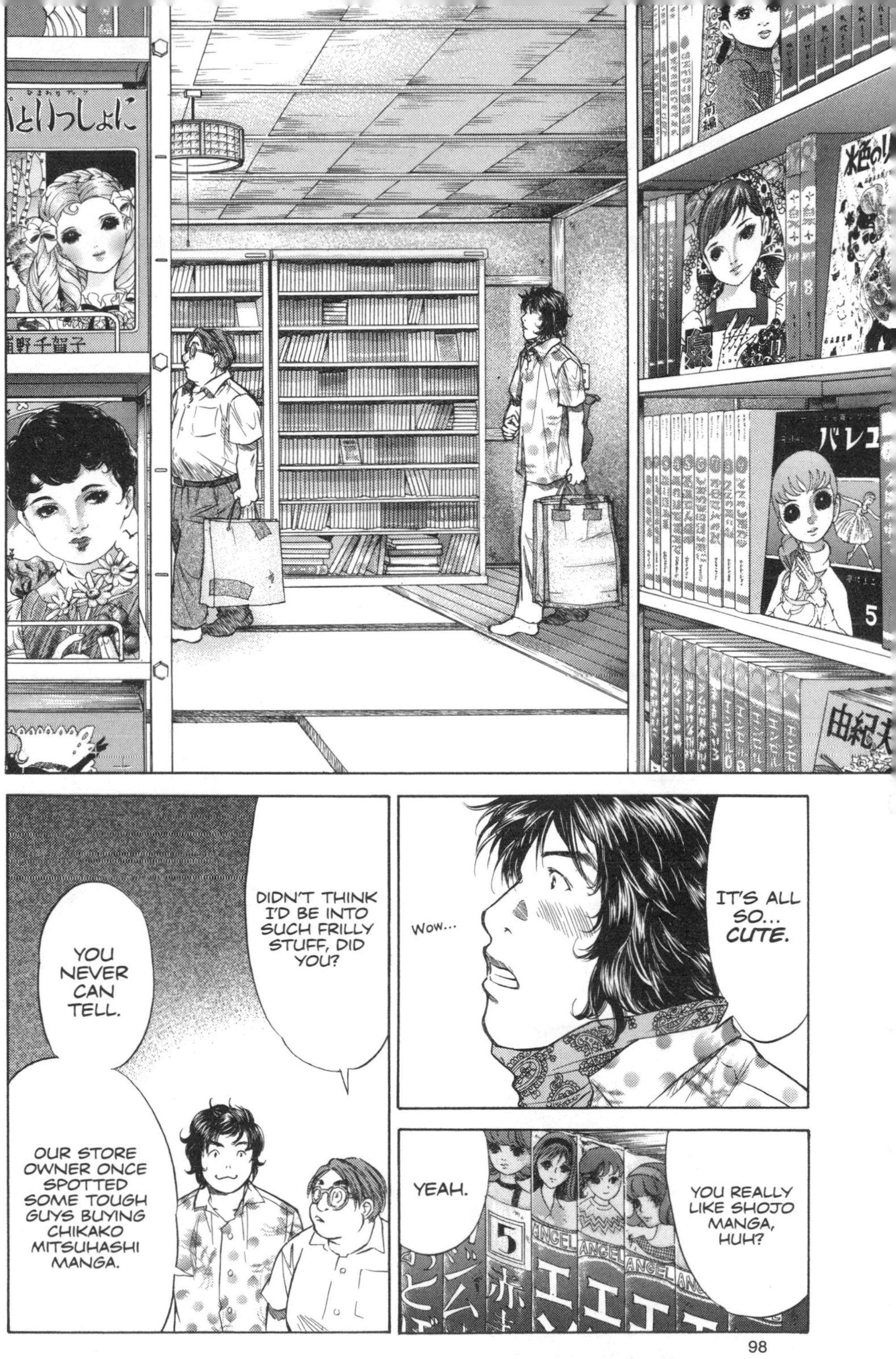
IT'S ALL SO... CUTE.
Wow...
YOU REALLY LIKE SHOJO MANGA, HUH?
YEAH.
DIDN'T THINK I'D BE INTO SUCH FRILLY STUFF, DID YOU?
YOU NEVER CAN TELL.
OUR STORE OWNER ONCE SPOTTED SOME TOUGH GUYS BUYING CHIKAKO MITSUHASHI MANGA.

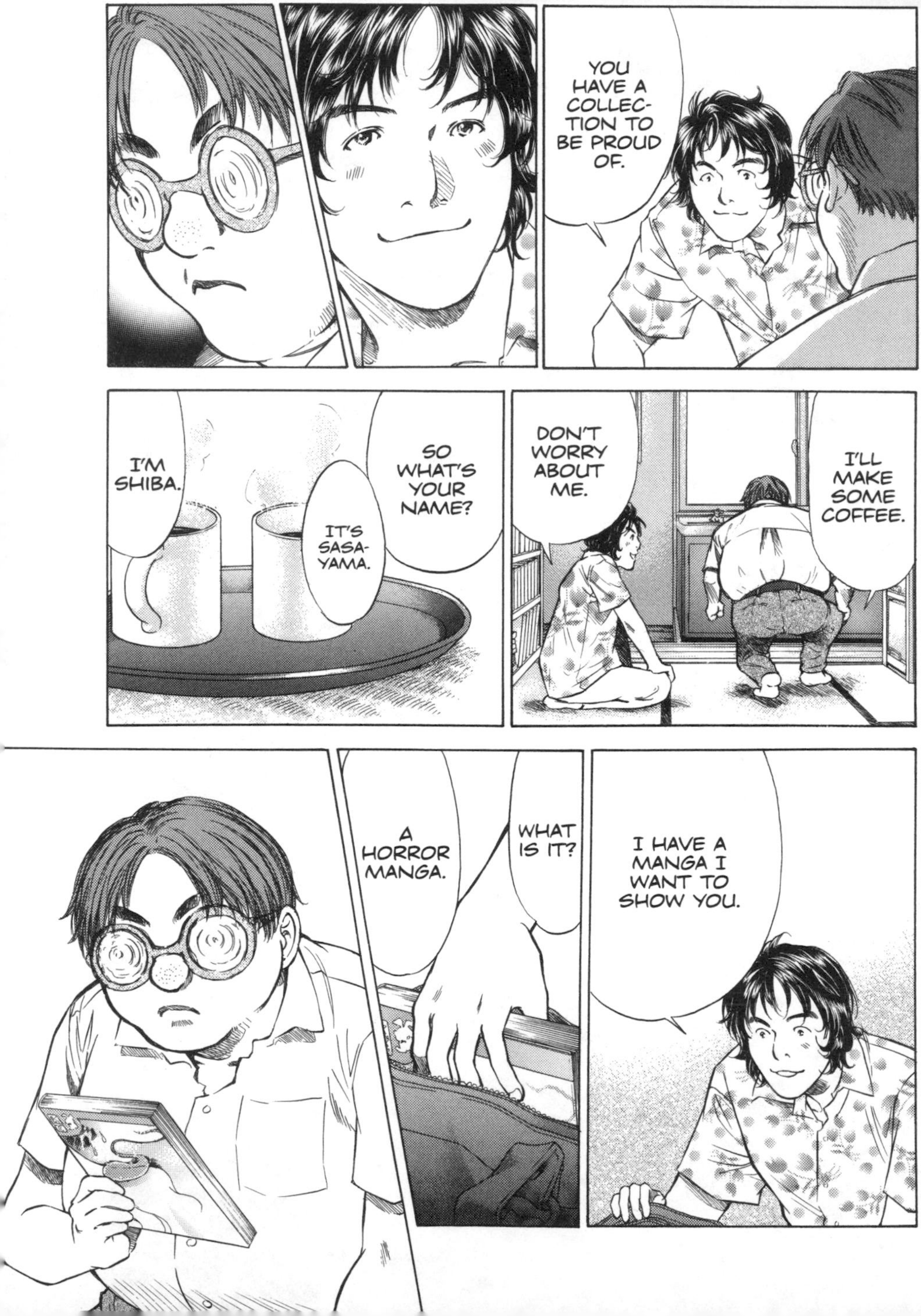
YOU HAVE A COLLECTION TO BE PROUD OF.
I'LL MAKE SOME COFFEE.
DON'T WORRY ABOUT ME.
SO WHAT'S YOUR NAME?
IT'S SASA-YAMA.
I'M SHIBA.
I HAVE A MANGA I WANT TO SHOW YOU.
WHAT IS IT?
A HORROR MANGA.

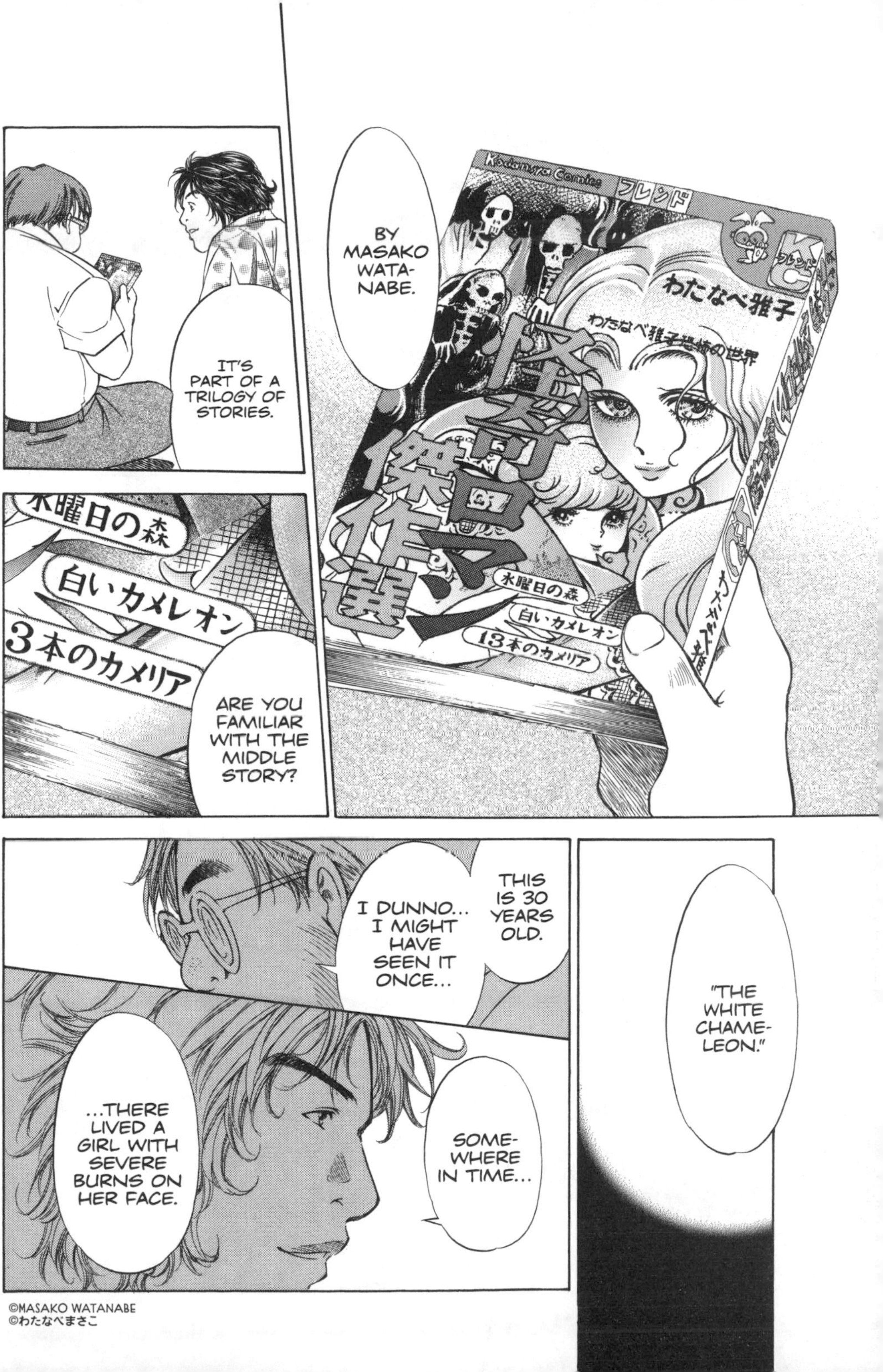
BY MASAKO WATA-NABE.
Kodansya Comics
フレンド
KC フレンド
わたなべ雅子
わたなべ雅子恐怖の世界
怪奇傑作選
水曜日の森
白いカメレオン
13本のカメリア
IT'S PART OF A TRILOGY OF STORIES.
水曜日の森
白いカメレオン
3本のカメリア
ARE YOU FAMILIAR WITH THE MIDDLE STORY?
"THE WHITE CHAME-LEON."
THIS IS 30 YEARS OLD.
I DUNNO... I MIGHT HAVE SEEN IT ONCE...
SOME-WHERE IN TIME...
...THERE LIVED A GIRL WITH SEVERE BURNS ON HER FACE.

"SUIYOUBI NO MORI" (WEDNESDAY'S FOREST), "SHIROI CHAMELEON" (THE WHITE CHAMELEON) AND "SANBON NO CAMELLIA" (THREE CAMELLIAS).

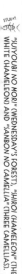

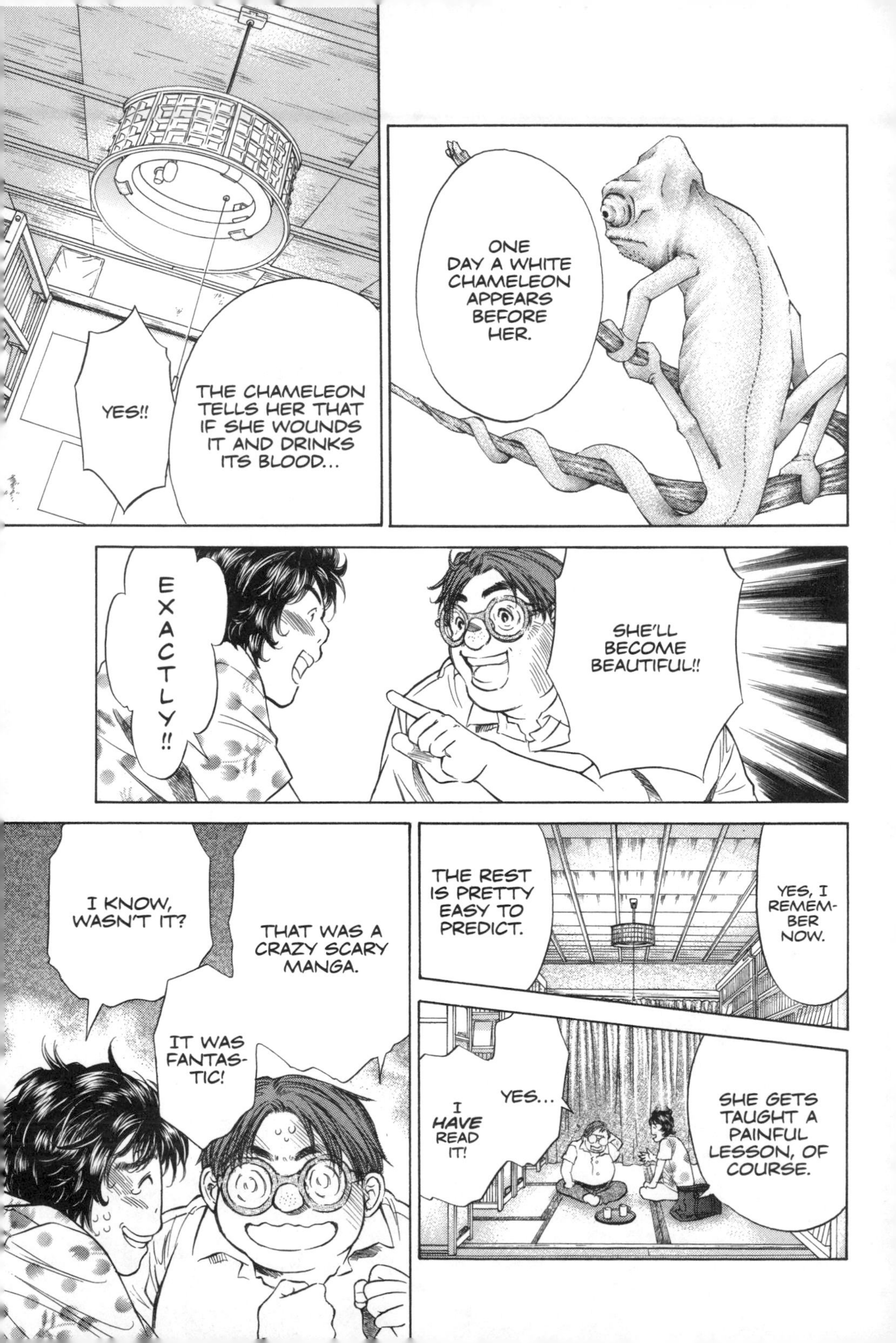
ONE DAY A WHITE CHAMELEON APPEARS BEFORE HER.
THE CHAMELEON TELLS HER THAT IF SHE WOUNDS IT AND DRINKS ITS BLOOD...
YES!!
SHE'LL BECOME BEAUTIFUL!!
EXACTLY!!
YES, I REMEM-BER NOW.
THE REST IS PRETTY EASY TO PREDICT.
SHE GETS TAUGHT A PAINFUL LESSON, OF COURSE.
YES...
I *HAVE* READ IT!
THAT WAS A CRAZY SCARY MANGA.
I KNOW, WASN'T IT?
IT WAS FANTAS-TIC!

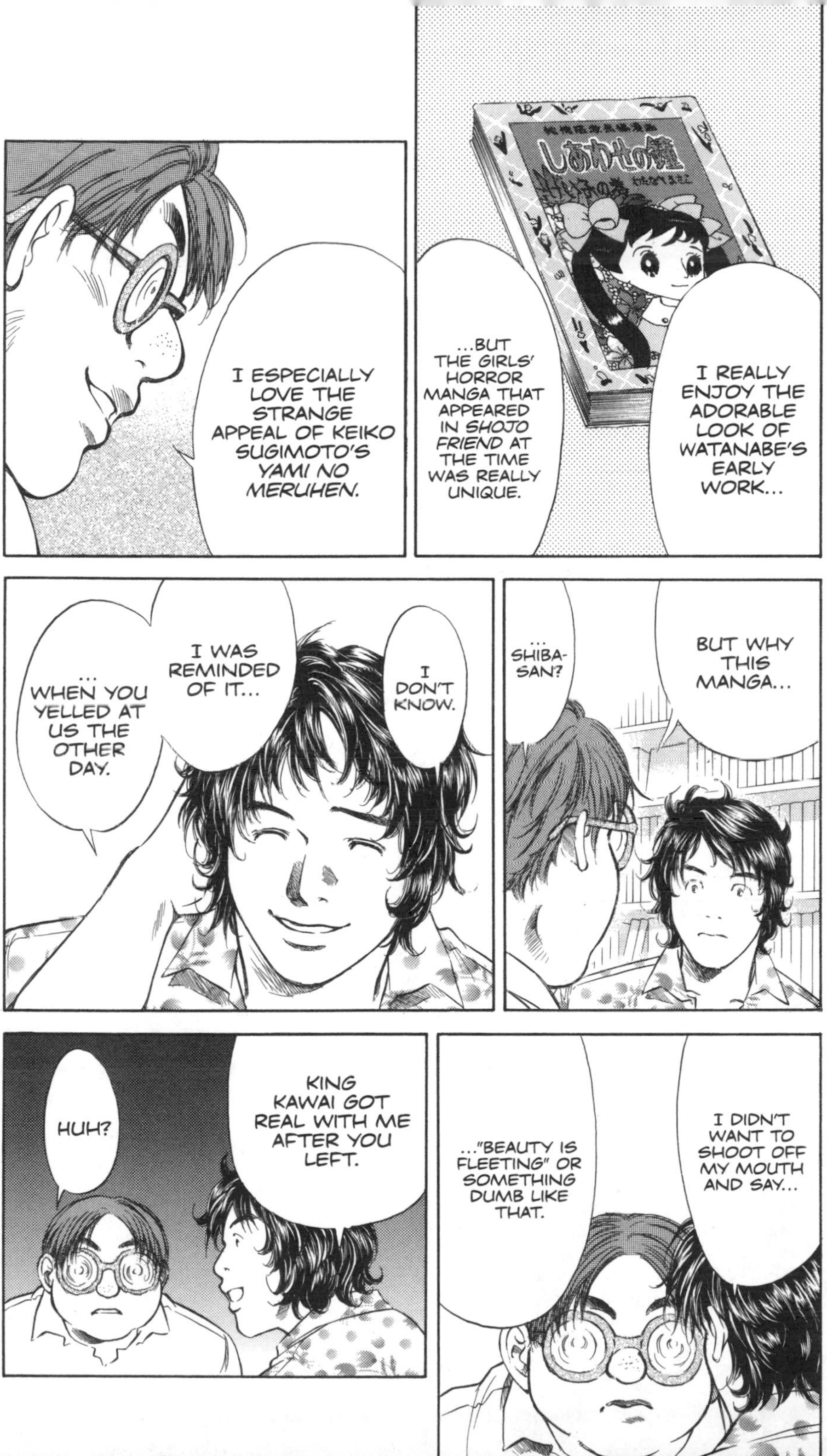
I REALLY ENJOY THE ADORABLE LOOK OF WATANABE'S EARLY WORK...
...BUT THE GIRLS' HORROR MANGA THAT APPEARED IN *SHOJO FRIEND* AT THE TIME WAS REALLY UNIQUE.
I ESPECIALLY LOVE THE STRANGE APPEAL OF KEIKO SUGIMOTO'S *YAMI NO MERUHEN*.
BUT WHY THIS MANGA...
...SHIBA-SAN?
I DON'T KNOW.
I WAS REMINDED OF IT...
...WHEN YOU YELLED AT US THE OTHER DAY.
I DIDN'T WANT TO SHOOT OFF MY MOUTH AND SAY...
..."BEAUTY IS FLEETING" OR SOMETHING DUMB LIKE THAT.
KING KAWAI GOT REAL WITH ME AFTER YOU LEFT.
HUH?

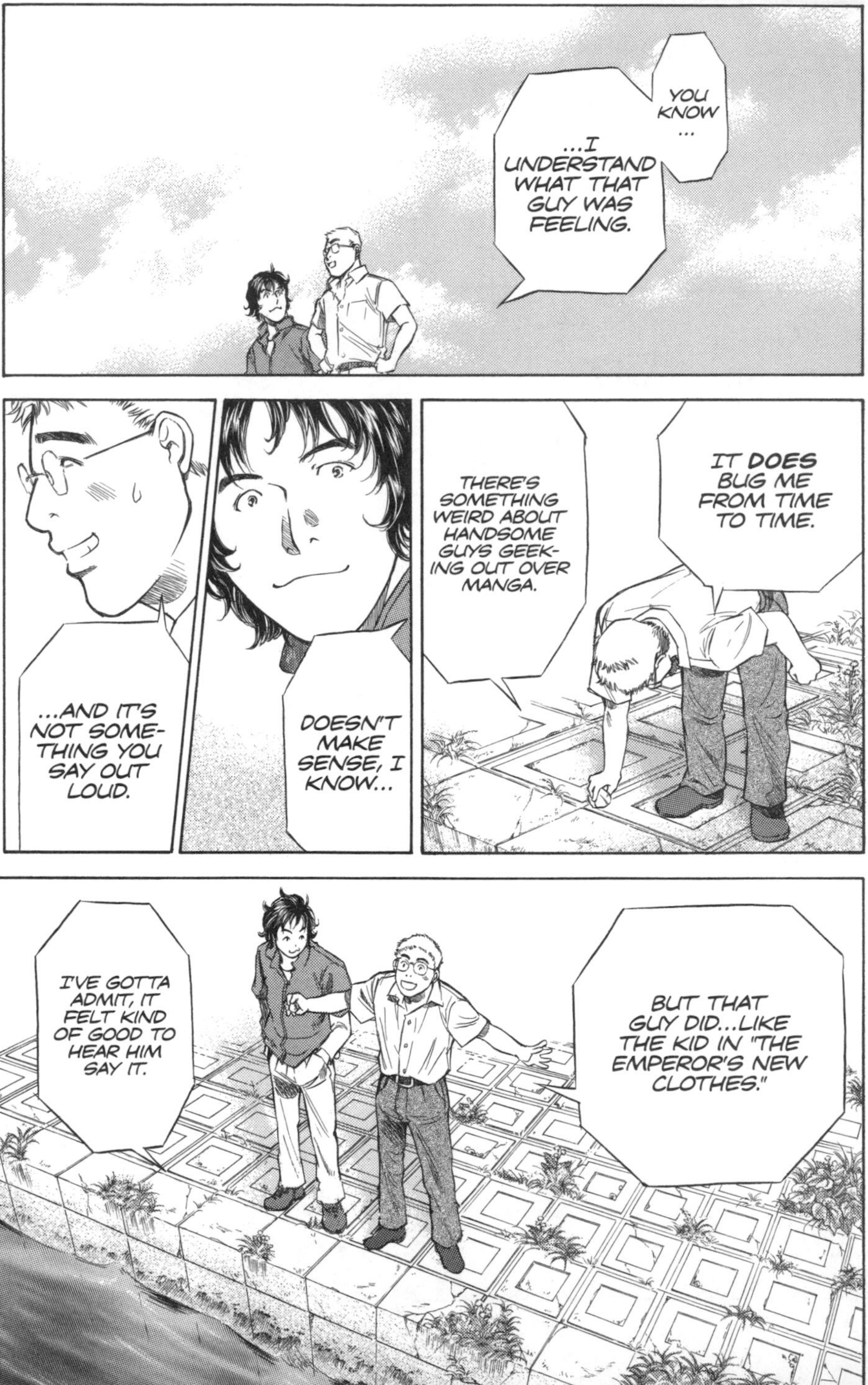
YOU KNOW...
...I UNDERSTAND WHAT THAT GUY WAS FEELING.
IT DOES BUG ME FROM TIME TO TIME.
THERE'S SOMETHING WEIRD ABOUT HANDSOME GUYS GEEK-ING OUT OVER MANGA.
DOESN'T MAKE SENSE, I KNOW...
...AND IT'S NOT SOME-THING YOU SAY OUT LOUD.
BUT THAT GUY DID...LIKE THE KID IN "THE EMPEROR'S NEW CLOTHES."
I'VE GOTTA ADMIT, IT FELT KIND OF GOOD TO HEAR HIM SAY IT.

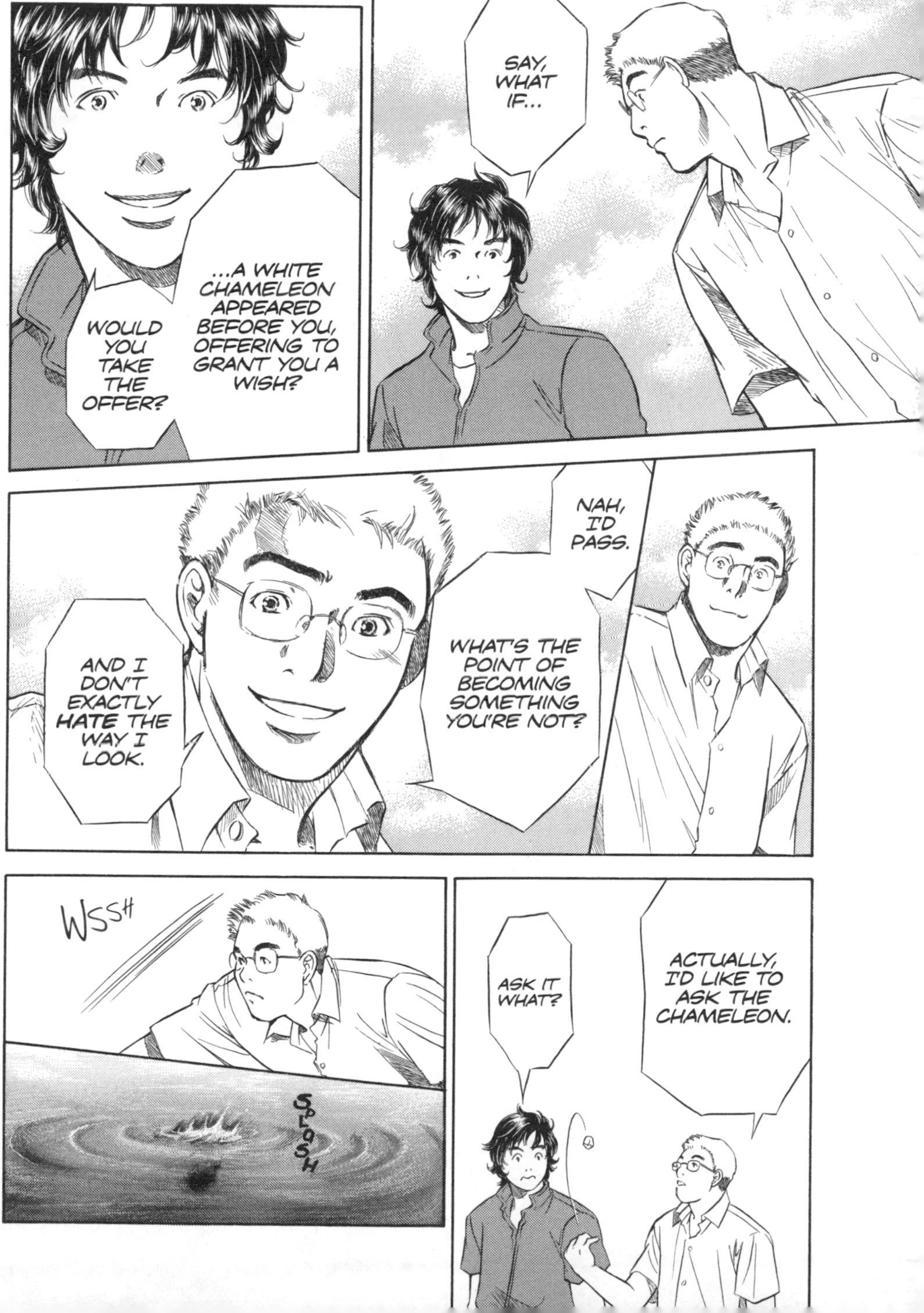
SAY, WHAT IF...
...A WHITE CHAMELEON APPEARED BEFORE YOU, OFFERING TO GRANT YOU A WISH?
WOULD YOU TAKE THE OFFER?
NAH, I'D PASS.
WHAT'S THE POINT OF BECOMING SOMETHING YOU'RE NOT?
AND I DON'T EXACTLY **HATE** THE WAY I LOOK.
ACTUALLY, I'D LIKE TO ASK THE CHAMELEON.
ASK IT WHAT?
WSSH
SPLOSH

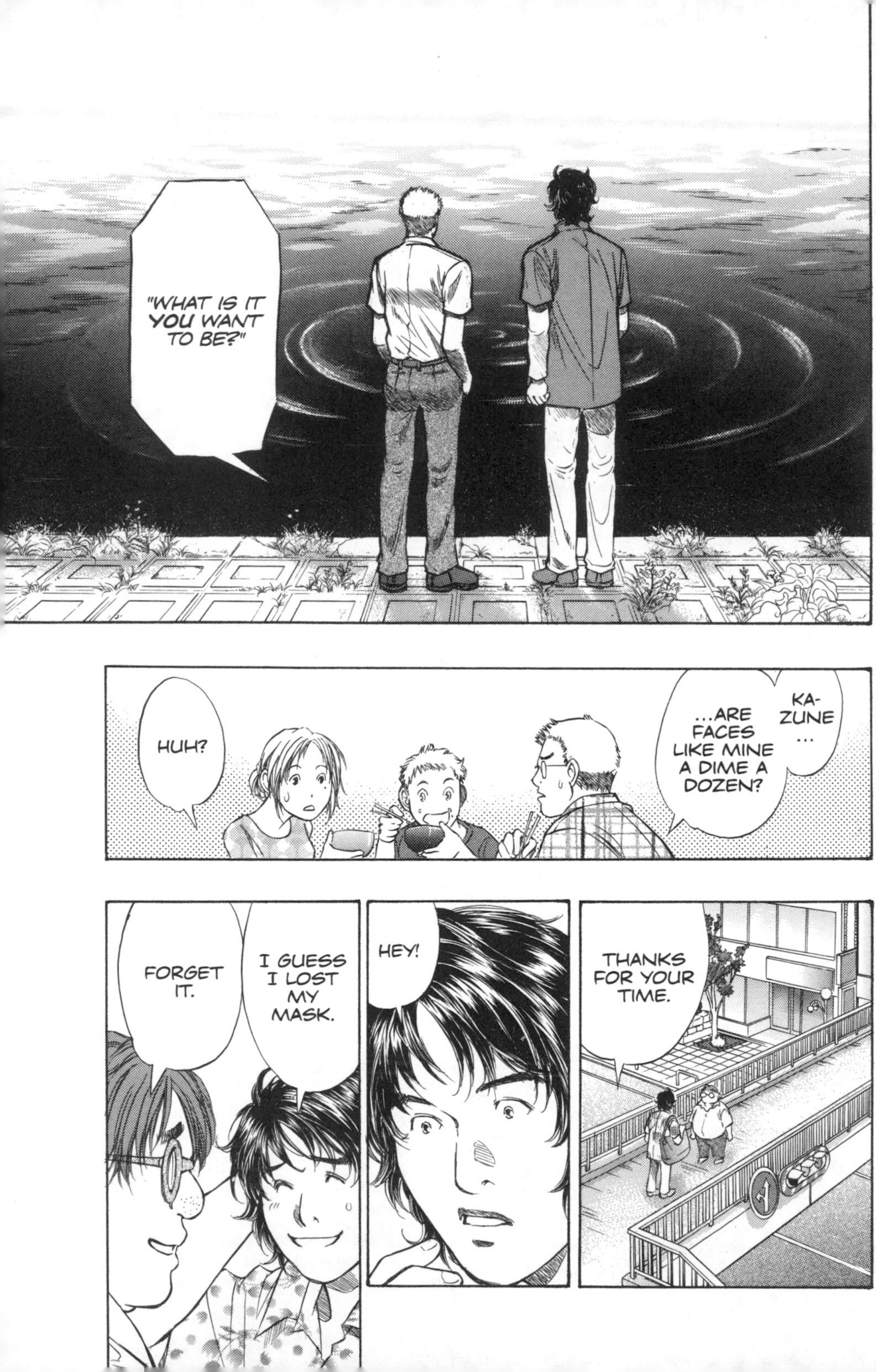
"WHAT IS IT YOU WANT TO BE?"
KA-ZUNE ...
...ARE FACES LIKE MINE A DIME A DOZEN?
HUH?
THANKS FOR YOUR TIME.
HEY!
I GUESS I LOST MY MASK.
FORGET IT.

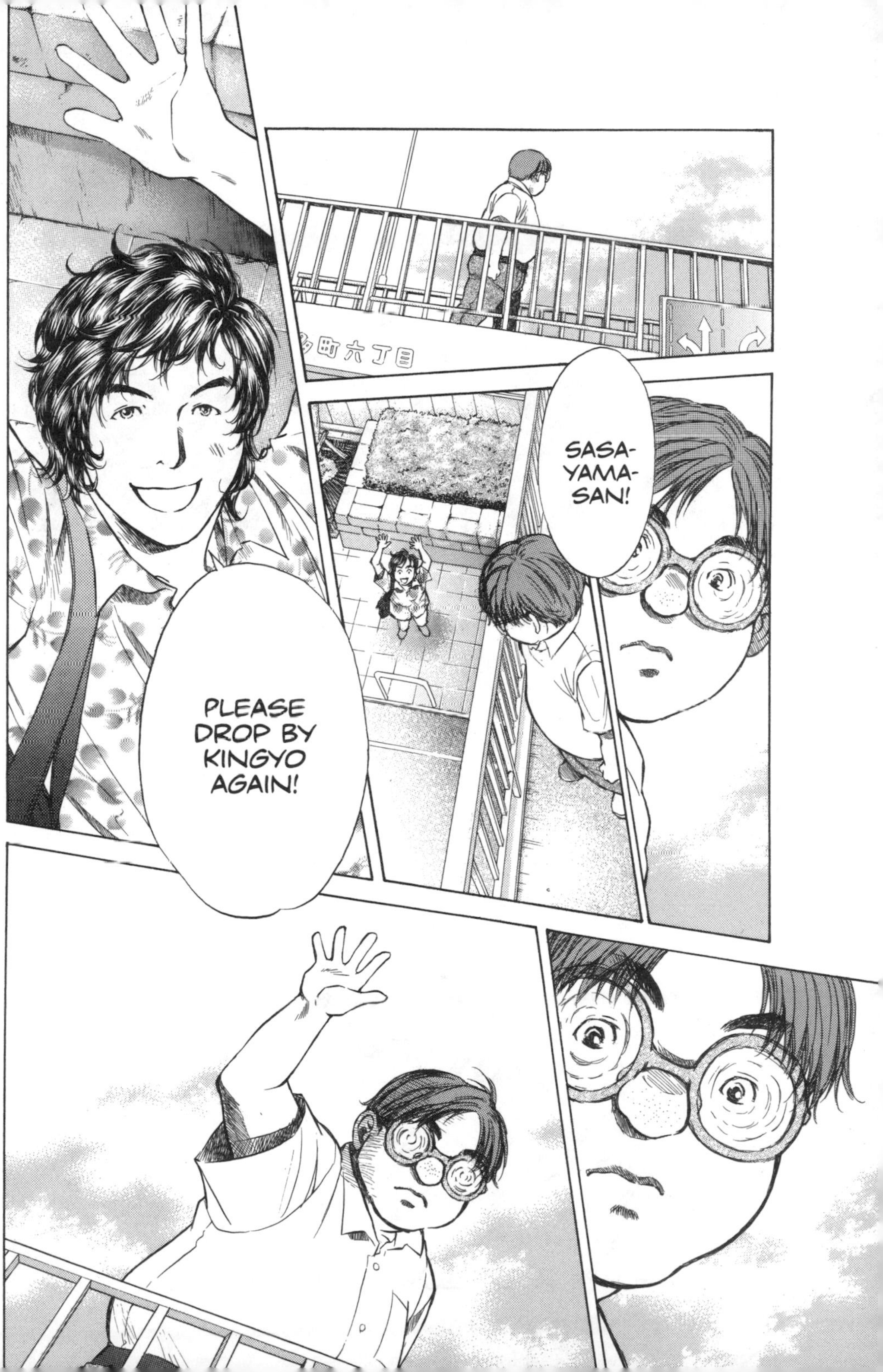
町六丁目
SASA-YAMA-SAN!
PLEASE DROP BY KINGYO AGAIN!

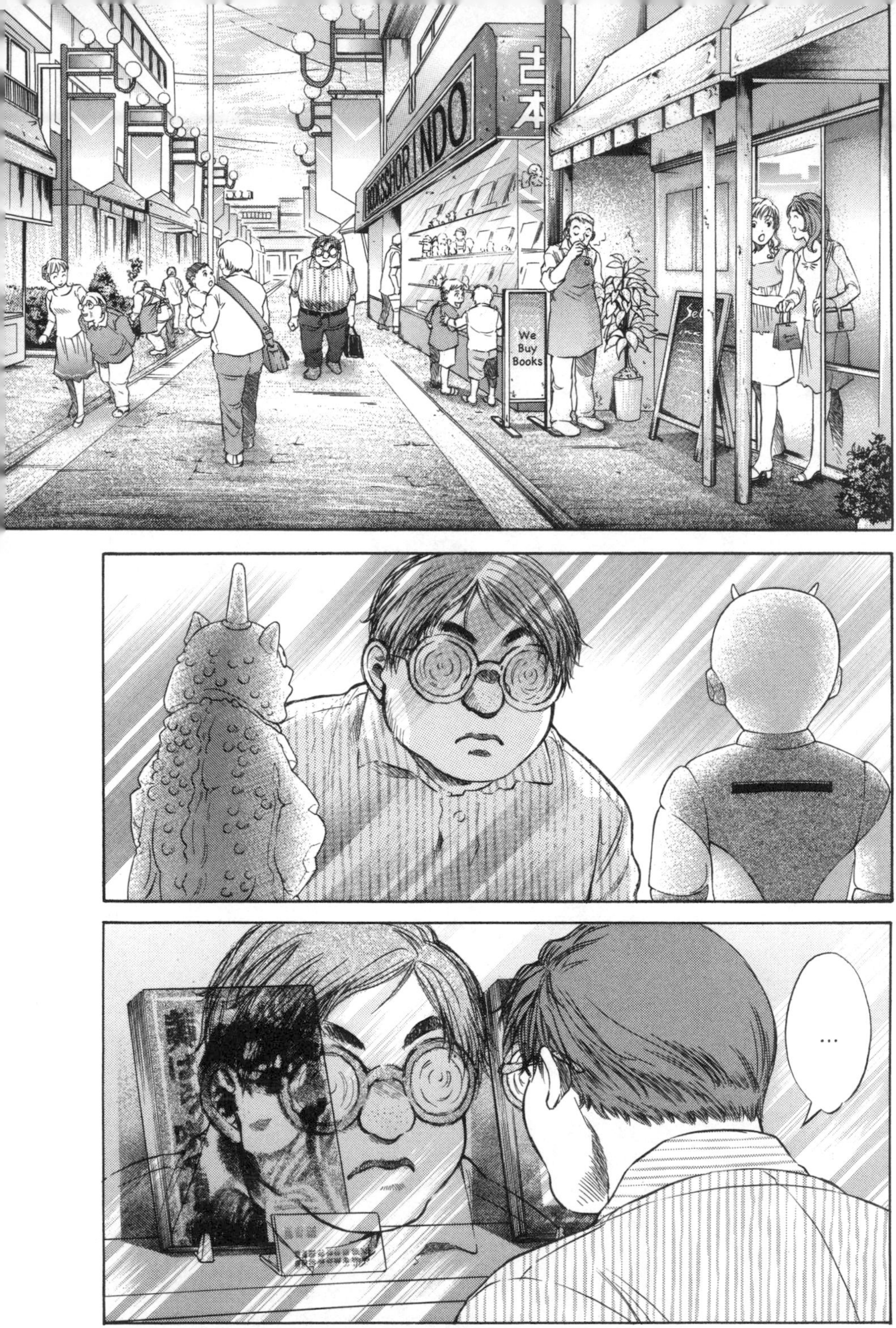
古本
We Buy Books
...

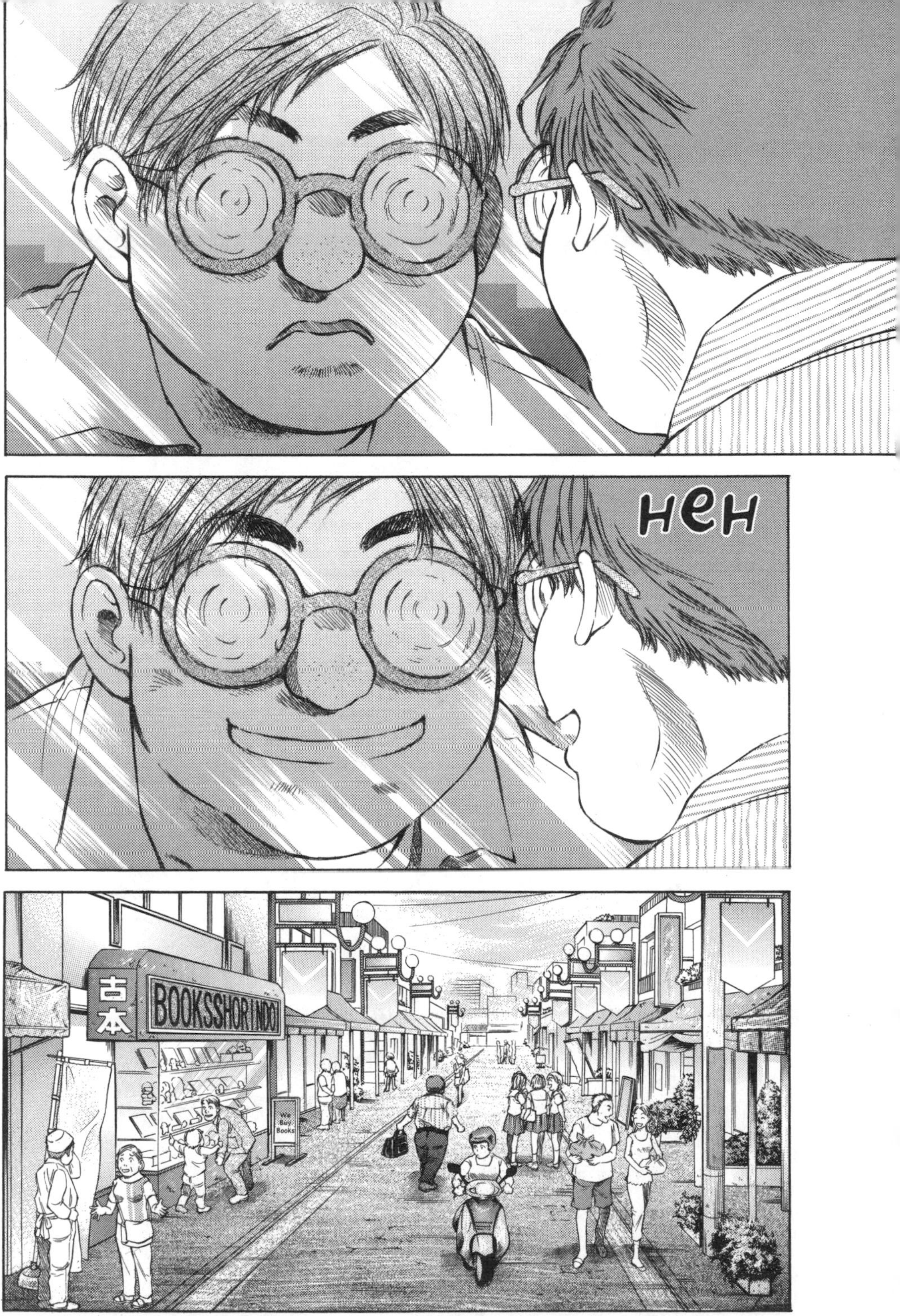
HEH
古本
BOOKSSHORINDO
We Buy Books

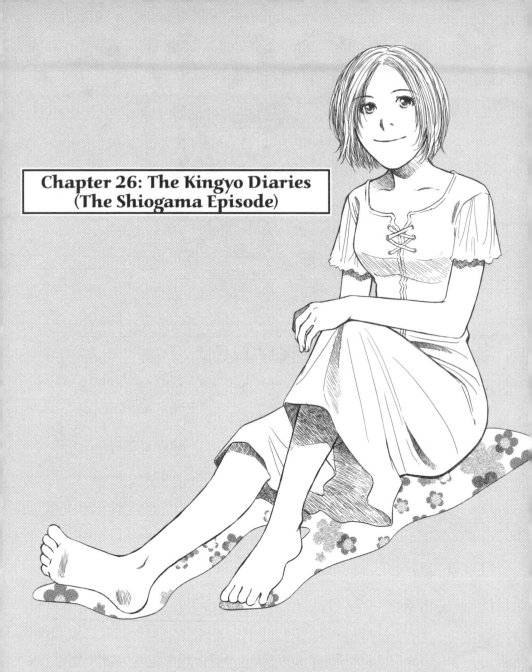

Chapter 26: The Kingyo Diaries
(The Shiogama Episode)

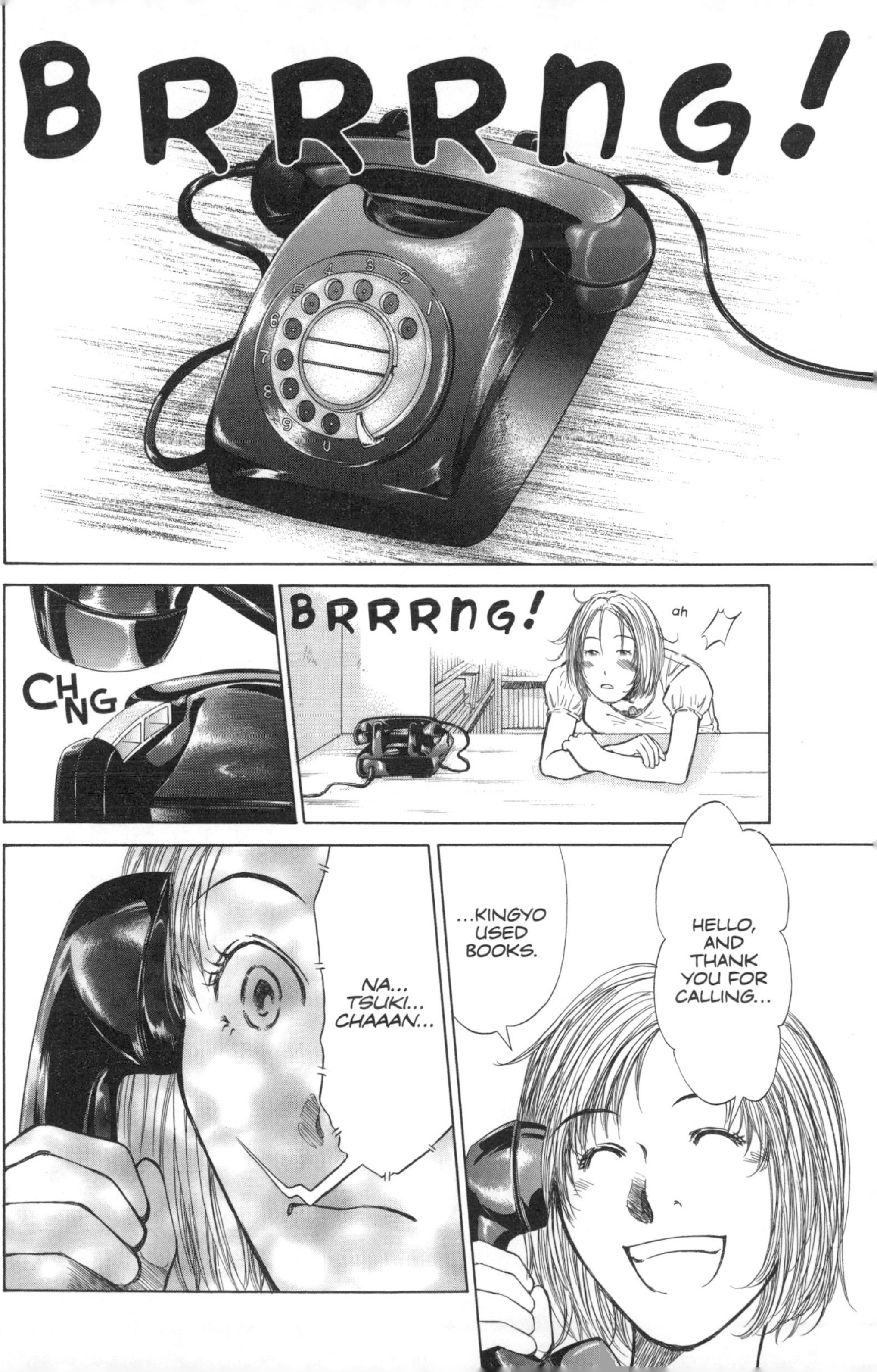
BRRRNG!
BRRRNG!
ah
CHNG
HELLO, AND THANK YOU FOR CALLING...
...KINGYO USED BOOKS.
NA... TSUKI... CHAAAN...

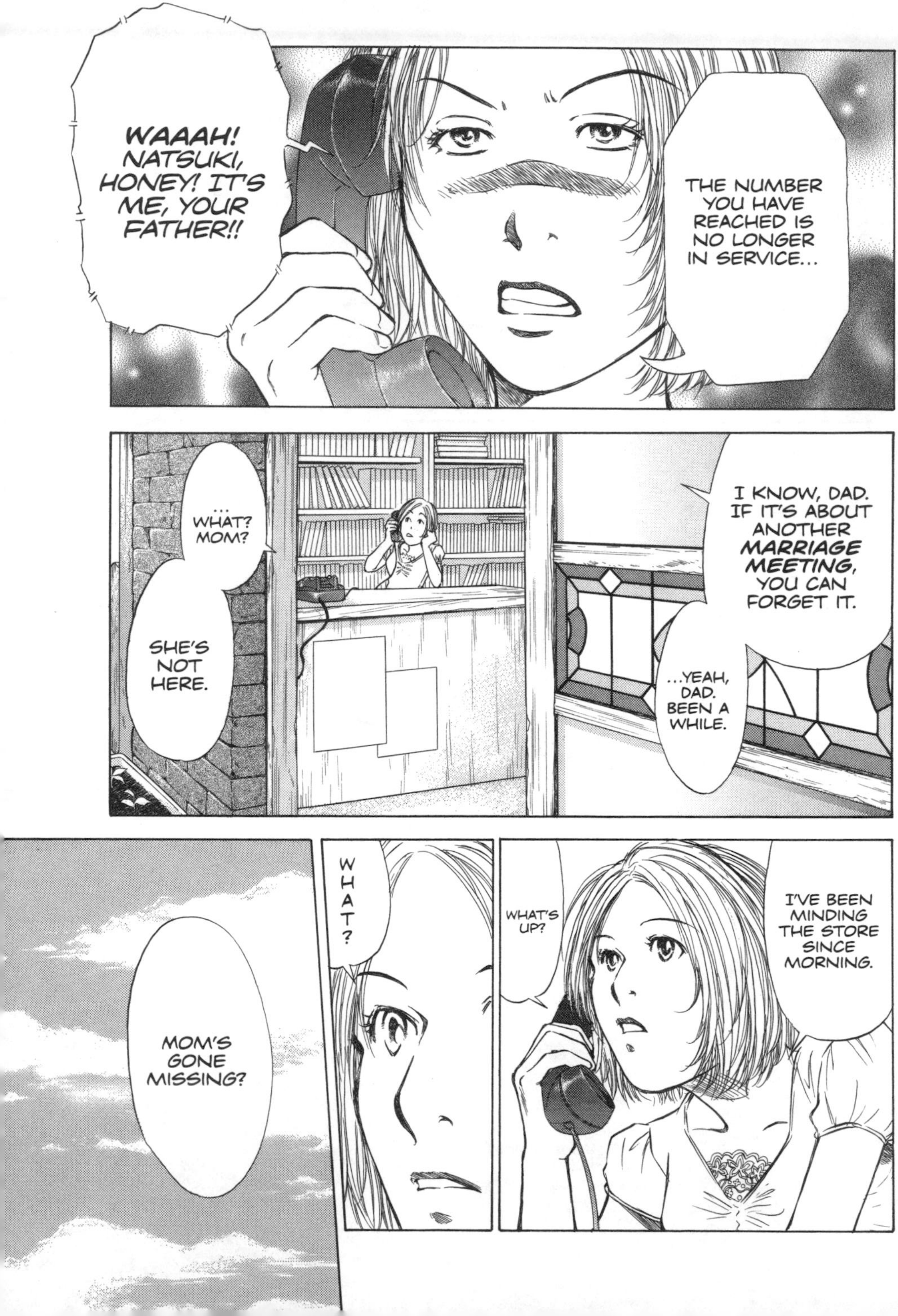
THE NUMBER YOU HAVE REACHED IS NO LONGER IN SERVICE...
WAAAH! NATSUKI, HONEY! IT'S ME, YOUR FATHER!!
I KNOW, DAD. IF IT'S ABOUT ANOTHER MARRIAGE MEETING, YOU CAN FORGET IT.
...YEAH, DAD. BEEN A WHILE.
...WHAT? MOM?
SHE'S NOT HERE.
I'VE BEEN MINDING THE STORE SINCE MORNING.
WHAT'S UP?
WHAT?
MOM'S GONE MISSING?

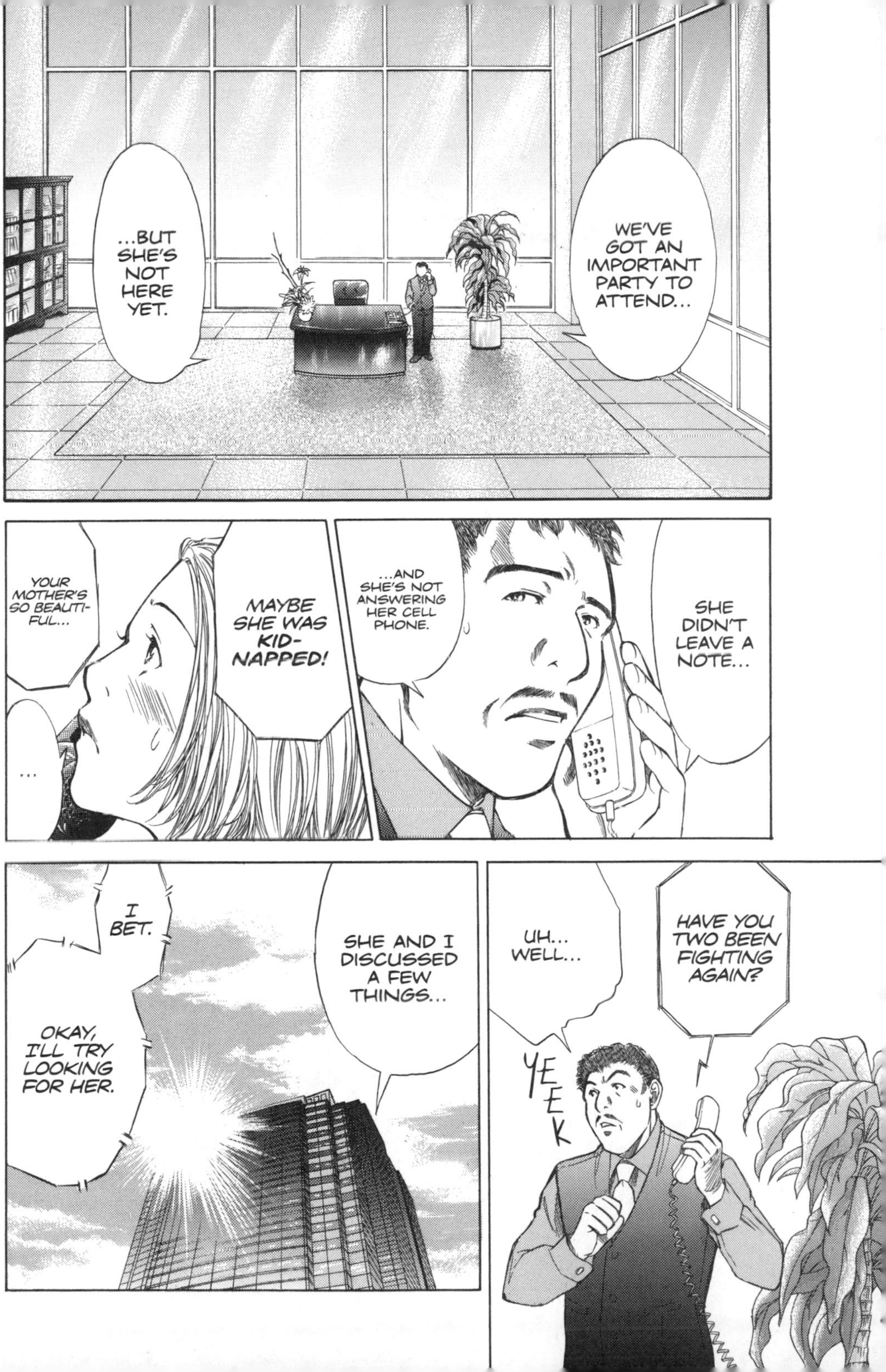
WE'VE GOT AN IMPORTANT PARTY TO ATTEND...
...BUT SHE'S NOT HERE YET.
SHE DIDN'T LEAVE A NOTE...
...AND SHE'S NOT ANSWERING HER CELL PHONE.
MAYBE SHE WAS KID-NAPPED!
YOUR MOTHER'S SO BEAUTI-FUL...
...
HAVE YOU TWO BEEN FIGHTING AGAIN?
UH... WELL...
YEEK
SHE AND I DISCUSSED A FEW THINGS...
I BET.
OKAY, I'LL TRY LOOKING FOR HER.

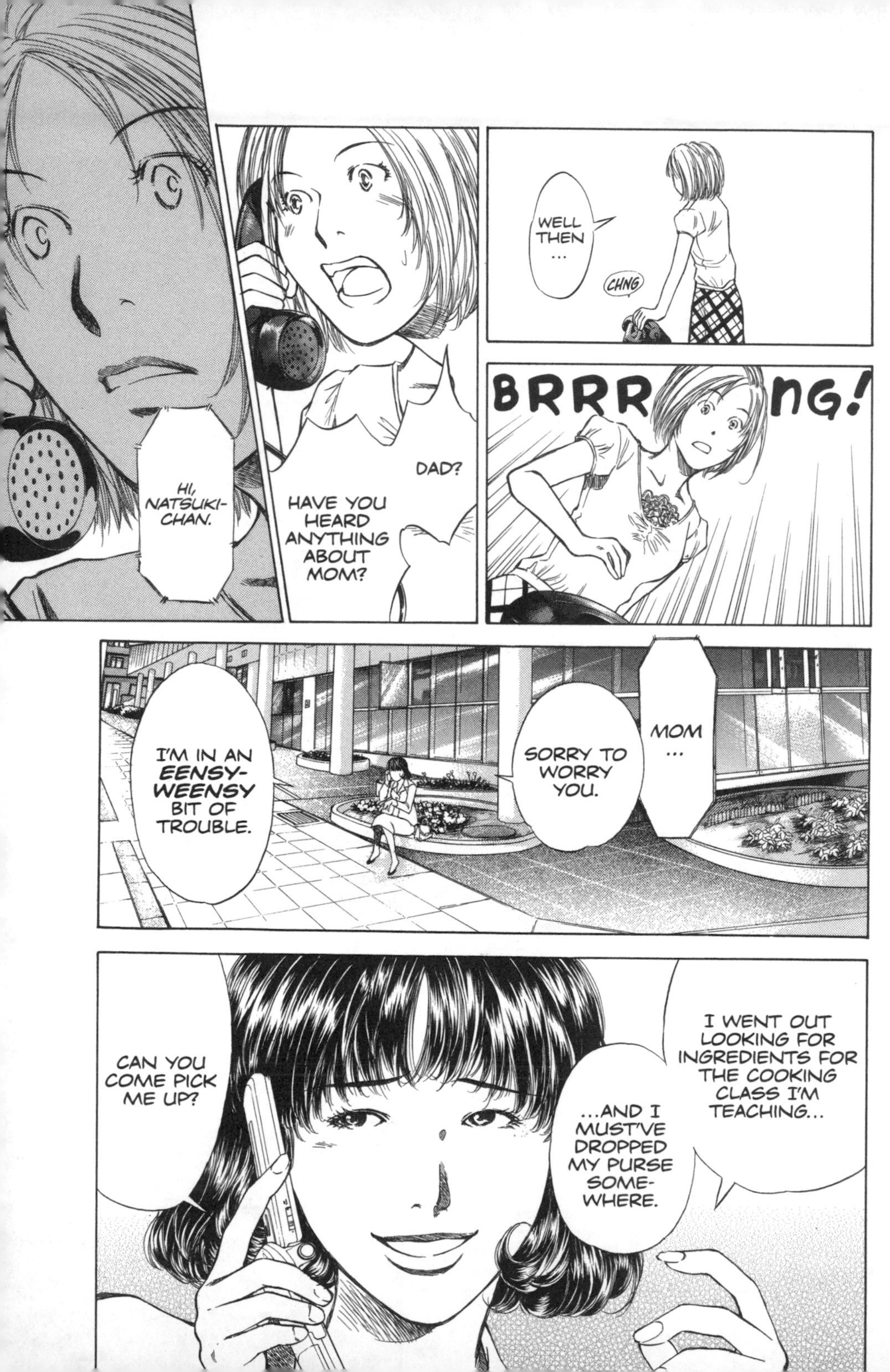
WELL THEN ...
CHNG
BRRRRING!
DAD?
HAVE YOU HEARD ANYTHING ABOUT MOM?
HI, NATSUKI-CHAN.
MOM ...
SORRY TO WORRY YOU.
I'M IN AN **EENSY-WEENSY** BIT OF TROUBLE.
I WENT OUT LOOKING FOR INGREDIENTS FOR THE COOKING CLASS I'M TEACHING...
...AND I MUST'VE DROPPED MY PURSE SOME-WHERE.
CAN YOU COME PICK ME UP?

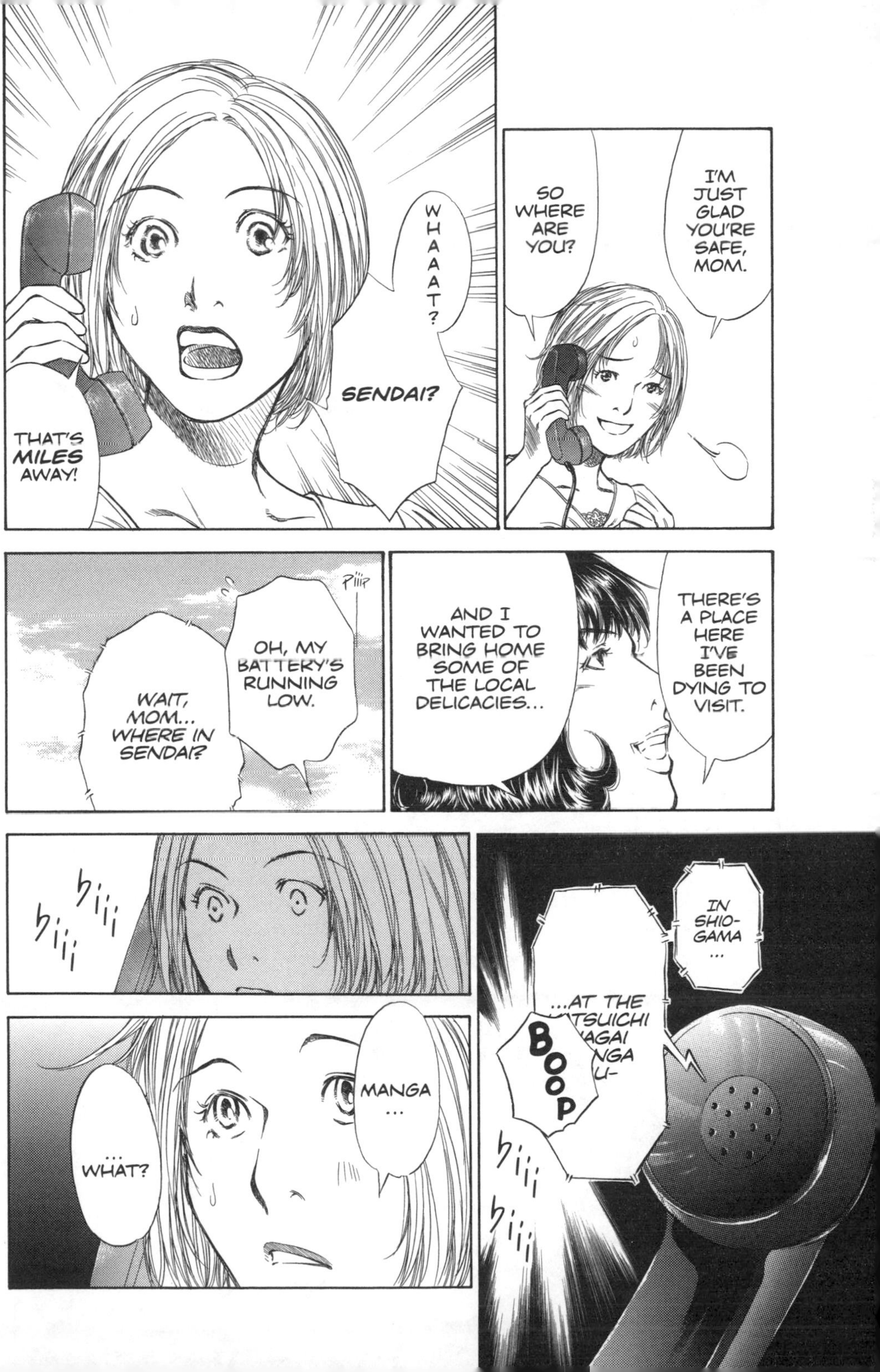
I'M JUST GLAD YOU'RE SAFE, MOM.
SO WHERE ARE YOU?
WHAAAT?
SENDAI?
THAT'S MILES AWAY!
THERE'S A PLACE HERE I'VE BEEN DYING TO VISIT.
AND I WANTED TO BRING HOME SOME OF THE LOCAL DELICACIES...
PIIIP
OH, MY BATTERY'S RUNNING LOW.
WAIT, MOM... WHERE IN SENDAI?
IN SHIO-GAMA...
...AT THE TSUICHI AGAI NGA U-
BOOP
hiii hiii
hiii hiii
MANGA...
...WHAT?

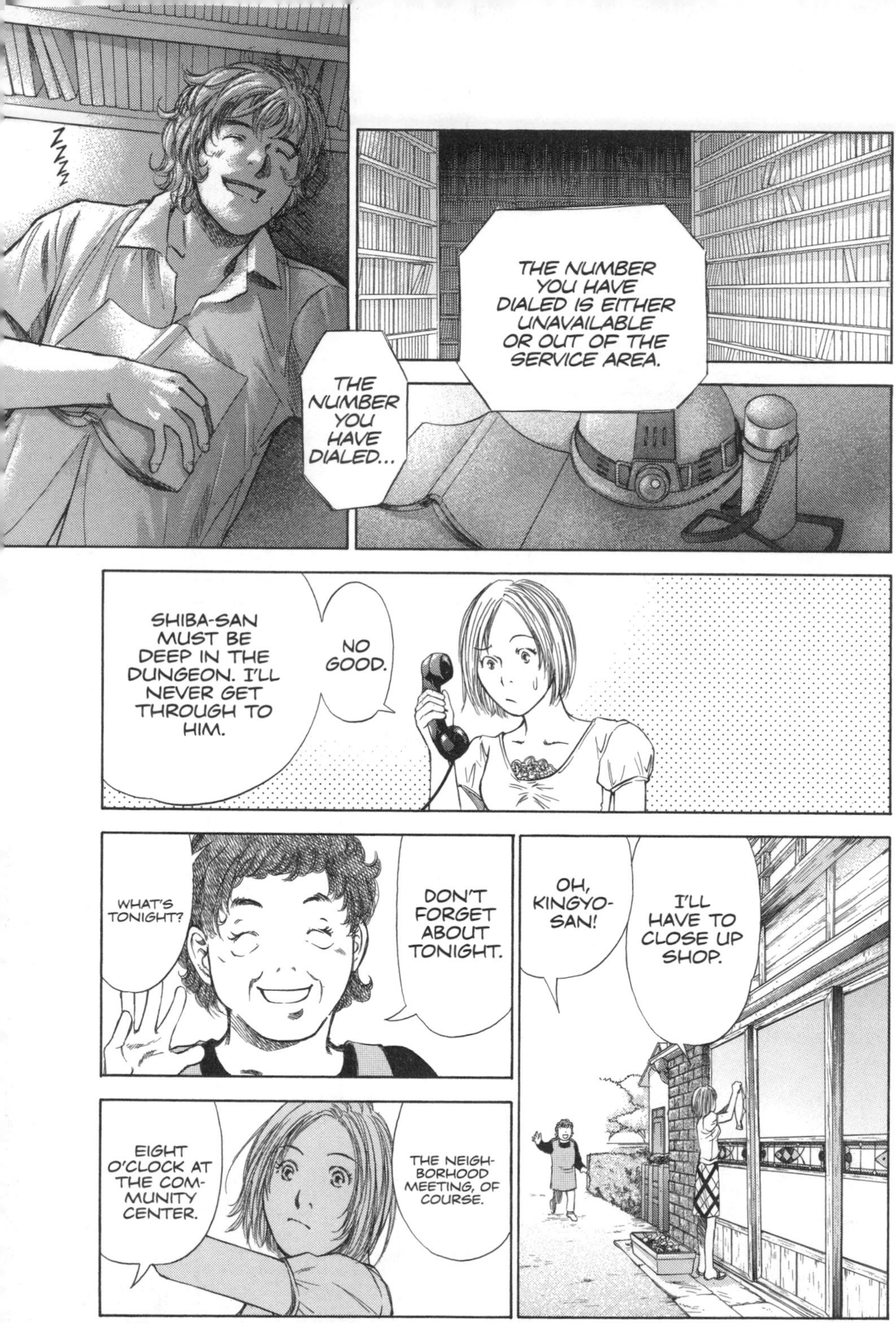
THE NUMBER YOU HAVE DIALED IS EITHER UNAVAILABLE OR OUT OF THE SERVICE AREA.
THE NUMBER YOU HAVE DIALED...
ZZZZ
NO GOOD.
SHIBA-SAN MUST BE DEEP IN THE DUNGEON. I'LL NEVER GET THROUGH TO HIM.
I'LL HAVE TO CLOSE UP SHOP.
OH, KINGYO-SAN!
DON'T FORGET ABOUT TONIGHT.
WHAT'S TONIGHT?
THE NEIGH-BORHOOD MEETING, OF COURSE.
EIGHT O'CLOCK AT THE COM-MUNITY CENTER.

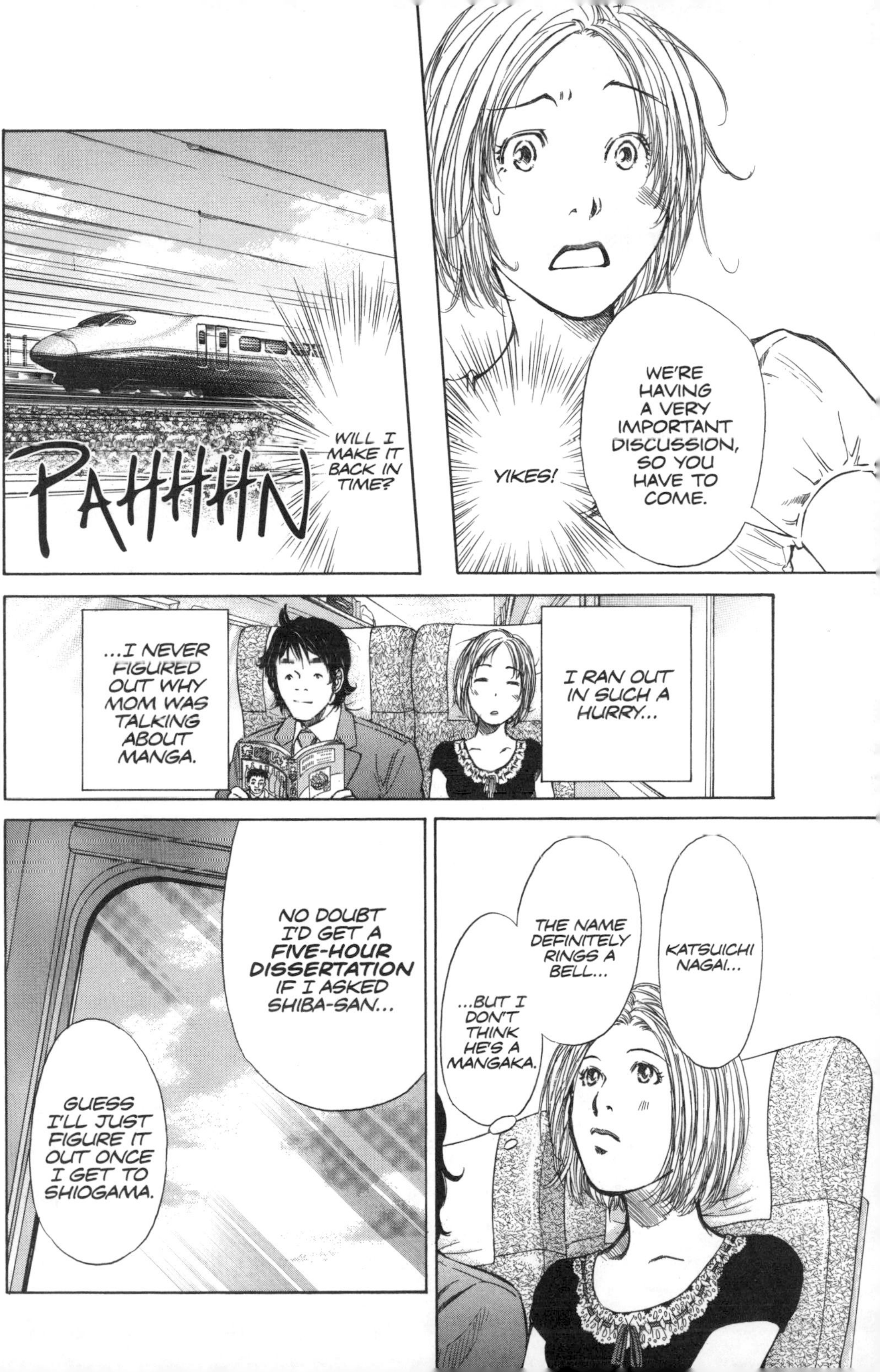
WE'RE HAVING A VERY IMPORTANT DISCUSSION, SO YOU HAVE TO COME.
YIKES!
WILL I MAKE IT BACK IN TIME?
PAHHHN
I RAN OUT IN SUCH A HURRY...
...I NEVER FIGURED OUT WHY MOM WAS TALKING ABOUT MANGA.
KATSUICHI NAGAI...
THE NAME DEFINITELY RINGS A BELL...
...BUT I DON'T THINK HE'S A MANGAKA.
NO DOUBT I'D GET A **FIVE-HOUR DISSERTATION** IF I ASKED SHIBA-SAN...
GUESS I'LL JUST FIGURE IT OUT ONCE I GET TO SHIOGAMA.

HEY!
THE NEW OISHINBO!
美味しんぼ
heh
I'M ACT-ING LIKE SHIBA-SAN.
How gauche...
PAHHHHN
WOW...
RICE FIELDS.
I'VE BEEN SO UP TO MY NECK IN BOOKS LATELY...
...LIVING IN MANGA, AROUND MANGA, FOR MANGA...
THIS IS A REFRESHING CHANGE OF SCENERY.
MMM, FEELS NICE!

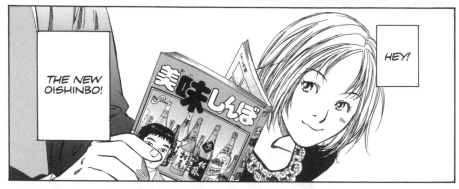

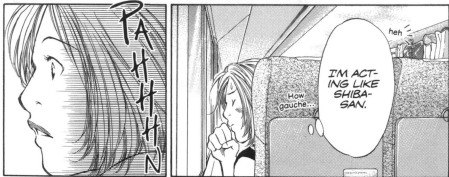

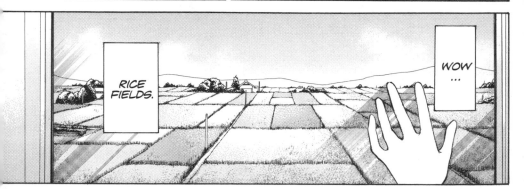

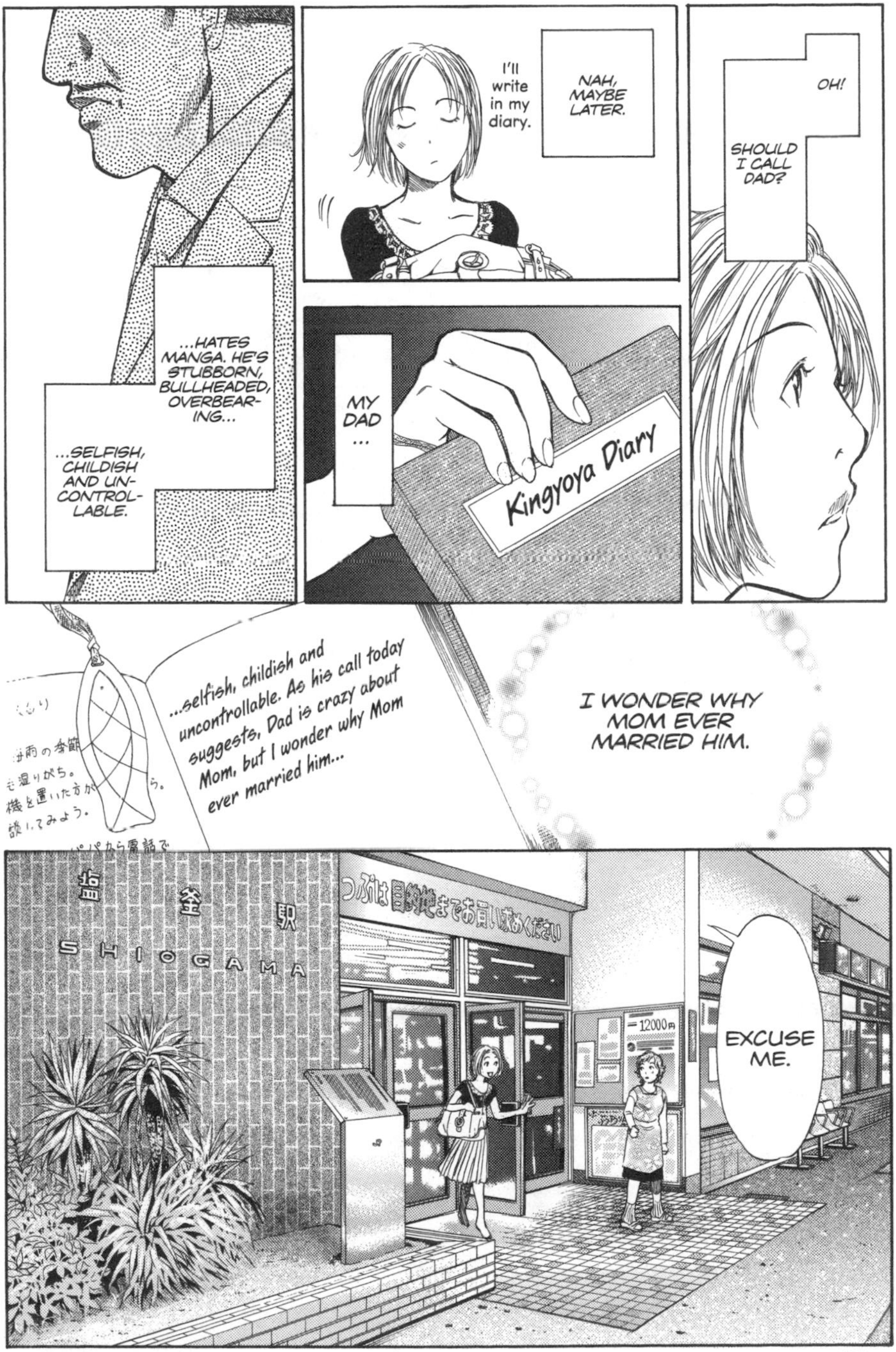
OH!
SHOULD I CALL DAD?
I'll write in my diary.
NAH, MAYBE LATER.
MY DAD...
Kingyoya Diary
...HATES MANGA. HE'S STUBBORN, BULLHEADED, OVERBEARING...
...SELFISH, CHILDISH AND UNCONTROLLABLE.
...selfish, childish and uncontrollable. As his call today suggests, Dad is crazy about Mom, but I wonder why Mom ever married him...
I WONDER WHY MOM EVER MARRIED HIM.
塩釜駅
SHIOGAMA
12000円
EXCUSE ME.

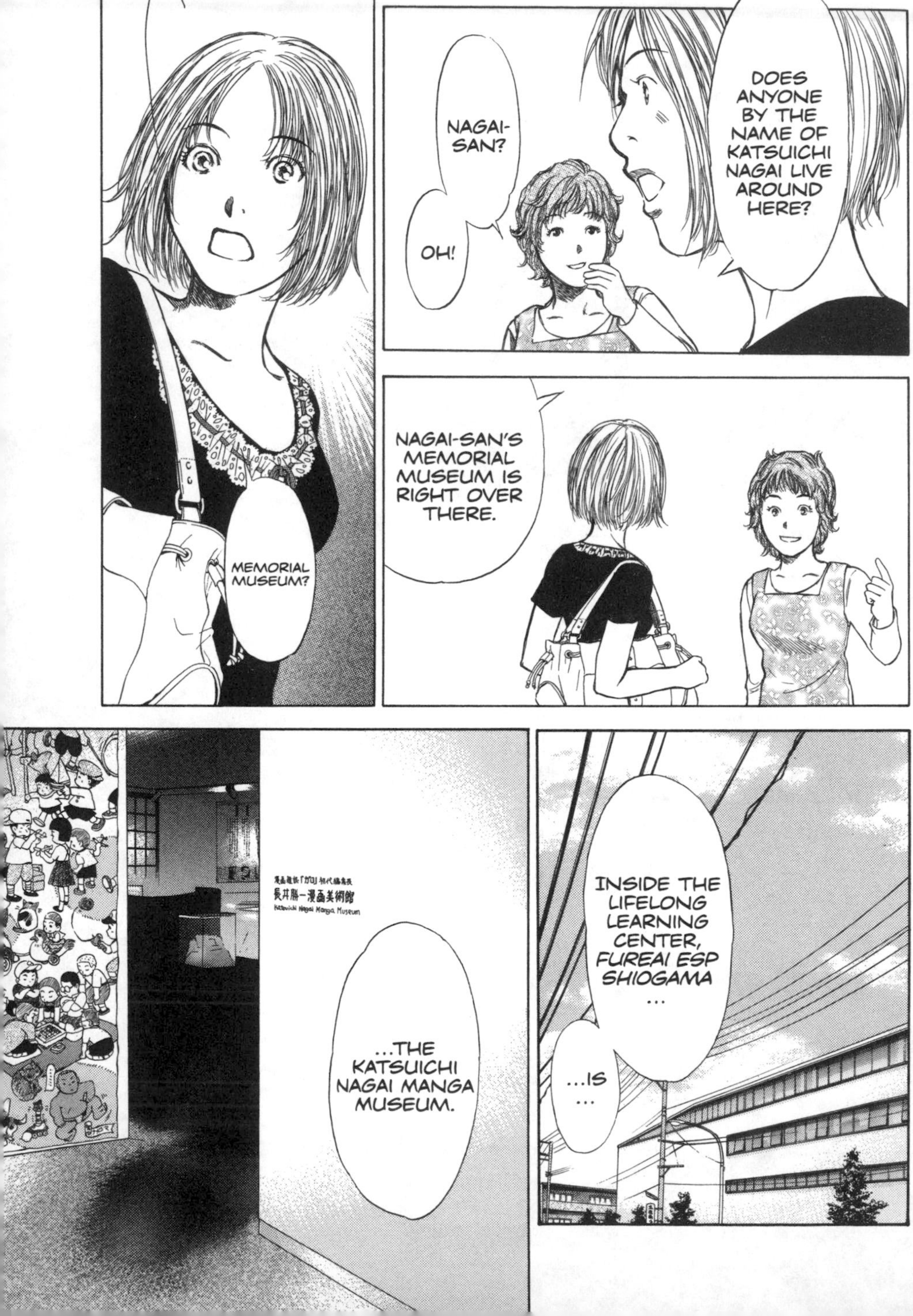
DOES ANYONE BY THE NAME OF KATSUICHI NAGAI LIVE AROUND HERE?
NAGAI-SAN?
OH!
NAGAI-SAN'S MEMORIAL MUSEUM IS RIGHT OVER THERE.
MEMORIAL MUSEUM?
INSIDE THE LIFELONG LEARNING CENTER, FUREAI ESP SHIOGAMA ...
...IS ...
漫画雑誌「ガロ」初代編集長
長井勝一漫画美術館
Katsuichi Nagai Manga Museum
...THE KATSUICHI NAGAI MANGA MUSEUM.

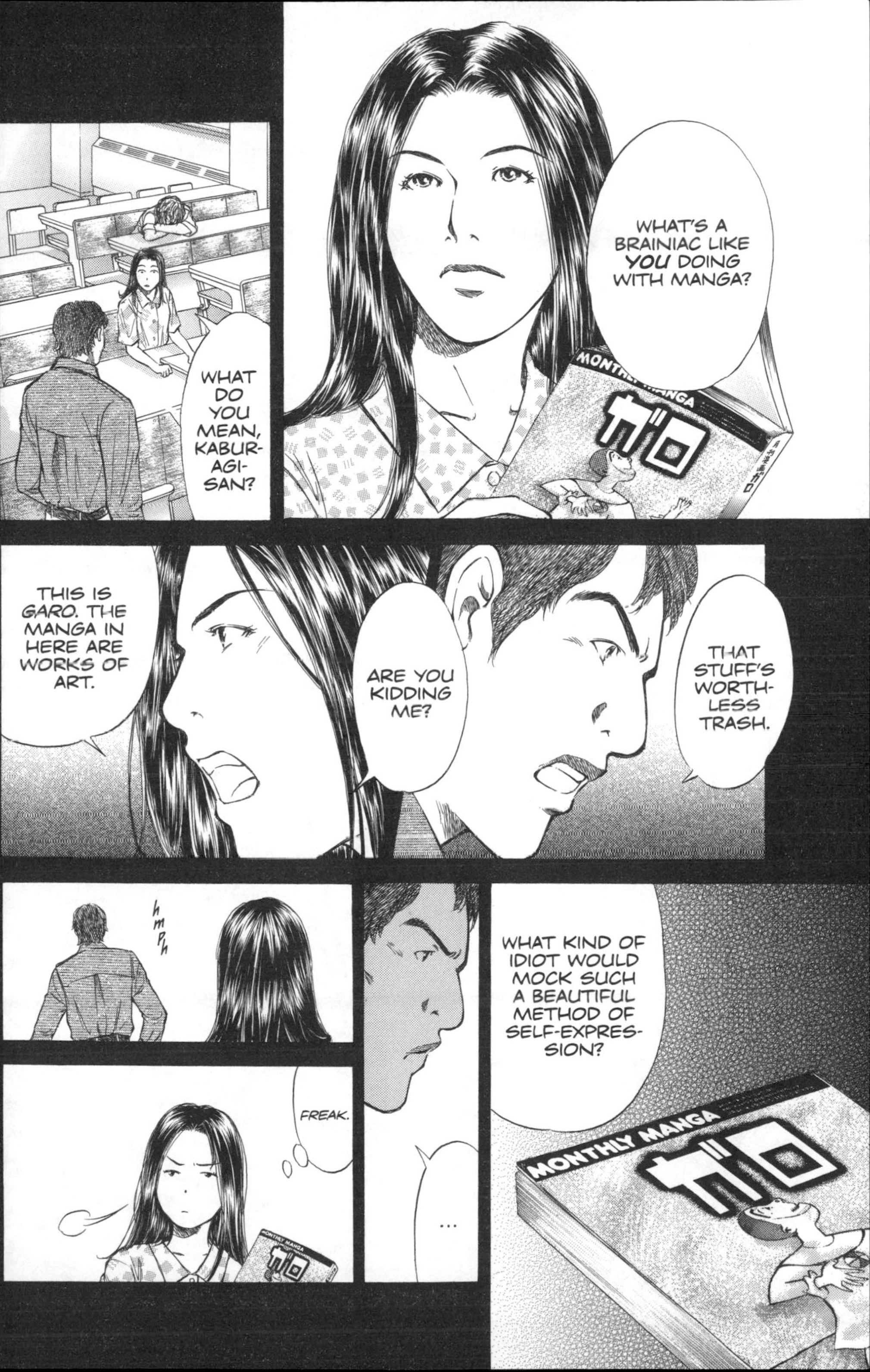
WHAT'S A BRAINIAC LIKE *YOU* DOING WITH MANGA?
MONTHLY MANGA
ガロ
WHAT DO YOU MEAN, KABURAGI-SAN?
THAT STUFF'S WORTHLESS TRASH.
ARE YOU KIDDING ME?
THIS IS GARO. THE MANGA IN HERE ARE WORKS OF ART.
WHAT KIND OF IDIOT WOULD MOCK SUCH A BEAUTIFUL METHOD OF SELF-EXPRESSION?
MONTHLY MANGA
ガロ
...
hmph
FREAK.
MONTHLY MANGA
ガロ

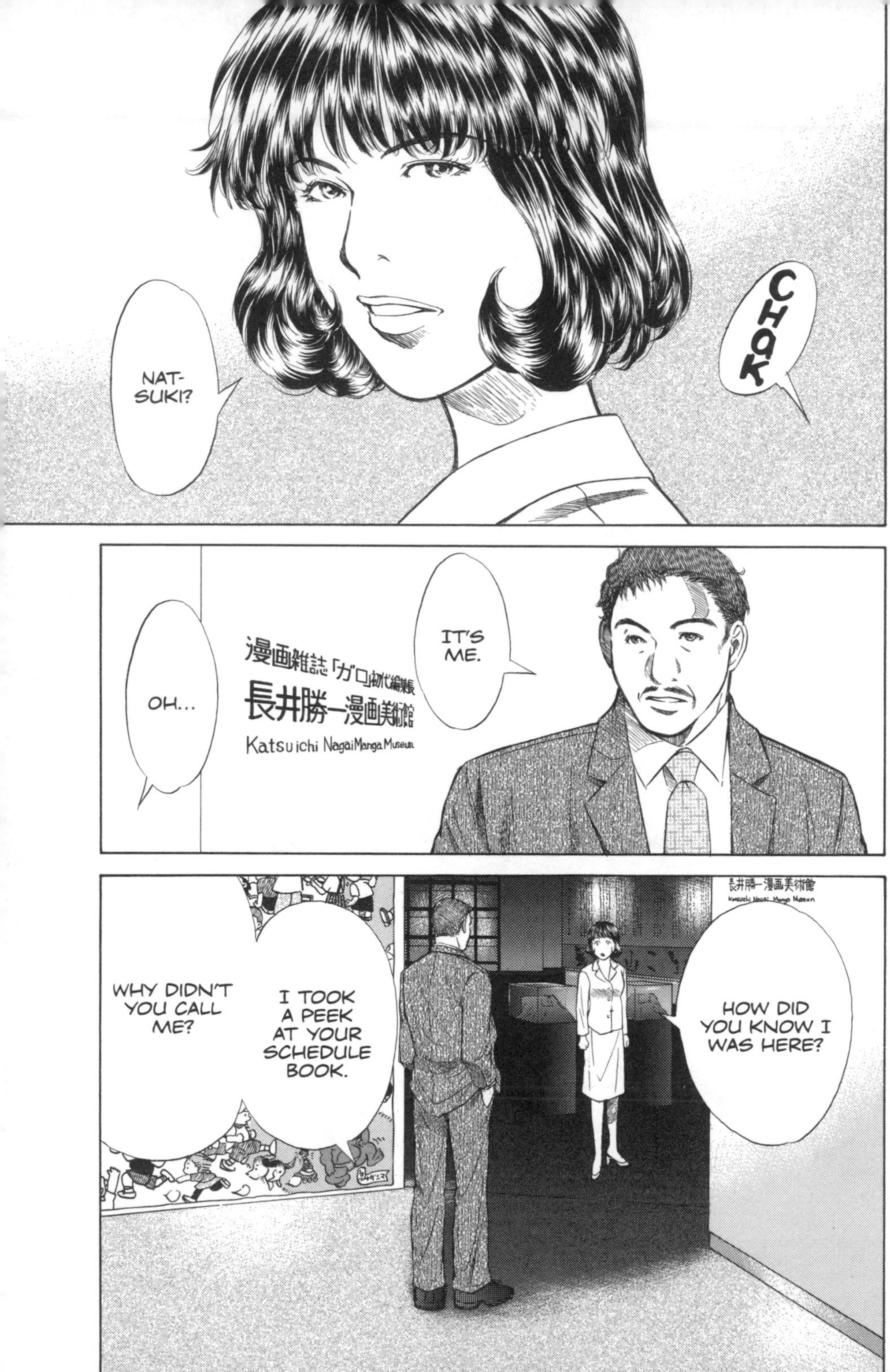
CHAK
NAT-SUKI?
IT'S ME.
漫画雑誌「ガロ」初代編集長
長井勝一漫画美術館
Katsuichi Nagai Manga Museum
OH...
長井勝一漫画美術館
HOW DID YOU KNOW I WAS HERE?
I TOOK A PEEK AT YOUR SCHEDULE BOOK.
WHY DIDN'T YOU CALL ME?

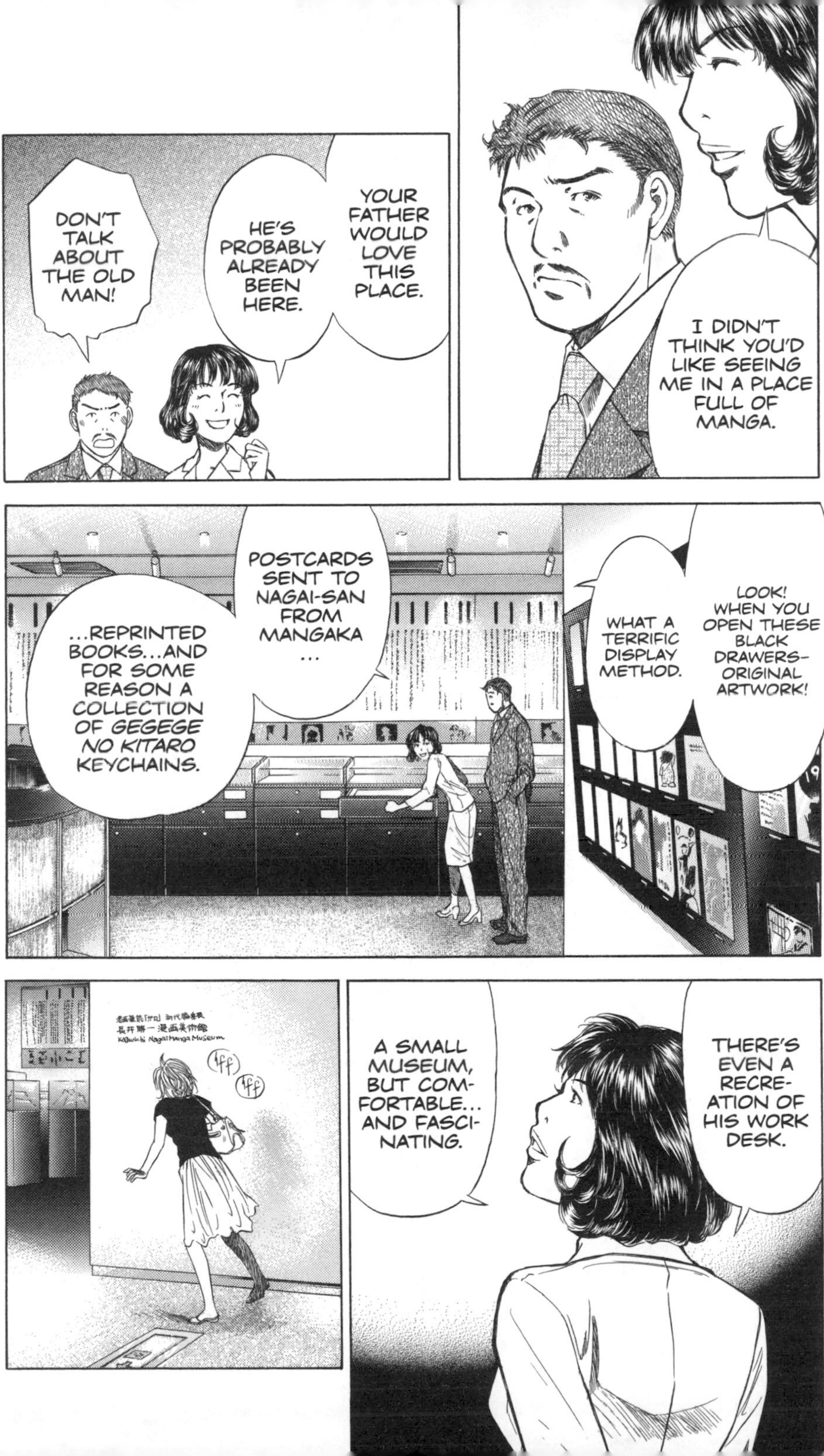
I DIDN'T THINK YOU'D LIKE SEEING ME IN A PLACE FULL OF MANGA.
YOUR FATHER WOULD LOVE THIS PLACE.
HE'S PROBABLY ALREADY BEEN HERE.
DON'T TALK ABOUT THE OLD MAN!
LOOK! WHEN YOU OPEN THESE BLACK DRAWERS- ORIGINAL ARTWORK!
WHAT A TERRIFIC DISPLAY METHOD.
POSTCARDS SENT TO NAGAI-SAN FROM MANGAKA ...
...REPRINTED BOOKS...AND FOR SOME REASON A COLLECTION OF GEGEGE NO KITARO KEYCHAINS.
THERE'S EVEN A RECREATION OF HIS WORK DESK.
A SMALL MUSEUM, BUT COMFORTABLE... AND FASCINATING.
漫画雑誌「ガロ」初代編集長
長井勝一漫画美術館
Katsuichi Nagai Manga Museum
fff
fff

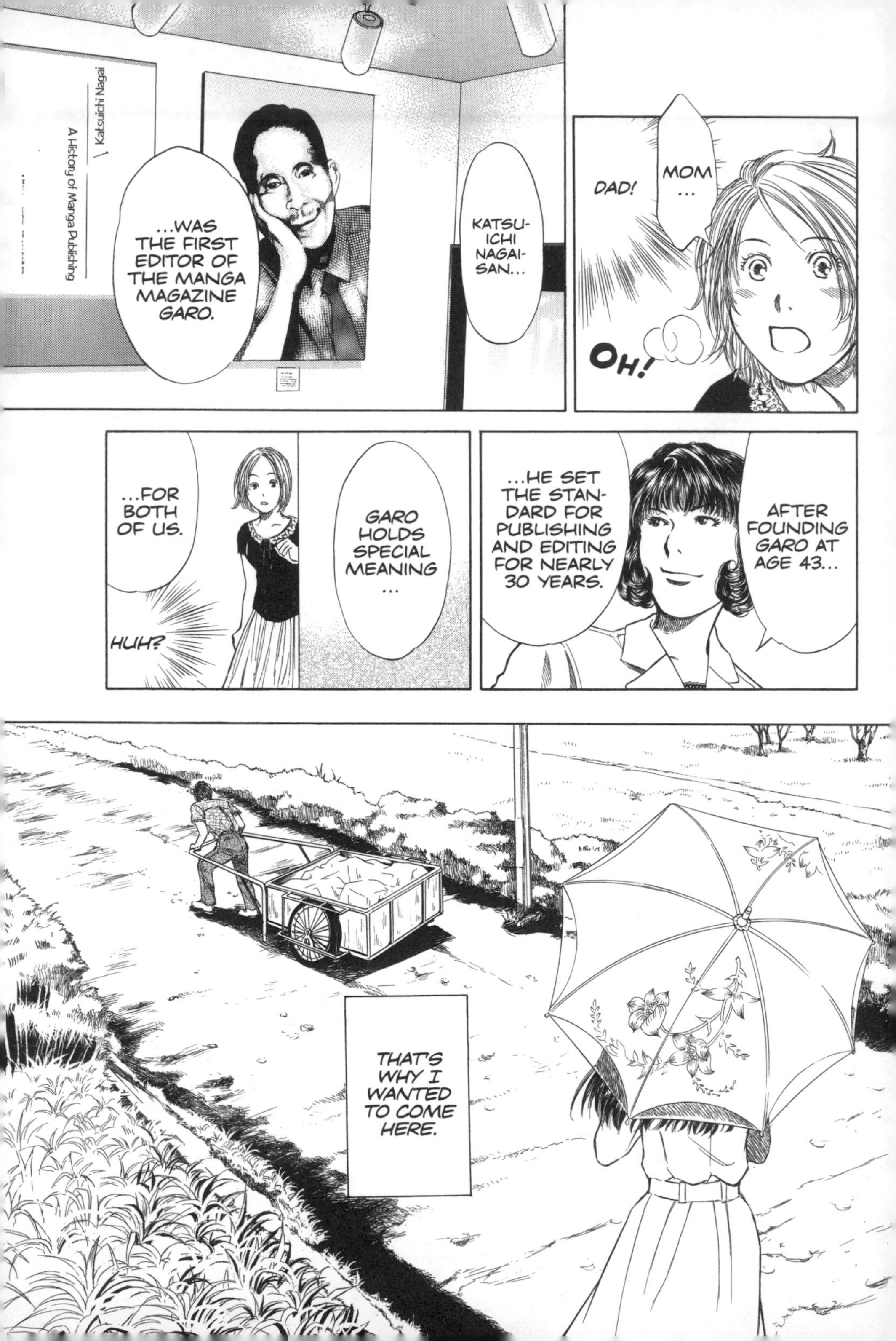
MOM ...
DAD!
OH!
KATSUICHI NAGAI-SAN...
Katsuichi Nagai
A History of Manga Publishing
...WAS THE FIRST EDITOR OF THE MANGA MAGAZINE GARO.
AFTER FOUNDING GARO AT AGE 43...
...HE SET THE STANDARD FOR PUBLISHING AND EDITING FOR NEARLY 30 YEARS.
GARO HOLDS SPECIAL MEANING ...
...FOR BOTH OF US.
HUH?
THAT'S WHY I WANTED TO COME HERE.

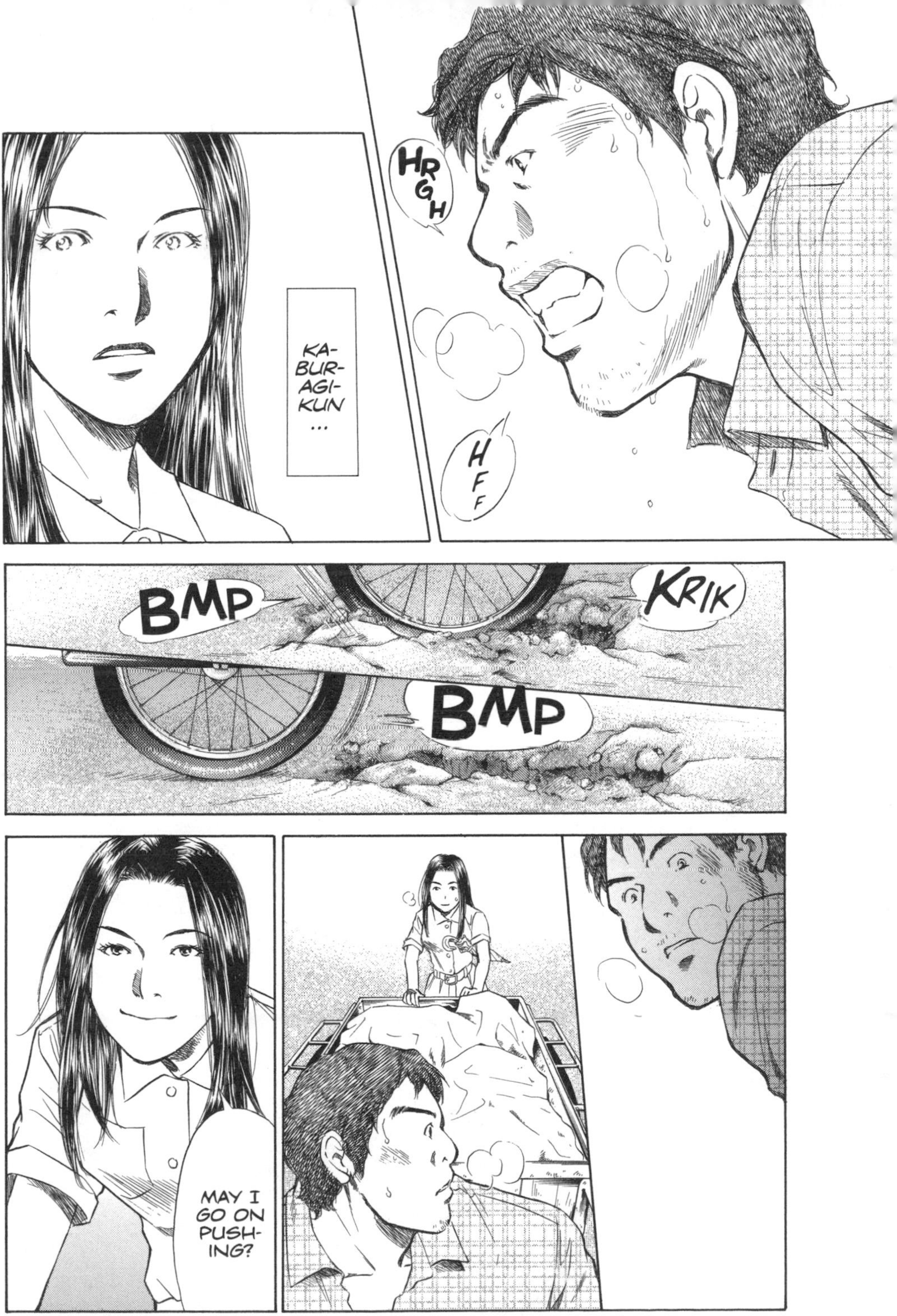
HRGH
HFF
KABURAGI-KUN...
KRIK
BMP
BMP
MAY I GO ON PUSHING?

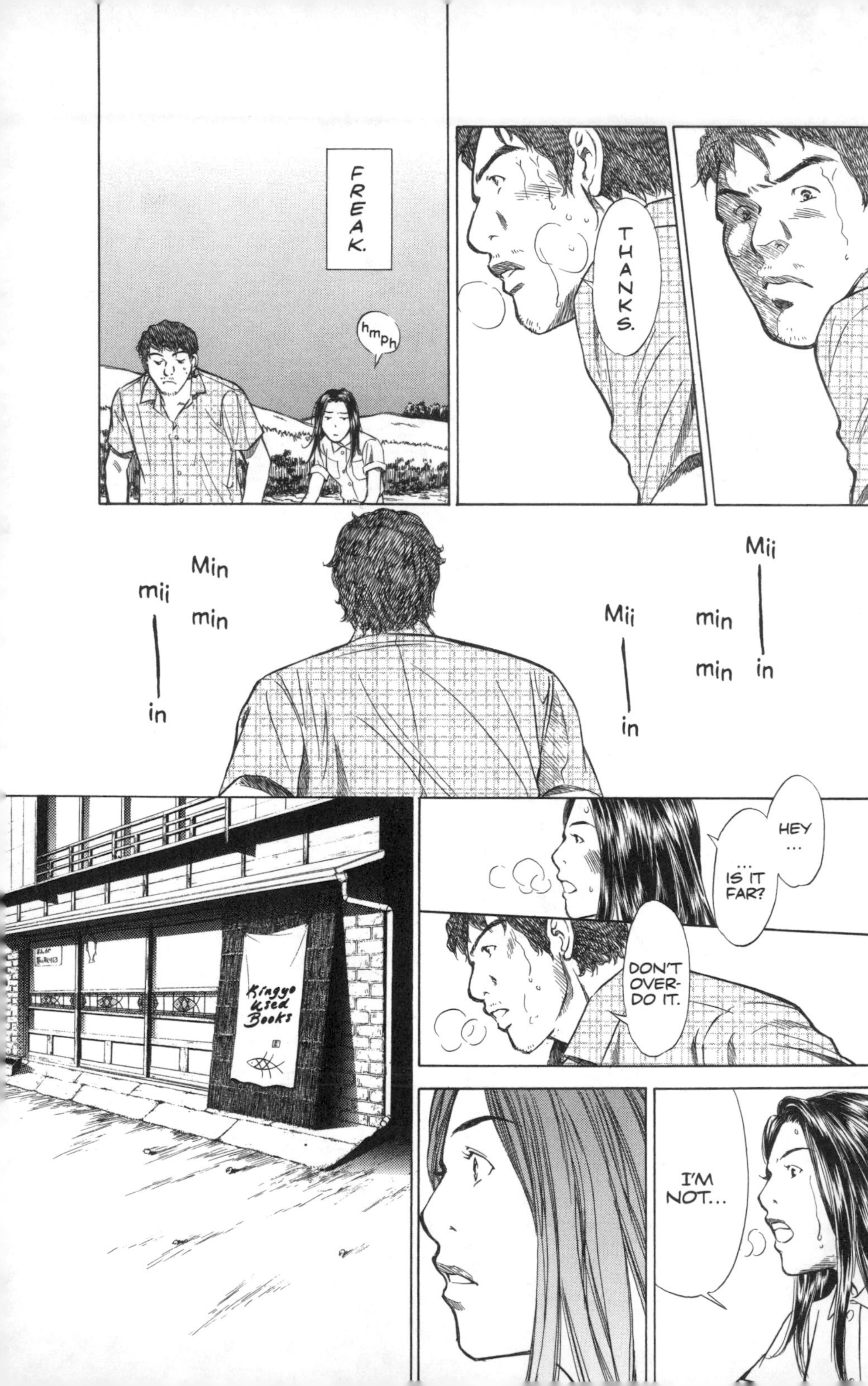
THANKS.
FREAK.
hmph
Mii— in
min
min
Mii— in
Min
min
mii— in
HEY...
...IS IT FAR?
DON'T OVER-DO IT.
I'M NOT...
Kingyo Used Books

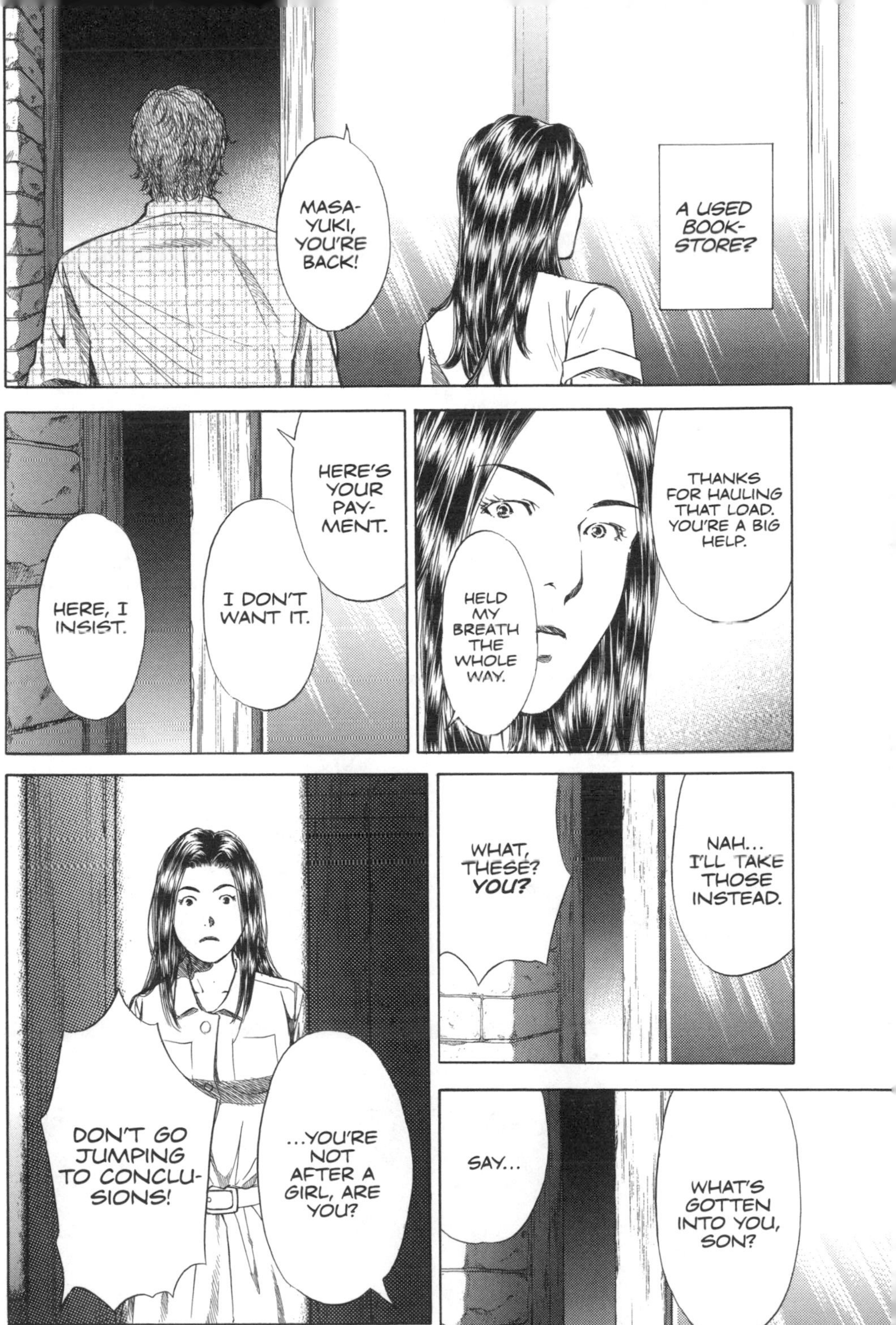
A USED BOOK-STORE?
MASA-YUKI, YOU'RE BACK!
THANKS FOR HAULING THAT LOAD. YOU'RE A BIG HELP.
HELD MY BREATH THE WHOLE WAY.
HERE'S YOUR PAY-MENT.
I DON'T WANT IT.
HERE, I INSIST.
NAH... I'LL TAKE THOSE INSTEAD.
WHAT, THESE? *YOU?*
WHAT'S GOTTEN INTO YOU, SON?
SAY...
...YOU'RE NOT AFTER A GIRL, ARE YOU?
DON'T GO JUMPING TO CONCLU-SIONS!

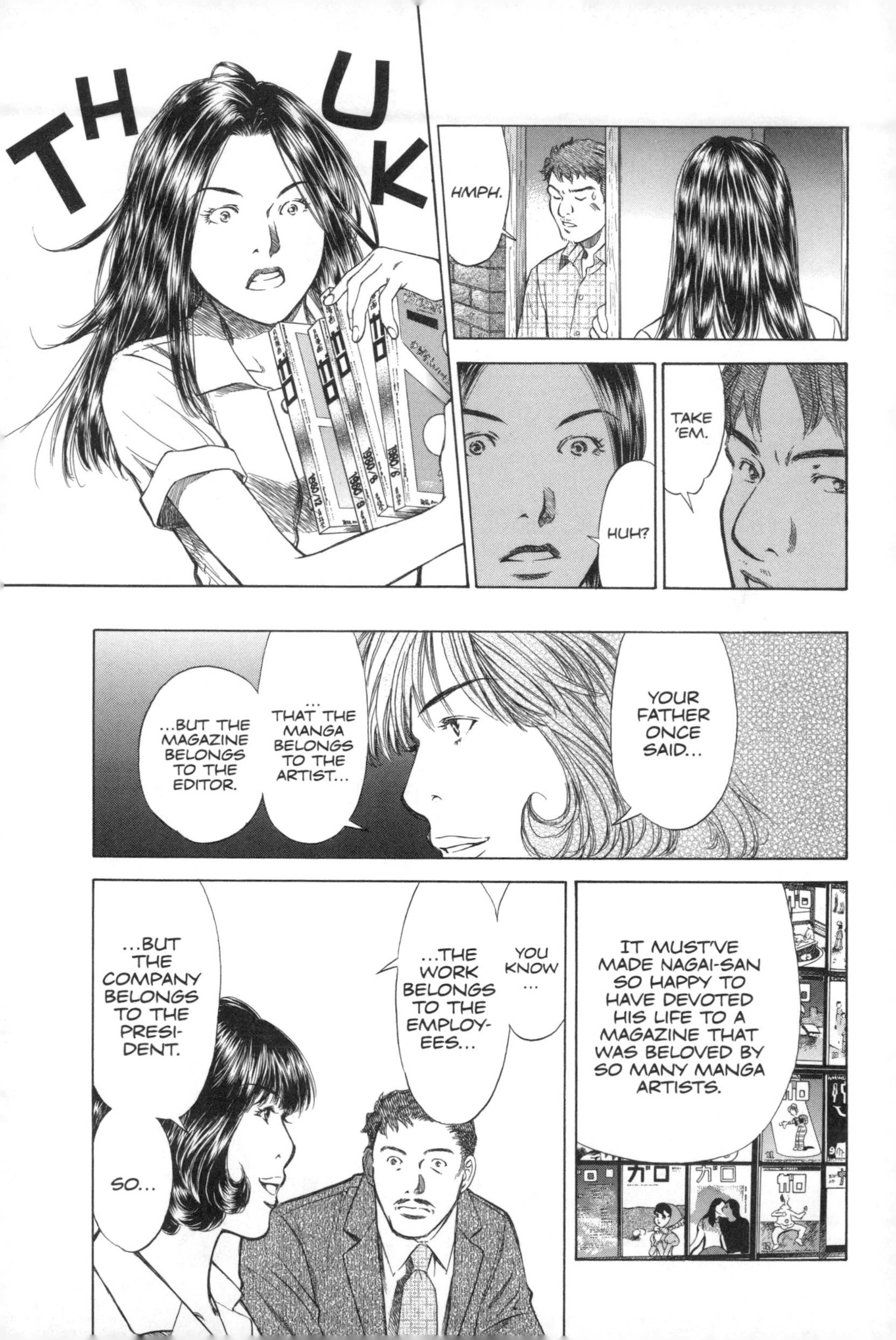
HMPH.
TAKE 'EM.
HUH?
THUK
YOUR FATHER ONCE SAID...
... THAT THE MANGA BELONGS TO THE ARTIST...
...BUT THE MAGAZINE BELONGS TO THE EDITOR.
IT MUST'VE MADE NAGAI-SAN SO HAPPY TO HAVE DEVOTED HIS LIFE TO A MAGAZINE THAT WAS BELOVED BY SO MANY MANGA ARTISTS.
YOU KNOW...
...THE WORK BELONGS TO THE EMPLOY-EES...
...BUT THE COMPANY BELONGS TO THE PRESI-DENT.
SO...

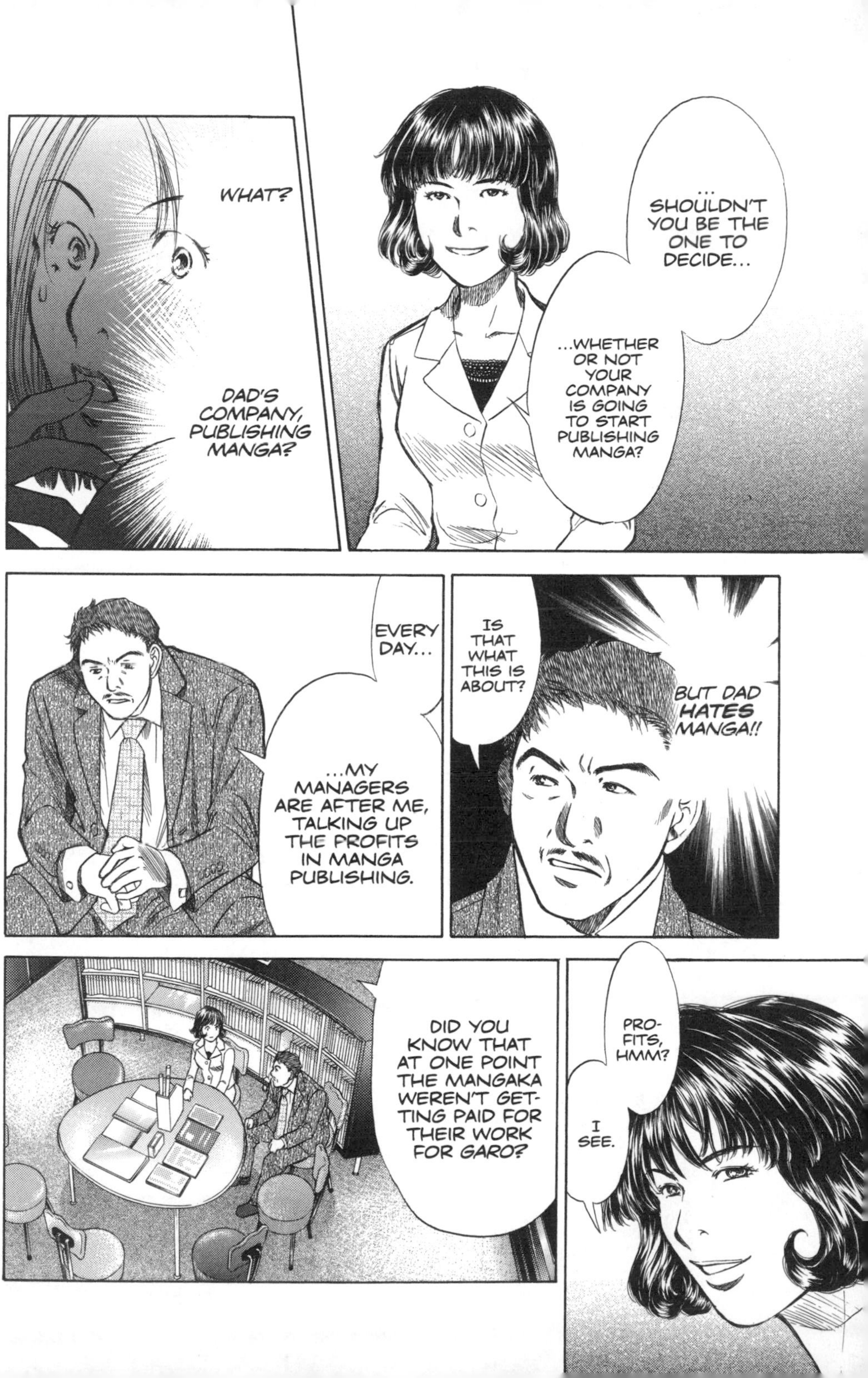
...SHOULDN'T YOU BE THE ONE TO DECIDE...
...WHETHER OR NOT YOUR COMPANY IS GOING TO START PUBLISHING MANGA?
WHAT?
DAD'S COMPANY, PUBLISHING MANGA?
IS THAT WHAT THIS IS ABOUT?
BUT DAD HATES MANGA!!
EVERY DAY...
...MY MANAGERS ARE AFTER ME, TALKING UP THE PROFITS IN MANGA PUBLISHING.
PRO-FITS, HMM?
I SEE.
DID YOU KNOW THAT AT ONE POINT THE MANGAKA WEREN'T GET-TING PAID FOR THEIR WORK FOR GARO?

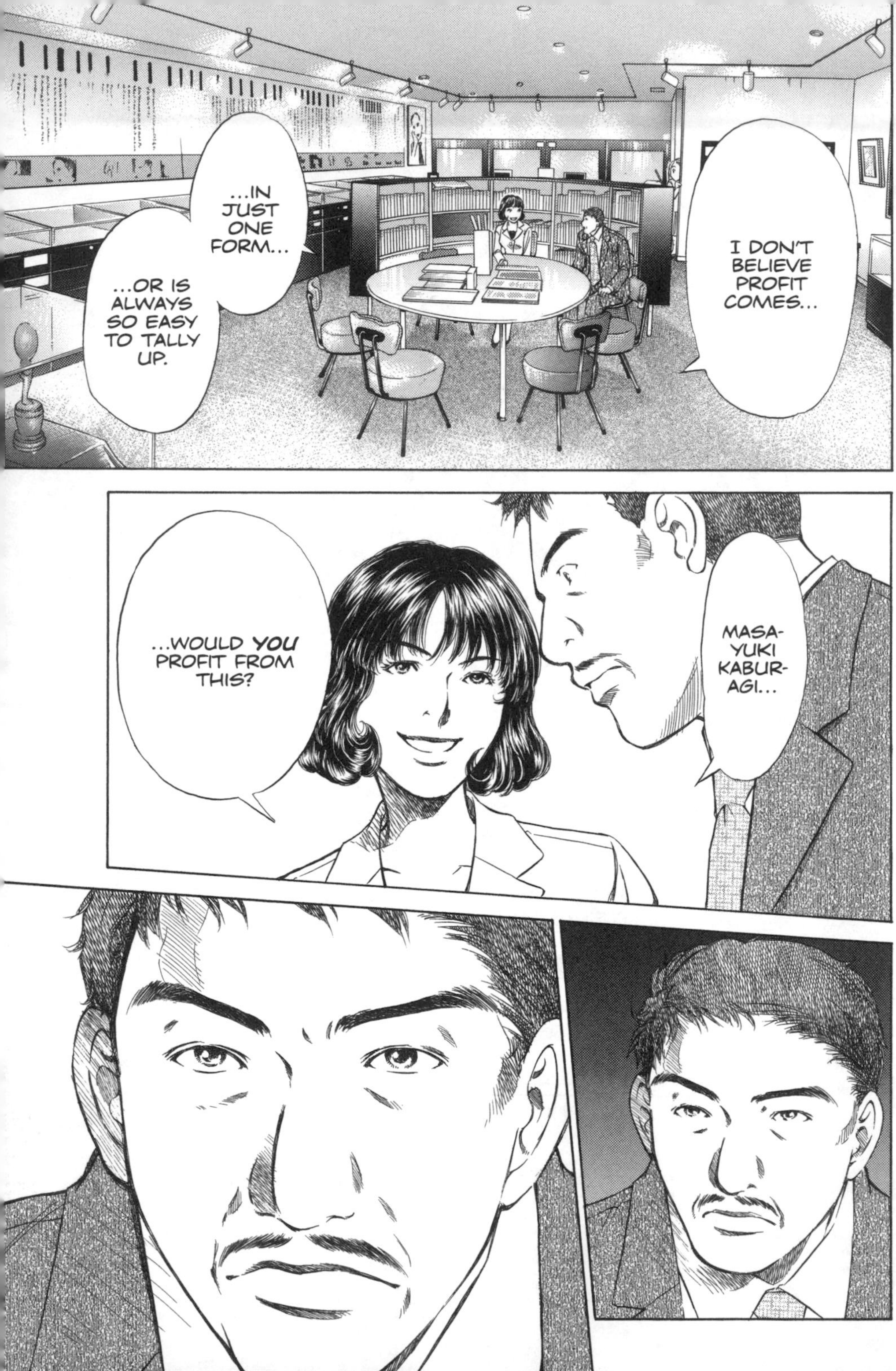
I DON'T BELIEVE PROFIT COMES...
...IN JUST ONE FORM...
...OR IS ALWAYS SO EASY TO TALLY UP.
MASA-YUKI KABUR-AGI...
...WOULD YOU PROFIT FROM THIS?

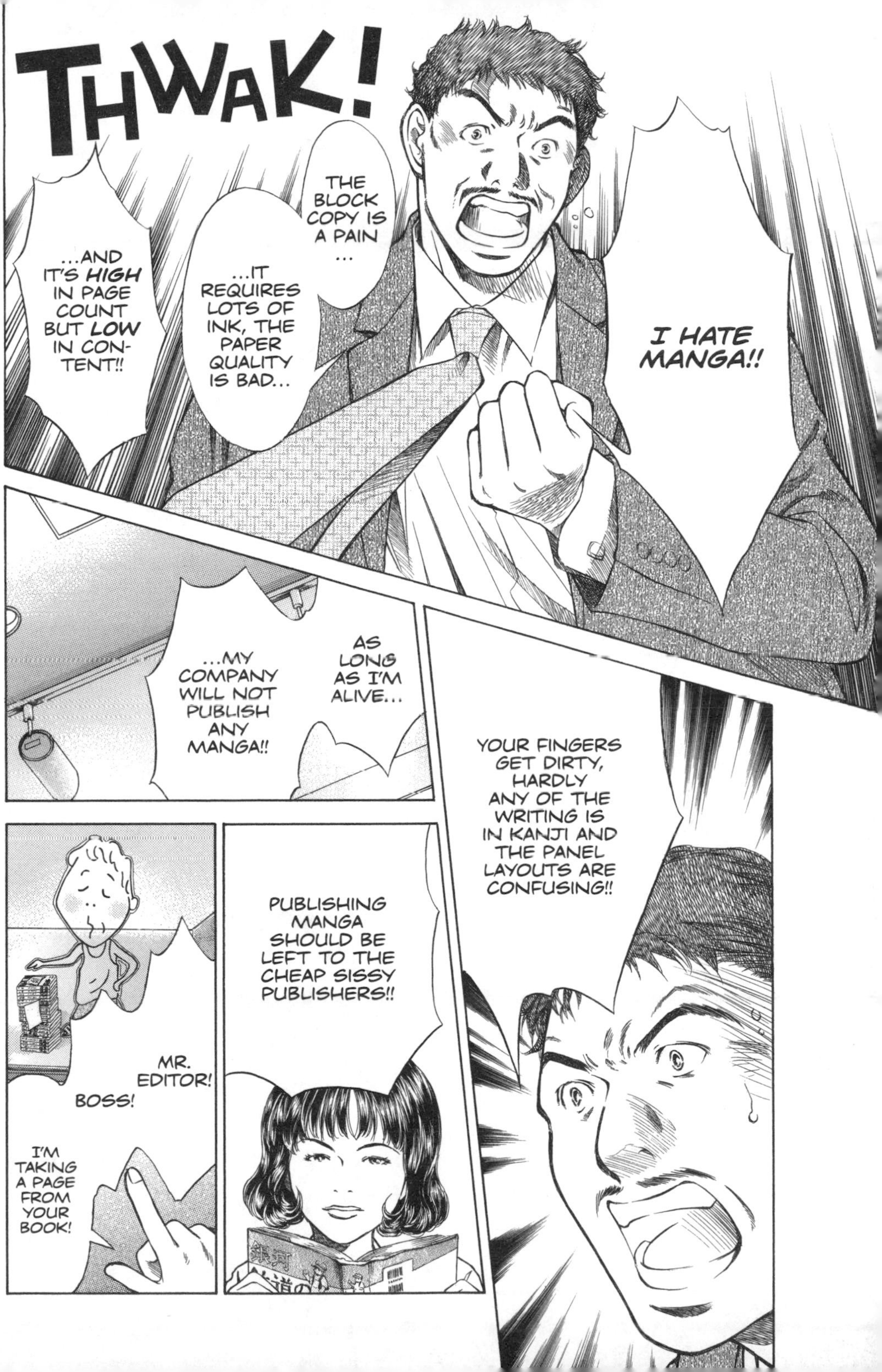
THWAK!
I HATE MANGA!!
THE BLOCK COPY IS A PAIN ...
...IT REQUIRES LOTS OF INK, THE PAPER QUALITY IS BAD...
...AND IT'S **HIGH** IN PAGE COUNT BUT **LOW** IN CONTENT!!
YOUR FINGERS GET DIRTY, HARDLY ANY OF THE WRITING IS IN KANJI AND THE PANEL LAYOUTS ARE CONFUSING!!
AS LONG AS I'M ALIVE...
...MY COMPANY WILL NOT PUBLISH ANY MANGA!!
PUBLISHING MANGA SHOULD BE LEFT TO THE CHEAP SISSY PUBLISHERS!!
MR. EDITOR!
BOSS!
I'M TAKING A PAGE FROM YOUR BOOK!

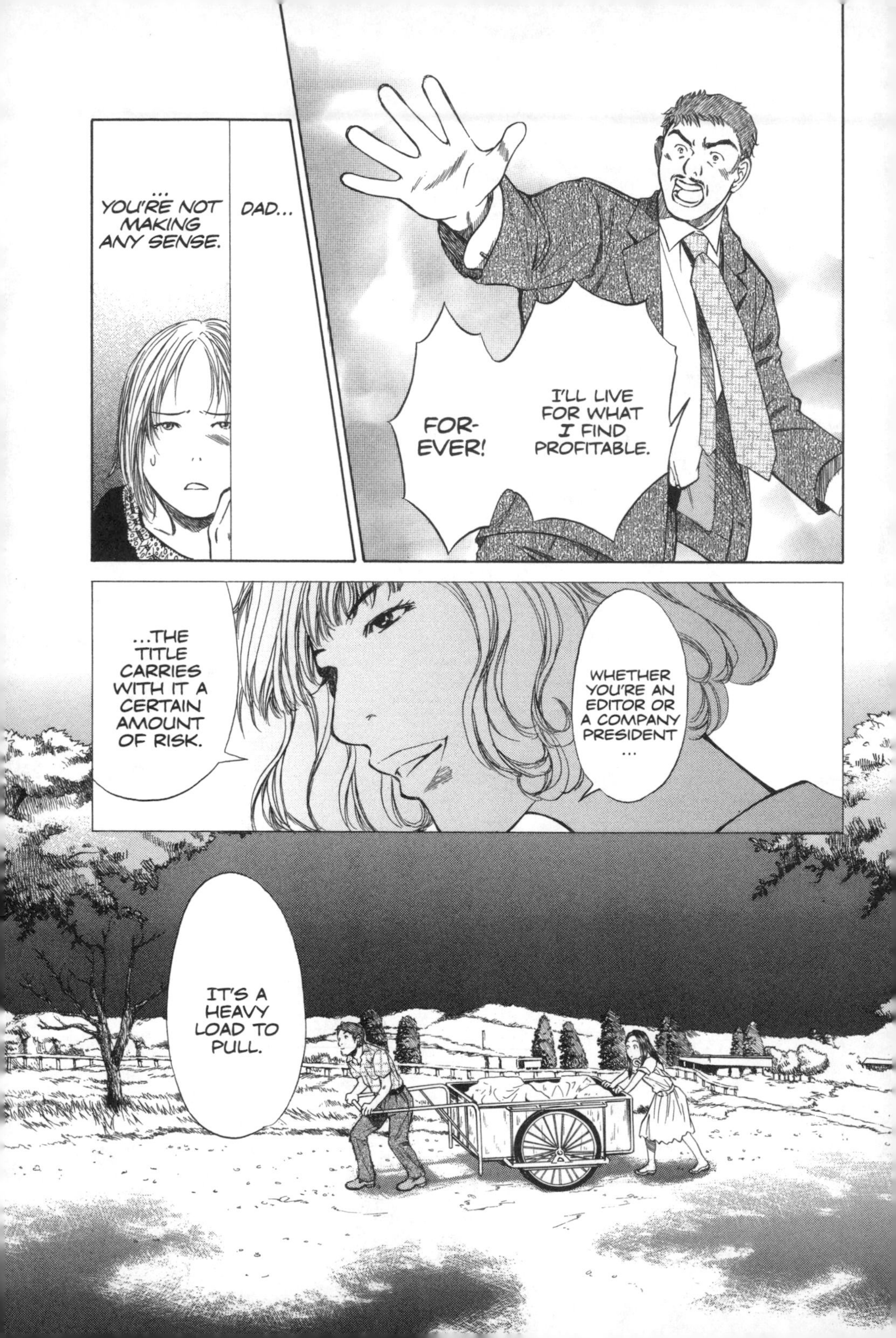
I'LL LIVE FOR WHAT I FIND PROFITABLE.
FOR-EVER!
DAD...
... YOU'RE NOT MAKING ANY SENSE.
WHETHER YOU'RE AN EDITOR OR A COMPANY PRESIDENT ...
...THE TITLE CARRIES WITH IT A CERTAIN AMOUNT OF RISK.
IT'S A HEAVY LOAD TO PULL.

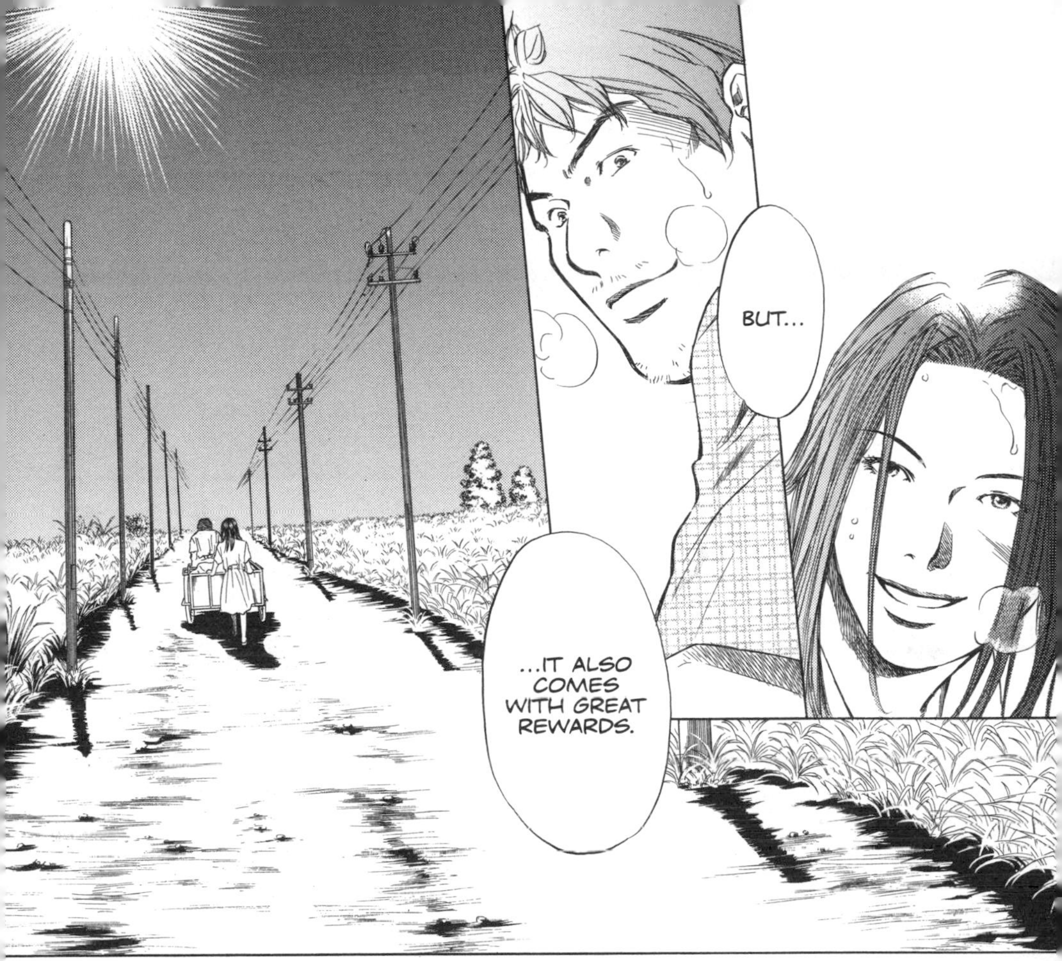
BUT...
...IT ALSO COMES WITH GREAT REWARDS.

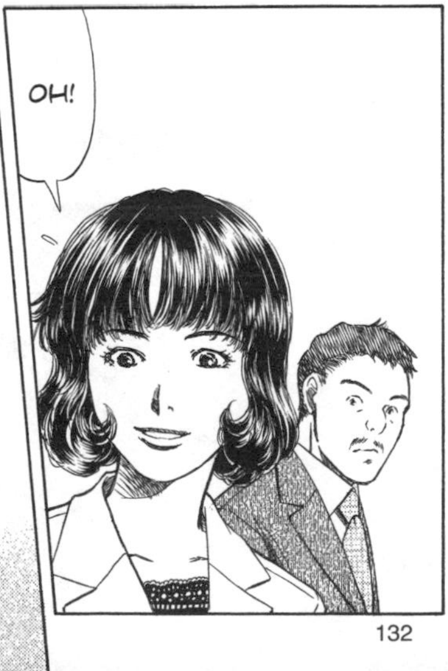
OH!

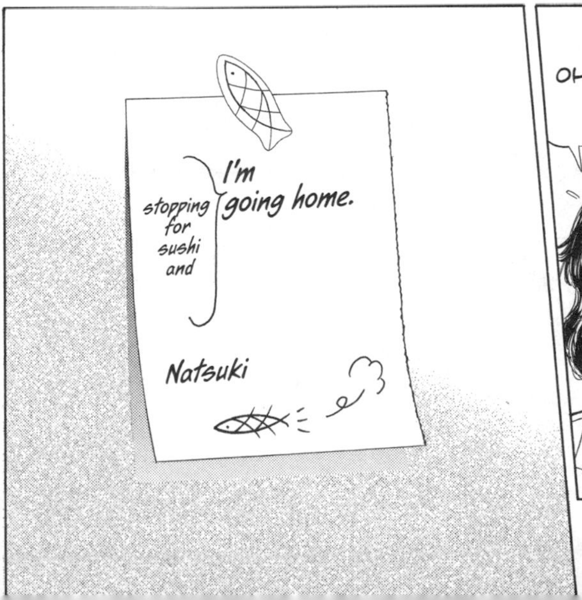
I'm going home.
stopping for sushi and
Natsuki

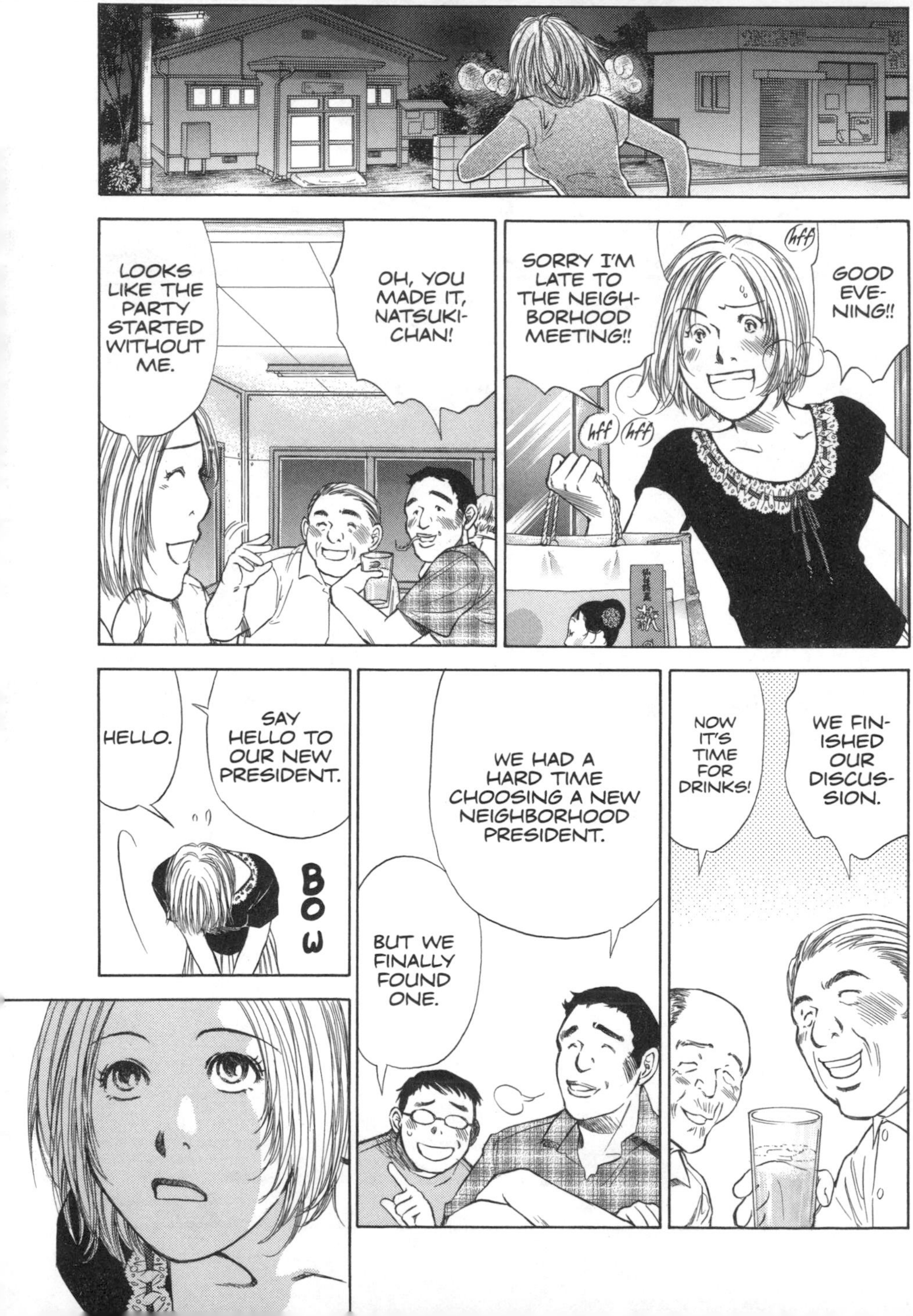
GOOD EVENING!!
hff
SORRY I'M LATE TO THE NEIGHBORHOOD MEETING!!
hff hff
OH, YOU MADE IT, NATSUKI-CHAN!
LOOKS LIKE THE PARTY STARTED WITHOUT ME.
WE FINISHED OUR DISCUSSION.
NOW IT'S TIME FOR DRINKS!
WE HAD A HARD TIME CHOOSING A NEW NEIGHBORHOOD PRESIDENT.
BUT WE FINALLY FOUND ONE.
SAY HELLO TO OUR NEW PRESIDENT.
HELLO.
BOW

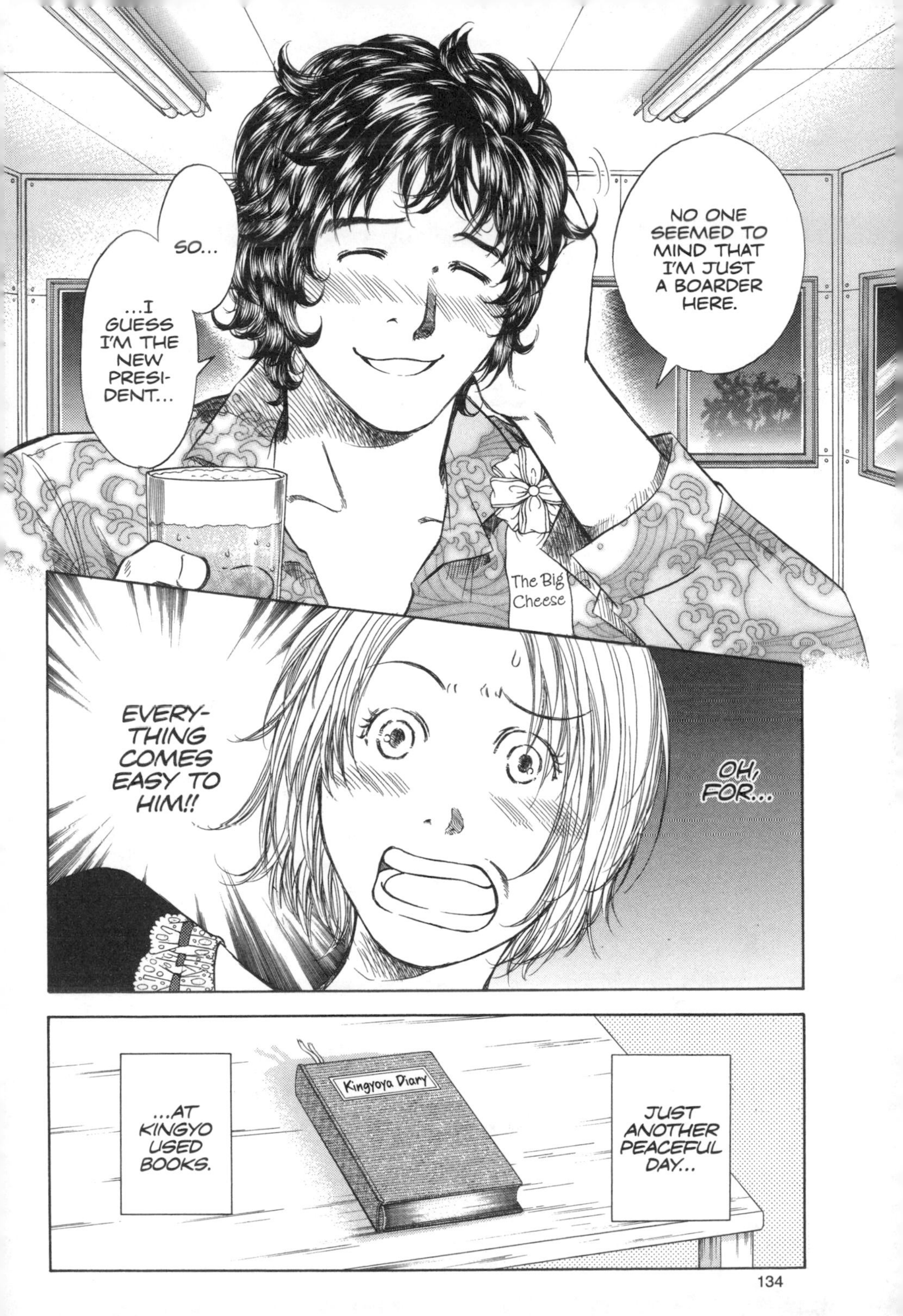
NO ONE SEEMED TO MIND THAT I'M JUST A BOARDER HERE.
SO...
...I GUESS I'M THE NEW PRESI-DENT...
The Big Cheese
OH, FOR...
EVERY-THING COMES EASY TO HIM!!
JUST ANOTHER PEACEFUL DAY...
Kingyoya Diary
...AT KINGYO USED BOOKS.

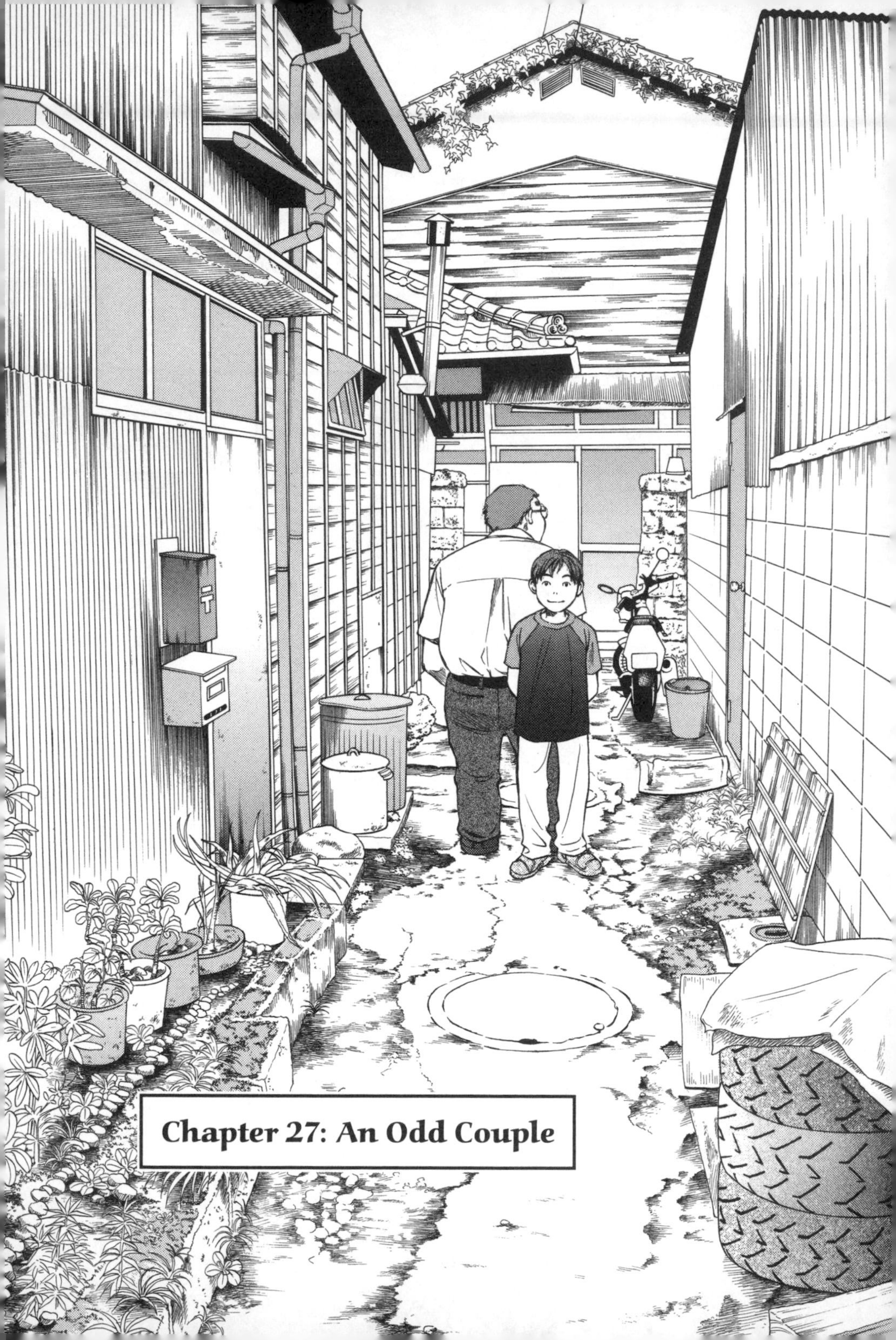
Chapter 27: An Odd Couple

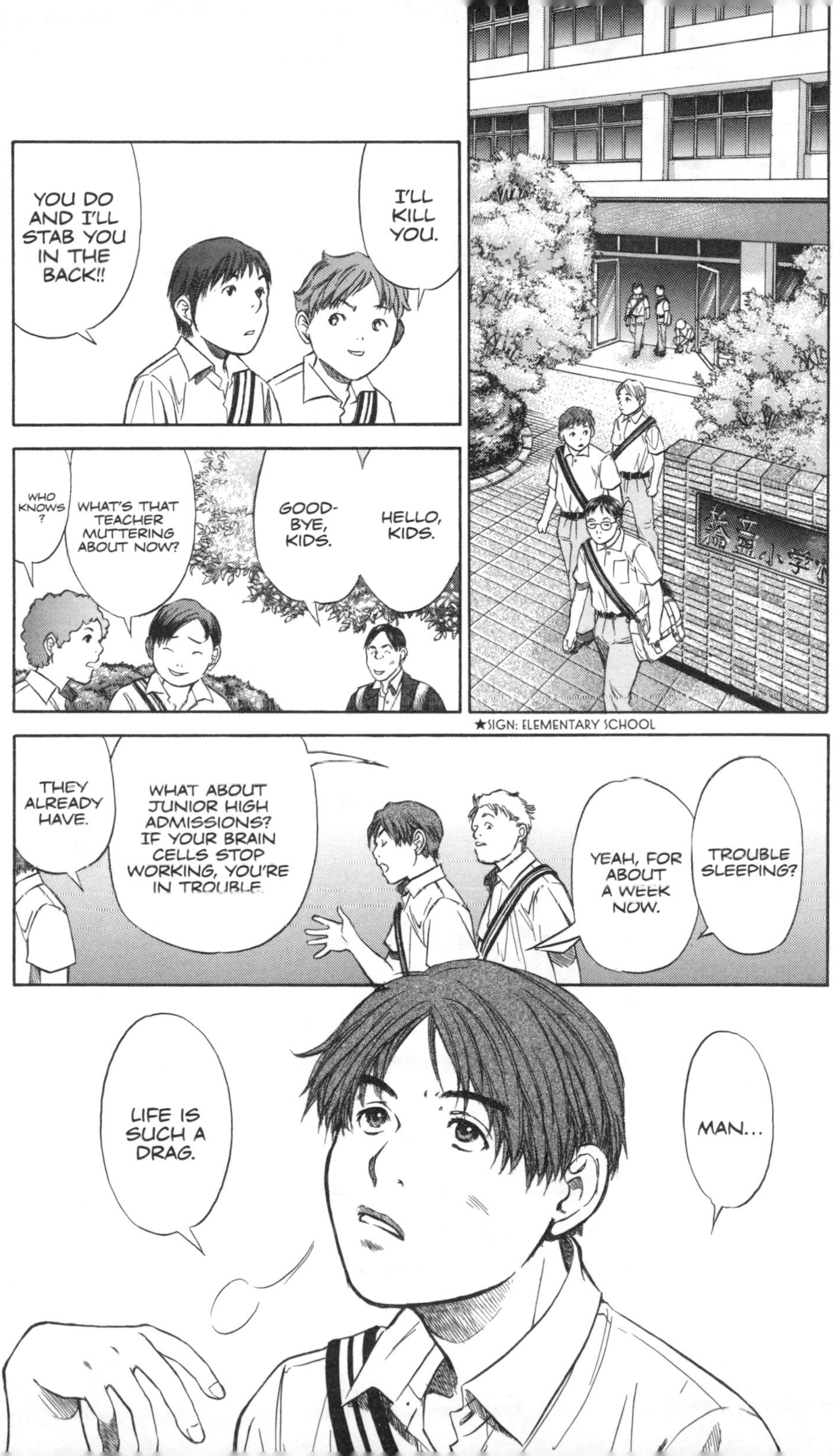
★SIGN: ELEMENTARY SCHOOL
I'LL KILL YOU.
YOU DO AND I'LL STAB YOU IN THE BACK!!
HELLO, KIDS.
GOOD-BYE, KIDS.
WHAT'S THAT TEACHER MUTTERING ABOUT NOW?
WHO KNOWS?
TROUBLE SLEEPING?
YEAH, FOR ABOUT A WEEK NOW.
WHAT ABOUT JUNIOR HIGH ADMISSIONS? IF YOUR BRAIN CELLS STOP WORKING, YOU'RE IN TROUBLE.
THEY ALREADY HAVE.
MAN...
LIFE IS SUCH A DRAG.

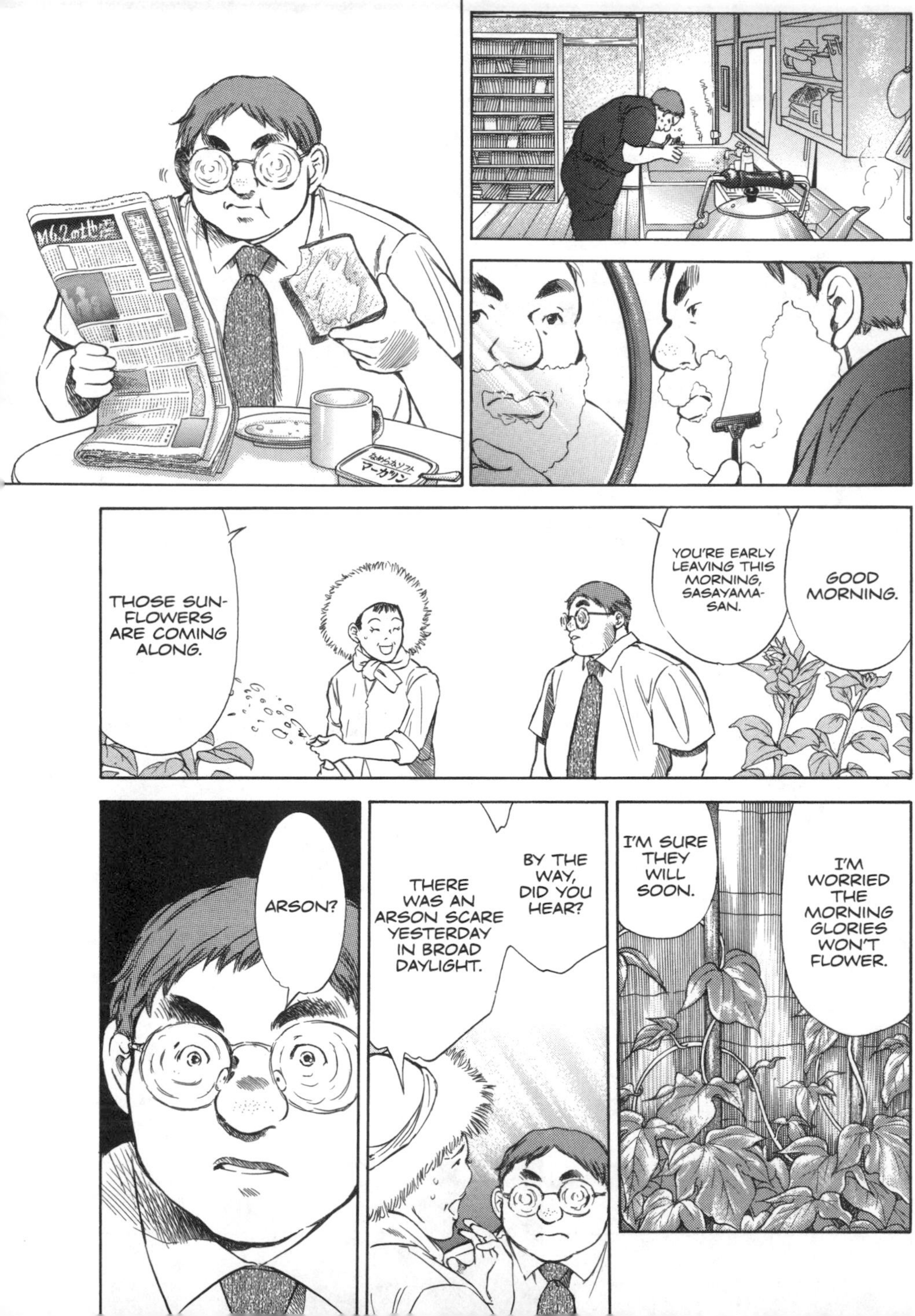
GOOD MORNING.
YOU'RE EARLY LEAVING THIS MORNING, SASAYAMA-SAN.
THOSE SUN-FLOWERS ARE COMING ALONG.
I'M WORRIED THE MORNING GLORIES WON'T FLOWER.
I'M SURE THEY WILL SOON.
BY THE WAY, DID YOU HEAR?
THERE WAS AN ARSON SCARE YESTERDAY IN BROAD DAYLIGHT.
ARSON?

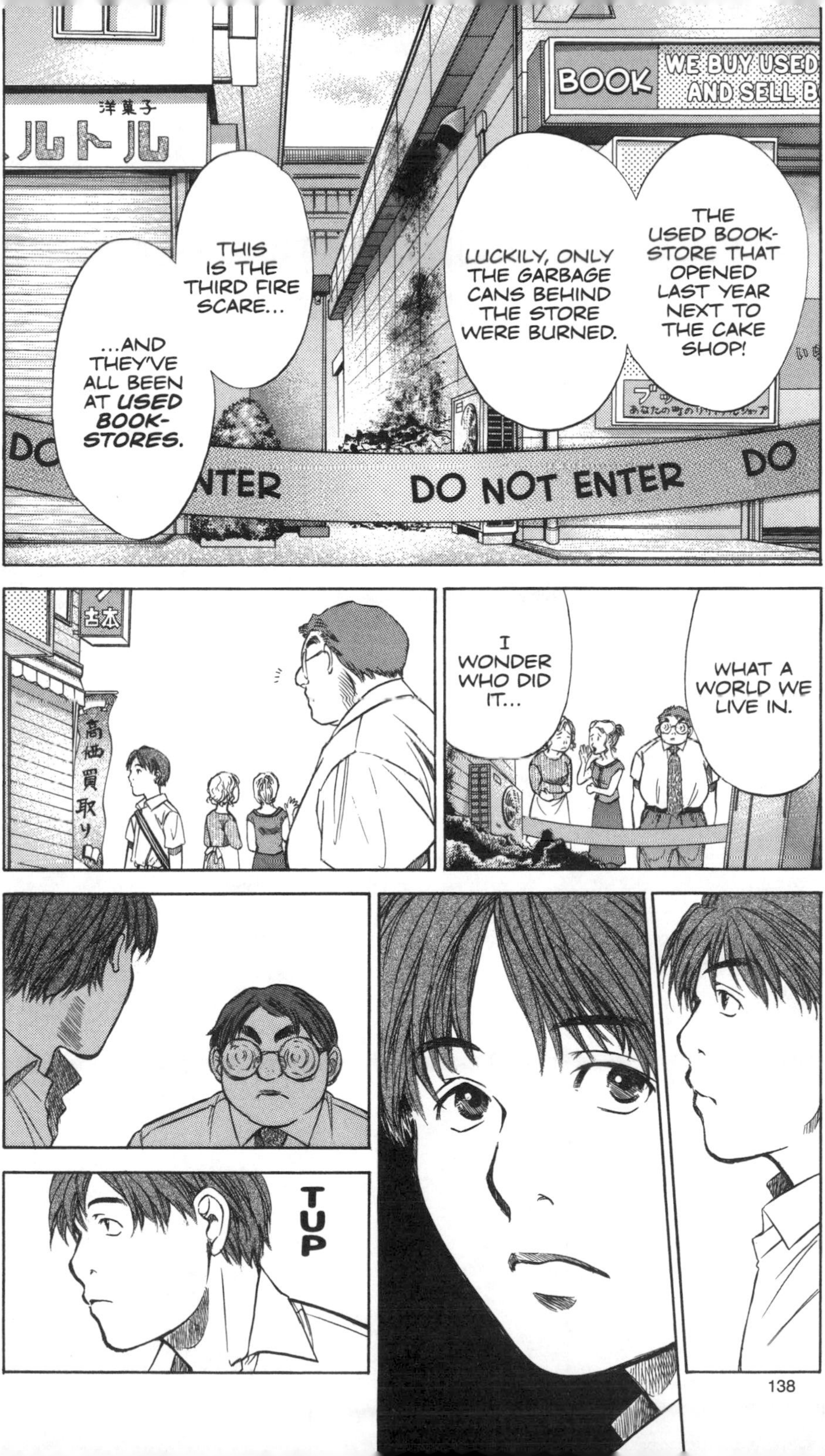

BOOK
WE BUY USED AND SELL B
洋菓子
THE USED BOOK-STORE THAT OPENED LAST YEAR NEXT TO THE CAKE SHOP!
LUCKILY, ONLY THE GARBAGE CANS BEHIND THE STORE WERE BURNED.
THIS IS THE THIRD FIRE SCARE...
...AND THEY'VE ALL BEEN AT ***USED BOOK-STORES.***
DO NOT ENTER
WHAT A WORLD WE LIVE IN.
I WONDER WHO DID IT...
古本
高価買取り
TUP

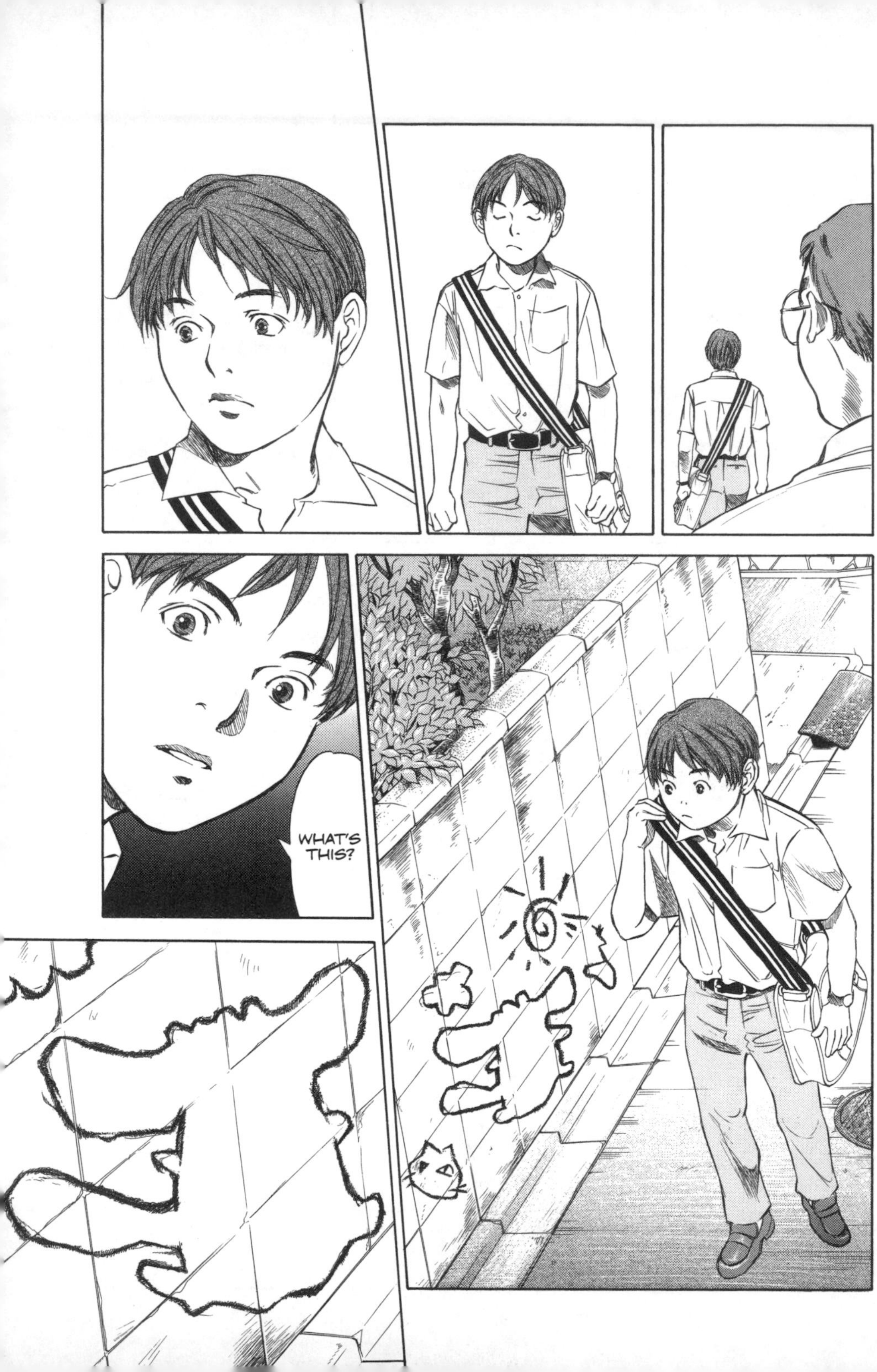
WHAT'S THIS?

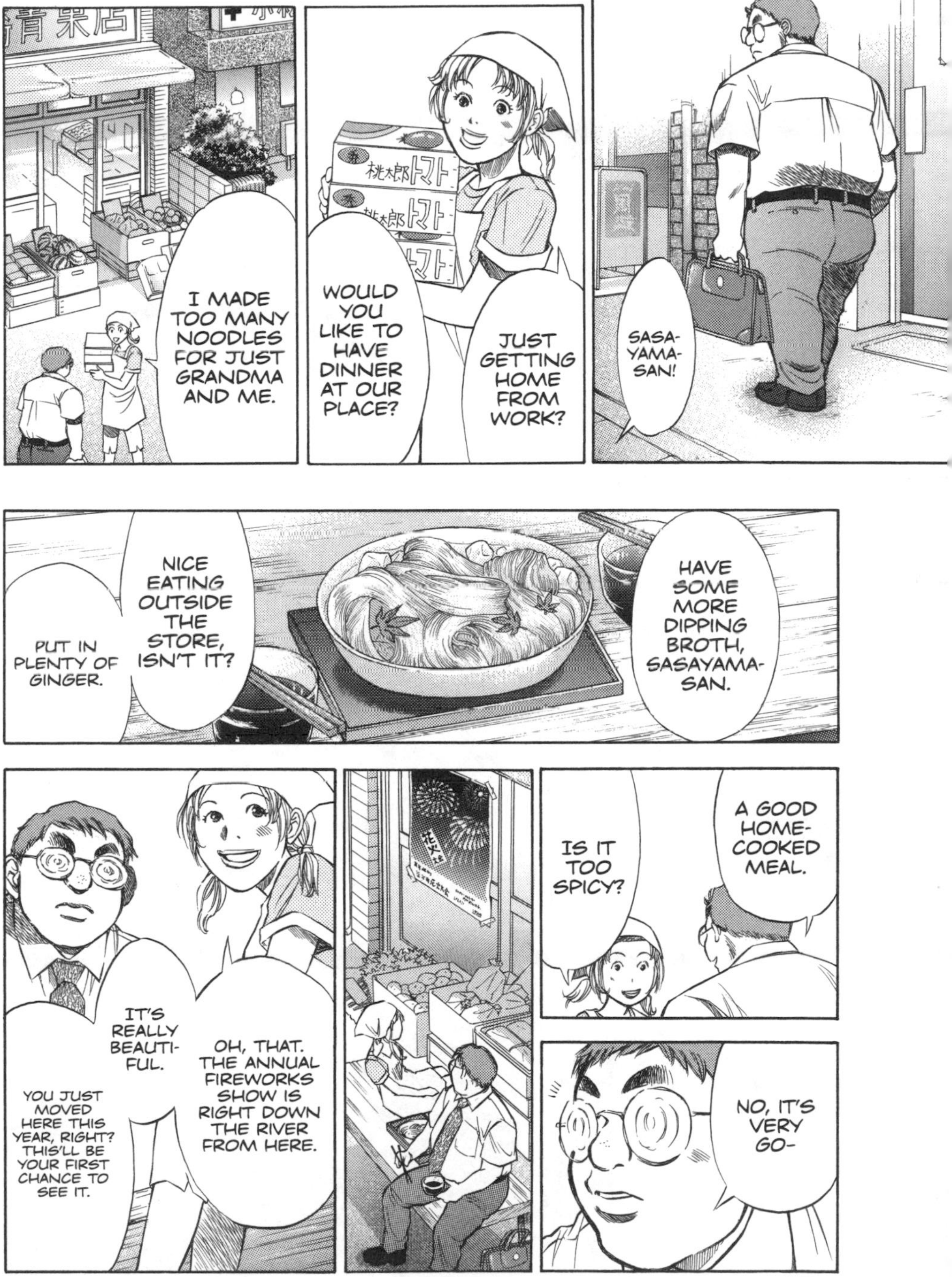
SASA-YAMA-SAN!
JUST GETTING HOME FROM WORK?
WOULD YOU LIKE TO HAVE DINNER AT OUR PLACE?
I MADE TOO MANY NOODLES FOR JUST GRANDMA AND ME.
HAVE SOME MORE DIPPING BROTH, SASAYAMA-SAN.
NICE EATING OUTSIDE THE STORE, ISN'T IT?
PUT IN PLENTY OF GINGER.
A GOOD HOME-COOKED MEAL.
IS IT TOO SPICY?
NO, IT'S VERY GO-
OH, THAT. THE ANNUAL FIREWORKS SHOW IS RIGHT DOWN THE RIVER FROM HERE.
IT'S REALLY BEAUTI-FUL.
YOU JUST MOVED HERE THIS YEAR, RIGHT? THIS'LL BE YOUR FIRST CHANCE TO SEE IT.

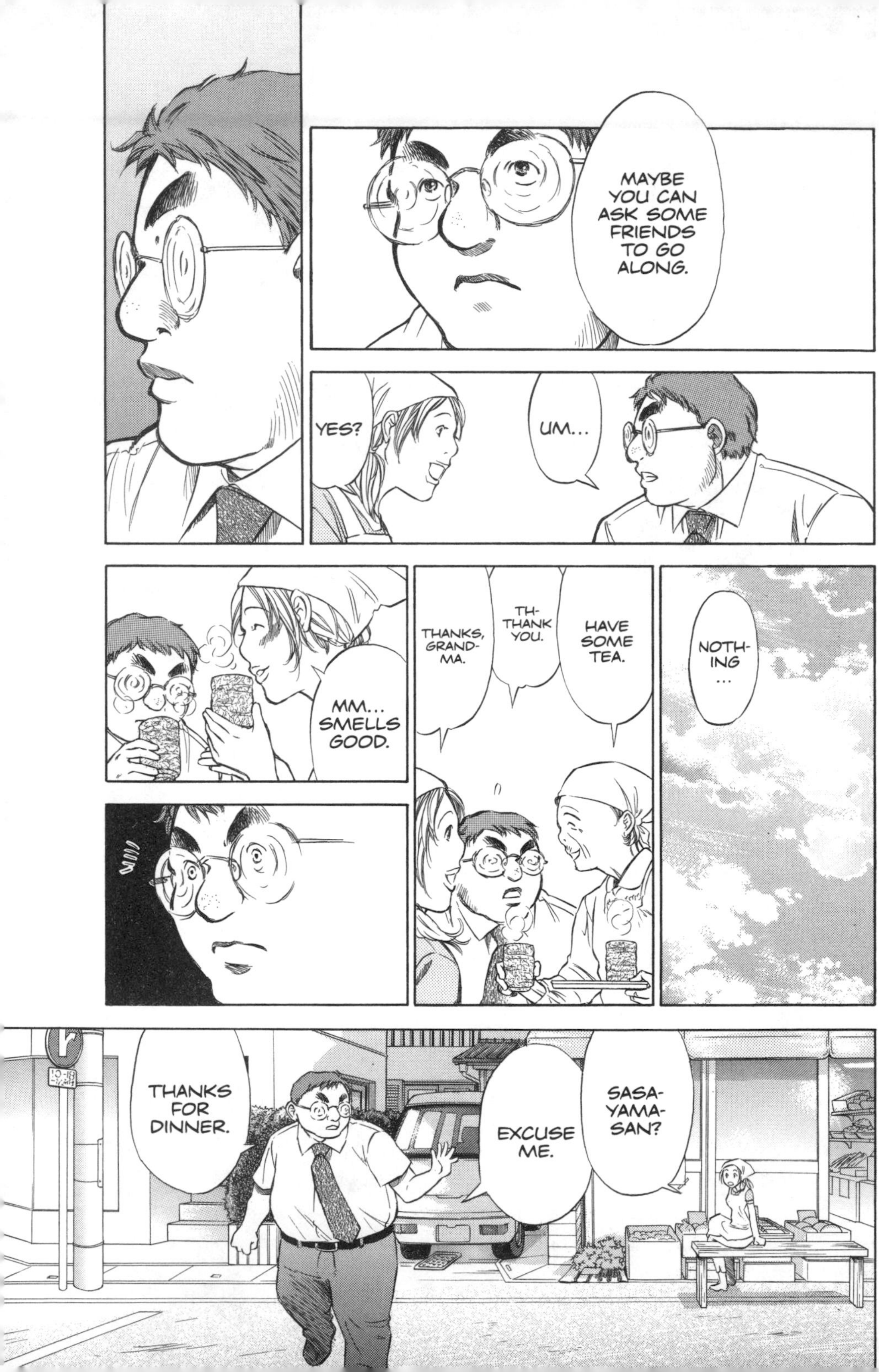
MAYBE YOU CAN ASK SOME FRIENDS TO GO ALONG.
UM...
YES?
NOTH-ING ...
HAVE SOME TEA.
TH-THANK YOU.
THANKS, GRAND-MA.
MM... SMELLS GOOD.
SASA-YAMA-SAN?
EXCUSE ME.
THANKS FOR DINNER.

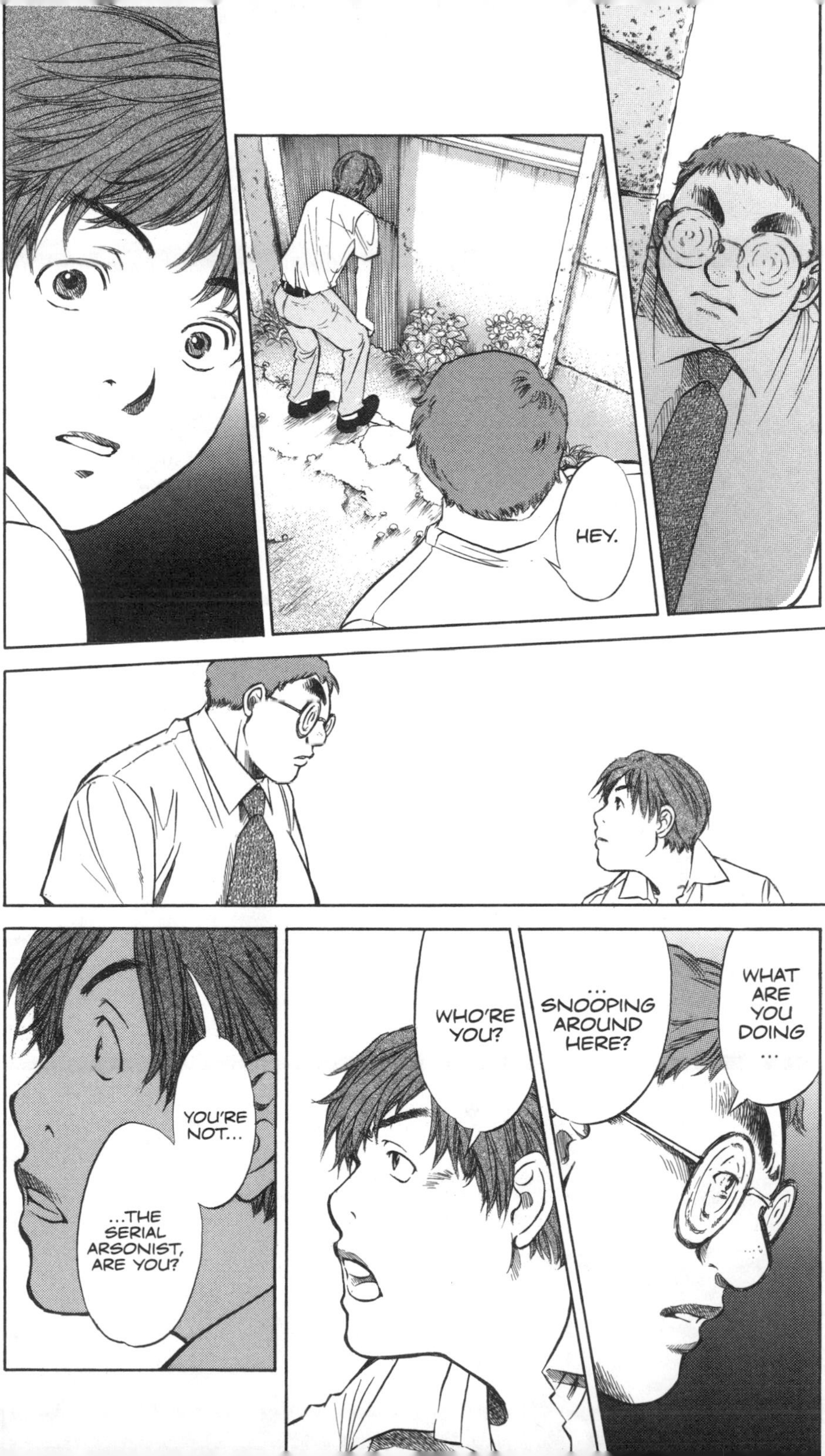
HEY.
WHAT ARE YOU DOING ...
... SNOOPING AROUND HERE?
WHO'RE YOU?
YOU'RE NOT...
...THE SERIAL ARSONIST, ARE YOU?

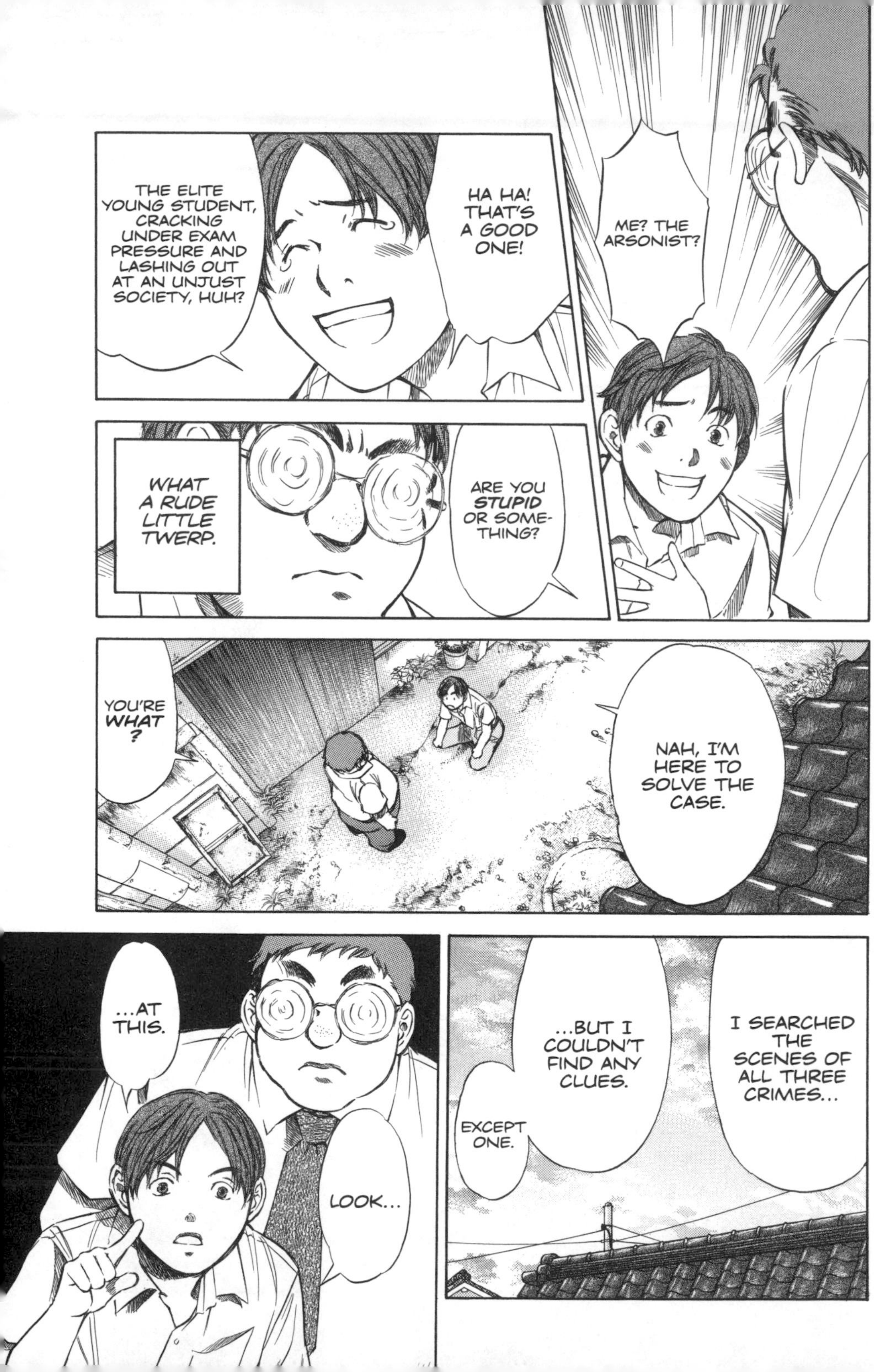
ME? THE ARSONIST?
HA HA! THAT'S A GOOD ONE!
THE ELITE YOUNG STUDENT, CRACKING UNDER EXAM PRESSURE AND LASHING OUT AT AN UNJUST SOCIETY, HUH?
ARE YOU STUPID OR SOME-THING?
WHAT A RUDE LITTLE TWERP.
NAH, I'M HERE TO SOLVE THE CASE.
YOU'RE WHAT?
I SEARCHED THE SCENES OF ALL THREE CRIMES...
...BUT I COULDN'T FIND ANY CLUES.
EXCEPT ONE.
LOOK...
...AT THIS.

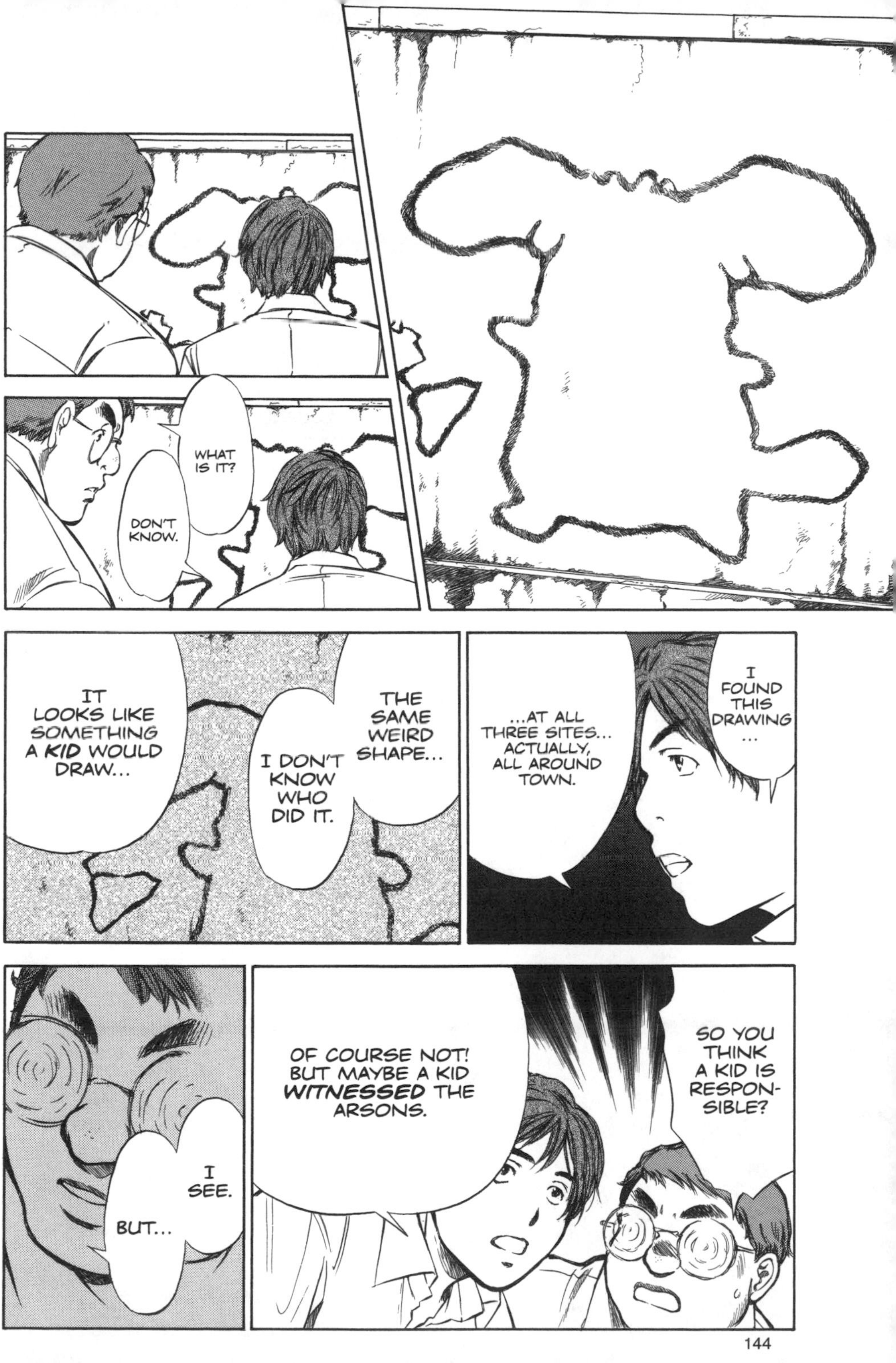

WHAT IS IT?
DON'T KNOW.
I FOUND THIS DRAWING...
...AT ALL THREE SITES... ACTUALLY, ALL AROUND TOWN.
THE SAME WEIRD SHAPE...
I DON'T KNOW WHO DID IT.
IT LOOKS LIKE SOMETHING A *KID* WOULD DRAW...
SO YOU THINK A KID IS RESPONSIBLE?
OF COURSE NOT! BUT MAYBE A KID *WITNESSED* THE ARSONS.
I SEE.
BUT...

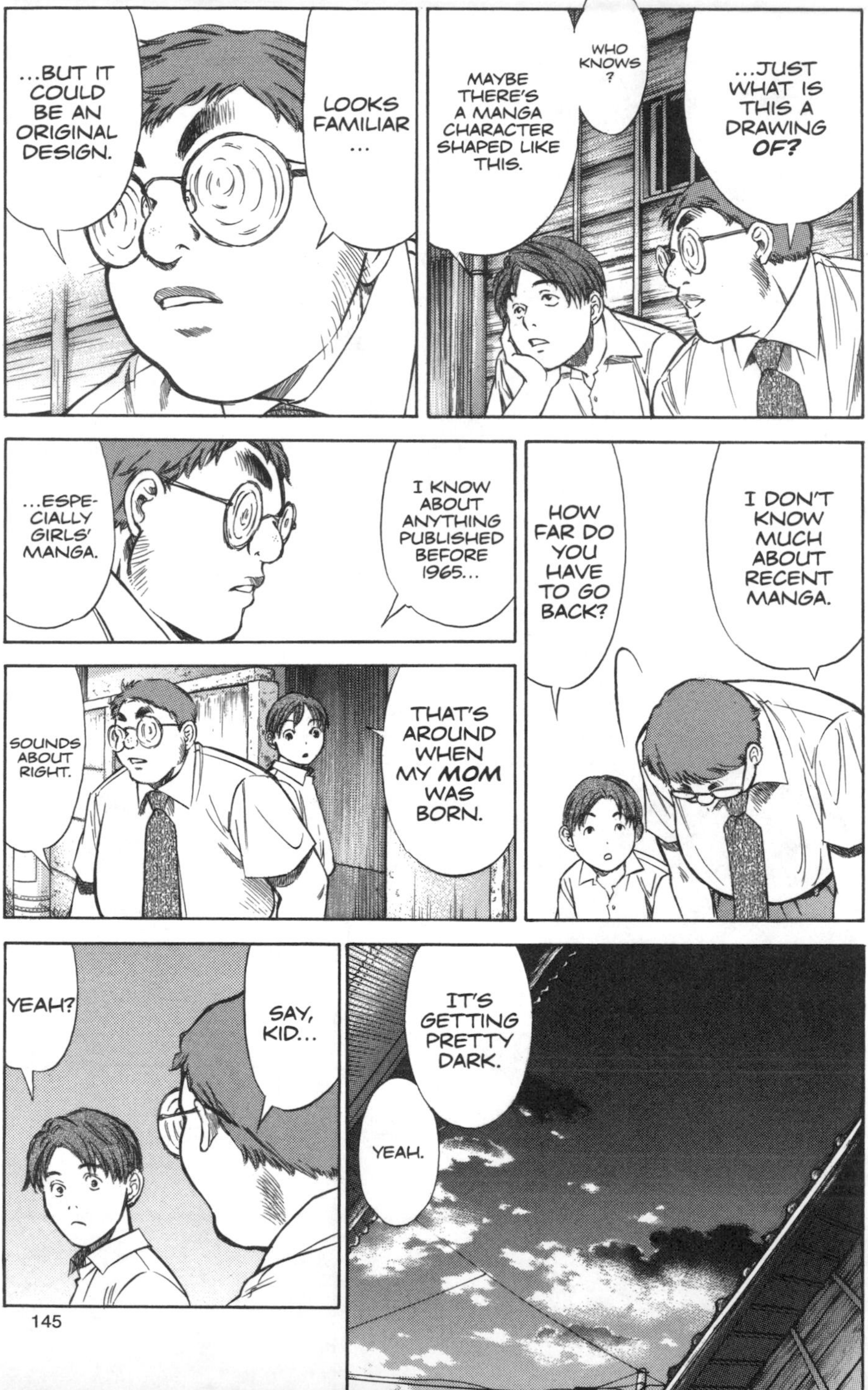
...JUST WHAT IS THIS A DRAWING OF?
WHO KNOWS?
MAYBE THERE'S A MANGA CHARACTER SHAPED LIKE THIS.
LOOKS FAMILIAR ...
...BUT IT COULD BE AN ORIGINAL DESIGN.
I DON'T KNOW MUCH ABOUT RECENT MANGA.
HOW FAR DO YOU HAVE TO GO BACK?
I KNOW ABOUT ANYTHING PUBLISHED BEFORE 1965...
...ESPECIALLY GIRLS' MANGA.
THAT'S AROUND WHEN MY MOM WAS BORN.
SOUNDS ABOUT RIGHT.
IT'S GETTING PRETTY DARK.
YEAH.
SAY, KID...
YEAH?

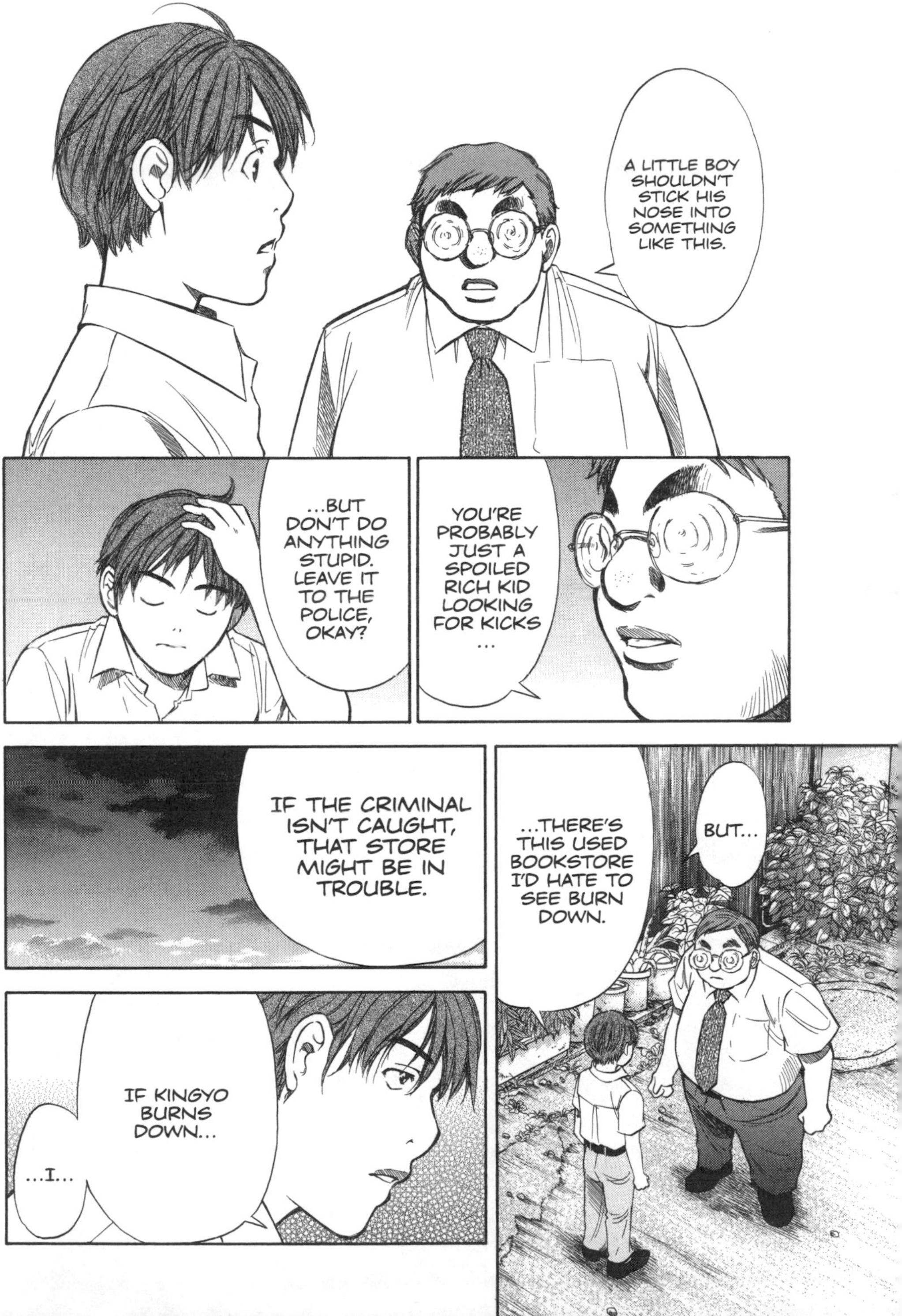
A LITTLE BOY SHOULDN'T STICK HIS NOSE INTO SOMETHING LIKE THIS.
YOU'RE PROBABLY JUST A SPOILED RICH KID LOOKING FOR KICKS ...
...BUT DON'T DO ANYTHING STUPID. LEAVE IT TO THE POLICE, OKAY?
BUT...
...THERE'S THIS USED BOOKSTORE I'D HATE TO SEE BURN DOWN.
IF THE CRIMINAL ISN'T CAUGHT, THAT STORE MIGHT BE IN TROUBLE.
IF KINGYO BURNS DOWN...
...I...

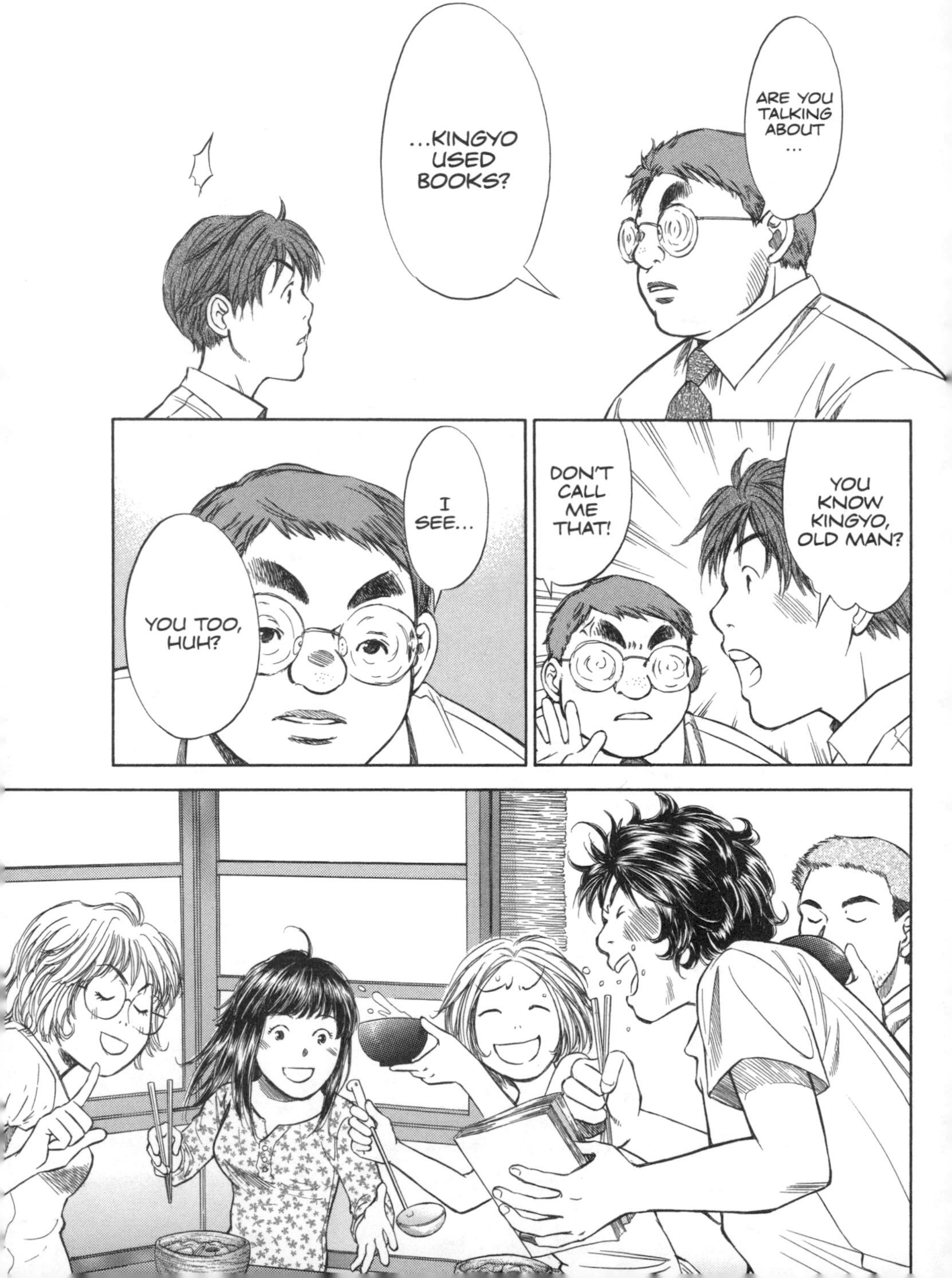
ARE YOU TALKING ABOUT ...
...KINGYO USED BOOKS?
YOU KNOW KINGYO, OLD MAN?
DON'T CALL ME THAT!
I SEE...
YOU TOO, HUH?

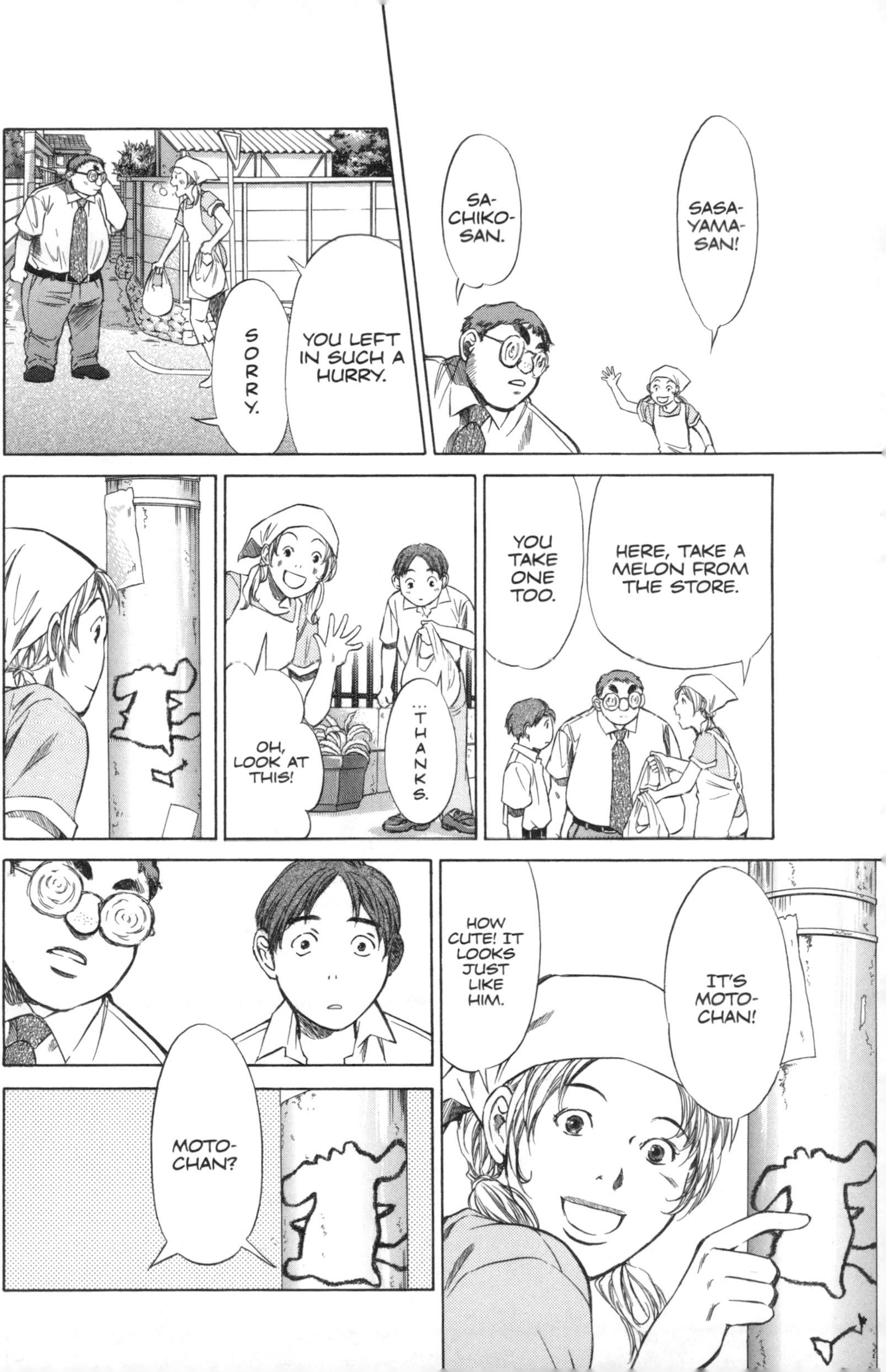
SASA-YAMA-SAN!
SA-CHIKO-SAN.
YOU LEFT IN SUCH A HURRY.
SORRY.
HERE, TAKE A MELON FROM THE STORE.
YOU TAKE ONE TOO.
...THANKS.
OH, LOOK AT THIS!
IT'S MOTO-CHAN!
HOW CUTE! IT LOOKS JUST LIKE HIM.
MOTO-CHAN?

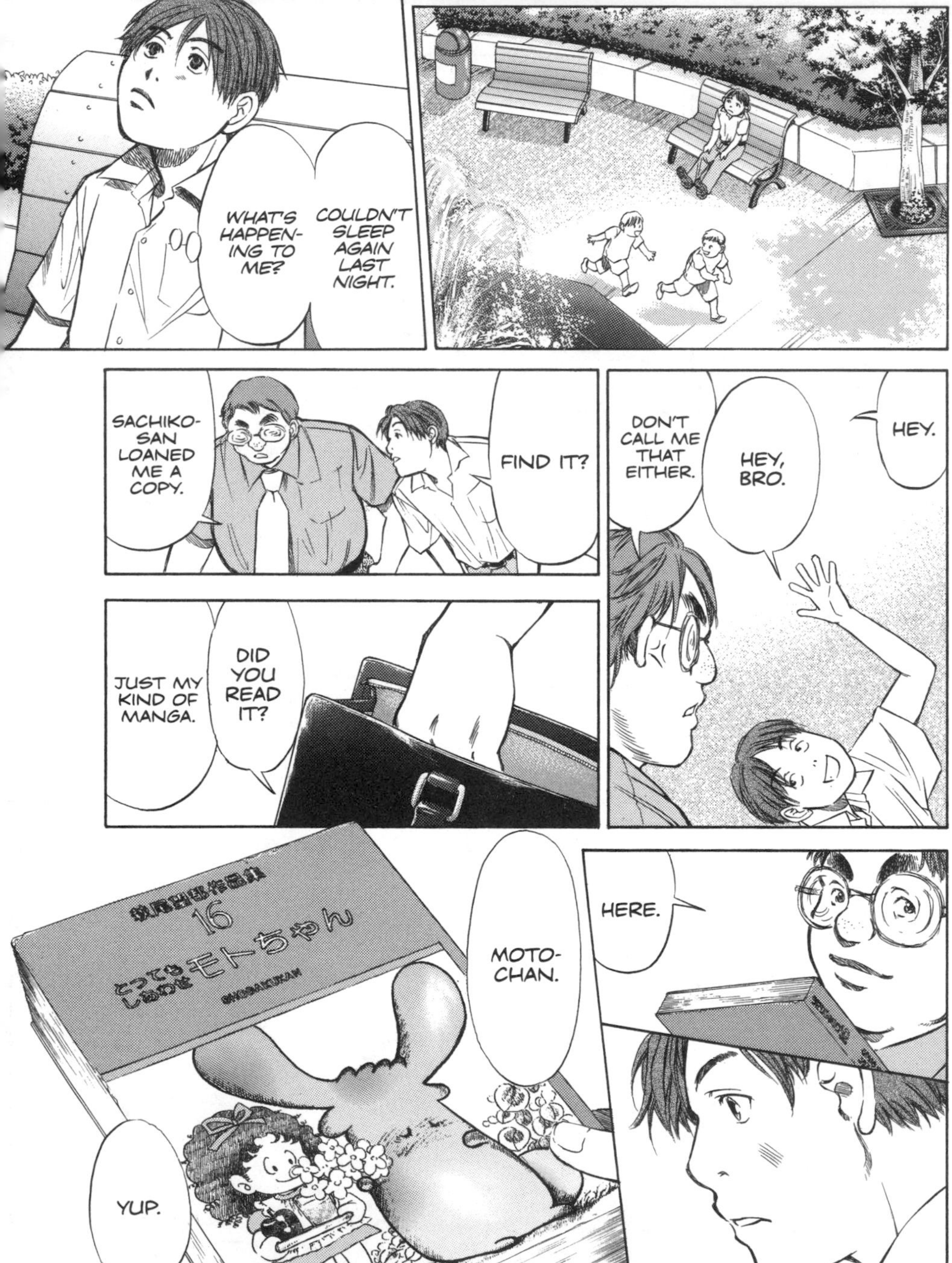
COULDN'T SLEEP AGAIN LAST NIGHT.
WHAT'S HAPPENING TO ME?
HEY.
HEY, BRO.
DON'T CALL ME THAT EITHER.
FIND IT?
SACHIKO-SAN LOANED ME A COPY.
DID YOU READ IT?
JUST MY KIND OF MANGA.
HERE.
MOTO-CHAN.
16
とってもしあわせモトちゃん
YUP.

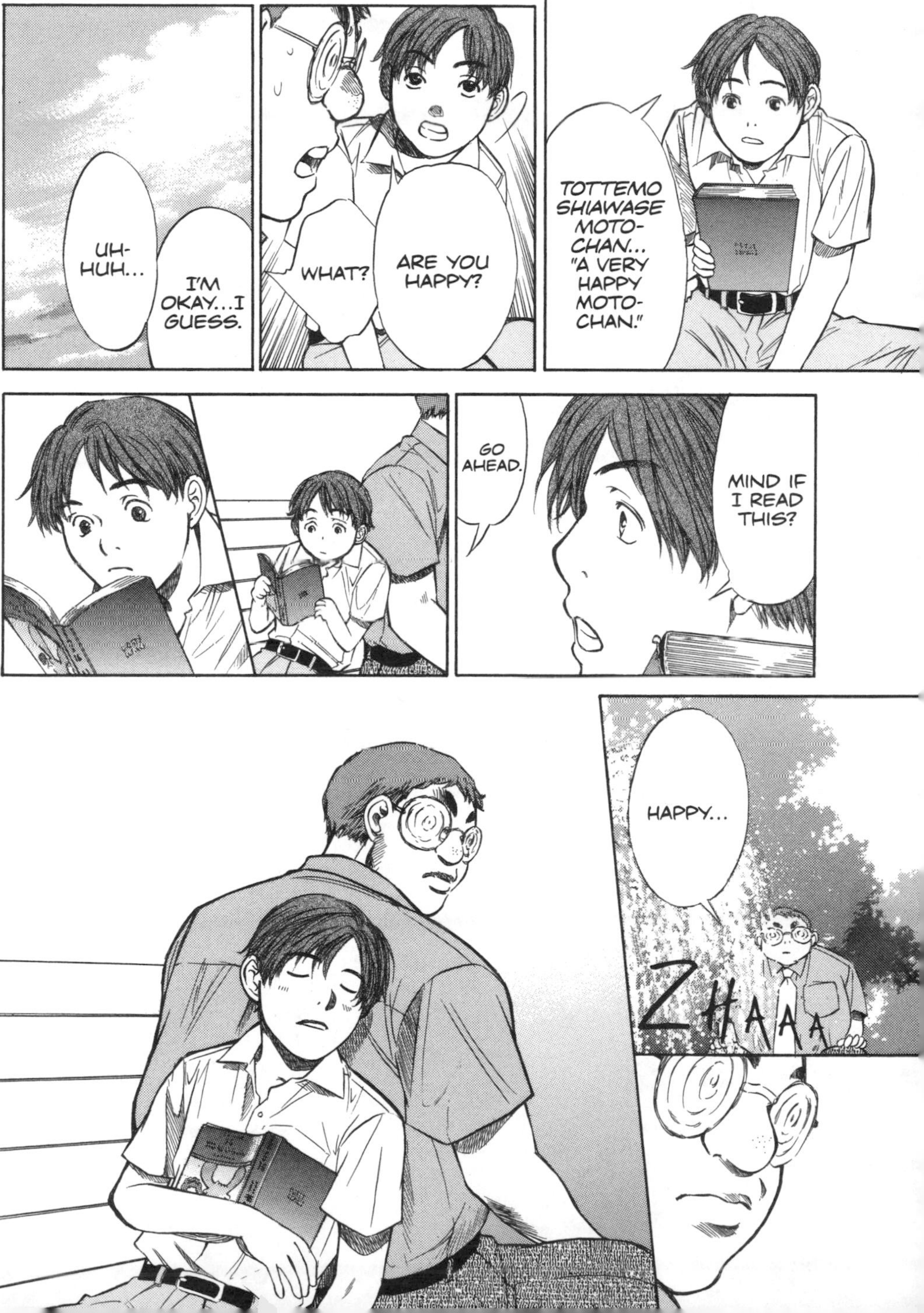
TOTTEMO SHIAWASE MOTO-CHAN... "A VERY HAPPY MOTO-CHAN."
ARE YOU HAPPY?
WHAT?
I'M OKAY...I GUESS.
UH-HUH...
MIND IF I READ THIS?
GO AHEAD.
HAPPY...
ZHAAA

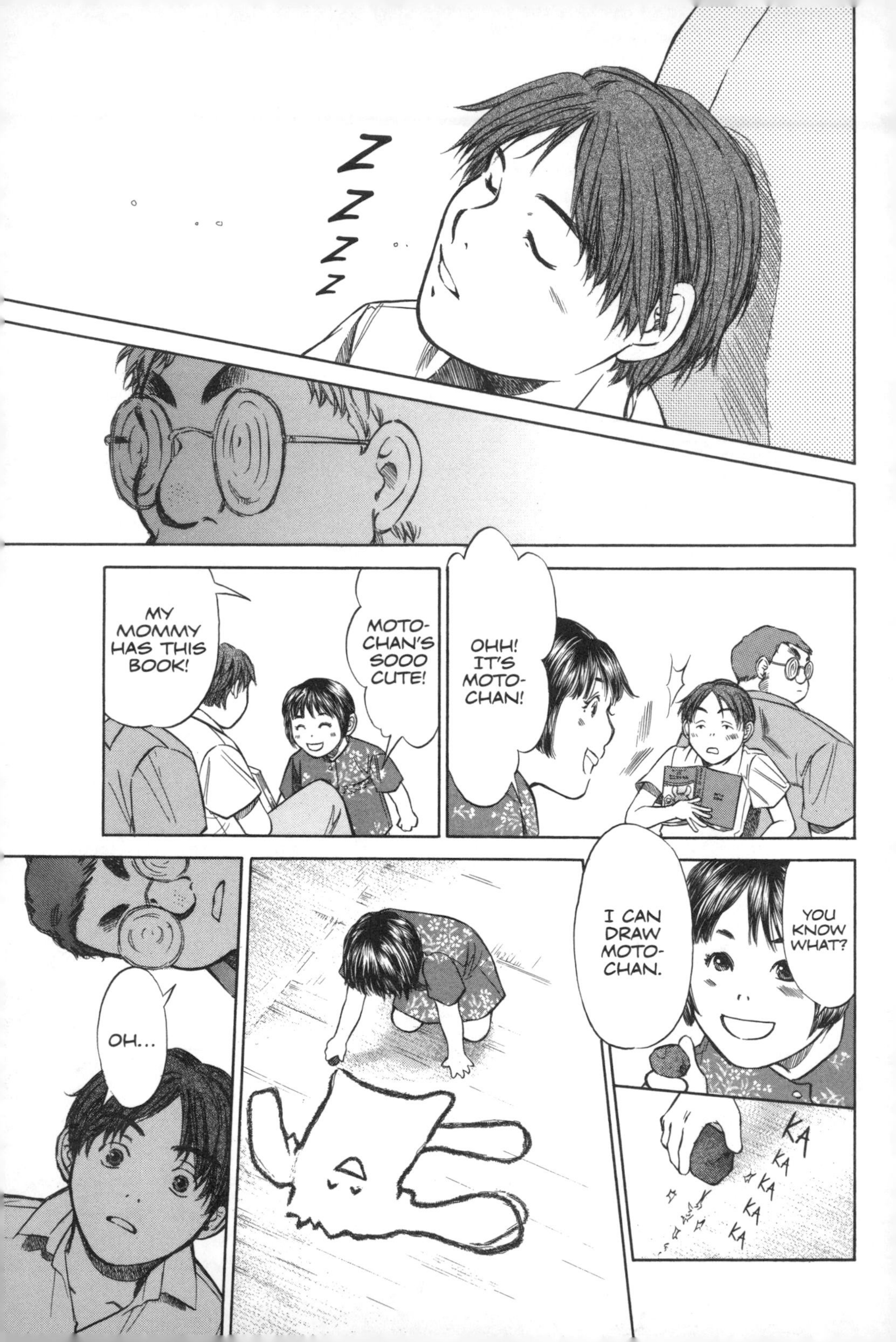
ZZZZ
OHH! IT'S MOTO-CHAN!
MOTO-CHAN'S SOOO CUTE!
MY MOMMY HAS THIS BOOK!
YOU KNOW WHAT?
I CAN DRAW MOTO-CHAN.
KA KA KA KA KA KA
OH...

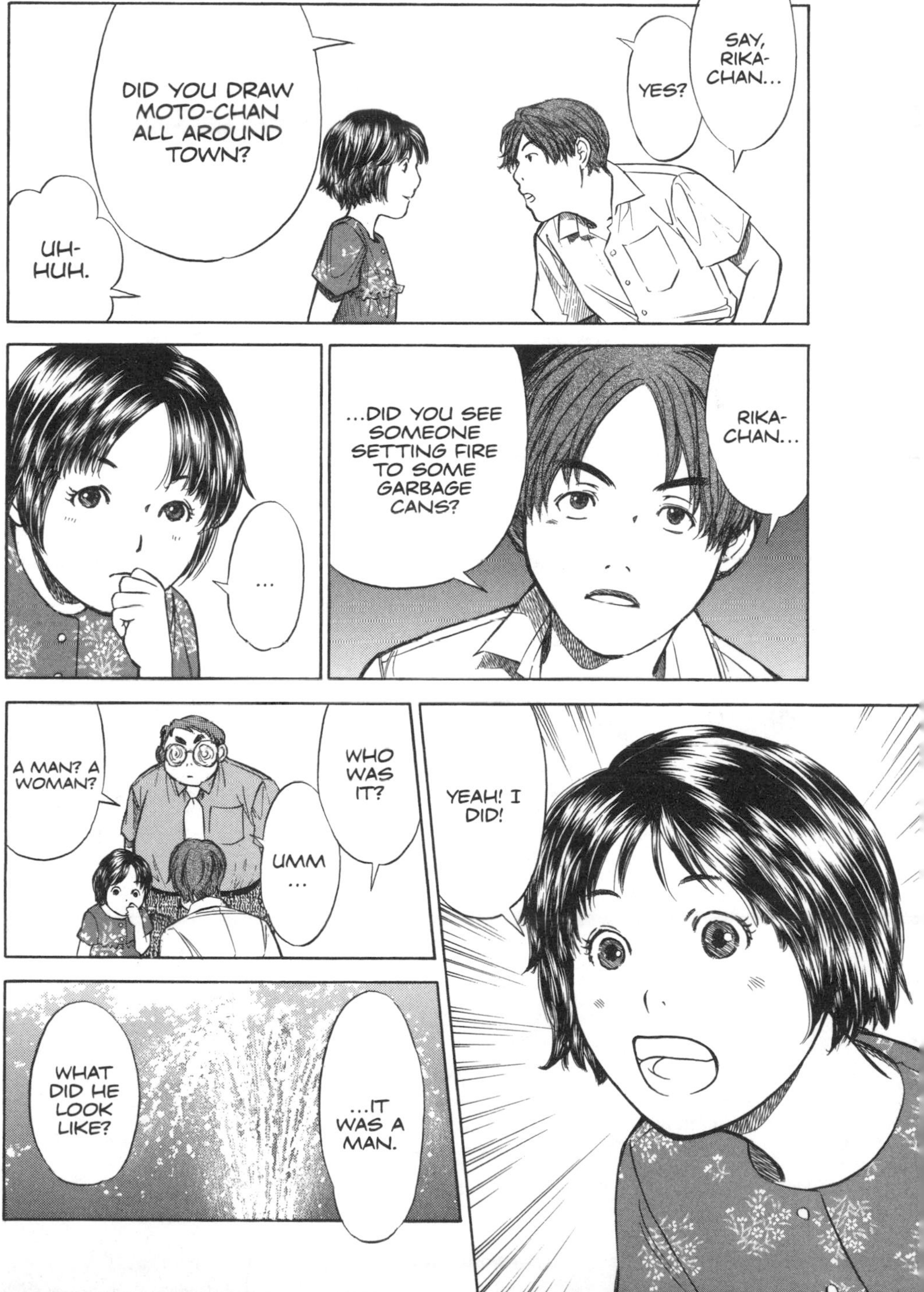
SAY, RIKA-CHAN...
YES?
DID YOU DRAW MOTO-CHAN ALL AROUND TOWN?
UH-HUH.
RIKA-CHAN...
...DID YOU SEE SOMEONE SETTING FIRE TO SOME GARBAGE CANS?
...
YEAH! I DID!
WHO WAS IT?
UMM ...
A MAN? A WOMAN?
...IT WAS A MAN.
WHAT DID HE LOOK LIKE?

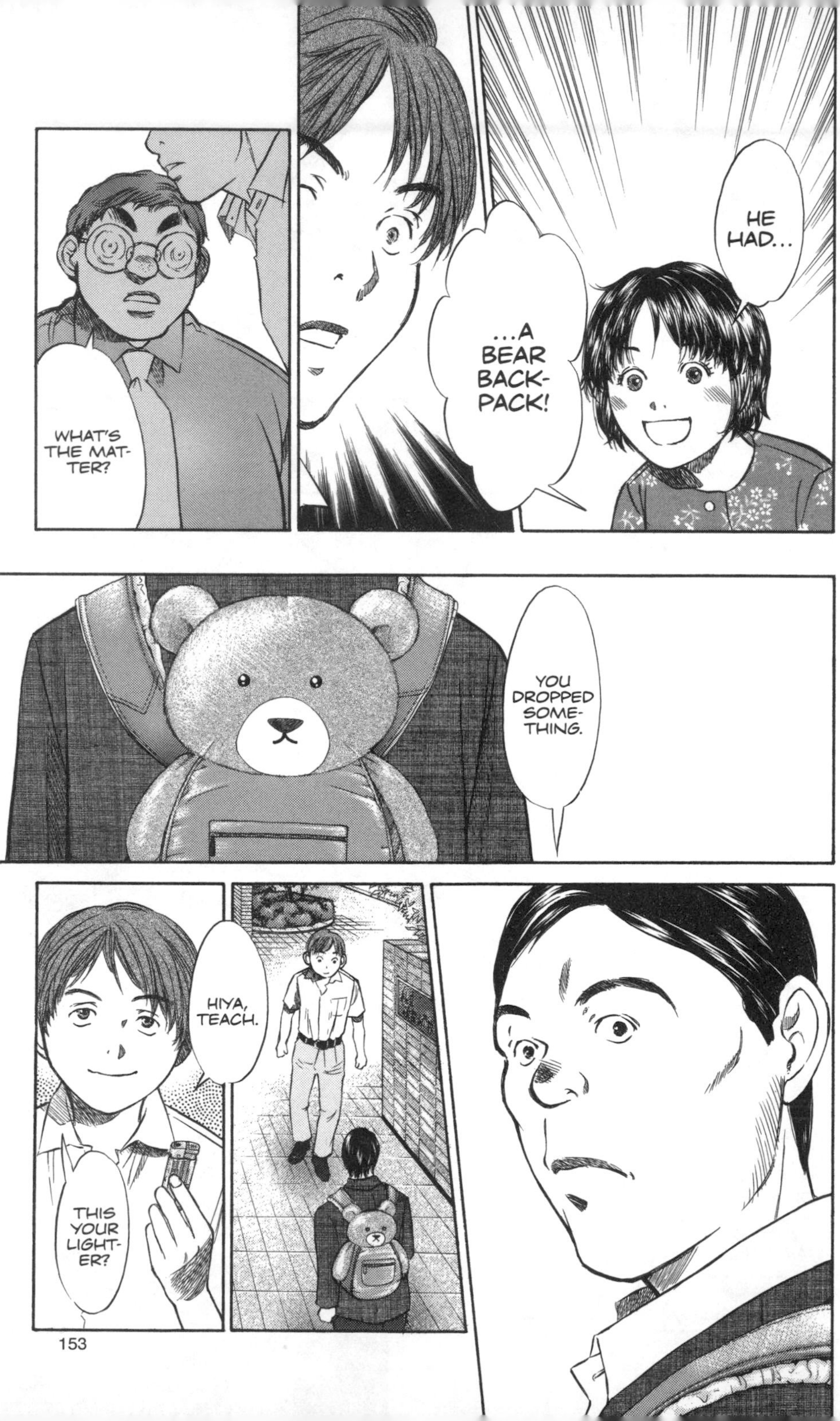
HE HAD...
...A BEAR BACKPACK!
WHAT'S THE MATTER?
YOU DROPPED SOMETHING.
HIYA, TEACH.
THIS YOUR LIGHTER?

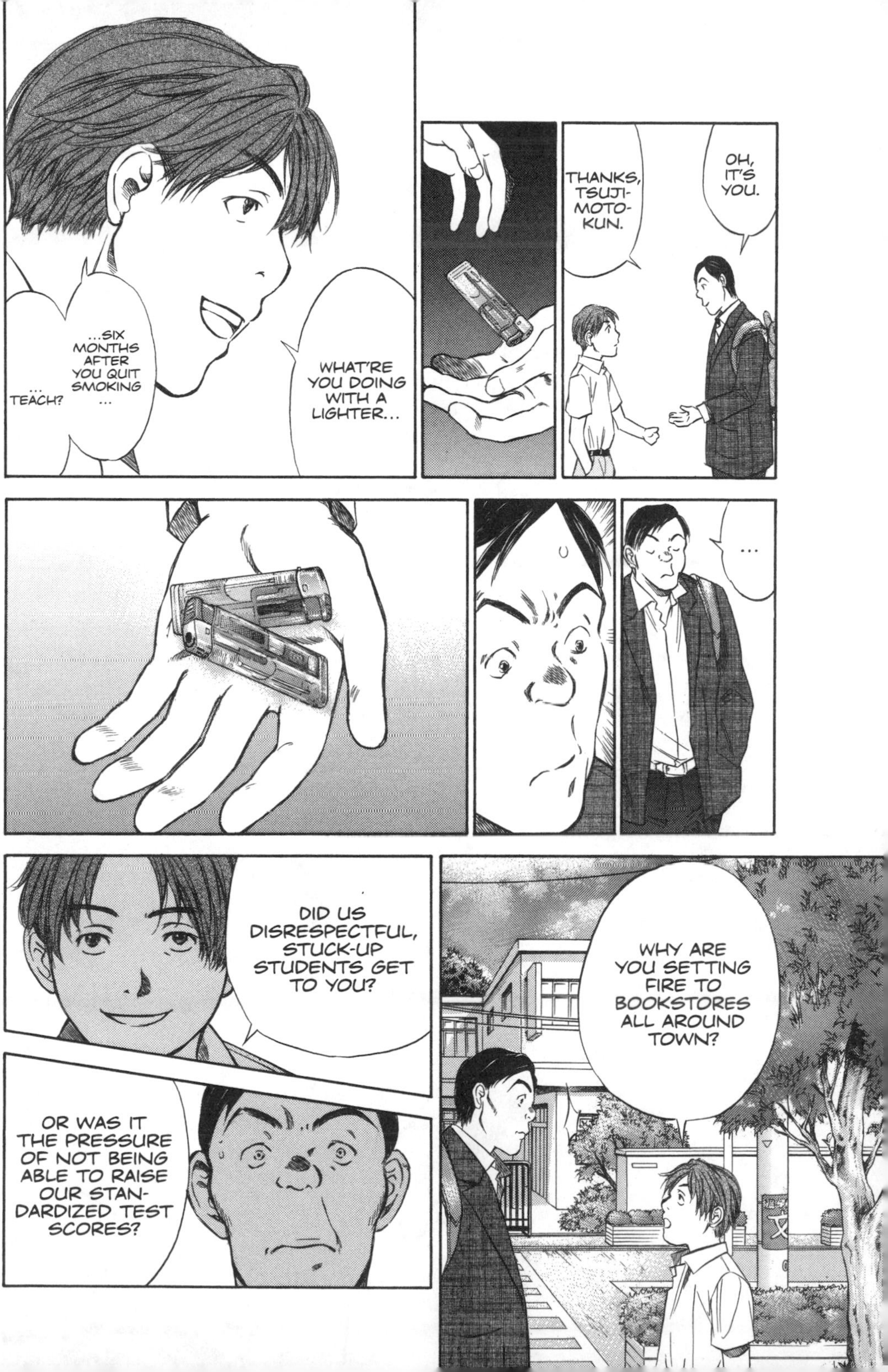
OH, IT'S YOU.
THANKS, TSUJI-MOTO-KUN.
WHAT'RE YOU DOING WITH A LIGHTER...
...SIX MONTHS AFTER YOU QUIT SMOKING...
...TEACH?
...
WHY ARE YOU SETTING FIRE TO BOOKSTORES ALL AROUND TOWN?
DID US DISRESPECTFUL, STUCK-UP STUDENTS GET TO YOU?
OR WAS IT THE PRESSURE OF NOT BEING ABLE TO RAISE OUR STAN-DARDIZED TEST SCORES?

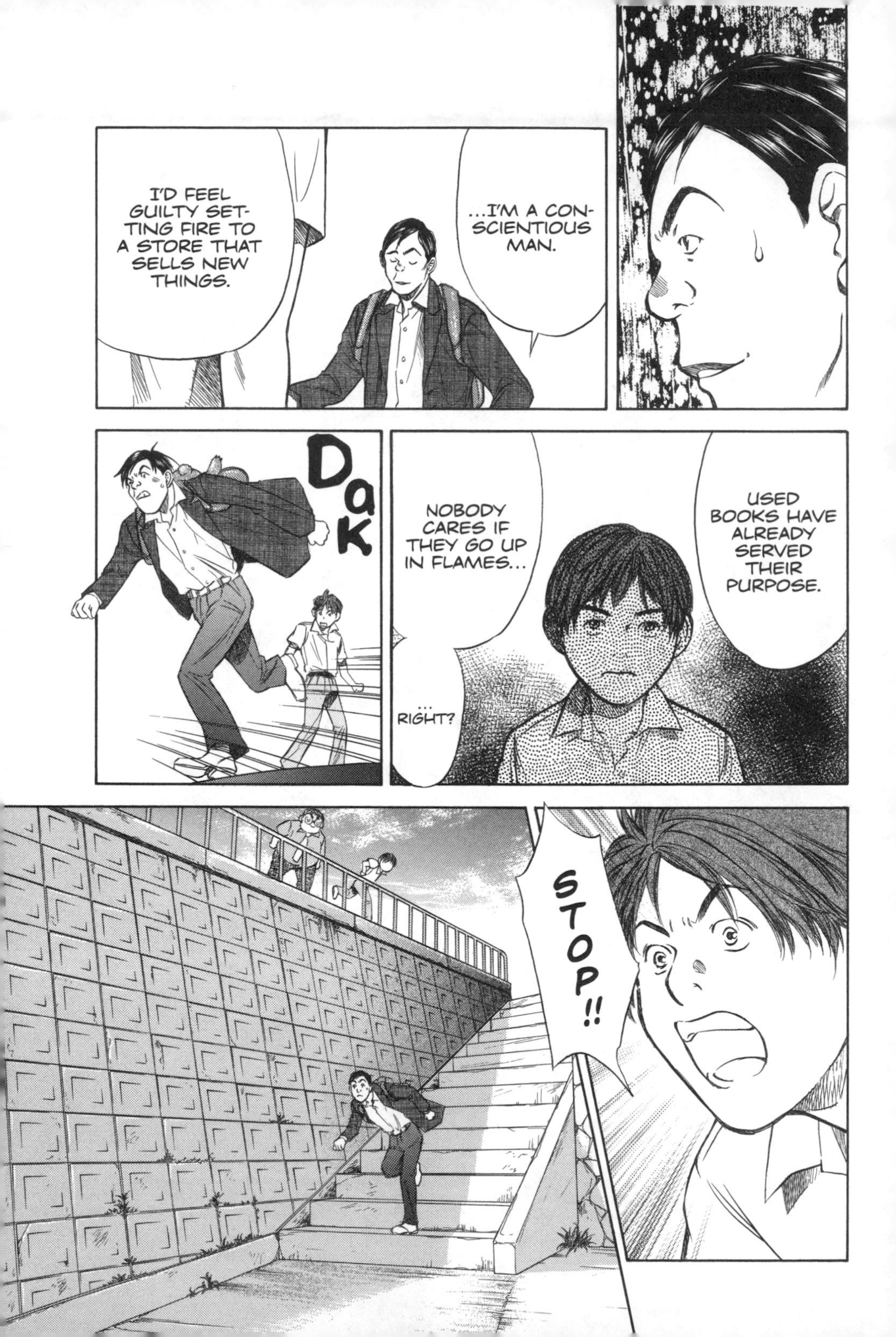
...I'M A CONSCIENTIOUS MAN.
I'D FEEL GUILTY SETTING FIRE TO A STORE THAT SELLS NEW THINGS.
USED BOOKS HAVE ALREADY SERVED THEIR PURPOSE.
NOBODY CARES IF THEY GO UP IN FLAMES...
...RIGHT?
DaK
STOP!!

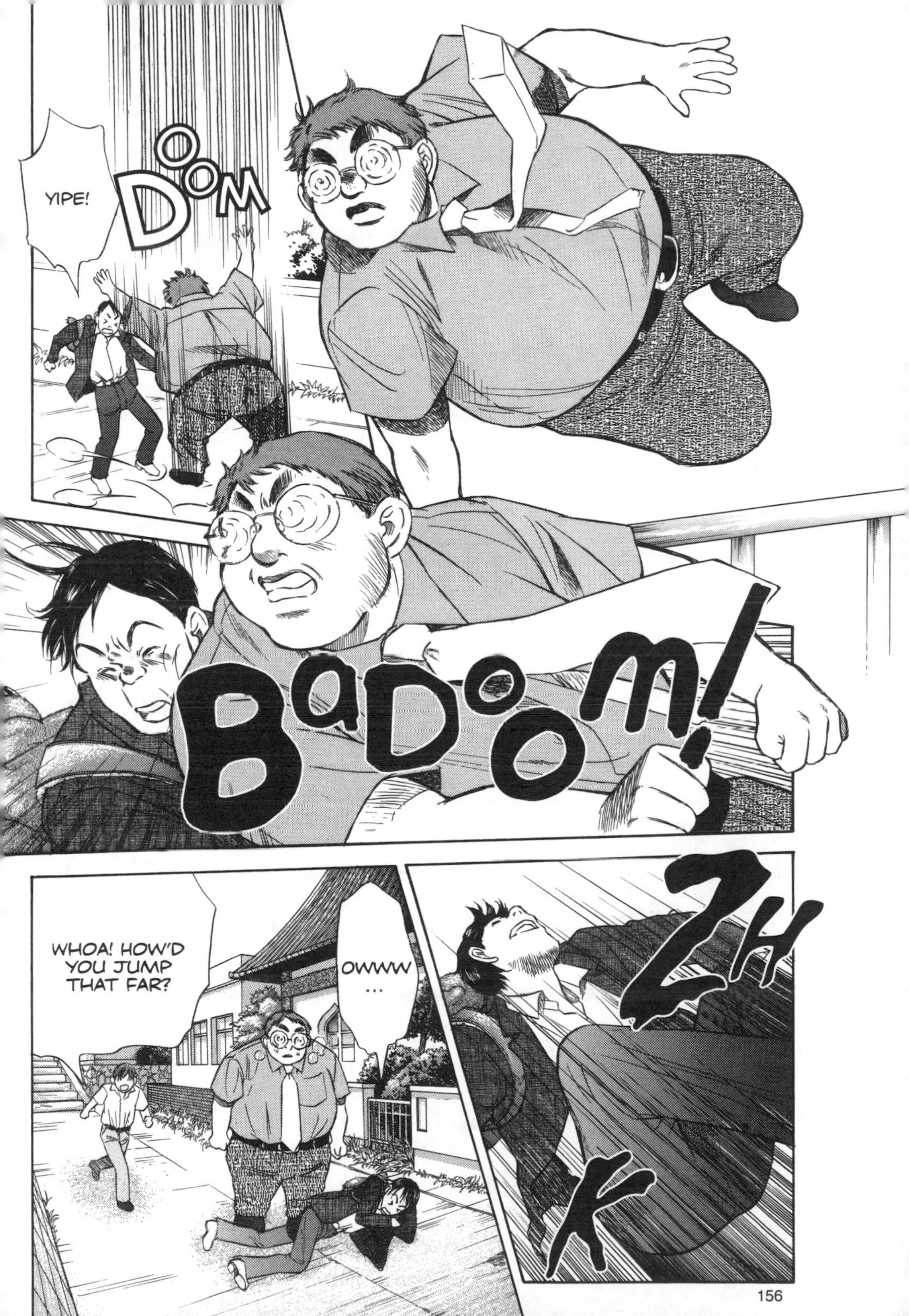
DOOM
YIPE!
BADOOM!
ZHK
OWWW ...
WHOA! HOW'D YOU JUMP THAT FAR?

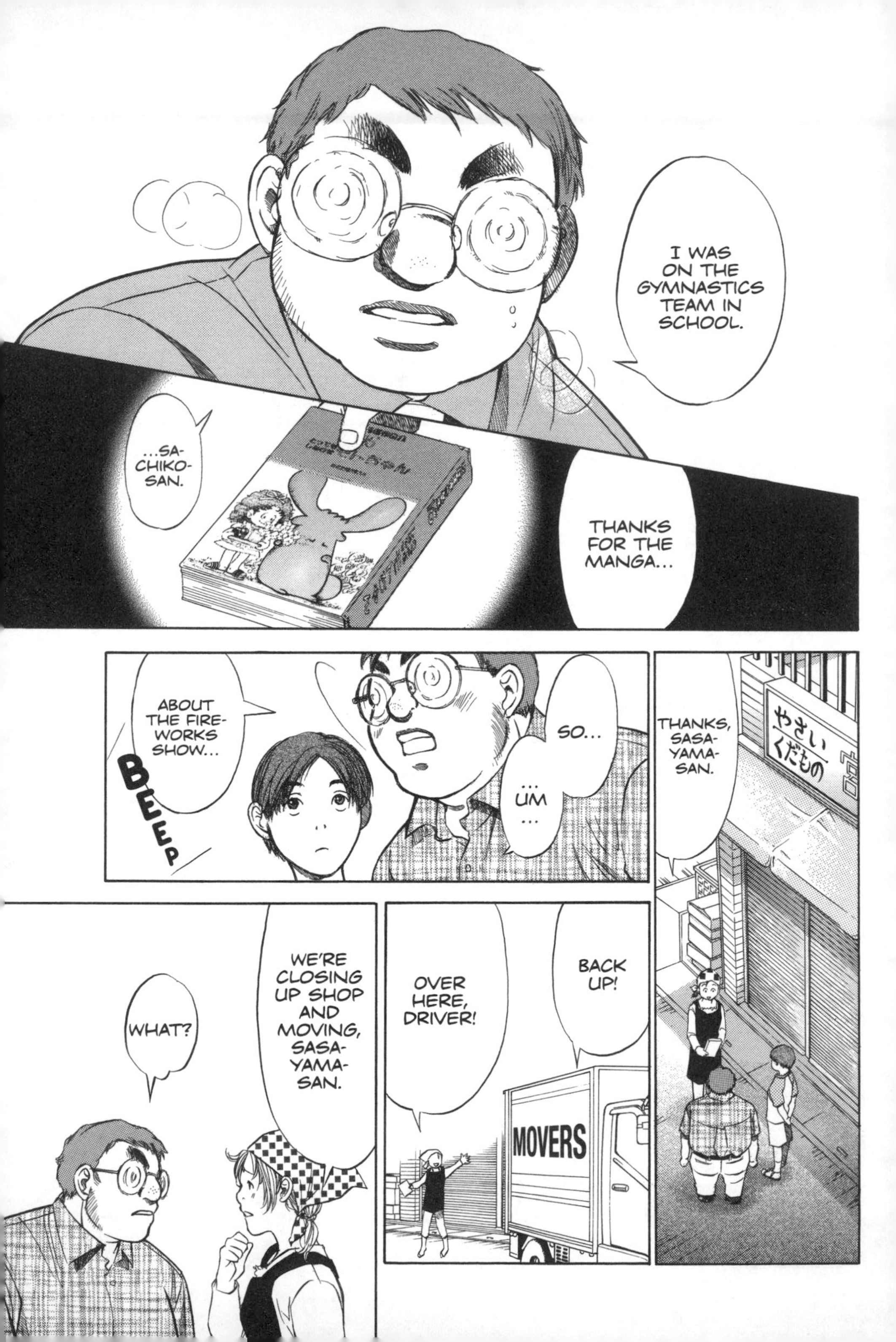
I WAS ON THE GYMNASTICS TEAM IN SCHOOL.
THANKS FOR THE MANGA...
...SA-CHIKO-SAN.
THANKS, SASA-YAMA-SAN.
やさい くだもの
SO...
...UM...
ABOUT THE FIRE-WORKS SHOW...
BEEP
BACK UP!
OVER HERE, DRIVER!
MOVERS
WE'RE CLOSING UP SHOP AND MOVING, SASA-YAMA-SAN.
WHAT?

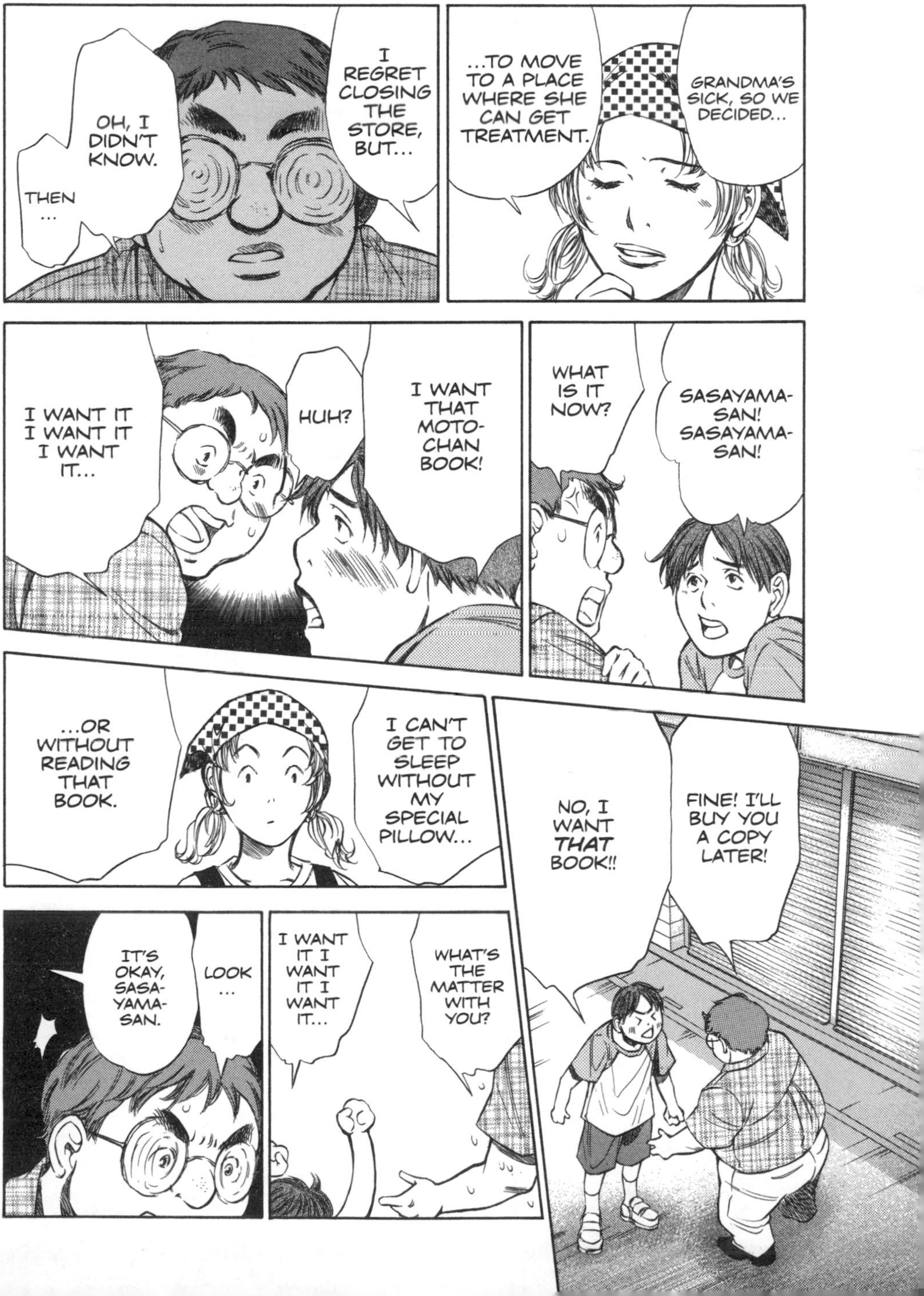
GRANDMA'S SICK, SO WE DECIDED...
...TO MOVE TO A PLACE WHERE SHE CAN GET TREATMENT.
I REGRET CLOSING THE STORE, BUT...
OH, I DIDN'T KNOW.
THEN ...
SASAYAMA-SAN! SASAYAMA-SAN!
WHAT IS IT NOW?
I WANT THAT MOTO-CHAN BOOK!
HUH?
I WANT IT I WANT IT I WANT IT...
FINE! I'LL BUY YOU A COPY LATER!
NO, I WANT *THAT* BOOK!!
I CAN'T GET TO SLEEP WITHOUT MY SPECIAL PILLOW...
...OR WITHOUT READING THAT BOOK.
WHAT'S THE MATTER WITH YOU?
I WANT IT I WANT IT I WANT IT...
LOOK ...
IT'S OKAY, SASA-YAMA-SAN.

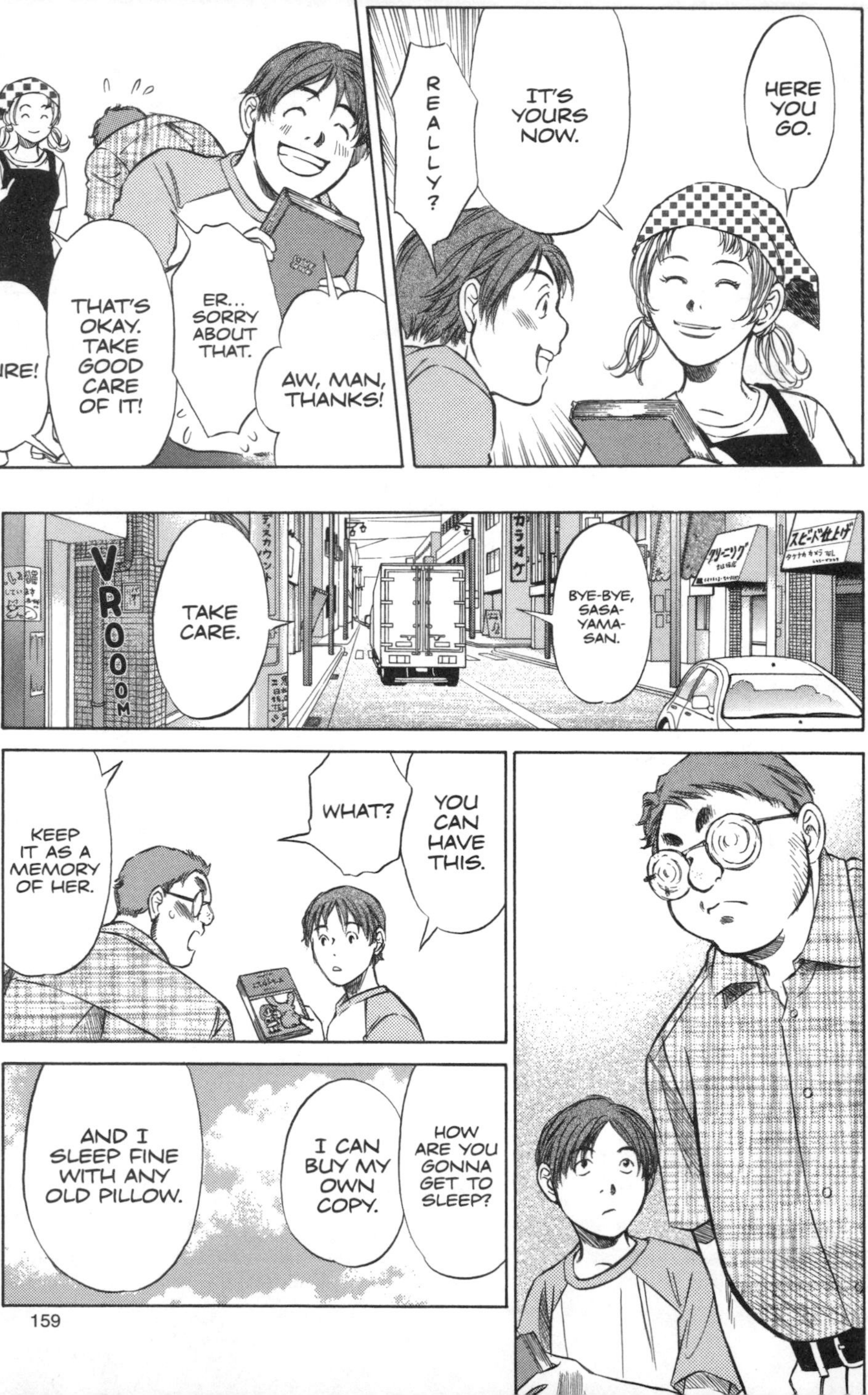
HERE YOU GO.
IT'S YOURS NOW.
REALLY?
AW, MAN, THANKS!
ER... SORRY ABOUT THAT.
THAT'S OKAY. TAKE GOOD CARE OF IT!
SURE!
スピード仕上げ
BYE-BYE, SASA-YAMA-SAN.
カラオケ
TAKE CARE.
VROOOOM
YOU CAN HAVE THIS.
WHAT?
KEEP IT AS A MEMORY OF HER.
HOW ARE YOU GONNA GET TO SLEEP?
I CAN BUY MY OWN COPY.
AND I SLEEP FINE WITH ANY OLD PILLOW.

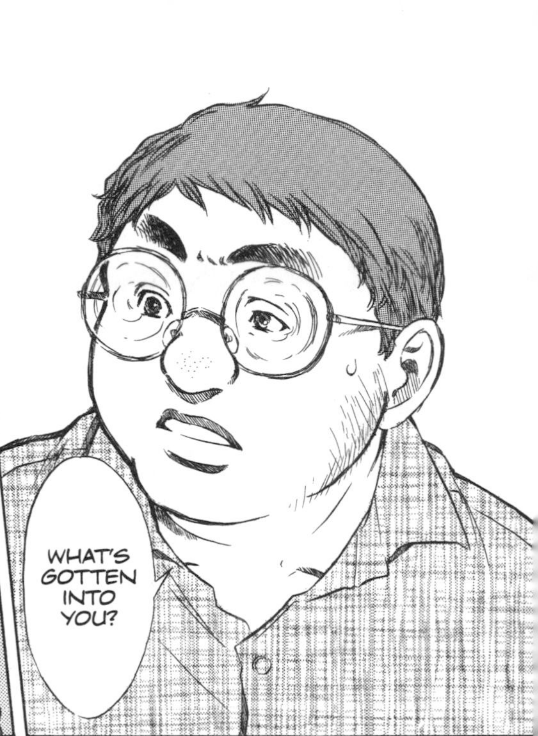
WHAT'S GOTTEN INTO YOU?
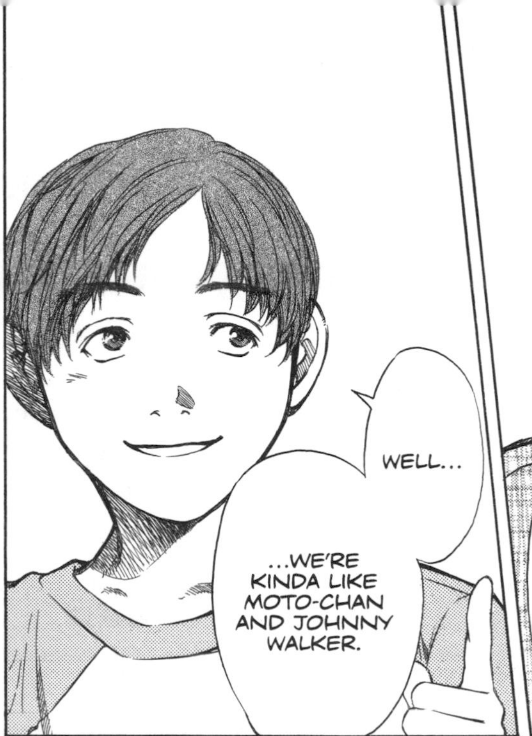
WELL...
...WE'RE KINDA LIKE MOTO-CHAN AND JOHNNY WALKER.
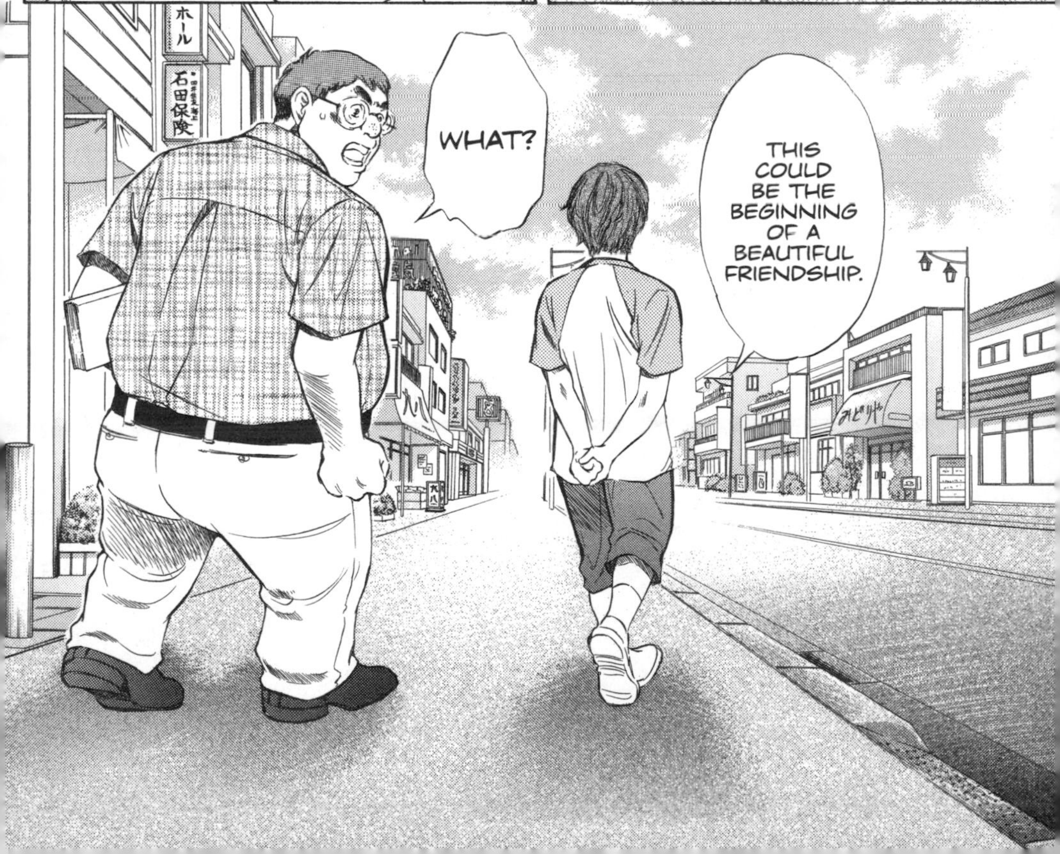
THIS COULD BE THE BEGINNING OF A BEAUTIFUL FRIENDSHIP.
WHAT?
ホール
石田保険

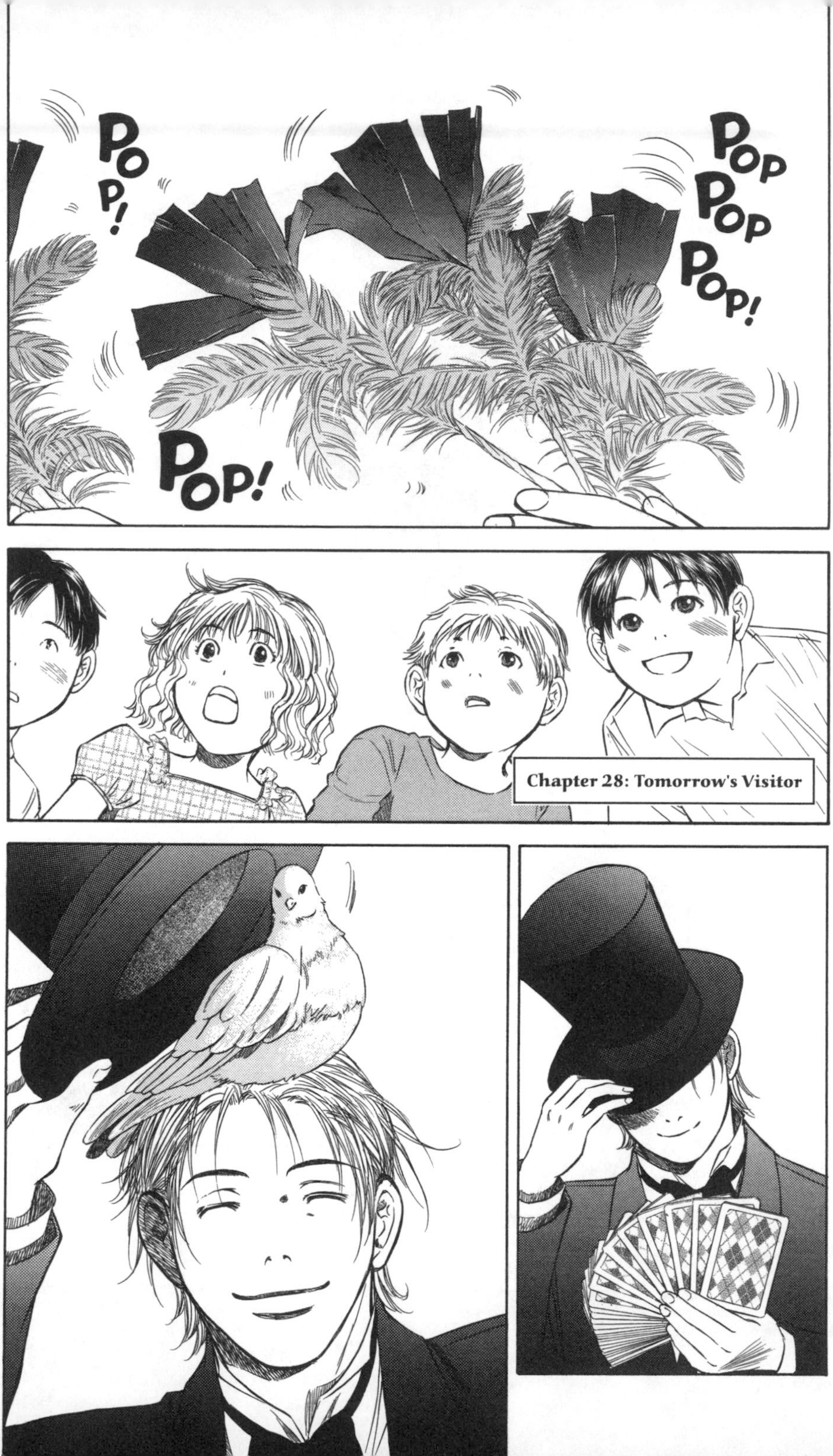
POP POP POP!
POP!
POP!
Chapter 28: Tomorrow's Visitor

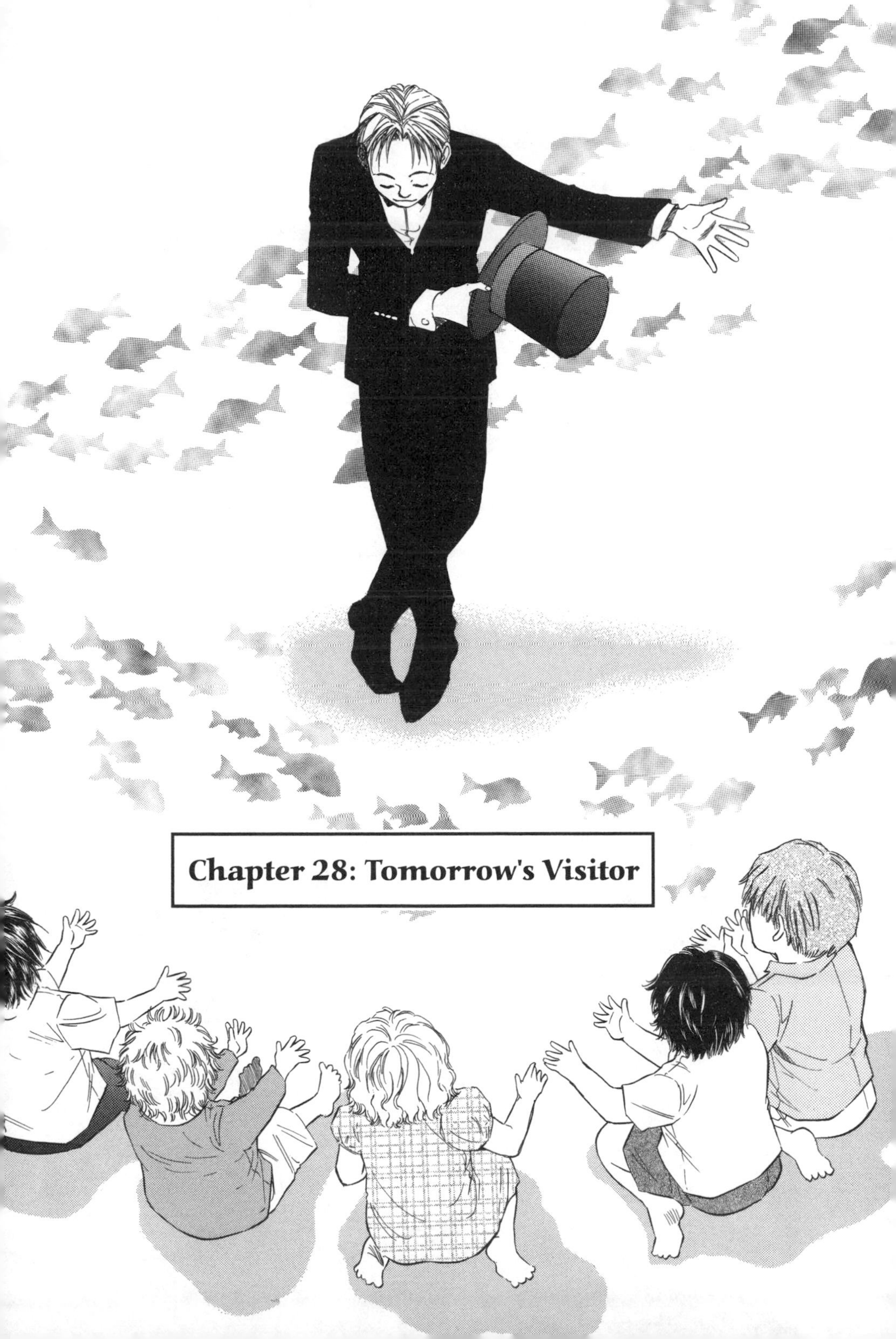
Chapter 28: Tomorrow's Visitor

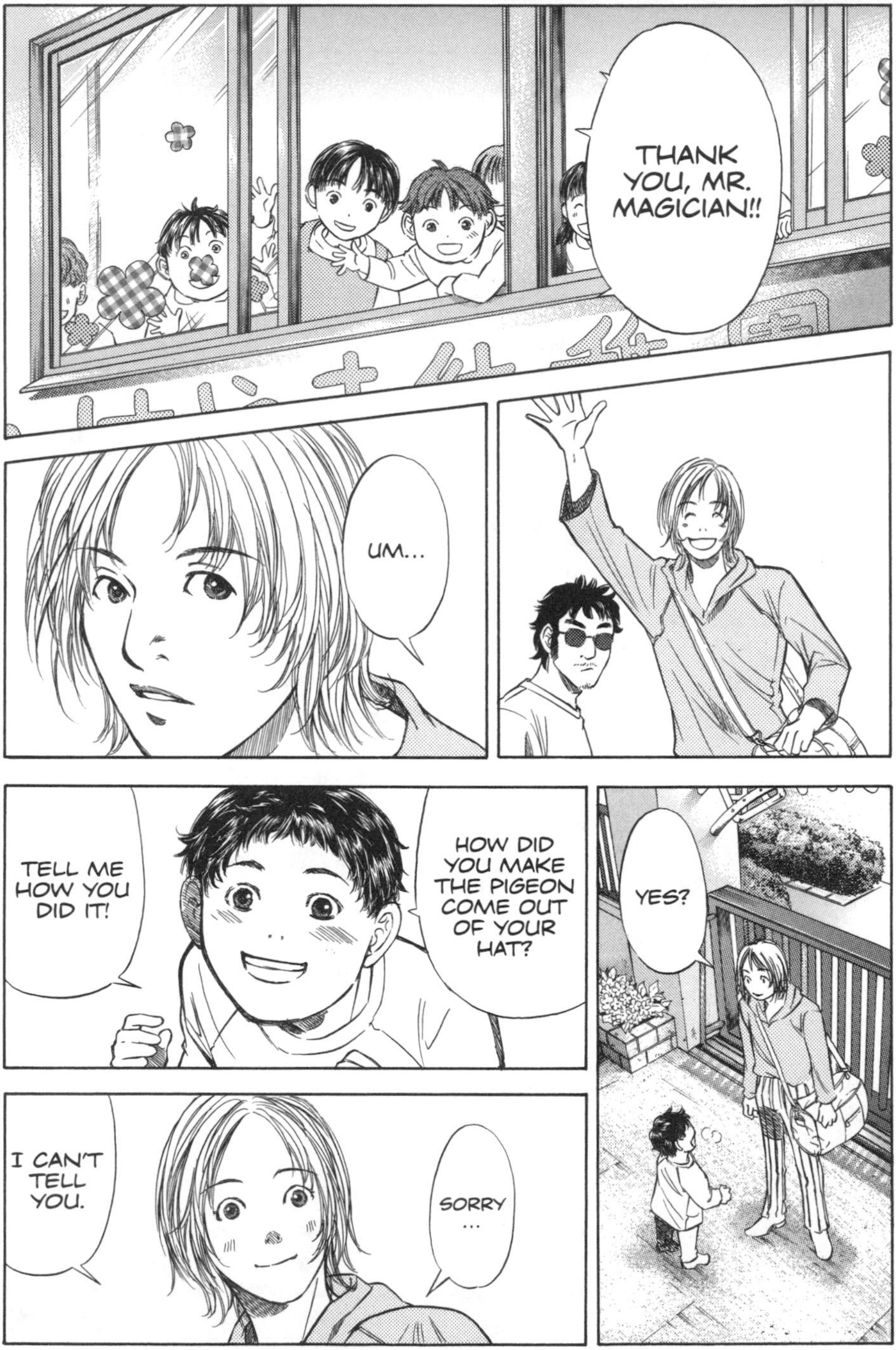
THANK YOU, MR. MAGICIAN!!
UM...
YES?
HOW DID YOU MAKE THE PIGEON COME OUT OF YOUR HAT?
TELL ME HOW YOU DID IT!
SORRY ...
I CAN'T TELL YOU.

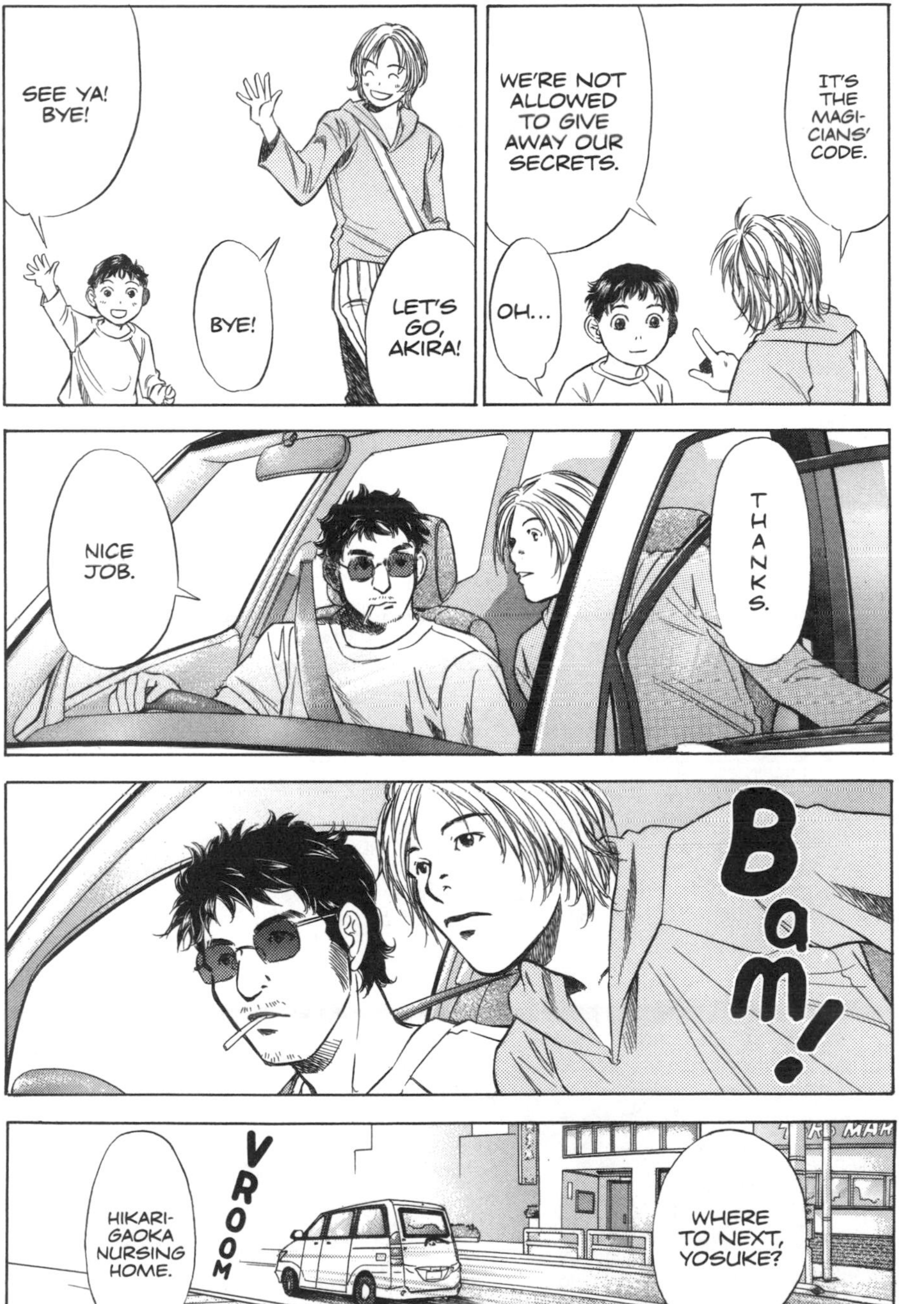

IT'S THE MAGICIANS' CODE.
WE'RE NOT ALLOWED TO GIVE AWAY OUR SECRETS.
OH...
LET'S GO, AKIRA!
BYE!
SEE YA! BYE!
NICE JOB.
THANKS.
BAM!
WHERE TO NEXT, YOSUKE?
VROOM
HIKARI-GAOKA NURSING HOME.

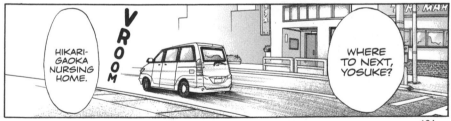

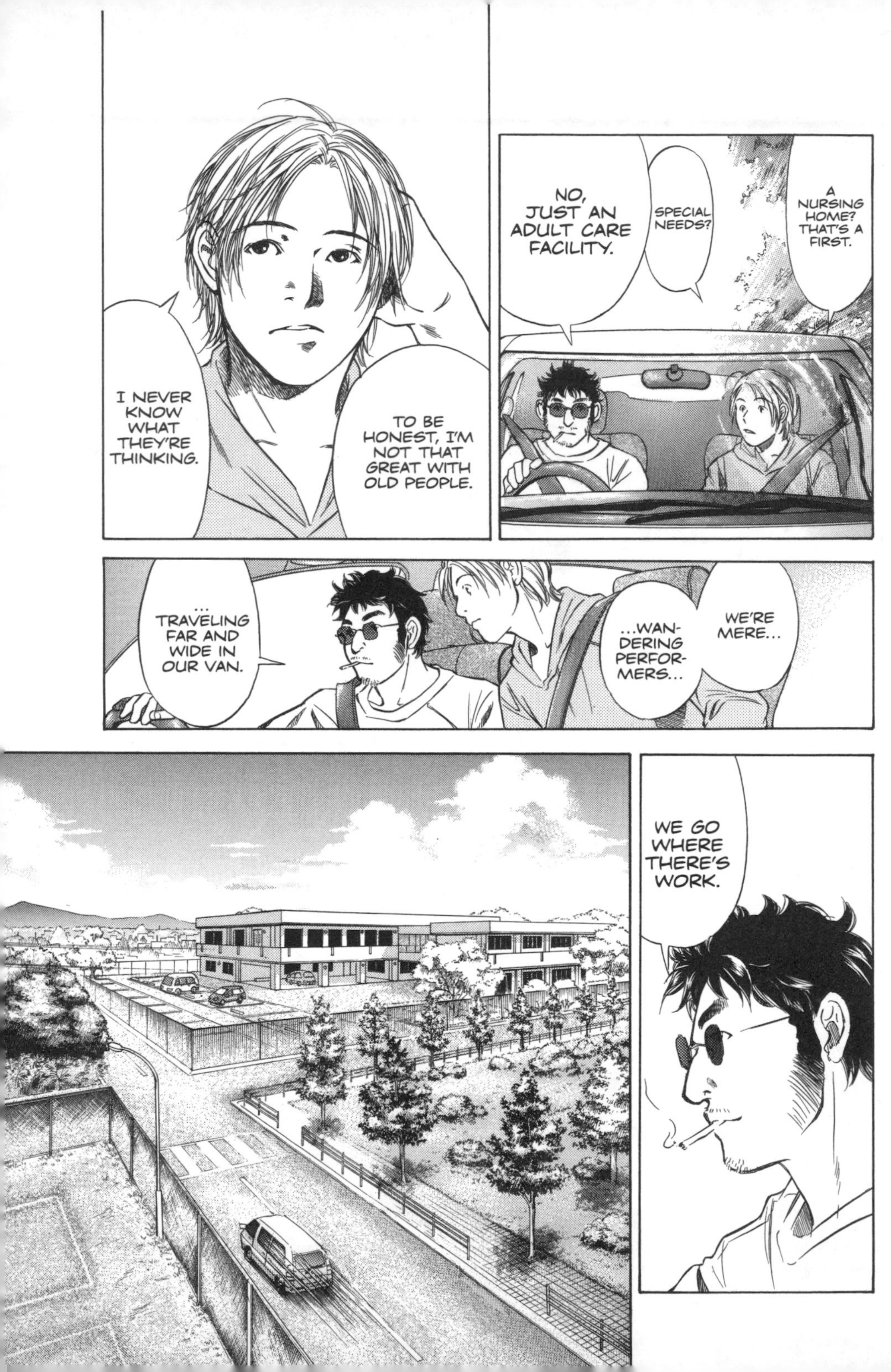
A NURSING HOME? THAT'S A FIRST.
SPECIAL NEEDS?
NO, JUST AN ADULT CARE FACILITY.
TO BE HONEST, I'M NOT THAT GREAT WITH OLD PEOPLE.
I NEVER KNOW WHAT THEY'RE THINKING.
WE'RE MERE...
...WAN-DERING PERFOR-MERS...
...TRAVELING FAR AND WIDE IN OUR VAN.
WE GO WHERE THERE'S WORK.

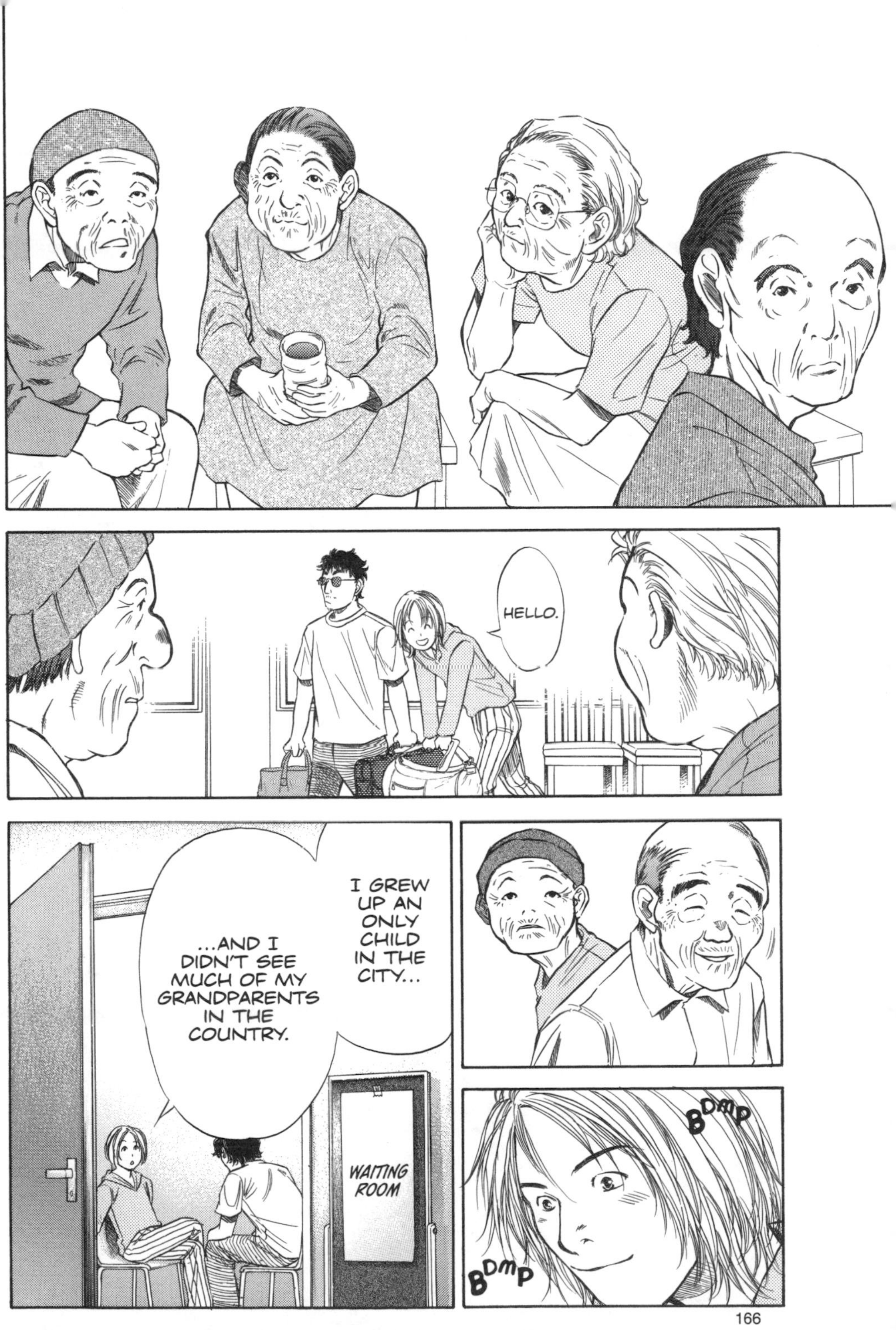
HELLO.
BDMP
BDMP
I GREW UP AN ONLY CHILD IN THE CITY...
...AND I DIDN'T SEE MUCH OF MY GRANDPARENTS IN THE COUNTRY.
WAITING ROOM

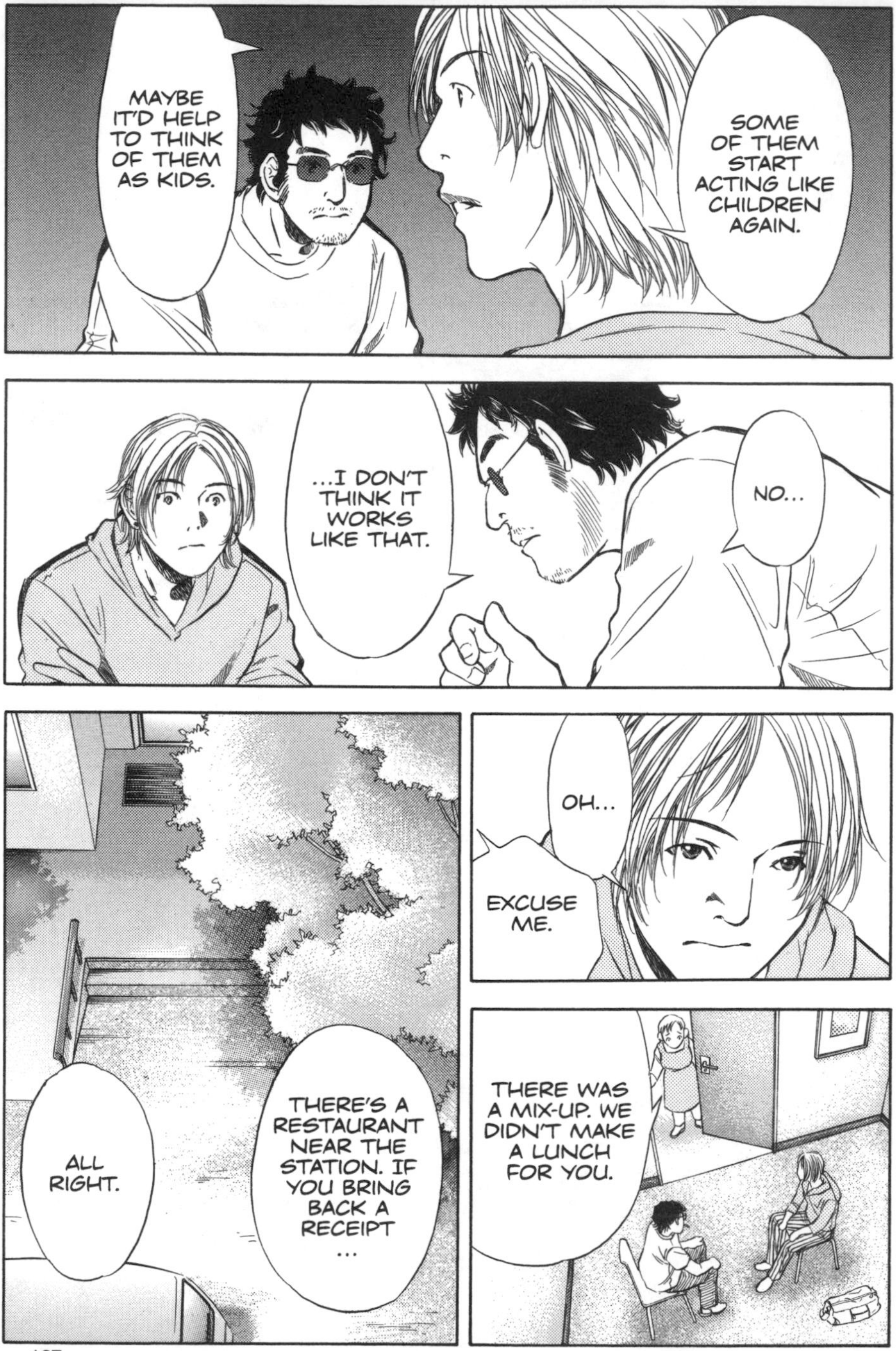
SOME OF THEM START ACTING LIKE CHILDREN AGAIN.
MAYBE IT'D HELP TO THINK OF THEM AS KIDS.
NO...
...I DON'T THINK IT WORKS LIKE THAT.
OH...
EXCUSE ME.
THERE WAS A MIX-UP. WE DIDN'T MAKE A LUNCH FOR YOU.
THERE'S A RESTAURANT NEAR THE STATION. IF YOU BRING BACK A RECEIPT ...
ALL RIGHT.

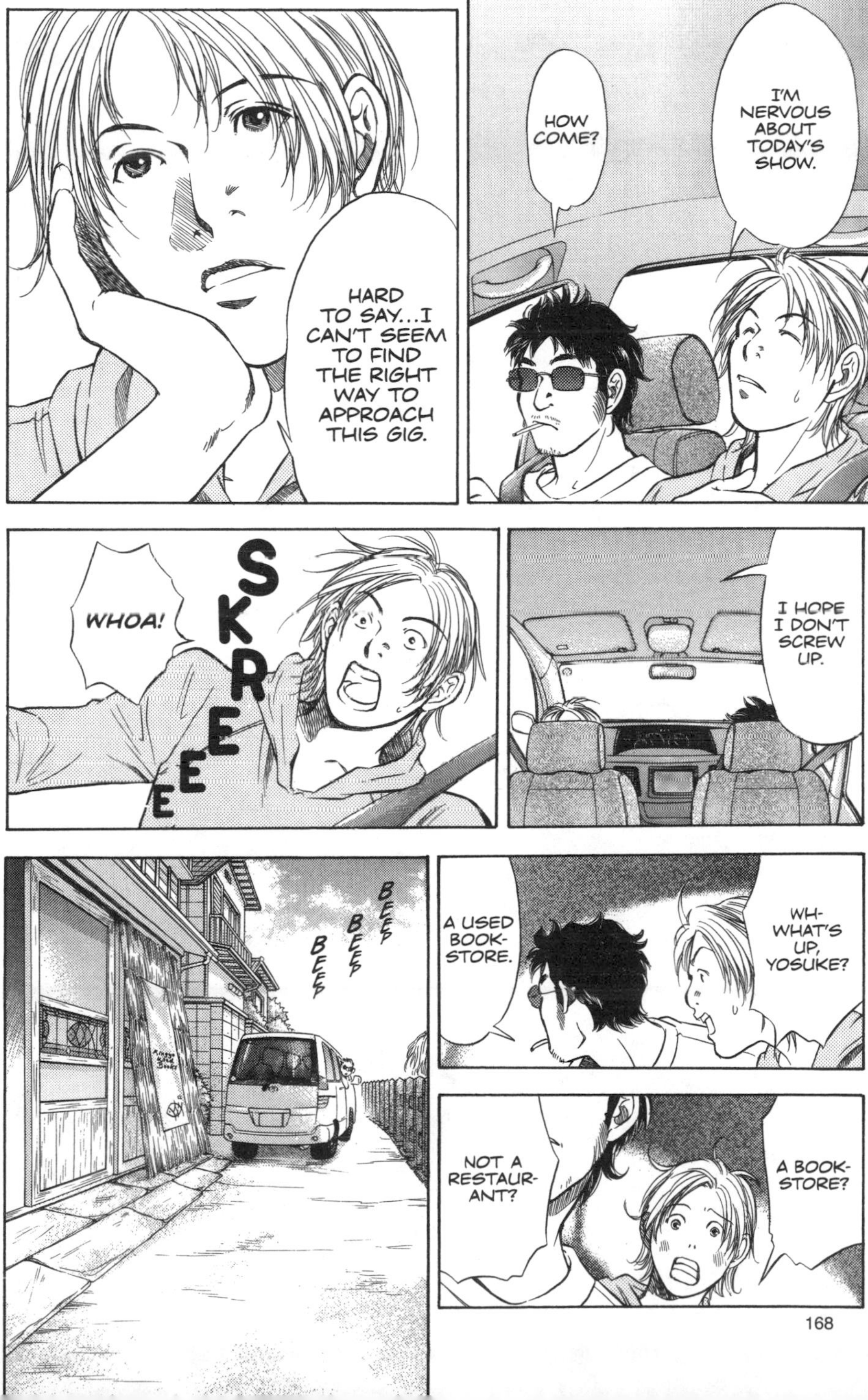
I'M NERVOUS ABOUT TODAY'S SHOW.
HOW COME?
HARD TO SAY...I CAN'T SEEM TO FIND THE RIGHT WAY TO APPROACH THIS GIG.
I HOPE I DON'T SCREW UP.
WHOA!
SKREEEE
WH- WHAT'S UP, YOSUKE?
A USED BOOK-STORE.
A BOOK-STORE?
NOT A RESTAURANT?
BEEP BEEP BEEP

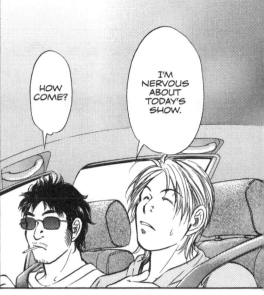

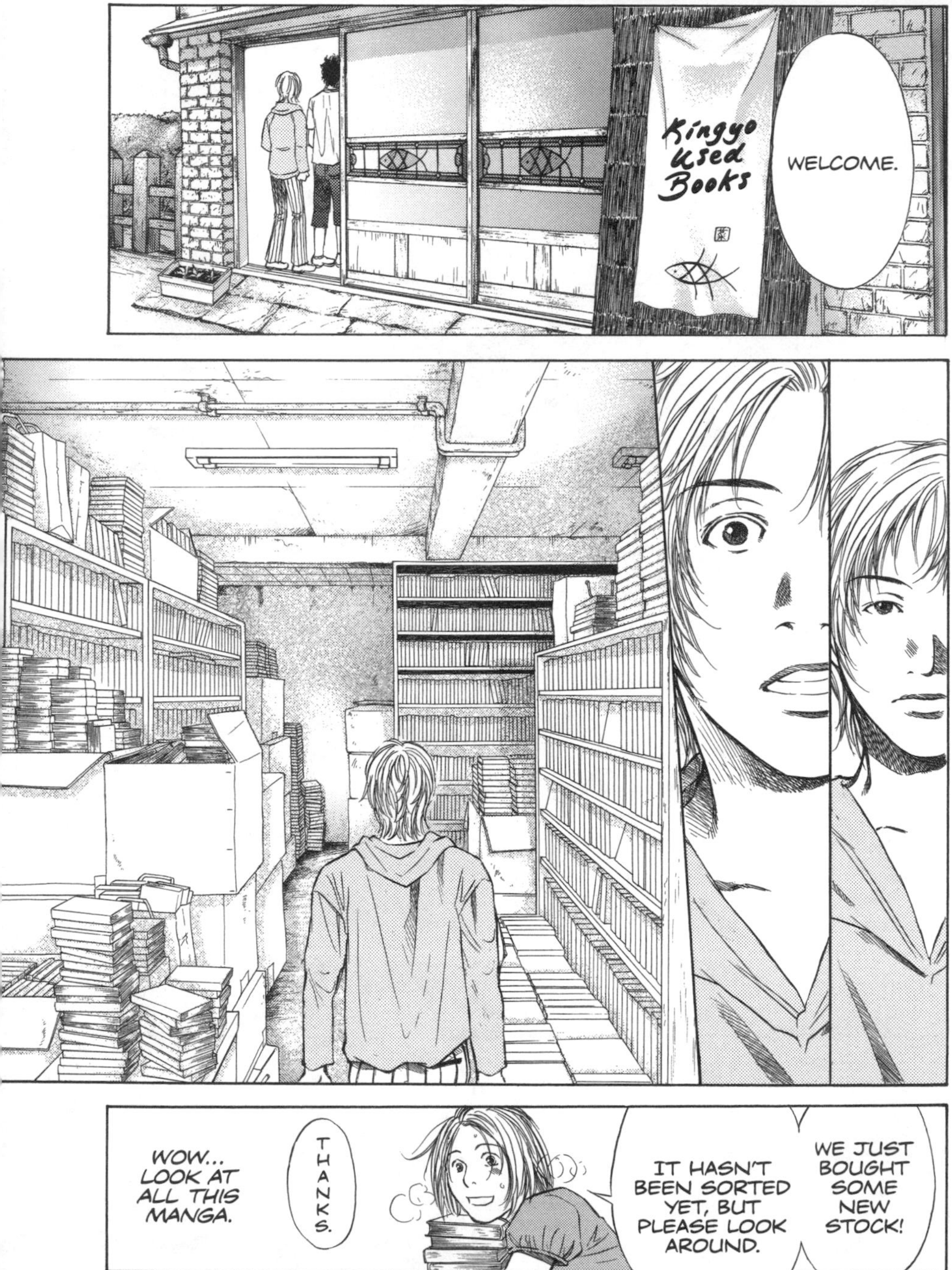
Kingyo Used Books
WELCOME.
WE JUST BOUGHT SOME NEW STOCK!
IT HASN'T BEEN SORTED YET, BUT PLEASE LOOK AROUND.
THANKS.
WOW... LOOK AT ALL THIS MANGA.

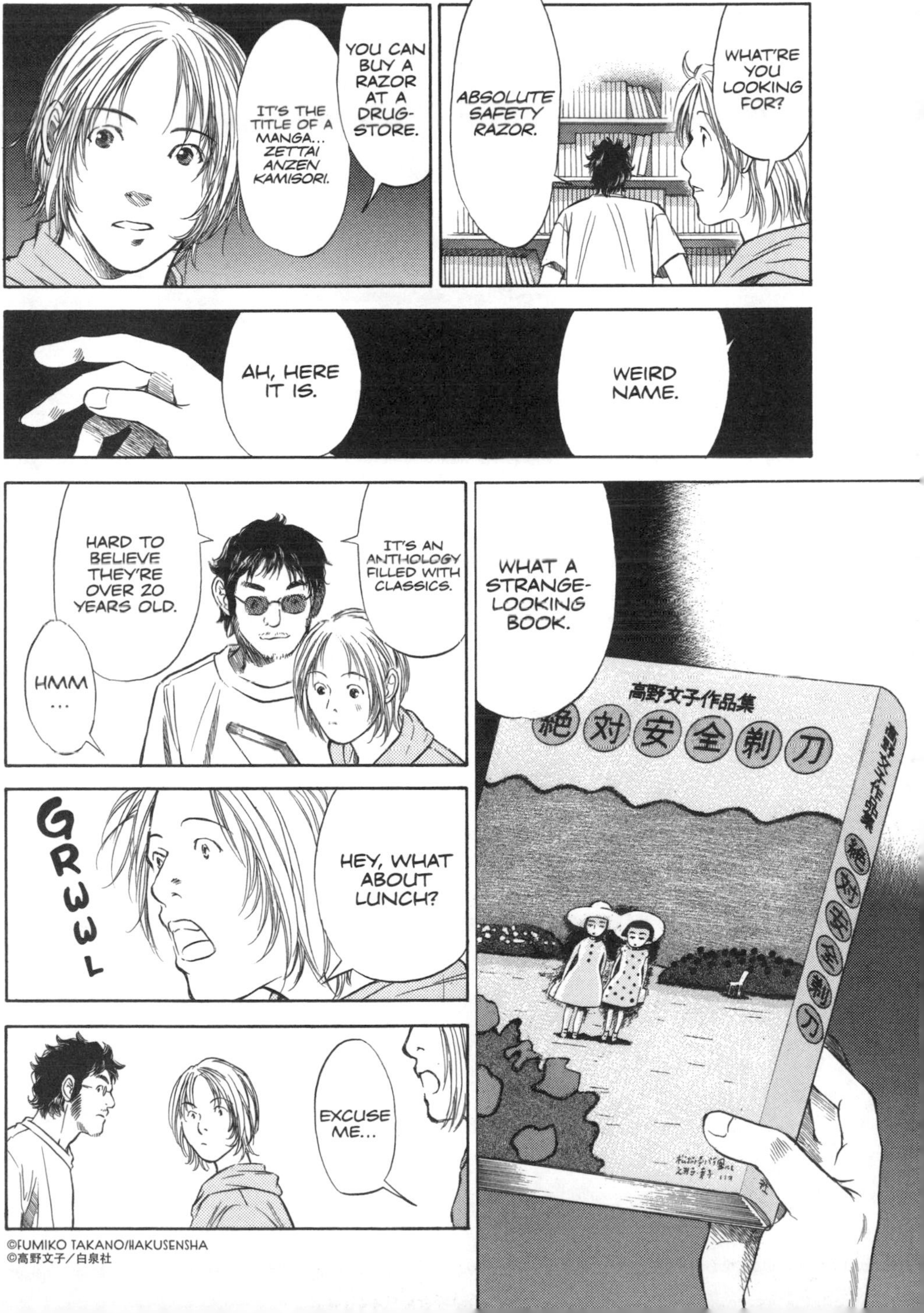

WHAT'RE YOU LOOKING FOR?
ABSOLUTE SAFETY RAZOR.
YOU CAN BUY A RAZOR AT A DRUG-STORE.
IT'S THE TITLE OF A MANGA... ZETTAI ANZEN KAMISORI.
WEIRD NAME.
AH, HERE IT IS.
WHAT A STRANGE-LOOKING BOOK.
高野文子作品集
絶対安全剃刀
IT'S AN ANTHOLOGY FILLED WITH CLASSICS.
HARD TO BELIEVE THEY'RE OVER 20 YEARS OLD.
HMM...
HEY, WHAT ABOUT LUNCH?
GRWWL
EXCUSE ME...

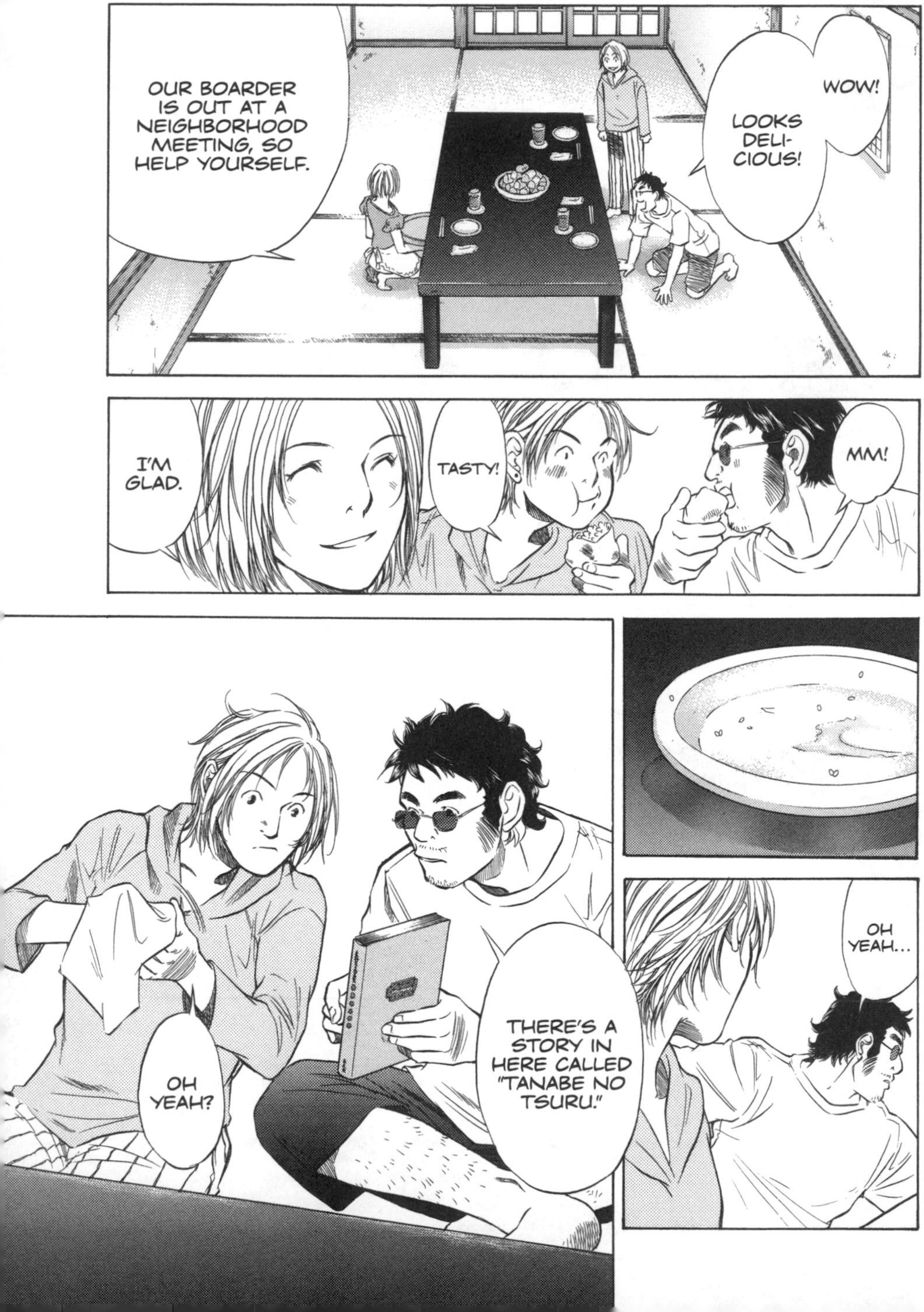
WOW!
LOOKS DELI-CIOUS!
OUR BOARDER IS OUT AT A NEIGHBORHOOD MEETING, SO HELP YOURSELF.
MM!
TASTY!
I'M GLAD.
OH YEAH...
THERE'S A STORY IN HERE CALLED "TANABE NO TSURU."
OH YEAH?

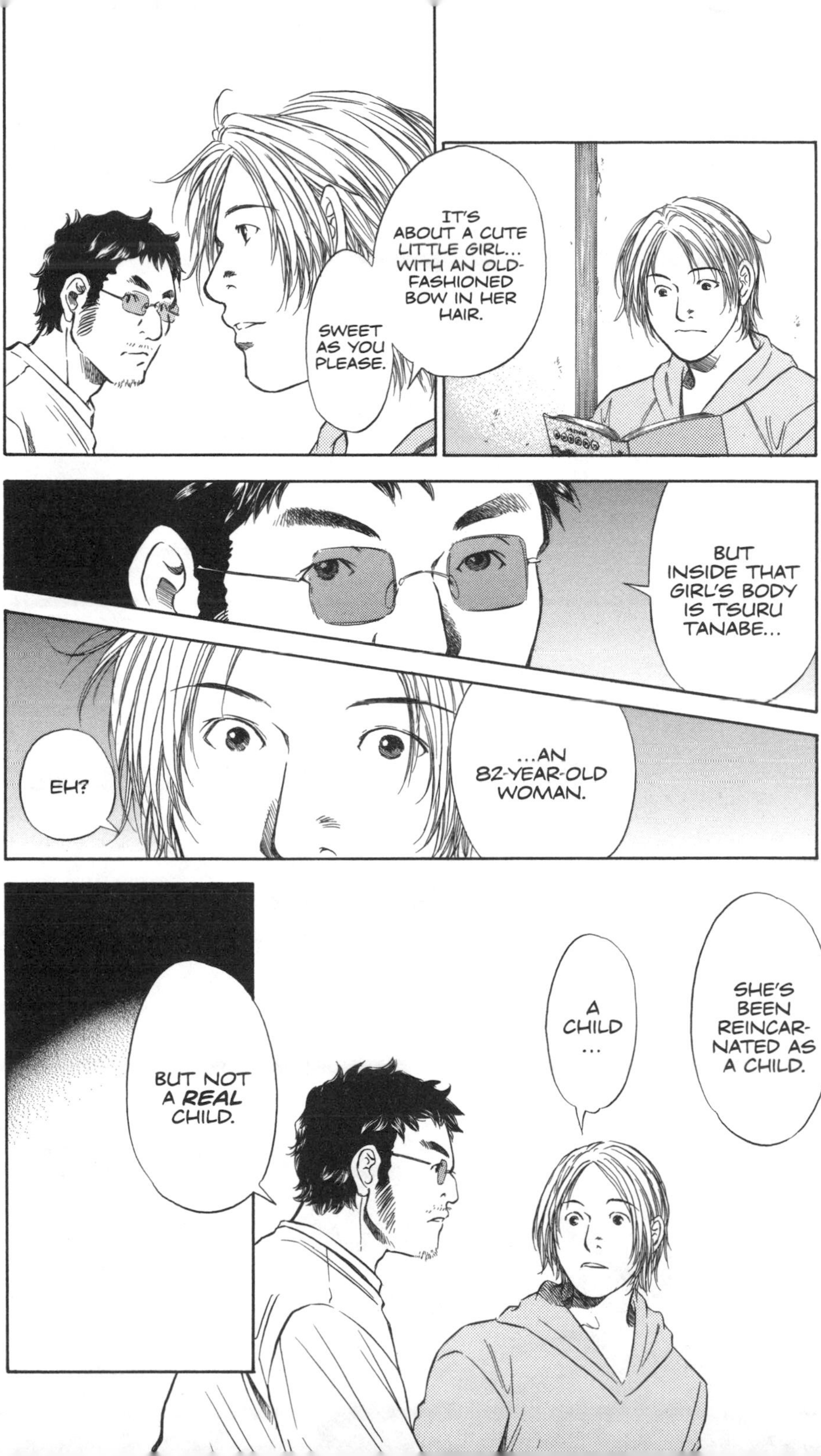
IT'S ABOUT A CUTE LITTLE GIRL... WITH AN OLD-FASHIONED BOW IN HER HAIR.
SWEET AS YOU PLEASE.
BUT INSIDE THAT GIRL'S BODY IS TSURU TANABE...
...AN 82-YEAR-OLD WOMAN.
EH?
SHE'S BEEN REINCAR-NATED AS A CHILD.
A CHILD...
BUT NOT A *REAL* CHILD.

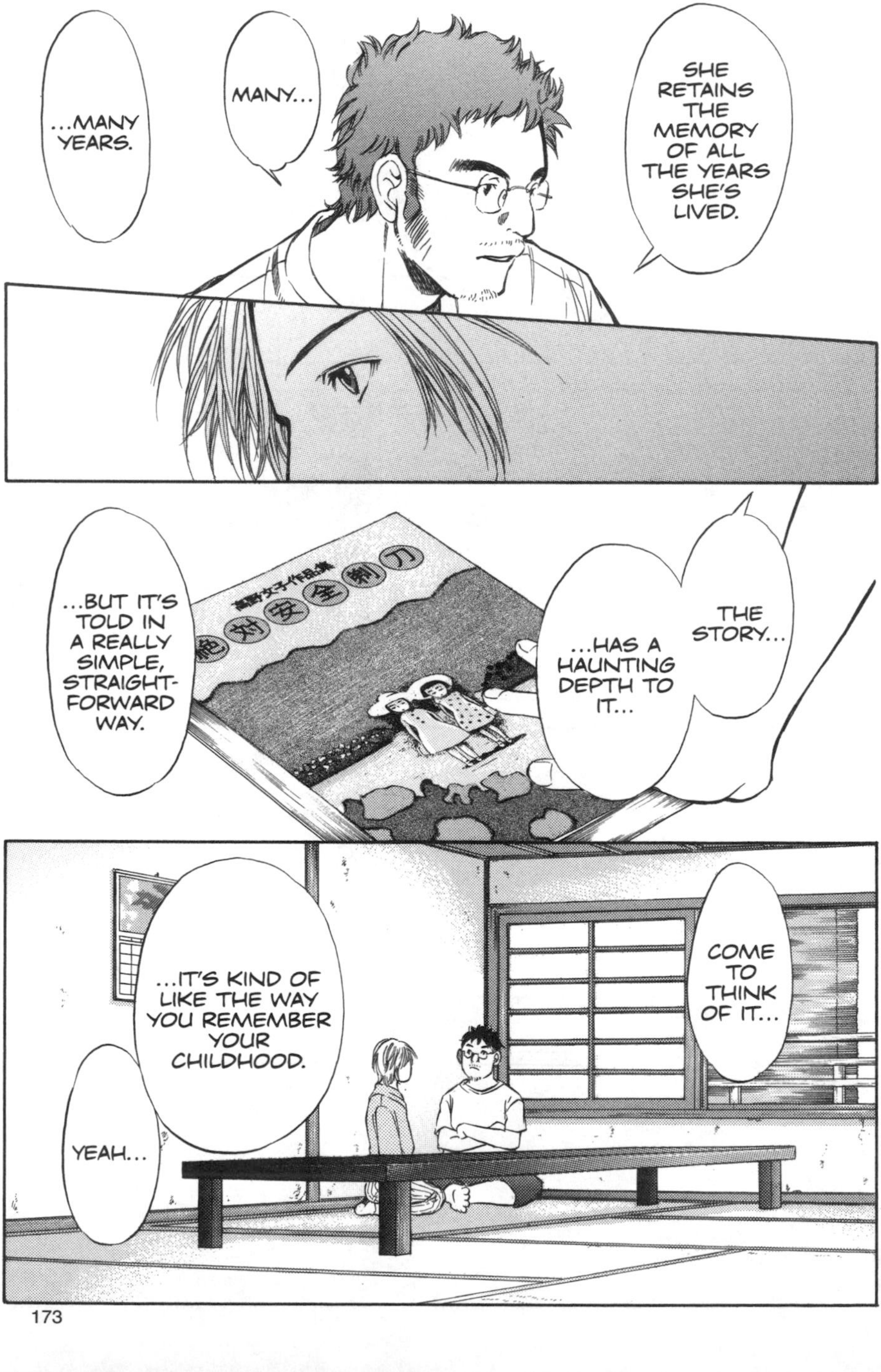
SHE RETAINS THE MEMORY OF ALL THE YEARS SHE'S LIVED.
MANY...
...MANY YEARS.
THE STORY...
...HAS A HAUNTING DEPTH TO IT...
...BUT IT'S TOLD IN A REALLY SIMPLE, STRAIGHT-FORWARD WAY.
絶対安全剃刀
COME TO THINK OF IT...
...IT'S KIND OF LIKE THE WAY YOU REMEMBER YOUR CHILDHOOD.
YEAH...

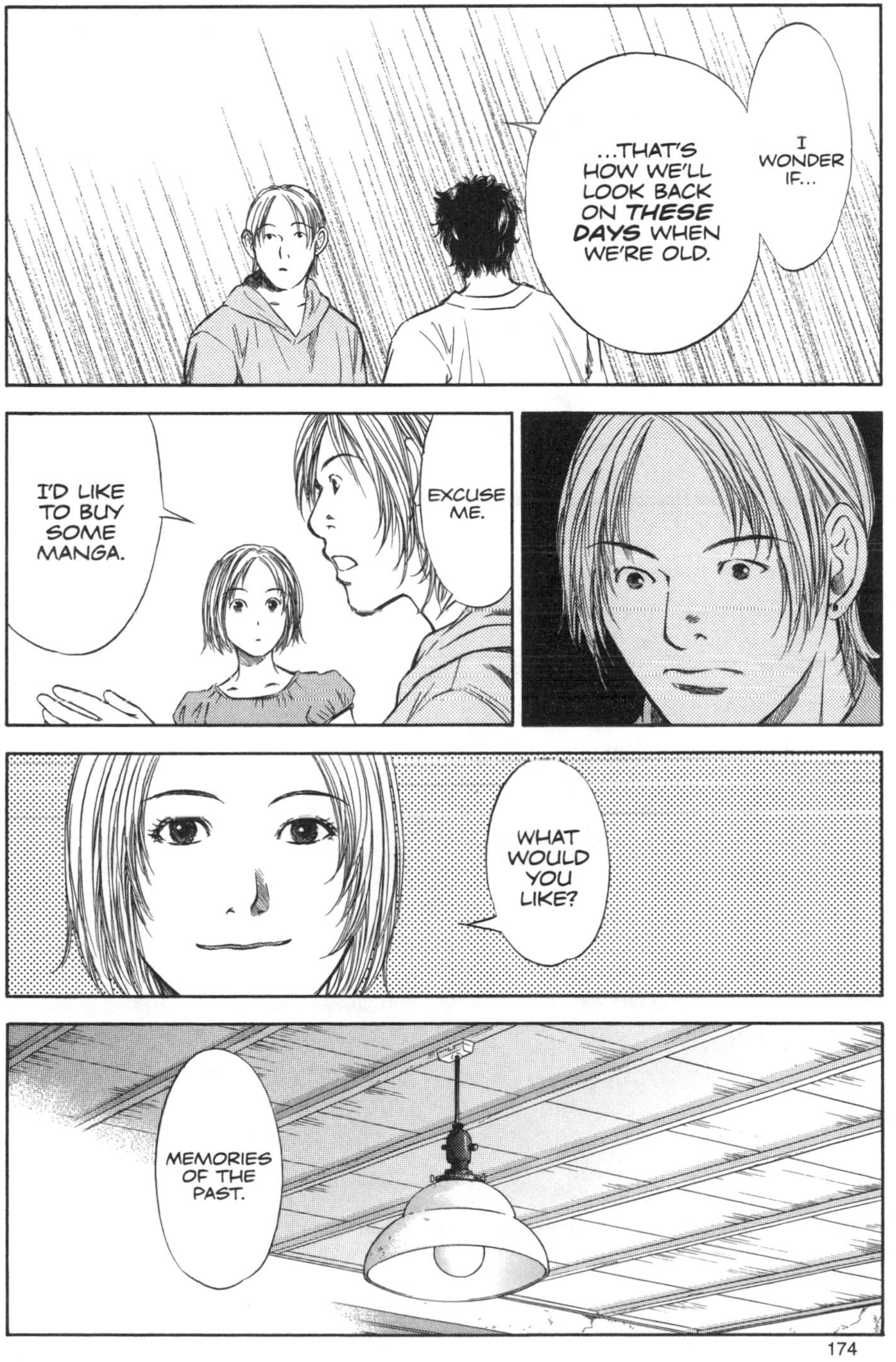
I WONDER IF...
...THAT'S HOW WE'LL LOOK BACK ON THESE DAYS WHEN WE'RE OLD.
EXCUSE ME.
I'D LIKE TO BUY SOME MANGA.
WHAT WOULD YOU LIKE?
MEMORIES OF THE PAST.

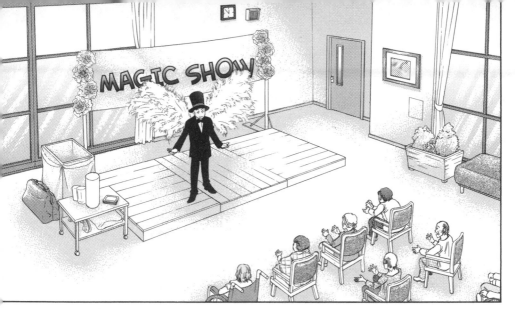

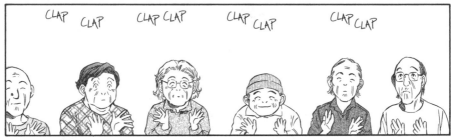

CLAP CLAP   CLAP CLAP   CLAP CLAP   CLAP CLAP

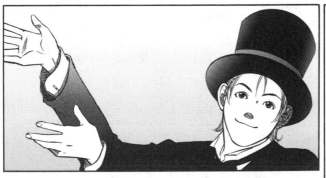

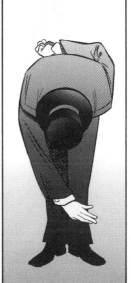

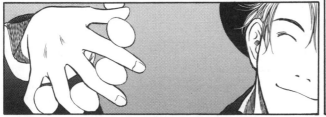

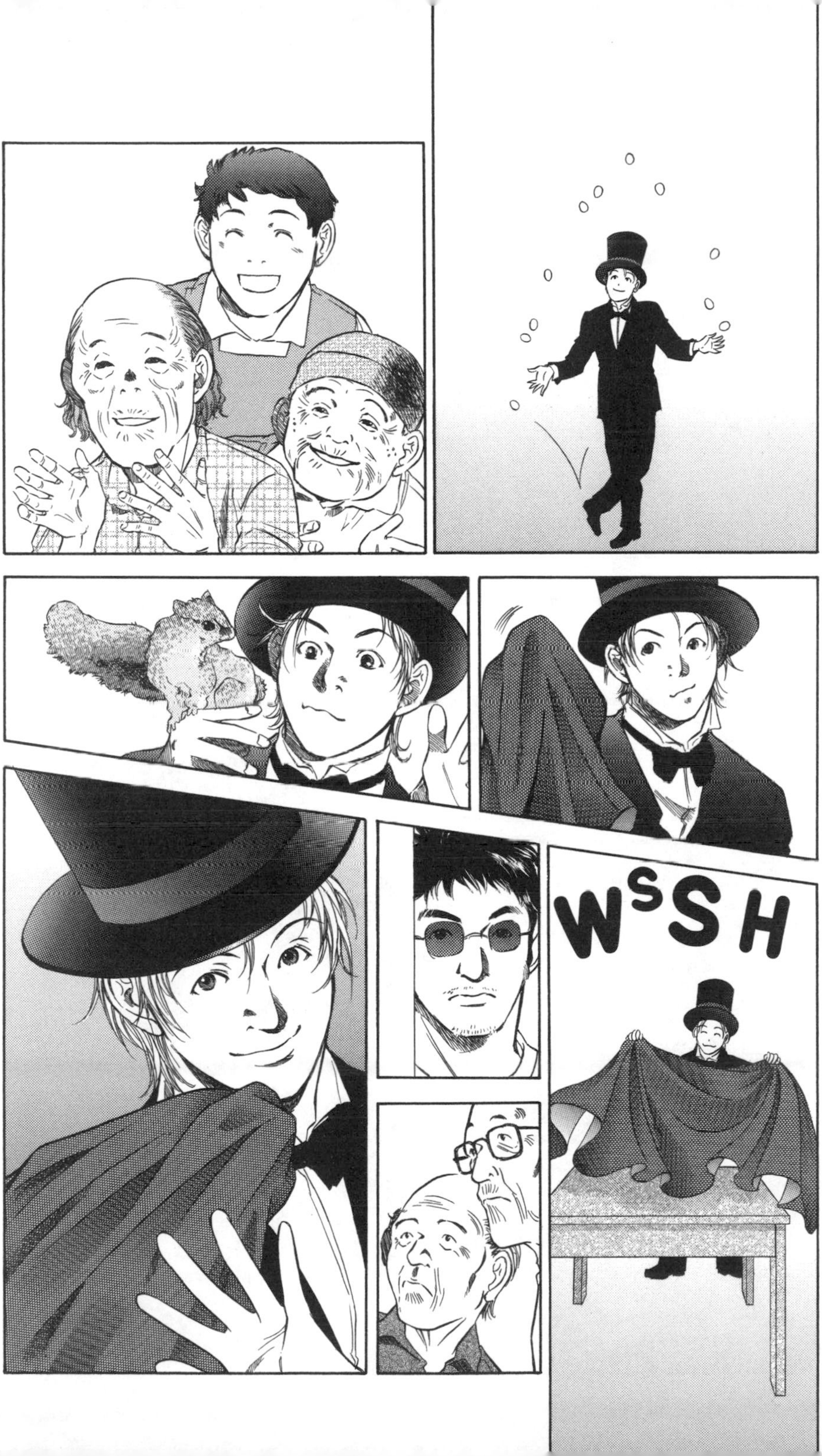
WSSH

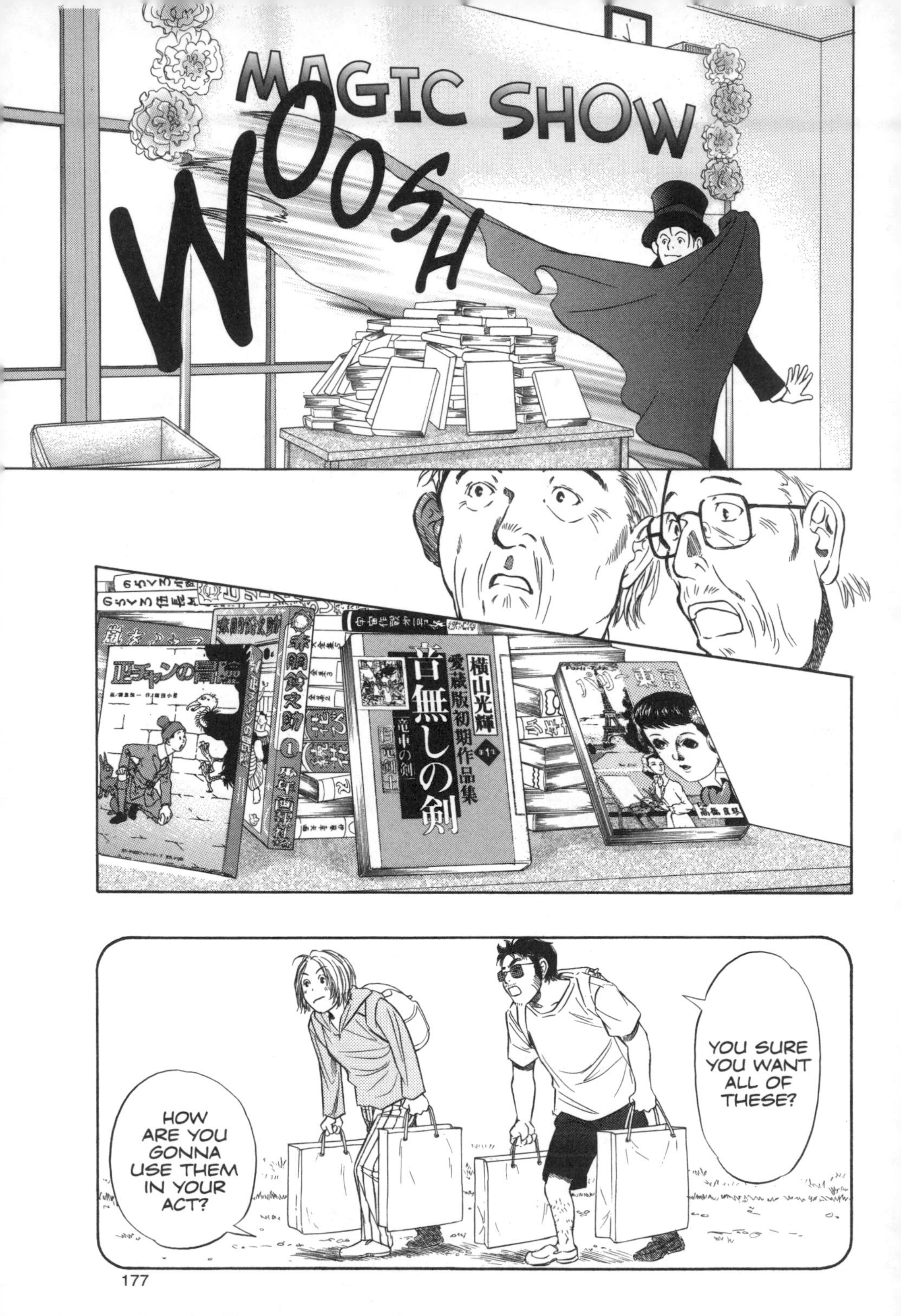
MAGIC SHOW
WOOSH
横山光輝
愛蔵版初期作品集
首無しの剣
YOU SURE YOU WANT ALL OF THESE?
HOW ARE YOU GONNA USE THEM IN YOUR ACT?

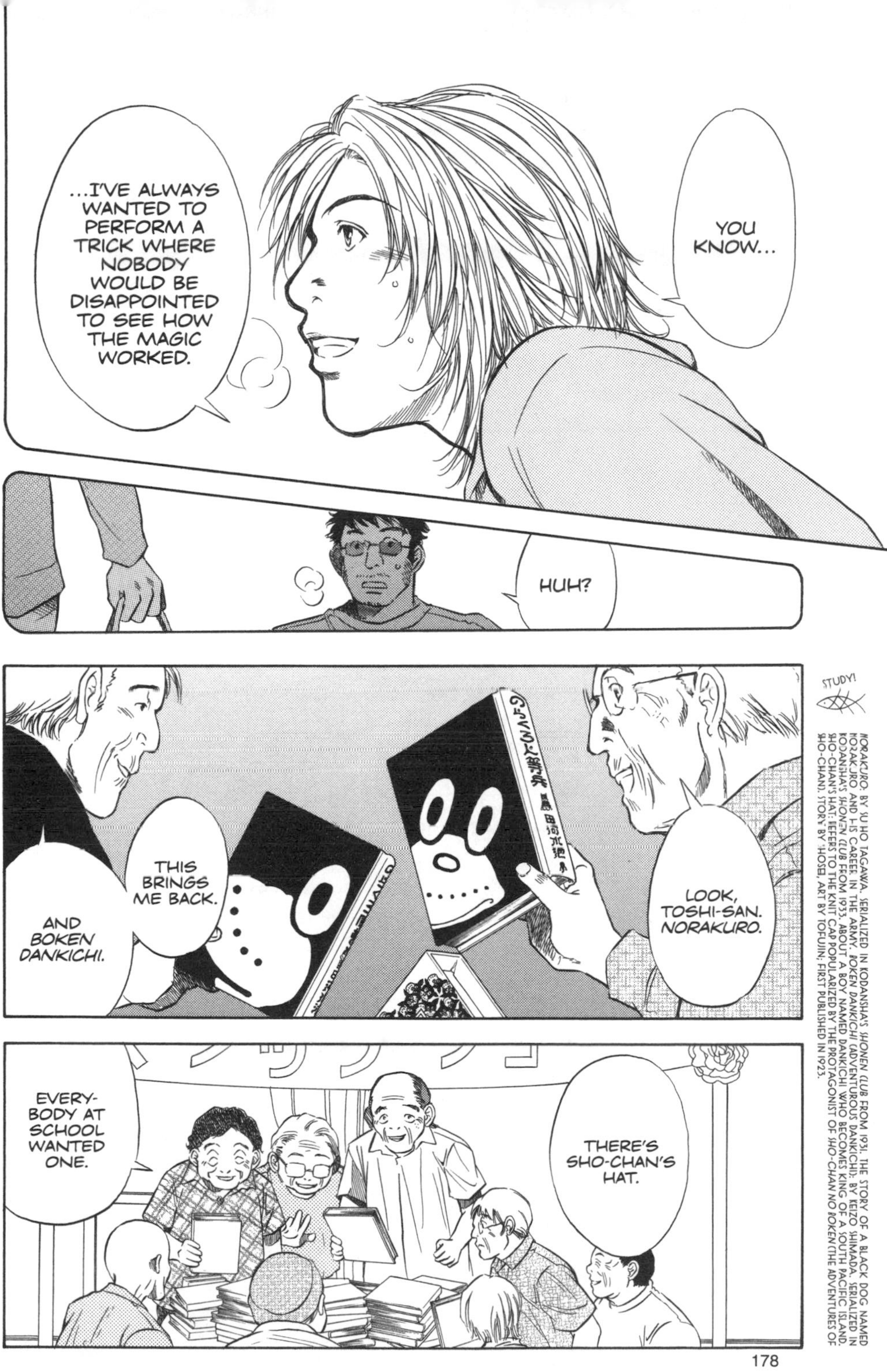
YOU KNOW...
...I'VE ALWAYS WANTED TO PERFORM A TRICK WHERE NOBODY WOULD BE DISAPPOINTED TO SEE HOW THE MAGIC WORKED.
HUH?
LOOK, TOSHI-SAN. NORAKURO.
THIS BRINGS ME BACK.
AND BOKEN DANKICHI.
THERE'S SHO-CHAN'S HAT.
EVERYBODY AT SCHOOL WANTED ONE.

STUDY!

NORAKURO: BY SU HO TAGAWA. SERIALIZED IN KODANSHA'S *SHONEN CLUB* FROM 1931. THE STORY OF A BLACK DOG NAMED NORAKURO AND HIS CAREER IN THE ARMY. *BOKEN DANKICHI* (ADVENTUROUS DANKICHI): BY KEIZO SHIMADA. SERIALIZED IN KODANSHA'S *SHONEN CLUB* FROM 1933. ABOUT A BOY NAMED DANKICHI WHO BECOMES KING OF A SOUTH PACIFIC ISLAND. SHO-CHAN'S HAT: REFERS TO THE KNIT CAP POPULARIZED BY THE PROTAGONIST OF *SHO-CHAN NO BOKEN* (THE ADVENTURES OF SHO-CHAN). STORY BY SHOSEI, ART BY TOFUJIN; FIRST PUBLISHED IN 1923.

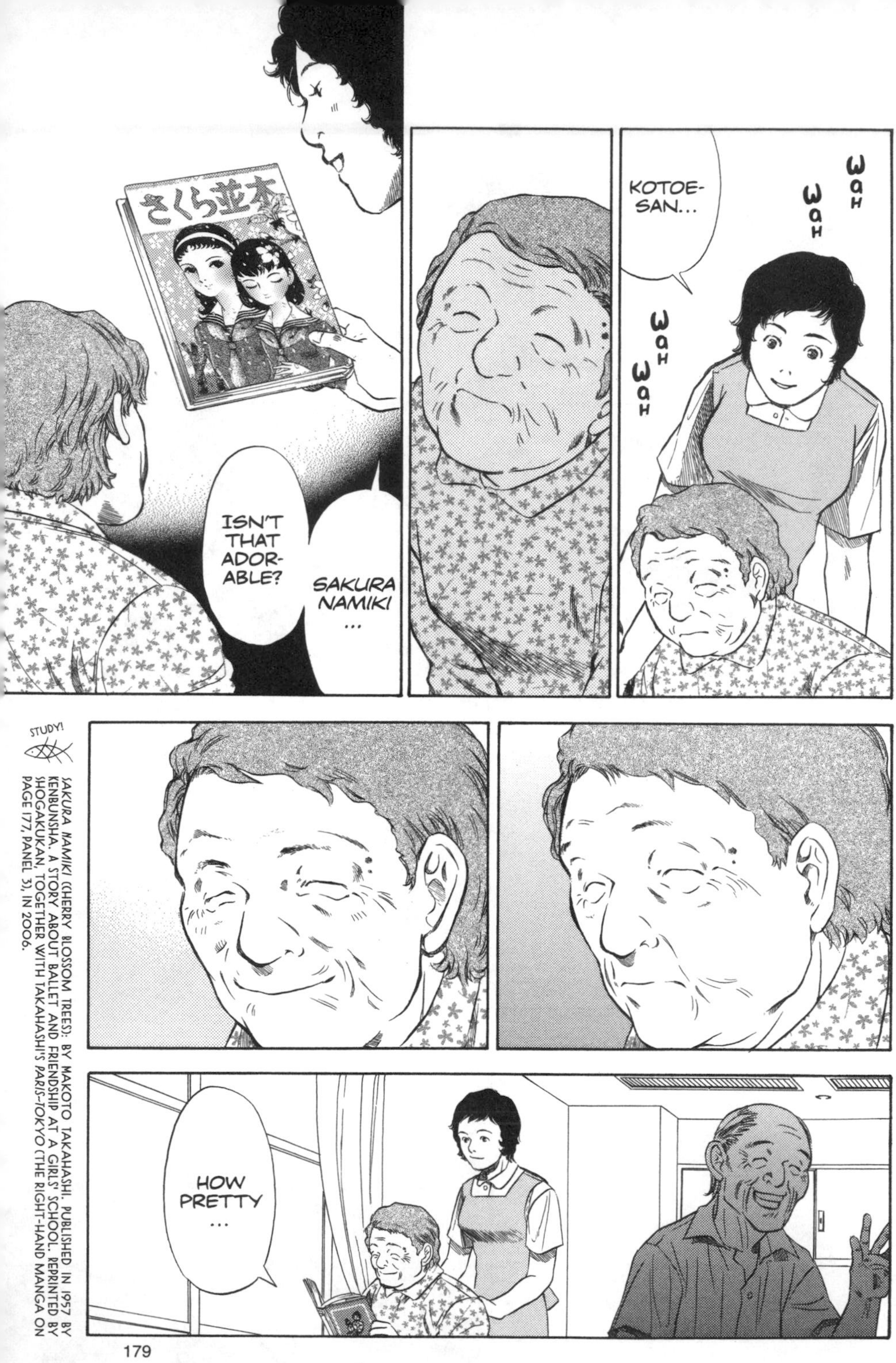
KOTOE-SAN...
WAH WAH WAH WAH WAH
SAKURA NAMIKI ...
ISN'T THAT ADORABLE?
HOW PRETTY ...

STUDY!

SAKURA NAMIKI (CHERRY BLOSSOM TREES): BY MAKOTO TAKAHASHI. PUBLISHED IN 1957 BY KENBUNSHA. A STORY ABOUT BALLET AND FRIENDSHIP AT A GIRLS' SCHOOL. REPRINTED BY SHOGAKUKAN, TOGETHER WITH TAKAHASHI'S *PARIS-TOKYO* (THE RIGHT-HAND MANGA ON PAGE 177, PANEL 3), IN 2006.

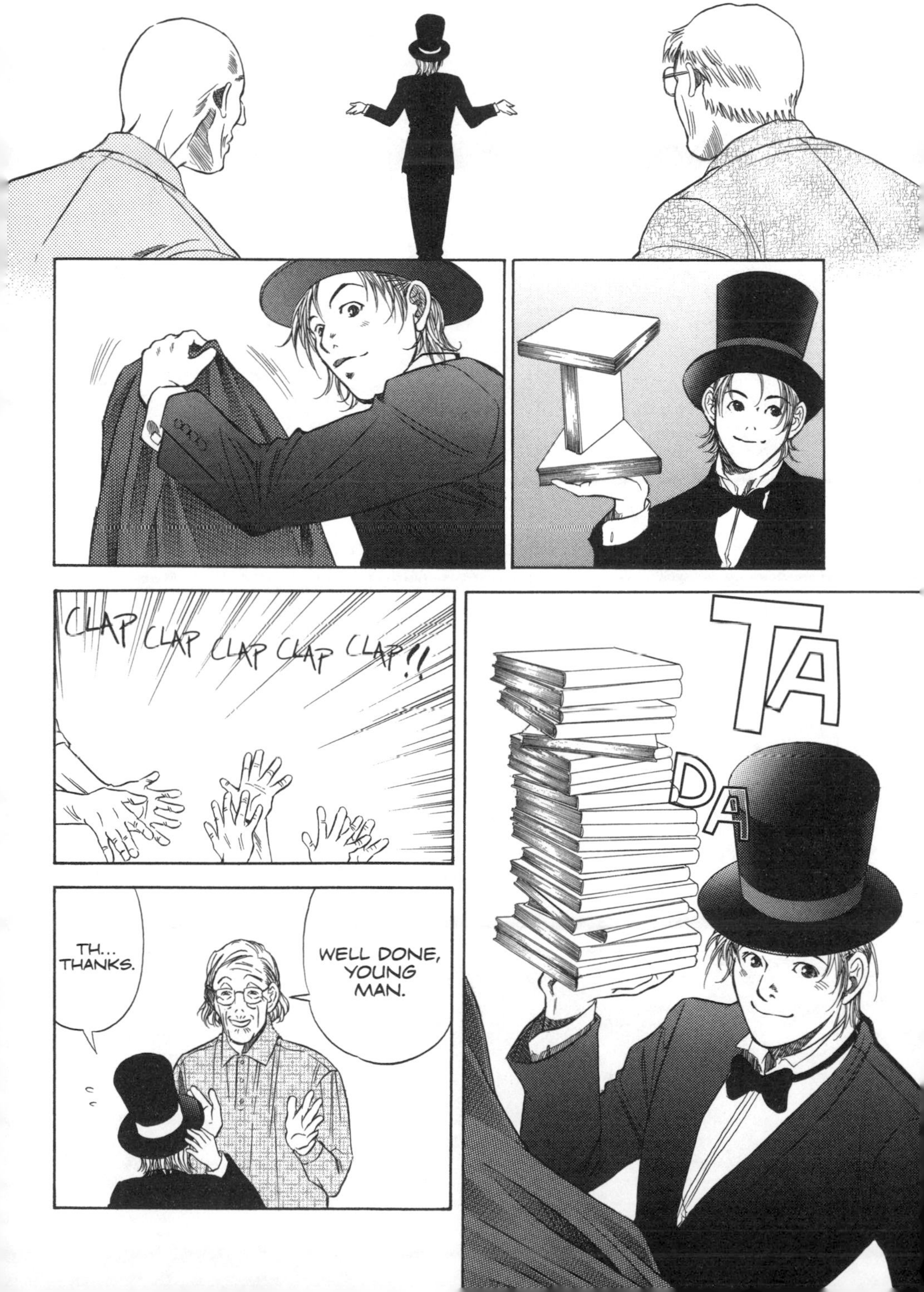
TA DA
CLAP CLAP CLAP CLAP CLAP!!
WELL DONE, YOUNG MAN.
TH... THANKS.

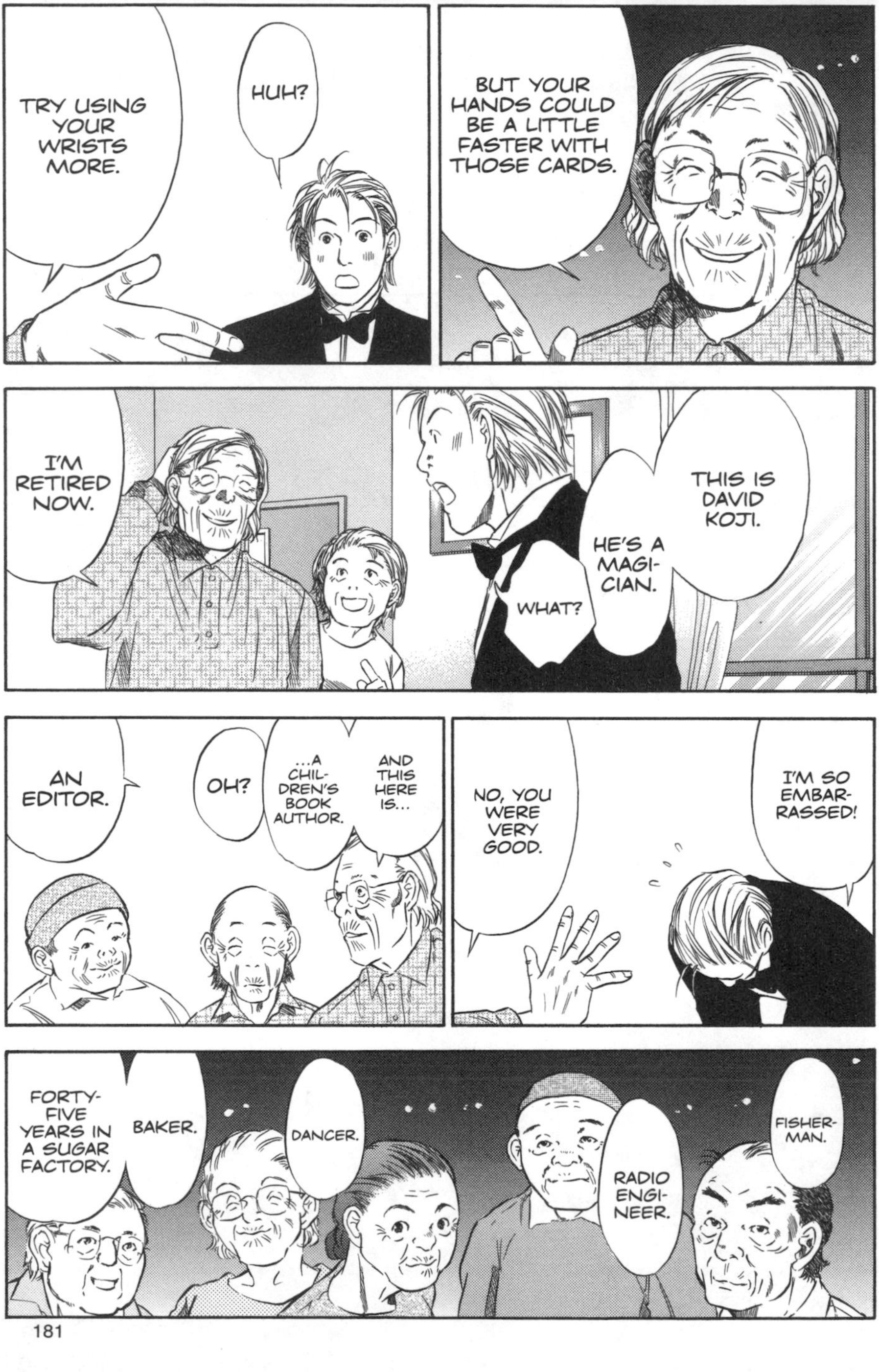
BUT YOUR HANDS COULD BE A LITTLE FASTER WITH THOSE CARDS.
HUH?
TRY USING YOUR WRISTS MORE.
THIS IS DAVID KOJI.
HE'S A MAGICIAN.
WHAT?
I'M RETIRED NOW.
I'M SO EMBARRASSED!
NO, YOU WERE VERY GOOD.
AND THIS HERE IS...
...A CHILDREN'S BOOK AUTHOR.
OH?
AN EDITOR.
FISHERMAN.
RADIO ENGINEER.
DANCER.
BAKER.
FORTY-FIVE YEARS IN A SUGAR FACTORY.

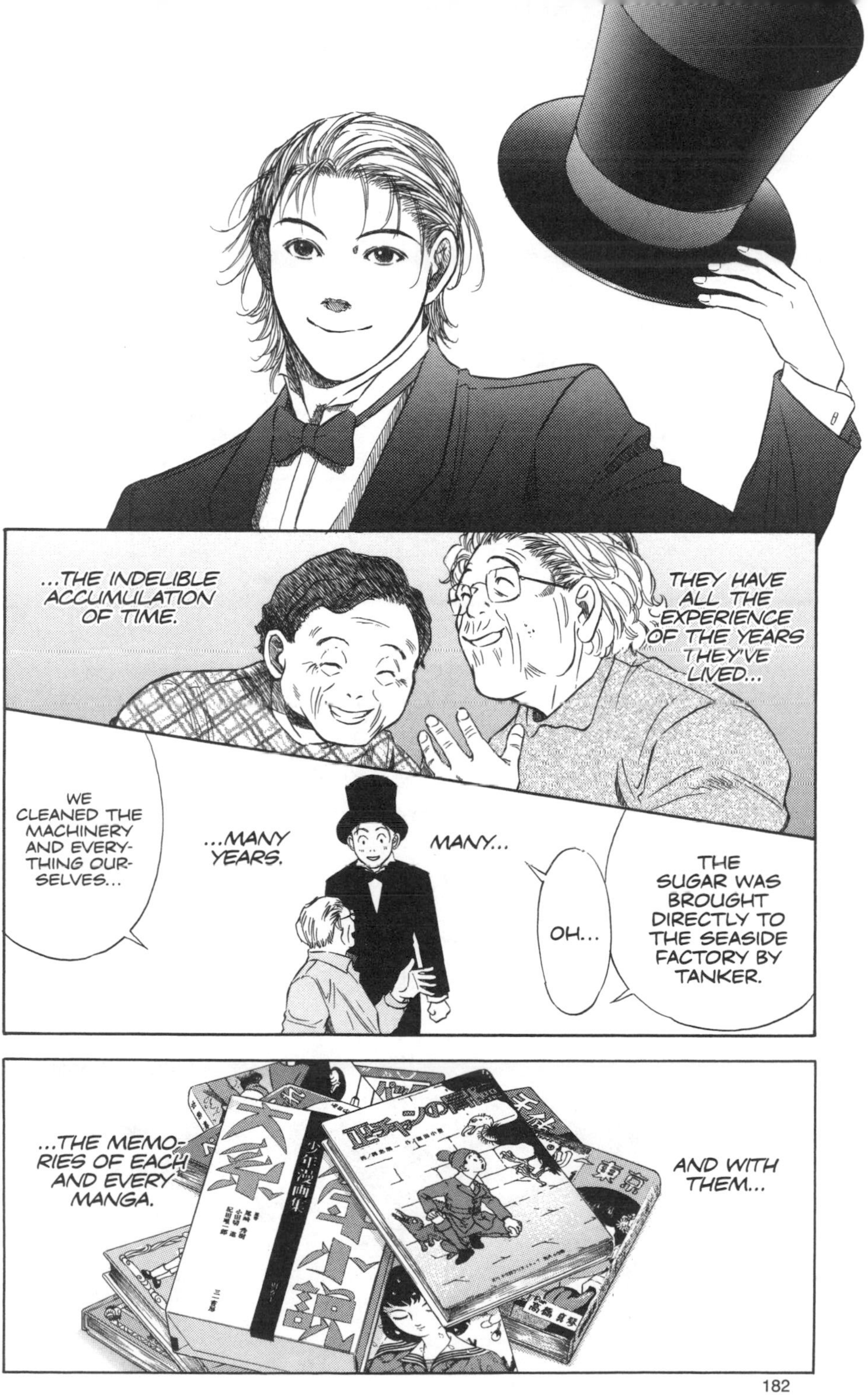
THEY HAVE ALL THE EXPERIENCE OF THE YEARS THEY'VE LIVED...
...THE INDELIBLE ACCUMULATION OF TIME.
THE SUGAR WAS BROUGHT DIRECTLY TO THE SEASIDE FACTORY BY TANKER.
OH...
MANY...
...MANY YEARS.
WE CLEANED THE MACHINERY AND EVERY-THING OUR-SELVES...
AND WITH THEM...
...THE MEMO-RIES OF EACH AND EVERY MANGA.

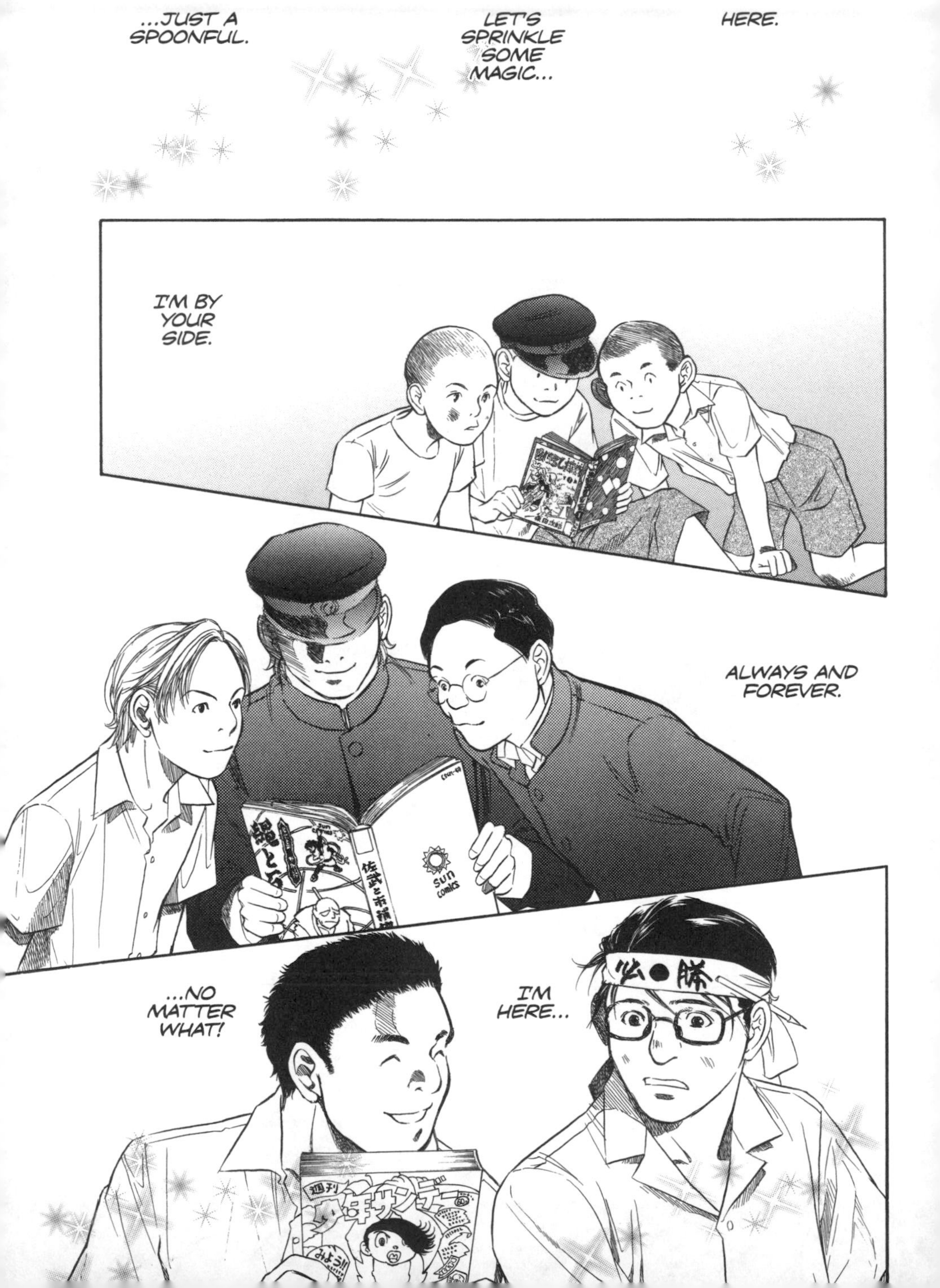
HERE.
LET'S SPRINKLE SOME MAGIC...
...JUST A SPOONFUL.
I'M BY YOUR SIDE.
ALWAYS AND FOREVER.
sun comics
必 勝
I'M HERE...
...NO MATTER WHAT!

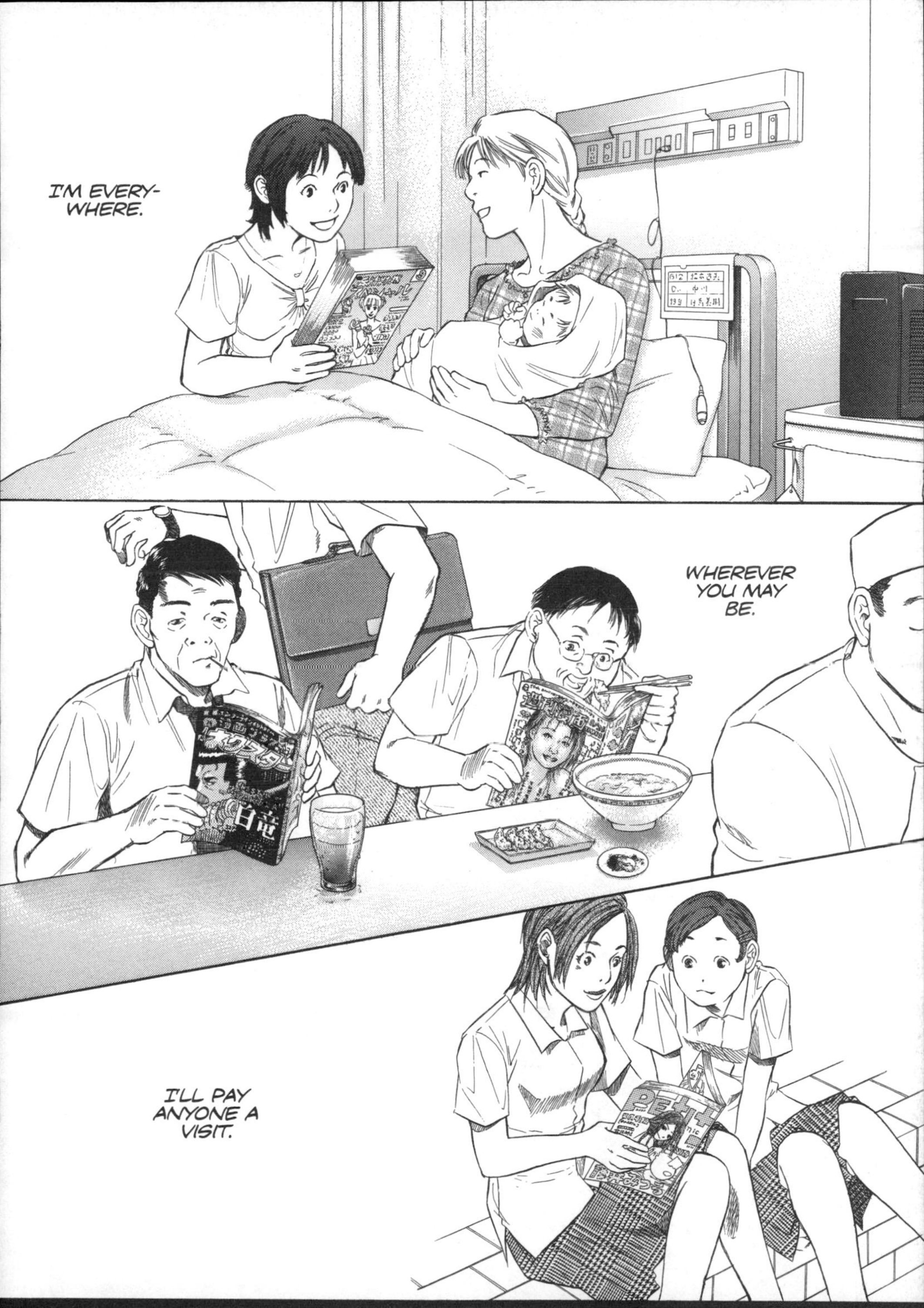
I'M EVERY-
WHERE.
WHEREVER
YOU MAY
BE.
I'LL PAY
ANYONE A
VISIT.

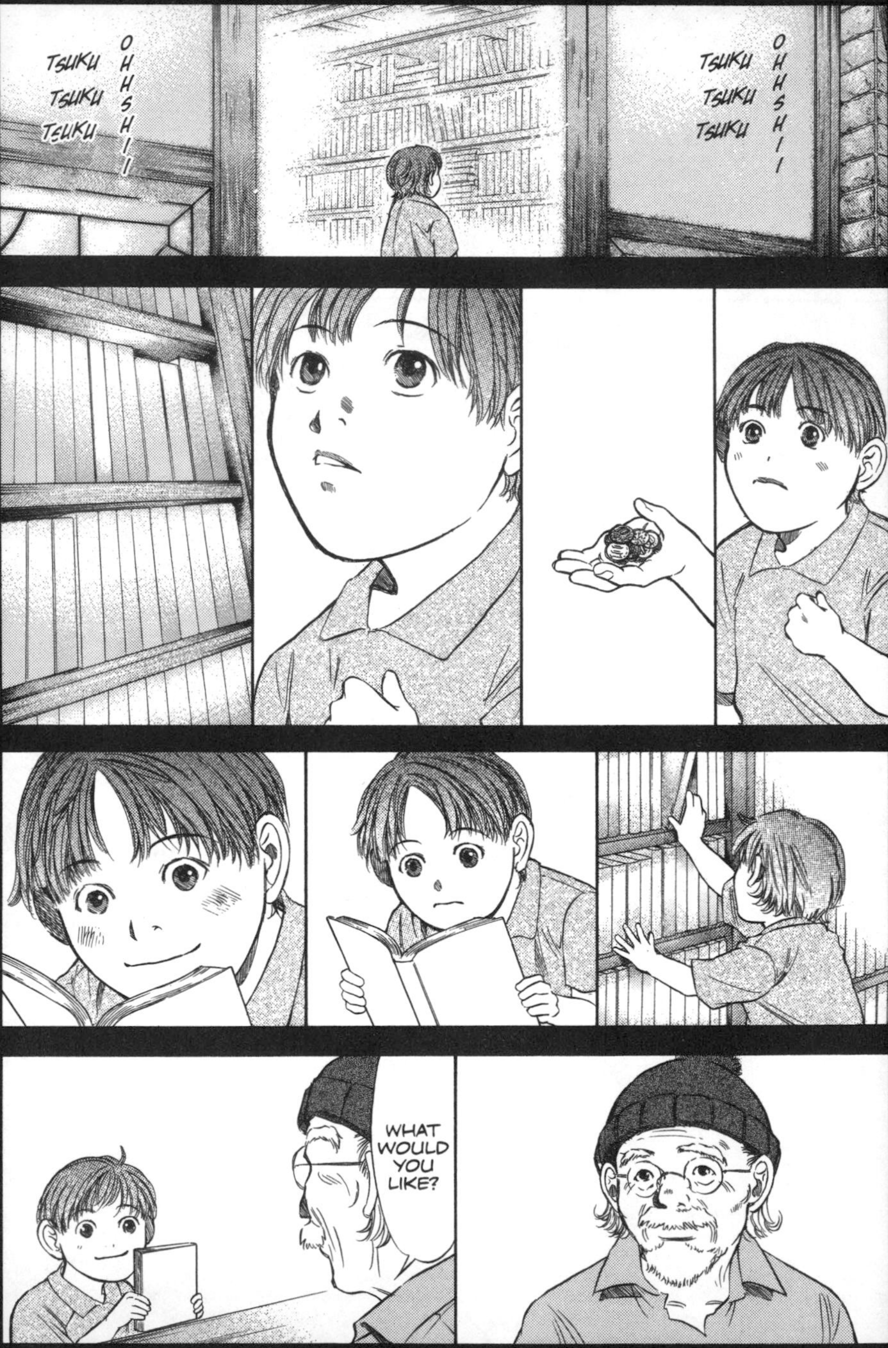
OHHSHII
TSUKU
TSUKU
TSUKU
OHHSHII
TSUKU
TSUKU
TSUKU
WHAT WOULD YOU LIKE?

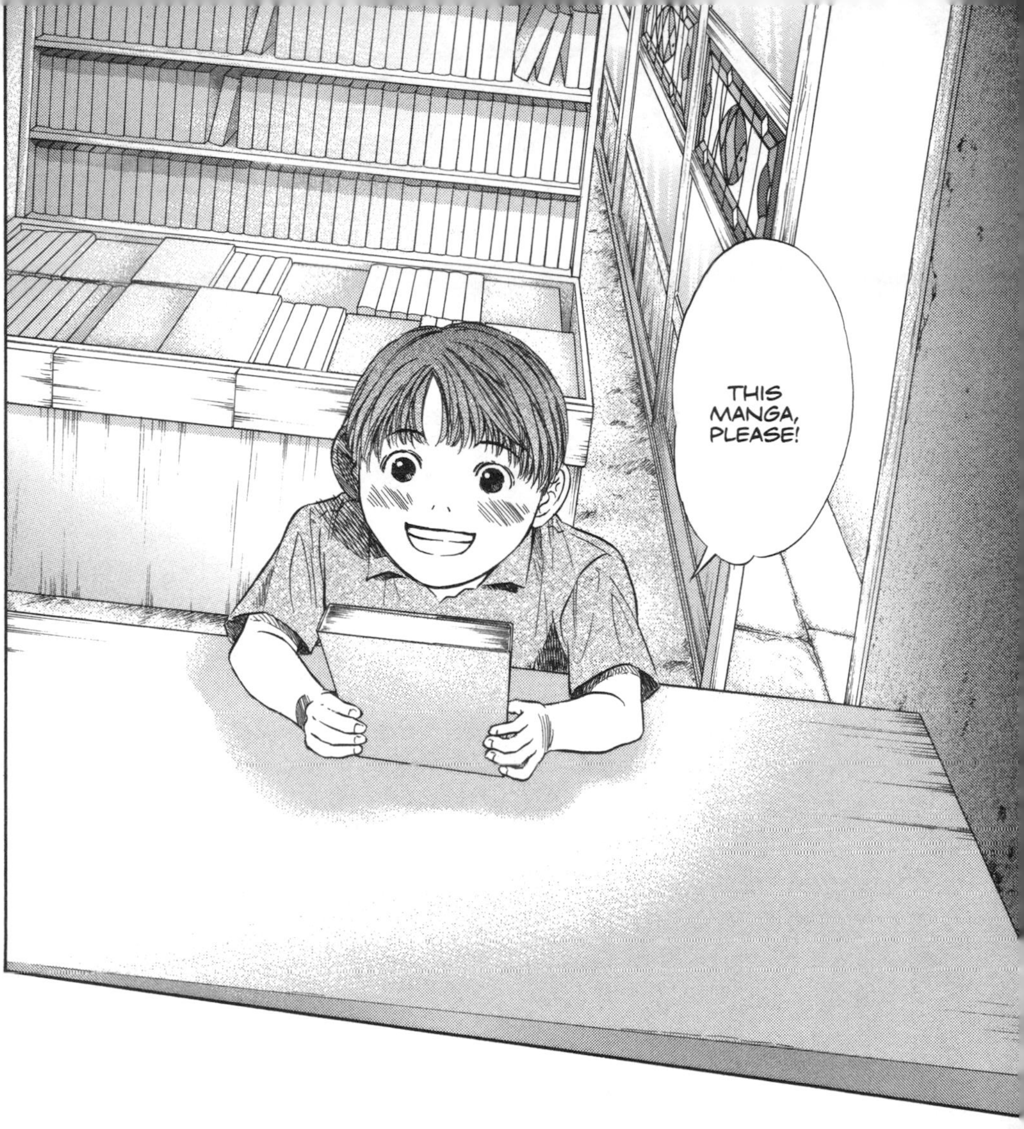
THIS MANGA, PLEASE!

EVERLASTING MEMORIES OF MANGA...

...ALWAYS BEGIN HERE.

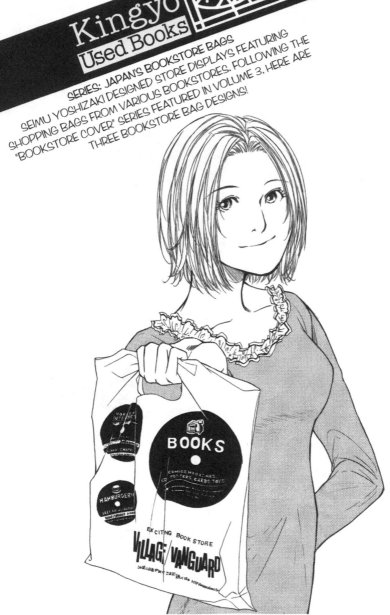

Kingyo Used Books

SERIES: JAPAN'S BOOKSTORE BAGS
SEIMU YOSHIZAKI DESIGNED STORE DISPLAYS FEATURING SHOPPING BAGS FROM VARIOUS BOOKSTORES. FOLLOWING THE "BOOKSTORE COVER" SERIES FEATURED IN VOLUME 3, HERE ARE THREE BOOKSTORE BAG DESIGNS!

BOOKS

COMICS, MAGAZINES, POSTERS, CARDS, TOYS

HAMBURGER IN

EXCITING BOOK STORE
VILLAGE/VANGUARD

VILLAGE VANGUARD

COMIC TORANOANA
SHIBUYA
TSUTAYA

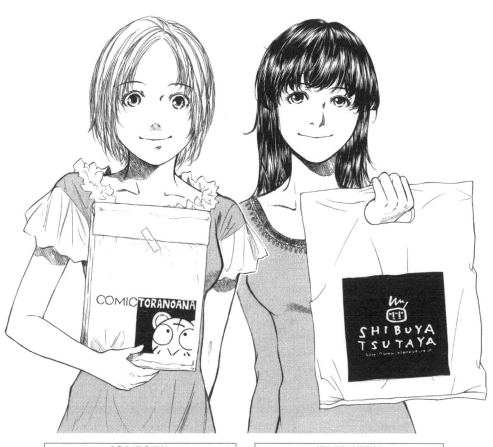

TORANOANA

SHIBUYA TSUTAYA

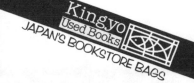

Kingyo Used Books
JAPAN'S BOOKSTORE BAGS

A 21st Century Gift

Billy and Grandpa's Curious Travelogue

Episode 4

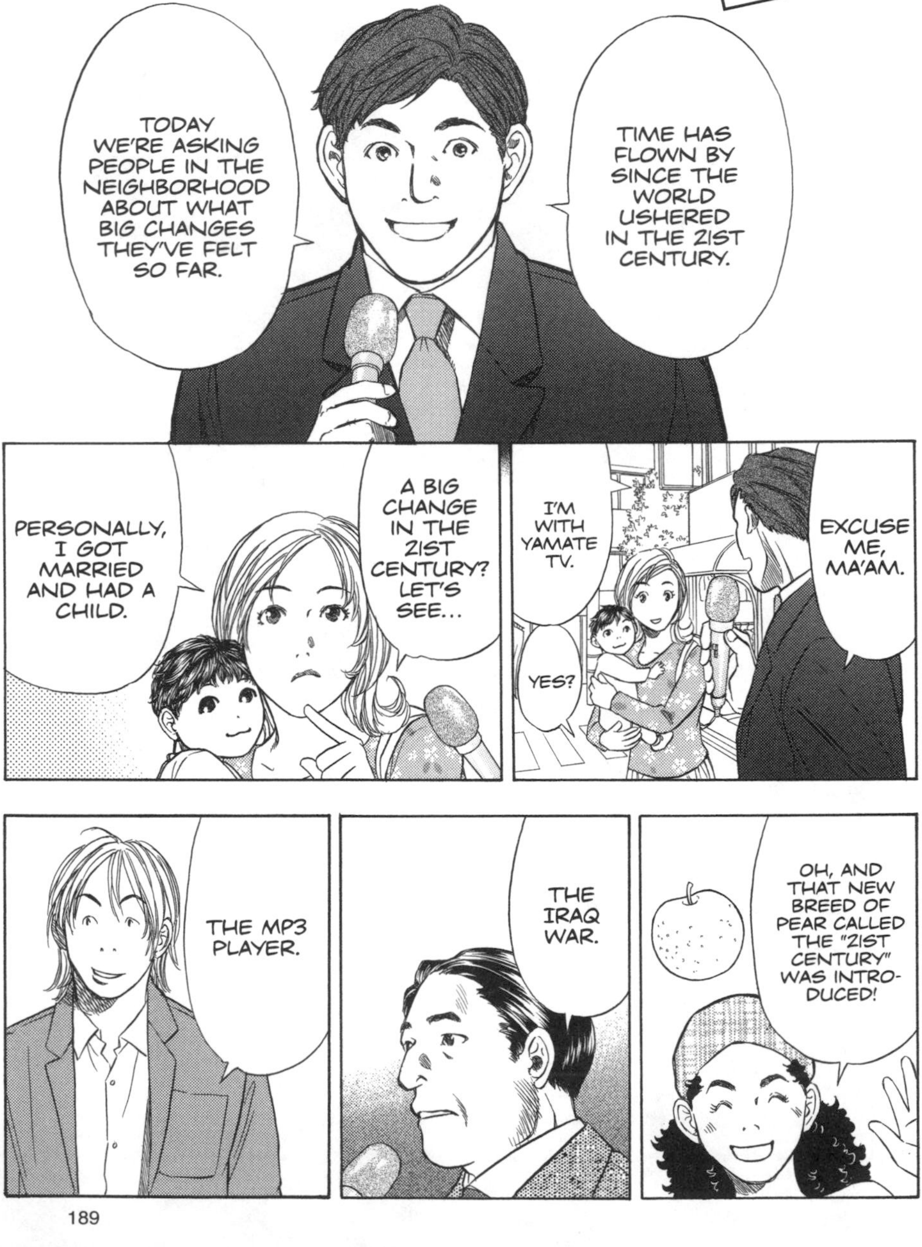

TIME HAS FLOWN BY SINCE THE WORLD USHERED IN THE 21ST CENTURY.
TODAY WE'RE ASKING PEOPLE IN THE NEIGHBORHOOD ABOUT WHAT BIG CHANGES THEY'VE FELT SO FAR.
EXCUSE ME, MA'AM.
I'M WITH YAMATE TV.
YES?
A BIG CHANGE IN THE 21ST CENTURY? LET'S SEE...
PERSONALLY, I GOT MARRIED AND HAD A CHILD.
OH, AND THAT NEW BREED OF PEAR CALLED THE "21ST CENTURY" WAS INTRO-DUCED!
THE IRAQ WAR.
THE MP3 PLAYER.

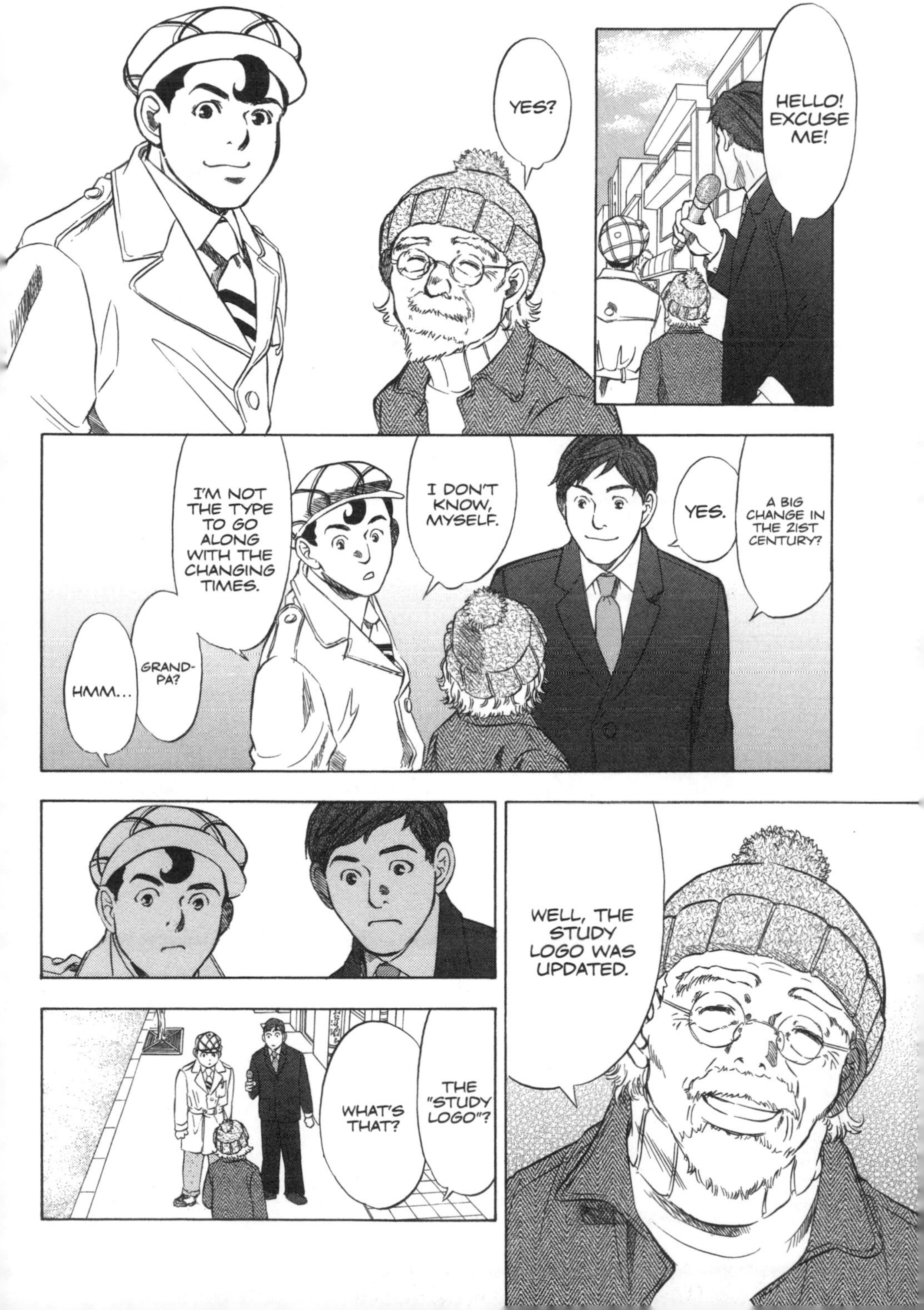
HELLO! EXCUSE ME!
YES?
A BIG CHANGE IN THE 21ST CENTURY?
YES.
I DON'T KNOW, MYSELF.
I'M NOT THE TYPE TO GO ALONG WITH THE CHANGING TIMES.
GRAND-PA?
HMM...
WELL, THE STUDY LOGO WAS UPDATED.
THE "STUDY LOGO"?
WHAT'S THAT?

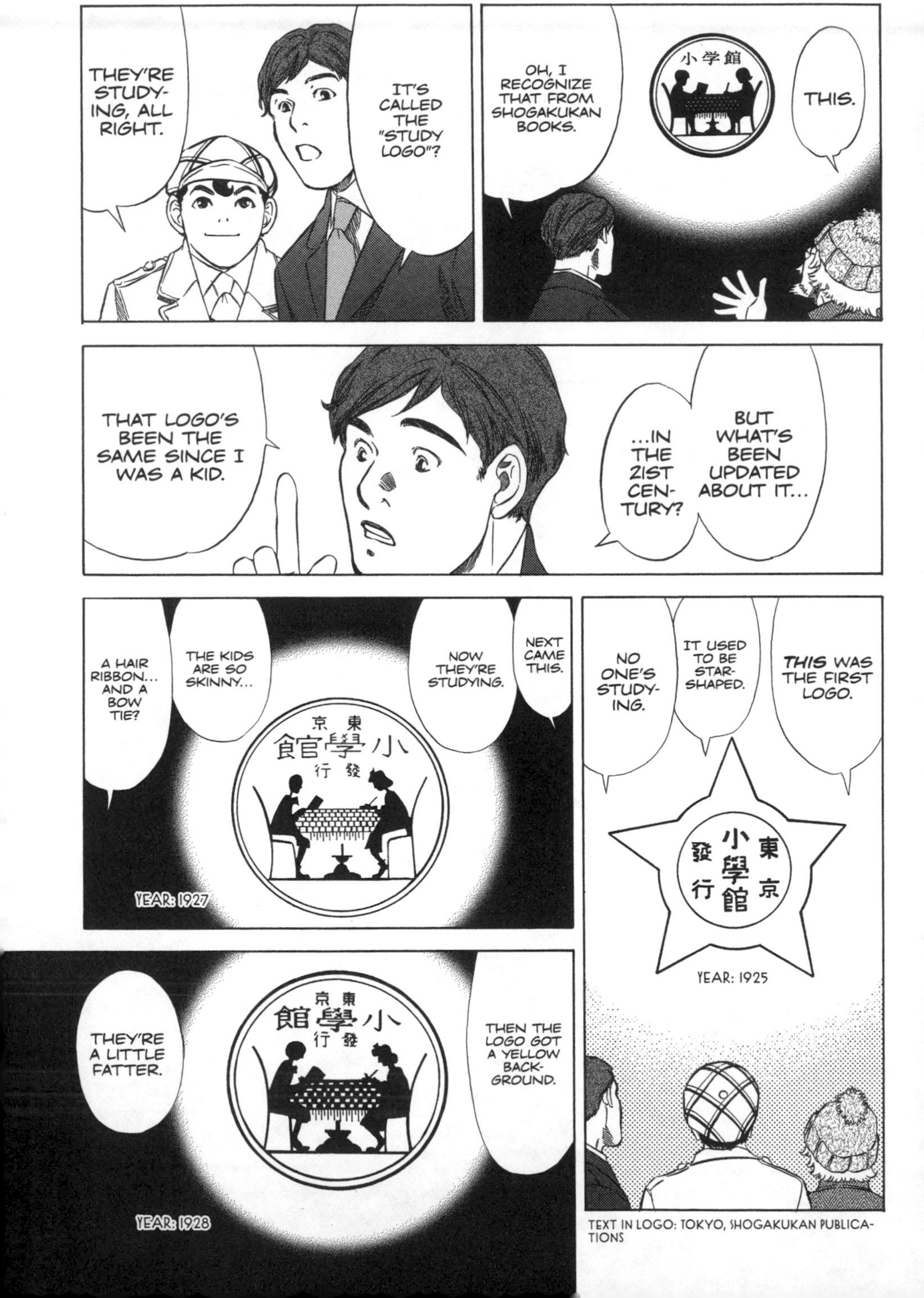
THIS.
OH, I RECOGNIZE THAT FROM SHOGAKUKAN BOOKS.
小学館
IT'S CALLED THE "STUDY LOGO"?
THEY'RE STUDYING, ALL RIGHT.
BUT WHAT'S BEEN UPDATED ABOUT IT...
...IN THE 21ST CENTURY?
THAT LOGO'S BEEN THE SAME SINCE I WAS A KID.
THIS WAS THE FIRST LOGO.
IT USED TO BE STAR-SHAPED.
NO ONE'S STUDYING.
東京 小學館 發行
YEAR: 1925
NEXT CAME THIS.
NOW THEY'RE STUDYING.
THE KIDS ARE SO SKINNY...
A HAIR RIBBON... AND A BOW TIE?
東京 小學館 發行
YEAR: 1927
THEN THE LOGO GOT A YELLOW BACKGROUND.
THEY'RE A LITTLE FATTER.
東京 小學館 發行
YEAR: 1928
TEXT IN LOGO: TOKYO, SHOGAKUKAN PUBLICATIONS

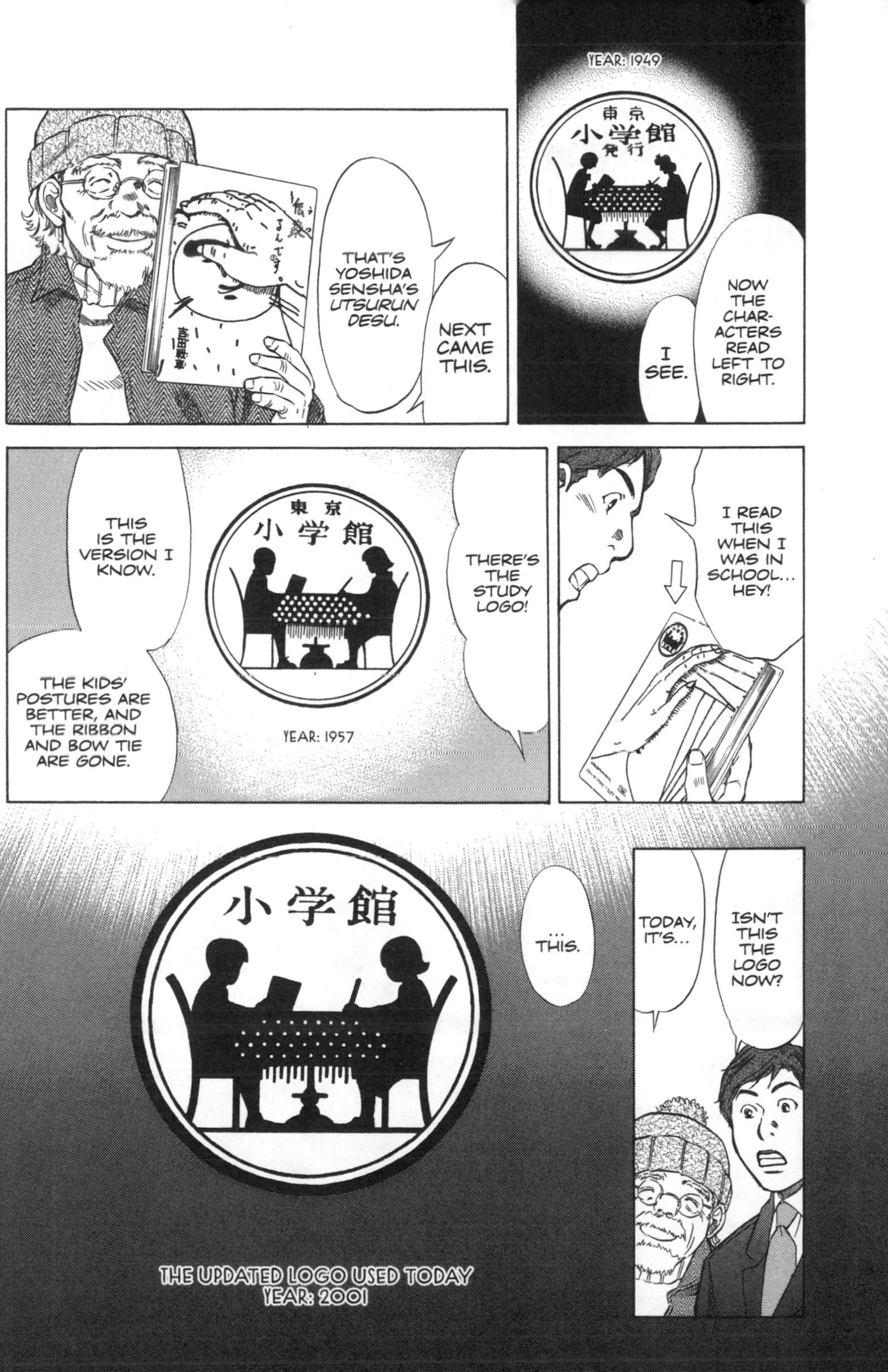
YEAR: 1949
東京
小学館
発行
NOW THE CHAR-ACTERS READ LEFT TO RIGHT.
I SEE.
THAT'S YOSHIDA SENSHA'S UTSURUN DESU.
NEXT CAME THIS.
I READ THIS WHEN I WAS IN SCHOOL... HEY!
THERE'S THE STUDY LOGO!
東京
小学館
THIS IS THE VERSION I KNOW.
THE KIDS' POSTURES ARE BETTER, AND THE RIBBON AND BOW TIE ARE GONE.
YEAR: 1957
ISN'T THIS THE LOGO NOW?
TODAY, IT'S...
...THIS.
小学館
THE UPDATED LOGO USED TODAY
YEAR: 2001

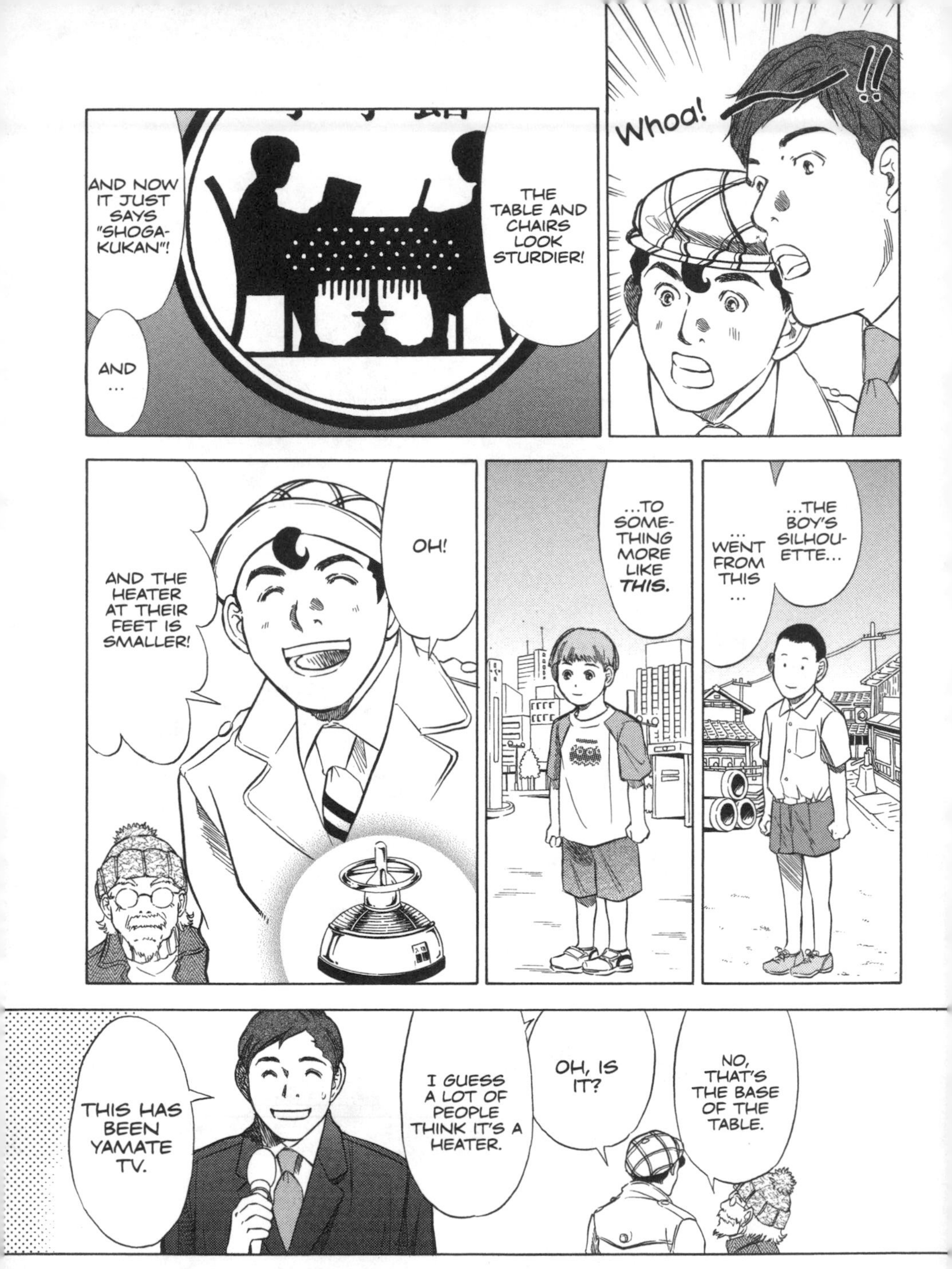
Whoa!
!!
THE TABLE AND CHAIRS LOOK STURDIER!
AND NOW IT JUST SAYS "SHOGA-KUKAN"!
AND ...
...THE BOY'S SILHOU-ETTE...
... WENT FROM THIS ...
...TO SOME-THING MORE LIKE *THIS.*
OH!
AND THE HEATER AT THEIR FEET IS SMALLER!
NO, THAT'S THE BASE OF THE TABLE.
OH, IS IT?
I GUESS A LOT OF PEOPLE THINK IT'S A HEATER.
THIS HAS BEEN YAMATE TV.

A SCREENSAVER OF THE STUDY LOGO CAN BE DOWNLOADED AT THIS WEBSITE:

HTTP://WWW.NETKUN.COM/DIGITAL/DESKTOP/SCREEN/INDEX.HTM

Kingyo Used Books, Volume 4 / The End

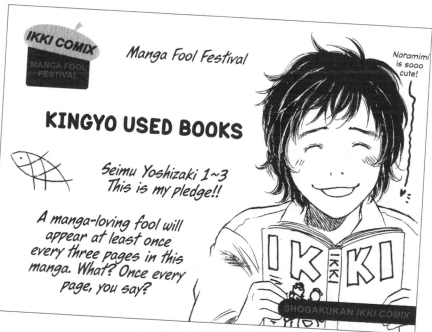

IKKI COMIX
MANGA FOOL FESTIVAL
Manga Fool Festival
KINGYO USED BOOKS
Seimu Yoshizaki 1~3
This is my pledge!!
A manga-loving fool will appear at least once every three pages in this manga. What? Once every page, you say?
Noramimi is sooo cute!
IKKI
SHOGAKUKAN IKKI COMIX

BONUS IMAGE: FOR BOOKSTORE DISPLAY 4

KINGYO USED BOOKS NOTEBOOK

More useful information about
the manga found on the shelves of
Kingyo Used Books!

Text by Hiroshi Hashimoto.

Born in 1948 in Kumamoto, Japan.
Owner of the used bookstore
Kirara Bunko. Aside from running
his bookstore, he also teaches at a
preparatory school and is active in
a nonprofit organization. Fellow
alumni of his elementary school
include manga commentators
Hiroshi Yonezawa and Yukari
Fujimoto. His dream is to build a
manga library in Aso. Hashimoto
was asked to write this column
when being interviewed for
information for this series.

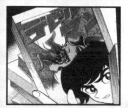

This series is featured in Chapter 22: Devil Power

Devilman (5 volumes)

By Go Nagai

Published by Kodansha beginning in 1972

"Do you have any good manga you can recommend?" is the single question I've heard most frequently during my nearly 20 years managing a manga bookstore in Kumamoto. At that point, I ask the customer about the intended reader's age, sex, education or profession and hobbies, as well as favorite authors, mangaka and music. Since people have different definitions of "good," it's a difficult question to answer without knowing something about the reader.

Of course, my own criterion for what constitutes a good manga is quite clear: it's whether or not the story has a satisfying ending. If I were to name three manga with truly satisfying endings that I've come across in all my years of reading, they would have to be *Ashita no Joe* (Tomorrow's Joe) (story by Asao Takamori, art by Tetsuya Chiba), *Kozure Okami* (Lone Wolf and Cub) (story by Kazuo Koike, art by Goseki Kojima), and Go Nagai's *Devilman*, featured in this chapter.

In particular, *Devilman* succeeds in capturing the author's unique postapocalyptic vision in five short tankobon volumes, leaving readers traumatized and influencing generations of writers here and abroad. The last scene, especially, is one of the great unforgettable endings, which is precisely why I've recommended the series to so many people as an undisputed classic.

Based on *Maoh Dante* (Demon Lord Dante), an earlier Nagai manga about the final battle between God and the devil serialized in *Bokura Magazine*, *Devilman* ran simultaneously as an anime and as a manga in Kodansha's *Shonen Magazine* from 1972 to 1973. You can read the series today through the Kodansha Manga Bunko series. Apparently enamored with his role-reversal of the villainous God and good devil, Nagai went on to create spinoffs and original titles with the same theme, including *Shin Devilman* (New Devilman), *Violence Jack*, *Devilman Lady*, *Shin Violence Jack* (New Violence Jack), and *AMON Devilman Mokujiroku* (Amon: The Apocalypse of Devilman).

An increasing number of readers lament the paucity of "good" manga today. While it's true that overall sales of manga magazines have declined, there are still plenty of great individual manga out there, not to mention many classic manga yet to be rediscovered. For those of you searching for a good manga, why not head down to Kingyo's dungeon and look for a manga or two that sparks your interest?

※ The setting and plot of the *Devilman* anime and manga are vastly different.

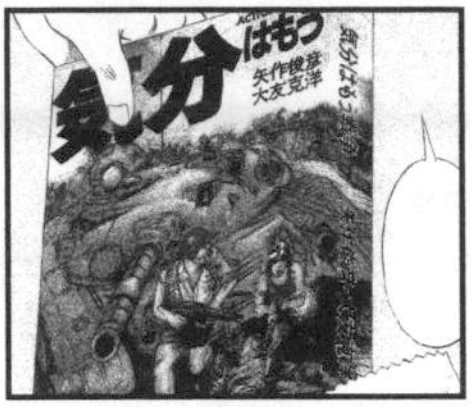
気分はもう
矢作俊彦
大友克洋

This manga is featured in Chapter 23:
A Man Ahead of His Time

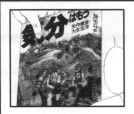

Kibun wa Mou Senso (1 volume)

Story by Toshihiko Yahagi, art by Katsuhiro Otomo

Published by Futabasha in 1982

The generation born between 1947 and 1949, known as the baby boom generation, is about to reach retirement age. The people of this generation have lived with manga since the dawn of the postwar manga boom and continue to embrace manga to this day, even as they've been derided as the generation that can't grow up. Okadome's father, appearing for the first time in this chapter, and his friend Kunimoto are both baby boomers. Having lived through campus uprisings and having discovered jazz, leftist ideology and manga during their college days in the 1960s, the two continue to fight losing battles throughout their lives. Now they're about to turn 60 without having grown very adept at surviving the times.

Both men mention *Kibun wa Mou Senso* (In the Mood for War or Already at War) as a shared memory. Okadome and Kunimoto identify with the depictions of characters rushing into war for different personal reasons, having been embroiled in the 1960s campus uprisings—now a precious shared experience for both men. This 1982 manga was released during the prime of mangaka Katsuhiro Otomo's career, along with his renowned titles *Domu* (A Child's Dream) and *AKIRA*, and is currently available from Futabasha and Kadokawa Shoten.

Katsuhiro Otomo was greatly influenced by French comic artist Moebius (Jean Giraud), featured in volume 1 of *Kingyo Used Books*, and Otomo's un-Japanese bold visual compositions and minutely detailed backgrounds had an immeasurable impact on the manga world. Even Osamu Tezuka, always pursuing new styles of expression in keeping with the changing times, realized all of his previous work had become history the moment he saw Otomo's artwork and said, "I surrender unconditionally before Otomo-san's work."

Truth be told, I'm also a baby boomer, born in 1948. I belong to a generation that's perpetually preoccupied with Kagemaru's last words in Sanpei Shirato's *Ninja Bugeicho* (Band of Ninja): "Where did we come from, and where are we going?" Having picked fights with our parents, universities, society, Japan and the world, and having said stuff like, "Demand solidarity, fear not isolation," in our youth, can we continue to stay connected to others and fight for our beliefs? I believe the answer has to be somewhere in the books we've already read and forgotten. Perhaps you'd like to open the time capsule of books at Kingyo to search for the answer and revisit that era again.

This series is featured in Chapter 24:
A Common Language

Ranma 1/2 (38 volumes)

By Rumiko Takahashi

Published by Shogakukan beginning in 1988

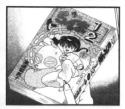

© Rumiko Takahashi

The series featured in this chapter, Rumiko Takahashi's *Ranma 1/2*, is, along with *Doraemon*, Shogakukan's most enormously popular flagship series. Appealing to the tween crowd, a decidedly younger readership than that of Takahashi's previous manga *Urusei Yatsura*, *Ranma 1/2* gained widespread popularity through an anime series, character merchandise, music and animated features. In addition, with the anime series televised overseas and the manga translated in over 20 countries, there are *Ranma* fans all over the world. *Ranma 1/2* truly has become synonymous with Japanese manga.

The manga is a slapstick comedy about Ranma Saotome, a teenage boy who turns into a girl when doused with water, and his bride-to-be Akane Tendo, along with Akane's sisters Kasumi and Nabiki and their friend Ryoga Hibiki. The diverse cast of characters and abundance of cursed hot springs with transformative powers combine to create Rumiko's intricately woven comedy world.

The manga began serialization in *Shonen Sunday* in 1987 and held on to its top manga status for nearly 10 years without ever losing steam during its run, which speaks to the manga's quality. You can read the 38-volume series in a new tankobon edition re-released by Shogakukan in 2002.

Why was the manga so popular with kids? I think the answer is in the dual personalities of the characters. Through the strange powers of the hot springs, Ranma Saotome turns into the female

Ranma, his father Genma into a panda, and Ryoga into P-chan the pig. For kids feeling constrained by the restrictions of childhood, having another identity, entirely different from one's own, must seem immensely appealing. The manga was especially popular among girls who fantasized about changing who they were.

Incidentally, each chapter of *Kingyo* has featured interesting developments in the human relationships surrounding Kingyo Used Books. Sudo-kun is crazy about Kinko-chan, the manga-loving regular, but he can't seem to carry on an extended conversation with her. He gets it into his head that he can't talk to her because they lack a common language. However, common ground isn't so easy to find, no matter how much two people love manga. That's because it has no fixed form.

When Kinko-chan pulls out a volume of *Ranma 1/2*, grade school memories come flooding back to both of them. Once they are able to recall how much they loved and laughed over manga back then, there is no need for words. What's important isn't finding the right words, but capturing the right spirit. Sudo-kun seems to have come to that realization with the help of this manga.

In the same way, people who are helplessly in love with manga gather at Kingyo, searching for the right spirit. Why don't you come down to Kingyo to get together with these lovable manga freaks?

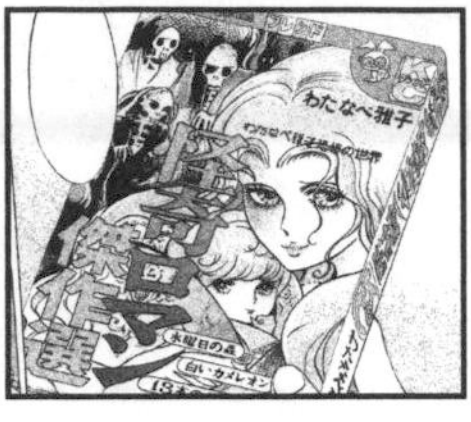

This manga is featured in Chapter 25: Beautiful People

Kaiki Roman Kessakushu **(1 volume)**

By Masako Watanabe

Published by Kodansha in 1974

This chapter of *Kingyo Used Books* introduces an unusual number of vintage manga. First is a classic loaner manga from Minoru Mori, pen name of the science fiction writer Sakyo Komatsu: *Daichiteikai* (Subterrocean), the first manga to deal with evolution and geotectonic changes. Said to be the model for the bestselling disaster epic *Nippon Chinbotsu* (Japan Sinks), it's a very rare book, with only a few confirmed copies in existence today. This chapter also casually mentions several vintage manga by Taku Horie, Kinya Ueki, Eiichi Fukui and Keiko Sugimoto, all currently sought after in the used-book world.

The recommended work this time is "*Shiroi Chameleon*" (The White Chameleon), first published in the 6/19/73 issue of *Shojo Friend*, which appears in Masako Watanabe's *Kaiki Roman Kessakushu* (The Best Mystery Romances) from Kodansha FC Friend. Masako Watanabe debuted in 1952 with *Suama-chan* from Wakagi Shobo and is considered the first major female artist of boys' manga. She is a master of her craft and, now in her 70s, continues to draw actively today. I once had the opportunity to talk to her at the Asian Manga Summit. She told me that her family was poor when she first started drawing, so she wanted to depict an elegant world in her manga and lavished every luxury on her young female protagonists. She also talked about how she thought to twine flowers around panel borders and put stars in the characters' eyes to accentuate the luxuriousness of the art. In other words, two key defining features of shojo manga—the flowers around the panels and the stars in the eyes—were both invented by Masako Watanabe.

The protagonist of "The White Chameleon" is Daphne, a girl who yearns to be beautiful to woo the boy she secretly likes. When a white chameleon appears before her to grant her wish, she drinks the chameleon's blood and succeeds in becoming as beautiful as her older sister. But the beauty she gains turns out to be temporary and a sad imitation of her sister's. As the effect of the chameleon's blood fades, she discovers that she is gradually becoming more disfigured than she was before. She resorts to killing the chameleon to become even more beautiful, which has horrific consequences in the end.

What did Shiba-san want to convey to Sasayama-san through this manga? Maybe he wanted to tell the insecure Sasayama-san, "Beauty is only fleeting. If you get hung up on looks, tragedy awaits you." But if the good-looking Shiba-san had told him that directly, Sasayama-san would only have gotten angrier.

"A white chameleon is in its natural uncolored state, so it has the potential to change to any color it chooses. And you have the capacity to genuinely love shojo manga, Sasayama-san. You should admire that pure and 'uncolored' part of yourself more." Perhaps that's what Shiba-san wanted to convey by showing Sasayama-san this manga.

In this way, the circle of Kingyo regulars continues to grow. Perhaps you'd like to join that circle too! Kingyo Used Books is truly a place where wonderful manga and people come together.

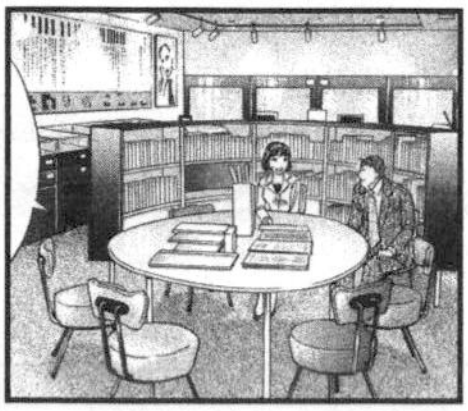

This museum is featured in Chapter 26: Kingyo Diaries (The Shiogama Episode)

The Katsuichi Nagai Manga Museum

Although there are a few museums devoted to mangaka, this is the only manga museum to honor an editor.

Who was Katsuichi Nagai?

The setting for this chapter of *Kingyo Used Books* is the Katsuichi Nagai Manga Museum in Shiogama, Miyagi Prefecture. The museum was built to commemorate the achievements of Katsuichi Nagai, the founder of *Garo*, a magazine that must be mentioned in any discussion of postwar manga history.

In recent years, museums collecting and exhibiting the works of mangaka have begun to pop up around Japan. But the Katsuichi Nagai Manga Museum is the only museum in the country honoring the achievements not of a mangaka, but of a manga editor. It's a testament to the tremendous legacy Nagai left behind. Nagai began his career publishing *kashihon manga* (loaner manga) after World War II while working as a street vendor and in the black market. He won initial acclaim for publishing the early works of Sanpei Shirato, like *Arashi no Ninja* (Storm Ninja), but left publishing temporarily due to an illness. Upon his return in 1964, he began publishing the manga magazine *Garo* at Seirindo. At this tiny publishing company, Nagai handled everything from marketing to sales. This helped turn *Garo* into a homegrown magazine unconstrained by profit margins, and Nagai succeeded in collecting top-notch manga titles. With Sanpei Shirato's popular *Kamui Den* (The Legend of Kamui) as its tentpole series, *Garo* published such masterpieces as Shigeru Mizuki's *Kitaro Yawa* (Kitaro Night Stories) and Yoshiharu Tsuge's short story "*Nejishiki*" (Screw-Style), boosting circulation exponentially and even prompting Shogakukan to offer to publish the magazine.

Garo is also responsible for introducing readers to the works of Takao Yaguchi, Hiroshi Masumura, Seiichi Hayashi, Ryoichi Ikegami, the trio of Shinichi Abe•Oji Suzuki•Masuzo Furukawa (known as the 1•2•3 Trio because their first names include the kanji for one, two and three), Shinji Nagashima, Kazuo Uemura, Yoshikazu Ebisu and Hinako Sugiura. Along with *COM* magazine, founded in 1967 by Osamu Tezuka's Mushi Productions, *Garo* became a pioneering force in the manga world. Many mangaka working today continue to look up to Nagai as a mentor because they still appreciate the early years when he took them under his wing both professionally and personally. You can read more about the history of *Garo* in *Garo Henshuucho* (Garo Editor) from Chikuma Bunko.

In this episode, there is a scene in which Natuski's parents, in their younger days, argue over *Garo*. Natsuki's father, the son of the owner of Kingyo Used Books, dismisses manga as worthless, to which Natsuki's mother fires back, "The manga in here are works of art. What kind of idiot would mock such a beautiful method of self-expression?" This manga holds a special memory for both of them because it's responsible for bringing them together.

Actually, *Garo* played a role in my marriage to my current wife. Our first date, after moving out to Tokyo from Kumamoto as college kids, happened to be in front of Seirindo. At the time, the characters from *Kamui Den*, like Kamui and Shosuke, seemed to speak for our generation, and the company responsible for publishing *Kamui* was hallowed ground. The wood-and-mortar building containing the editorial offices stood before us. Although we never had the courage to go inside, we met in front of Seirindo many times to talk about manga and politics, only to fall in love and later marry. Over 30 years later, we continue to talk about manga while managing a manga bookstore together.

And so, for Natsuki's parents and for my wife and me, *Garo* continues to live on along with the unforgettable memories of our younger days.

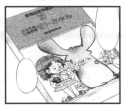

This series is featured in Chapter 27:
An Odd Couple

Tottemo Shiawase Moto-chan (1 volume)

By Moto Hagio

Published by Shogakukan in 1977

This episode is about an unusual friendship between two people who love Kingyo dearly: Tsujimoto-kun and Sasayama-san. When they set out in search of an arsonist who's setting fire to the used bookstores around town, they discover curious drawings of a big-eared creature near the crime scenes. The drawings are of the title character from *Tottemo Shiawase Moto-chan* (A Very Happy Moto-chan).

Moto-chan is a strange olive-colored creature that flies with its enormous ears. The story of Moto-chan's odd friendship with Johnny Walker, this fantastical six-*koma* (six-panel) comic strip first appeared in the October 1972 issue of Shogakukan's *Bessatsu Shojo Friend* (Special Edition Shojo Friend) and ran until the July 1976 issue of *Ohisama* (Sun). Among the readers who discovered this manga as kids, there are many who have never forgotten its cozy tone and count *Moto-chan* as their favorite of Moto Hagio's many works. The 1977 tankobon of this manga from the *Meruhen Leaf Series* (Fairy Tale Leaf Series) is considered the rarest of Hagio's works; a fierce battle erupts on the rare occasions when we get copies in our store. But don't worry: you can also read *Moto-chan* in the Shogakukan Manga Bunko series.

A revolutionary figure in shojo manga, Moto Hagio pushed the boundaries of artistic expression through her ingenious stories, fundamentally superior sense of design, psychological rendering of characters, diversity of subject matter and overall literary excellence. She is often called the Osamu Tezuka of the shojo manga world.

Moto Hagio is a baby boomer like myself and is often mentioned as a member of the Forty-Niners or Year 24 Group. This group of female mangaka born around the year 1949 (Showa 24 in the Japanese calendar) includes Yasuko Aoike, Riyoko Ikeda, Keiko Takemiya, Yumiko Oshima, Toshie Kihara, Ryoko Yamagishi, Minori Kimura, Nanae Sasaya and Mineko Yamada, many of whom continue to draw manga today. The Forty-Niners are said to have blown the doors off the shojo manga world, attracting male readers who previously had shied away from girls' manga.

Although Tokiwa-so, the apartment building where classic shonen mangaka like Osamu Tezuka, Fujiko Fujio, Fujio Akatsuka, Shotaro Ishimori and Hiro-o Terada all worked, is well known to manga fans, few people know that there was also such a place where shojo mangaka met. The Forty-Niners gathered at an apartment shared by Moto Hagio and Keiko Takemiya, where they talked manga and worked collaboratively, forming the most cutting-edge group of manga artists of the era. Called the "Oizumi Salon" because the apartment was located in Nerima Ward in Oizumi, it had a tremendous influence on the shojo mangaka known as the Post-Forty-Niners. No doubt the Oizumi Salon was a place where manga-lovers could meet casually in the same way the characters gather at Kingyo.

Incidentally, there's a scene in this episode where Tsujimoto-kun falls asleep on Sasayama-san's back, despite suffering from insomnia. Although he's often rude, he's really a sweet, manga-loving kid. And Sasayama-san seems to be hard on others at first, but he turns out to be a perfectly charming (more or less) manga-loving guy. Being around Kingyo seems to have the strange power to soothe and comfort people. The people who come together at Kingyo must be very happy, just like Moto-chan!

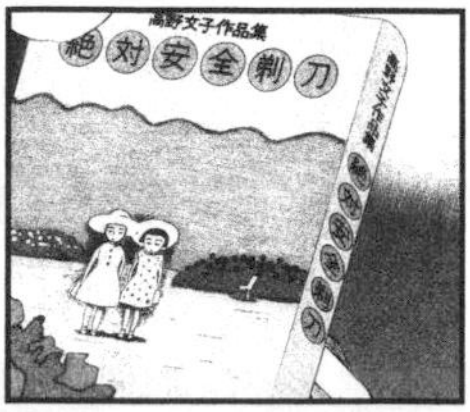
高野文子作品集
絶対安全剃刀

This manga is featured in Chapter 28: Tomorrow's Visitor

Zettai Anzen Kamisori (1 volume)

By Fumiko Takano

Published by Hakusensha in 1982

The manga featured in this chapter is Fumiko Takano's *Zettai Anzen Kamisori* (Absolute Safety Razor), published by Hakusensha. Takano, a leading figure in the manga New Wave movement, brought about a revolutionary change in visual expression. Along with Katsuhiro Otomo, Hisashi Eguchi, Noma Sabea and Yosuke Takahashi, she left a huge mark on the manga world.

From the late 1970s to the early 1980s, a number of magazines launched that were somewhere between *dojinshi* (self-published comics) and *shogyoushi* (commercial magazines), such as *Manga Kisou Tengai* (Out of This World Manga), *Rakugakikan*, *JUNE*, *Comic Again* and *Mankincho*. These magazines featured innovative methods of expression, manga titles that ignored commercial concerns and new mangaka with unique styles. The 1980s was a decade when manga artists, publishers and fans truly shone.

Takano made a name for herself by publishing in most of the aforementioned magazines. These short stories are collected in her 1982 debut tankobon, *Zettai Anzen Kamisori* (Absolute Safety Razor), currently available from Hakusensha. Among them is "*Tanabe no Tsuru*," published in the inaugural issue of *Mankincho* in 1982, a masterpiece that left a huge impression on readers.

The story follows Tsuru (Crane), an 82-year-old woman who believes she's the same bob-haired little girl she was in her youth. As the story unfolds, we observe Tsuru's internal world, in which she appears as a little girl, even as we realize she has all the experience of her 82 years in the external or "real" world. The conflict between these two worlds is deeply moving. Although philosophical, the story is rendered with Takano's uniquely light touch.

In this episode, a young magician comes across Takano's story at Kingyo, providing him with the inspiration for a new show to present at a nursing home. The biggest difference between children and the elderly is that the elderly have the experience of the many years they've lived. Even at 82, Tsuru still has the heart of a little girl. And so it occurs to the magician that perhaps the elderly might enjoy recapturing the heart of childhood.

That's where the power of manga comes in. In the field of geriatric psychology, music therapy is used to revitalize the elderly through the music they used to sing and play in their youth. Perhaps getting the eldery at the nursing home to read the manga they used to read as children works as a kind of comics therapy.

Once the magician casts a therapeutic spell over his audience, lo and behold, it's their turn to cast a spell over him! The story ends happily with the world-weary magician energized by their stories and experiences. And so the greatest magician in this episode is really Kingyo Used Books!

The information in this volume is current up to November 2006. This includes all manga footnotes and all the columns comprising the Kingyo Used Books Notebook.

Thanks to every creator, publisher and property owner of manga titles mentioned in this volume for your understanding and cooperation.

Information provided by Gendai Manga Toshokan/Kirara Bunko. Additional research in cooperation with the Katsuichi Nagai Manga Museum.

KINGYO USED BOOKS
Volume 4
VIZ Signature Edition

Story and Art by SEIMU YOSHIZAKI

© 2005 Seimu YOSHIZAKI/Shogakukan
All rights reserved.
Original Japanese edition "KINGYOYA KOSHOTEN"
published by SHOGAKUKAN Inc.

Original Japanese cover design by Kei Kasai

Translation: Takami Nieda
Touch-up Art & Lettering: Erika Terriquez
Design: Fawn Lau
Editor: Shaenon K. Garrity

The stories, characters and incidents mentioned
in this publication are entirely fictional.

Printed in Canada

Published by VIZ Media, LLC
P.O. Box 77010
San Francisco, CA 94107

10 9 8 7 6 5 4 3 2 1
First printing, October 2011

www.viz.com

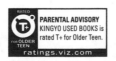
PARENTAL ADVISORY
KINGYO USED BOOKS is
rated T+ for Older Teen.
ratings.viz.com

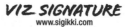
www.sigikki.com

>⋊⋉⋊⋉ Kingyo = Goldfish ⋊⋉⋊⋉<

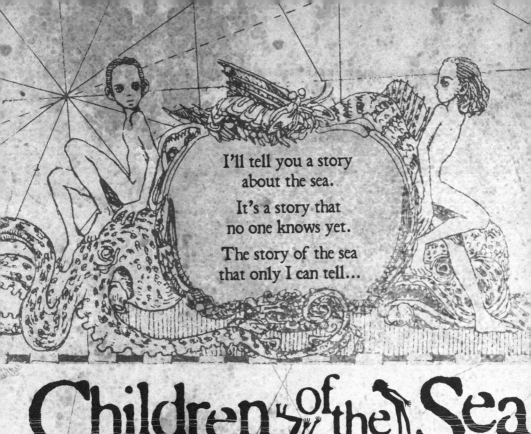
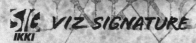
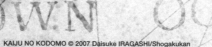

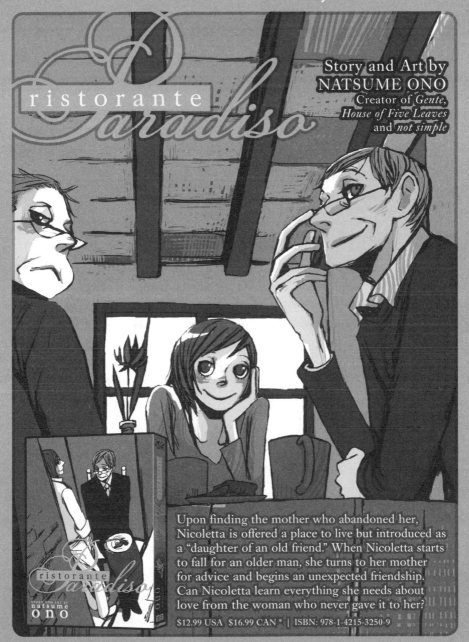
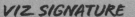

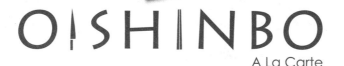

My parents are clueless.

My boyfriend's a mooch.

My boss is a perv.

But who cares? I sure don't.
At least they know who they are.

Being young and dissatisfied
really makes it hard to care
about anything in this world...

solanin

STORY & ART BY INIO ASANO

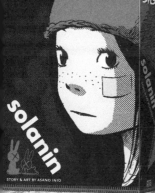